THE DRIVING INSTRUCTOR'S HANDBOOK

THE DRIVING INSTRUCTOR'S HANDBOOK

A REFERENCE AND TRAINING MANUAL

REVISED FIFTH EDITION

JOHN MILLER and NIGEL STACEY

KOGAN
PAGE

First published in 1982 by
Kogan Page Ltd
120 Pentonville Road, London N1 9JN
Second edition 1983
Third edition 1986
Fourth edition 1988
Fifth edition 1989
Reprints
Revised fifth edition 1990

British Library Cataloguing in Publication Data

A CIP catalogue record for this book is available from the British Library.

ISBN 0 7494 0145 1

Printed in Great Britain by Biddles Ltd, Guildford, Surrey

The Authors

John Miller runs a driving school at Chichester and a training centre based at Goodwood Motor Circuit specialising in courses for commercial vehicle drivers and for driving instructors. He and Nigel Stacey have worked as driver training consultants on various projects for organisations, local authorities and industry both at home and abroad. He is an RAC Registered Instructor, an HGV/RTITB Class 1 approved instructor, and a Department of Transport ADI.

Nigel and Margaret Stacey operated their own driving school for 21 years and more recently have specialised in instructor training. Since Nigel's death in 1987, Margaret has co-edited **The Driving Instructor's Handbook** and continues to run an instructor training facility in Derbyshire.

Millers Motor School
57 North Street
Chichester
West Sussex PO19 1NB

Autodriva
The Mount
53 Heanor Road
Ilkeston
Derbyshire DE7 8DY

Contents

Introduction   *11*

1 | Driving Instruction as a Career   12

The Qualities of a Good Instructor *13*
Qualifications *15*
Business Opportunities *17*
Starting Your Own School *19*
Instructor Associations *20*

2 | Defensive Driving   26

Road Accidents – An Epidemic *26*
An Introduction to Defensive Driving *27*
Influences on Driver Behaviour *28*

3 | Factors Affecting Vehicle Stability   48

Factors Affecting the Stability of Vehicles in Motion *48*

4 | The Learning Process   62

Some Theoretical Considerations *62*
Motivating Students *70*

5 | Learning Aids   74

Text and Reference Books *74*
Visual Aids *75*

6 | Teaching in a Classroom   82

Rules for the Use of Learning Aids *83*

7 | Driver Training   87

Route Planning *87*
Giving Route Directions *89*
The Use of Instructions and Terminology *92*
Structuring a Course of Driving Instruction *101*

8 | Assessments and Standards   **118**

Methods of Assessment *118*
Assessment Records *127*
'L' Driver Errors *129*

9 | Disabilities, Minor Handicaps and other Impairments   **137**

Teaching People with Disabilities *137*
Other Handicaps *138*
Impairments and Distractions *143*

10 | The 'L' Test   **147**

Driving Examiners *171*

11 | The HGV and PSV Tests   **173**

The HGV Driving Test *173*
The PSV Driving Test *177*

12 | Motorcycle Test   **194**

13 | Advanced Driving Tests   **204**

The Institute of Advanced Motorists *204*
The Institute of Advanced Motorists Test *205*
IAM Fleet Training *208*
The RoSPA Advanced Driving Test *208*
RoAD Association *210*
RoSPA Defensive Driving Courses *210*

14 | The ADI Register   **213**

Department of Transport Approved Driving
 Instructor Register *213*
The Test of Continued Ability and Fitness *222*
Instructor Grading *225*
Licence to Give Instruction *225*
The Right to Appeal *228*

15 | The ADI Examinations   **238**

The Qualifying Examination *238*

16 | ADI Training and Supervision of Licence Holders   **255**

Training for the Examination *255*
Supervision and Training of Licence Holders *267*

17 | Driver and Vehicle Licensing   **273**

Driver Licensing *273*

18 | Vehicle and Traffic Regulations   **285**

Legal Obligations of a Supervising Driver *285*
Vehicle Regulations *286*
Accident Procedure *292*
MOT Test *293*

19 | Motor Vehicle Insurance   **295**

Types of Insurance *295*
EC Requirements *297*
Motor Insurance for Driving Schools and
    Instructors *297*
Tuition in Customer's Own Vehicle *299*

20 | Driving and Traffic Offences   **301**

Driving Offences *302*
Fixed Penalties *303*
Driving Licence Endorsements *305*

21 | Driving School Administration   **308**

Legal Structure *308*
Franchising *310*
Registration of Businesses *311*
Disclosure of Business Ownership *311*
Employing Staff *312*
Conditions and Contract of Employment *313*
Equipment and Services *314*
Tuition Vehicles *316*
Documentation *319*
Standard Procedures *321*
Bookkeeping in a Small Business *324*

Appendix I: Vehicle Controls and Operation   **328**

Vehicle Operation *328*
Types of Automatic Transmission *335*

Appendix II: Mechanical Principles   **337**

The Engine *337*
The Fuel System *338*
The Ignition System *339*
Engine Lubrication *341*
The Cooling System *342*
Clutch *343*
Gearbox *344*
Differential *345*
Brakes *346*

Parking Brake *348*
Suspension *348*
Shock Absorbers *350*
Tyres *350*
Preventive Maintenance and Service Requirements *352*
Seasonally *355*

Appendix III: Useful Addresses   **357**

Appendix IV: ADI Examination Part III   **365**

Introduction

In this, the fifth edition of the *Driving Instructor's Handbook*, several significant changes have been made, including a revision of the text and the introduction of a soft-back version to replace the original hardback.

By changing to a soft cover it is felt that the cost of the *Handbook* will be kept to an acceptable level without any loss of contents; more frequent reprints or corrections will be possible and there will be less time lapse between the authors' corrections and a publication date. This last point is particularly important as the *Handbook* is to be used in conjunction with the Department of Transport Approved Driving Instructor examinations.

Some of the chapters cover the same subject matter as in previous editions, while other sections are regularly updated and corrected. The next edition of the *Handbook* will include further news on the implications of the harmonisation within the EC of driving licences and driving tests. In the meantime, for the present edition the contents have been corrected and updated to provide a source of reference for all instructors and trainees.

As the *Handbook* will be produced at more frequent intervals it is intended to include more detailed information in future editions in an enlarged section of 'useful addresses'. The authors would, therefore, appreciate any information from organisations or individuals who feel that an inclusion would be beneficial to the readership.

At the same time, any constructive comments regarding items or subjects which could, or should, be included in future editions of the *Handbook* would be welcomed by the authors.

The *Handbook* could not possibly be produced without a tremendous amount of co-operation and support from a variety of sources. This year I must express my gratitude to those individuals and organisations who helped in various ways to ensure that the compilation of the book has been as accurate as possible. In particular, my thanks to Margaret Stacey who, since Nigel's death in December 1987, has co-edited the *Handbook*.

While every effort has been made to ensure that the material contained in the *Handbook* is as accurate as possible, the progress of legislation means that we are not always able to be completely up to date.

John Miller
November 1989

Chapter 1

Driving Instruction as a Career

Driving schools and driving instructors are now part of a long established and proven industry providing an essential service for most of the one million new drivers who take to our roads each year.

Driver training is a vast potential market. It is estimated that over £300 million is spent annually on learning to drive. More than two million driving tests are conducted each year at a total cost in excess of £36 million. It is usually accepted that over 90 per cent of all test candidates have at least some professional driving instruction. In addition, there are over 30 million full licence holders who would benefit from some form of training.

Years ago – long before the driving test was introduced in 1935 – it was a different story. At that time the driver would take perhaps only a couple of hours of tuition from the salesman who sold him the car. Indeed, up until the 1950s driving schools were often attached to car sales offices. Today's new driver expects a very different service. However, it was from that modest beginning that the driving instruction industry grew, accelerated by the introduction of the driving test in 1935.

In those earlier times the motor car was an uncomfortable, noisy and generally less reliable vehicle than it is today. They were more difficult to control and temperamental to drive, with totally inadequate braking systems compared with modern standards. As the motor car developed through the decades, so the techniques required for driving them changed.

Learner drivers today are faced with a completely different set of problems compared with those of 50 years ago. Traditional 'hit and miss' teaching methods are inadequate when dealing with the complexity, speed and density of modern traffic. In addition, the driving instructor and his pupil have to cope with a mass of legislation, regulations and procedures which were unknown in those early days.

The European Community, by way of various directives, calls for harmonisation of driving tests throughout the EC. It seems to be generally accepted that the UK test fails to satisfy the spirit of these directives, and that the Department of Transport will have to look carefully at the possibility of introducing a revised syllabus for the driving test. It is now thought that the basic proposals will be agreed for implementation some time after 1992. This will provide further opportunities for instructors capable of widening their activities.

In today's conditions there is much more to learning to drive than simply passing the test. The modern driving school needs to offer more than the basic, traditional 'L' driver training facility:

1. Education authorities are implementing their own training schemes which place more emphasis on attitudes and awareness.
2. The Department of Transport is encouraging newly-qualified drivers to take motorway lessons.
3. Defensive driving techniques are being recognised as an effective way of reducing road accidents.
4. Fleet operators are becoming more aware of the financial benefits of training.
5. The government is currently reviewing the extent of its powers for the retraining of traffic offenders.
6. European Community regulations will involve a restructuring of the classifications of driving licences including the introduction of a new licence group for light commercial and passenger vehicles.

Driving schools and instructors will need to organise themselves to take advantage of these new opportunities – particularly as there will be a diminishing number of 17-year-old pupils over the next few years.

Newly qualified drivers continue to be over-proportionately involved in road accidents. Experts agree that more emphasis needs to be placed on improving safe attitudes and the acquisition of hazard recognition skills to reduce the scale of these accidents. Traditional methods of repetitive practice combined with the simple recitation of rules and regulations do not necessarily produce a skilled and informed driver.

Most road traffic accidents are caused by deficiencies in the information-processing task and perception skills. Human abilities are limited and drivers are often exposed to situations where too many things are happening at once. Faced with more than they can efficiently cope with, the driver may attend to some aspects of the task while remaining completely oblivious to others. The main aim of training should be to reduce the risk of accident involvement. Traditional methods of training need to be re-examined and strategies used which result in a safer driver behaviour pattern.

Emphasis should be placed on developing higher levels of attention, improving self-control and increasing the driver's awareness. Training should encourage the use of effective visual scanning techniques and should provide learners with controlled experience in recognising and responding to danger signals. Drivers must learn to predict events, assess the consequences of them and avoid the circumstances which lead to conflict. Reducing road accidents requires a systematic training programme combined with its professional delivery by suitably qualified instructors. It requires an integrated system of instructional materials and aids to stimulate learning and to reinforce safe behaviour.

The Qualities of a Good Instructor

Driving instructors' personalities are as diverse as those of the learners they teach. As an instructor you will meet all kinds of people from all walks of life. They will all differ in personality, attitude and ability. Consequently they will all require a different approach.

First and foremost, to become an instructor you will need a thorough working knowledge of the rules, procedures and techniques involved in driving a motor car. You will need to be able to demonstrate the skills involved. You must have proper attitudes towards other people because your student will try to copy you.

Good instructors are sensitive to the needs and hopes of their students. You will need to be aware of these needs and have a genuine concern for the well-being of your students. You must be able to communicate easily with them.

You must learn to plan routes which avoid or incorporate specific conditions according to the student's ability. You must advise, show, encourage, assess and protect students while they learn.

As an instructor you must be patient, understanding and tactful. Learners need reassurance and emotional support. This can be very tiring at times, so you will need plenty of physical and mental stamina. There will also be times when you must be firm. This may be needed for safety or teaching reasons, or because of the legal responsibilities you must accept as an instructor.

The qualities required of a good instructor are similar, in many respects, to those needed by the good driver.

Responsibility: a good driver will have a proper concern for the safety of his passengers and other road users. A good instructor must have the same concern for the future safety of his students.

Concentration is essential when driving. A moment's distraction can result in tragedy. As an instructor you will also need to concentrate on how your student is responding to the surroundings.

Anticipation is the driver's ability to predict and therefore avoid potentially dangerous incidents. As an instructor you will also need to predict your students' actions and needs.

The ability to communicate is one of the instructor's main assets. You must be able to pass on ideas, information and opinions; provide opportunities for practice and then assess the learner's performance.

Patience: if a driver loses his temper when someone else does something wrong, or because he is held up, he becomes a source of potential danger. If you lose your temper because a student makes a mistake, you will destroy his confidence and cause even more problems.

Confidence: this is part of the driver's attitude. Good drivers know their own limitations. Over-confidence leads to carelessness and mistakes. This is true of both drivers and instructors. The qualities discussed depend very much on having good instruction right from the start. Unprofessional training can ruin the confidence of new drivers and new instructors. Perfection in driving is rare, if it exists at all. However, it is something every driving instructor should aim for. Take pride in being an example to others!

Knowledge: although driving is mainly a skill, a thorough and up-to-date working knowledge of rules and procedures is essential. You must develop an open mind and be prepared to change, adapt and adopt the ideas of others.

Knowing your vehicle will help you drive it sympathetically and economically. Although a detailed knowledge is not absolutely essential to the driving instructor, you will need to know the laws relating to vehicle roadworthiness and have a basic understanding of mechanical and operating principles. Your knowledge in this area must be adequate to answer questions posed by your students. It is also an area tested in the written examination.

Qualifications

ADI Register

The Department of Transport Register of Approved Driving Instructors was introduced over 20 years ago on a voluntary basis. It became compulsory in 1970. Its purpose is to ensure that any person teaching another to drive a motor car for money (or money's worth) can meet the minimum standards laid down by the department. It is an offence for you to give instruction in driving a motor car unless your name is on the Register of Approved Driving Instructors, or you hold a trainee licence (a temporary licence to give instruction).

To qualify you must:

(a)   have held a full licence for driving a motor car for at least four years out of the six preceding your application. Periods after passing your driving test may be counted as a full licence providing you held a provisional during this time;

(b)   not have been disqualified from driving during any part of the four years preceding your application;

(c)   be a fit and proper person. Motoring and non-motoring convictions are taken into account in assessing your application;

(d)   pass the qualifying examinations.

You must pass the written examination before applying for the practical. The practical examination is taken in two parts. The first tests your eyesight and driving technique and the second your instructional ability. After passing all three examinations you have to pay the current initial registration fee. You will then receive your official certificate and can call yourself a Department of Transport Approved Driving Instructor.

Registration is renewable every four years on payment of the current fee. A condition of your continued registration is that you must, from time to time, undergo tests of continued ability and fitness to give instruction. These tests involve the attendance of your supervising examiner during one of your lessons.

Further Qualifications

The level of competence proved by passing the Department of Transport ADI examination is the minimum standard of instruction required by law. Many instructors continue to further their education by taking one of the advanced training and refresher courses which are offered by the main trade associations such as MSA and DIA. Some of the available courses lead to a formal qualification of an examining board.

The City and Guilds 730 course is a further education teacher's certificate. Courses are usually one-year, part-time with two sessions per week at a local college. Alternatively, the course is available through the Motor Schools Association on a distance learning basis in association with the North Worcestershire College at Bromsgrove. The '730' course is relevant for anyone who is involved in adult education and for others who may want to understand more about teaching techniques. The City and Guilds 725 course is a certificate in direct training. The overall aim is to provide an understanding of the principles and practice of direct training and an opportunity for trainers to achieve appropriate planning, presentation and evaluation skills.

The Diploma in Driving Instruction is a professional qualification awarded jointly by the Associated Examining Board and Driving Instructors' Association. Its overall aims are to improve standards of driver instruction and provide wider public recognition of professional services. It consists of five modules, each tested in a two-hour examination. The modules are:

1. *Legal obligations and regulations*
   Aims: to promote an understanding of the legal obligations of the driver and enable the instructor to carry out his professional duties within the law. To develop an understanding of the Department of Transport driving test and administration and regulations.
2. *Management of a small driving school*
   Aims: To provide an understanding of the financial, administrative and professional skills involved in the operation of a small driving school.
3. *Vehicle maintenance and mechanical principles*
   Aims: To develop an awareness of the importance of maintaining motor vehicles in a roadworthy and clean condition and provide a sound basic knowledge of the working principles. To provide an understanding of the instructor's responsibilities concerning maintenance and servicing requirements.
4. *Driving theory, skills and procedures*
   Aims: To develop a thorough knowledge and understanding of the responsibilities of driving and the physical and psychological requirements involved. To develop a general understanding of the attitude, skills and procedures involved in reduced risk driving.
5. *Instructing: practices and procedures*
   Aims: To provide a basic understanding of the principles of learning as they relate to driving instruction and assist the instructor to design and develop appropriate courses. To develop valid methods of assessing driving competence and provide a thorough understanding of the objectives, syllabus and methods of assessment used by the DTp driving test examiners.

A certificate for each module is awarded to successful candidates. When all five module examinations are passed, candidates are eligible for the award of the diploma.

Entering for the Examination

Examinations are held in November of each year. Entries will be accepted at any registered AEB centre which takes external candidates; these are mostly colleges of further education. A register of AEB examination centres which accept entries is available upon application to the AEB (The Secretary General ED/5), Stag Hill House, Guildford, Surrey GU2 5XJ.

Studying for the Examinations

A detailed syllabus for each module is available from the Driving Instructors Association (DIA). Study materials designed for independent learning have been specially prepared and are available from the DIA.

Business Opportunities

In spite of strong competition, opportunities still exist for the extension of traditional driving school services and the provision of new ones. Getting yourself and your services known is one of the essentials. It involves going out and telling the public what you can do for them and why they should come to you rather than your competitors. The telephone will not ring unless you are prepared to make the initial contact.

Good public relations are what you make of them and can mean the difference between dragging your feet and taking off; between paying for your own advertising or obtaining free publicity. For example, a short congratulatory letter to clients after passing their tests will help to increase future recommendations.

Brochures and leaflets should clearly describe the kind of services you provide and any conditions you may want to attach to them. They must be honest, not misleading. Decide on the main message you want to get over and keep the following ground rules in mind when preparing them: get the material laid out professionally with sufficient emphasis on the main message; make sure the advertising states where, when and how to obtain your services; make the text sufficiently compelling to motivate potential customers; point out the benefits and give potential customers reasons for selecting your services rather than your competitors'. An excellent example of a professional approach to this aspect is shown in the 'Code of Conduct' which is issued by the Motor Schools Association and supplied to its members.

New drivers benefit from properly structured and more intensive training, together with the wider introduction of group training facilities. Instructor training, remedial, defensive and pre-driver courses are the four main areas with potential. There is room for improving the quality of training services and potential for instructors to increase their activities in:

- more efficient, structured training for new drivers
- refresher training courses
- remedial training for traffic offenders
- theory training linked to EC proposals for the driving test
- various types of defensive driving courses

- pre-driver and traffic education courses
- full-time/residential 'L' driver courses.

'L' Driver Training

Traditionally, driving lessons usually mean one or two sessions per week over a prolonged period of time. This spreads the cost but increases the number of lessons needed, whereas condensed training reduces both. Group learning is another way to reduce costs and improve standards. Credit facilities are available to clients wishing to take more concentrated courses. Full-time courses, however, are not completely without their problems as difficulty may be experienced in arranging test appointments. There is also the risk that the client may not be ready for the test after completing the course.

There is still tremendous public resistance to tuition in automatic vehicles. However, they do make learning easier especially for the disabled, older people and others with minor handicaps. The provision of this type of service will require an extremely high population density to support it.

Some aspects of driving can be learned more effectively in a classroom away from the stress caused by traffic. Although the public are still a little sceptical about this kind of training, there are opportunities for instructors with the appropriate skills. Running courses through adult education services provides a sound source of new pupils for practical lessons.

There are opportunities for instructors to negotiate contracts with industry, the Armed Forces or the Manpower Training Services who frequently require the services of driving instructors to train students where driving is a necessary part of their subsequent work. Pre-driver courses are already run by some education authorities and there are many opportunities for instructors in both state and private schools. Instructors are advised to attain suitable training before embarking on any schemes involving classroom teaching.

Advanced/Defensive Driving

The main difference between these is that advanced driving is often learned on a trial-and-error basis from real-life experience, while defensive driving can be learned from contrived experiences. Defensive driving involves learning to identify specific risk factors and to respond to them in a manner which will minimise the danger.

Courses in defensive and economy driving techniques for experienced motorists can be a refreshing change. You will need to convince companies that the cost of these courses can be recouped from more economical and efficient drivers and reduced insurance, repairs and running costs.

Diversification/Use of Existing Facilities

Provisional licence holders and newly qualified drivers spend millions of pounds each year on books and services. Instructors should have copies of the Highway Code and other study materials in the car for on-sale to the learner. There is no reason why they should not also sell driving shoes, gloves and sunglasses or receive introductory commissions on new or secondhand vehicles, act as agents for car insurance and membership subscriptions to motoring or breakdown organisations. Sales could net an extra £1000 per annum.

Motor insurance agents with expensive offices in the high streets might like to reduce their costs by sharing facilities with a driving school. In addition both businesses should benefit from their association with each other. Car dealers also need new ways of enticing the public into their showrooms. Negotiate the use of their facilities for group training nights, pre-driver sessions and pre-test demonstrations.

Groups of local instructors can cut the cost of opening High Street offices or classrooms by sharing the expense. This enables instructors to provide a wider range of services, professional reception and booking facilities and makes expansion into other fields easier and less risky. Negotiating new and larger contracts from industry is also made simpler.

Starting Your Own School

Many instructors start up their own school, only after a great deal of investigation and consideration. Others tend to drift in with less of an idea of what is involved. The skills required to run a successful driving school are more complex than those required of a good instructor. As a driving school proprietor, you will have to deal with other people and make decisions concerning them. Contrary to popular belief, the customer may not always be right! Sometimes, you may have to adopt a firm line with a client who presents himself for a lesson after a lunchtime session at the pub, or a dangerously incompetent one insisting on taking a test.

Are you aware of the law as it may affect you and your new business? Check on possible 'changes of use' to either your home or office with the local planning department. Remember, too, that you will need to inform the local tax inspector of your changed circumstances.

Starting up your own school may result in a temporary lowering of your lifestyle while your business is becoming established and it can be a long hard struggle without the moral support of close relatives. Working for yourself means making decisions which involve others. Be realistic about the risks you are taking. Decide on the minimum weekly income you need to meet existing commitments, such as mortgage, rates, gas, electricity, hire purchase payments, insurance and housekeeping. What additional commitments will be incurred by the business?

Before making any decision, the following are some of the factors you ought to consider:

1. The capital requirements of establishing a driving school extend far beyond the cost of the tuition vehicle and include such items as road tax, dual controls, insurance, signs, telephone, teaching aids, stationery, office equipment and the cost of promotional brochures and financing the first three months' advertising. Various ways in which the tuition vehicle can be financed are looked at in Chapter 21.

2. Costs will be incurred whether the vehicle is operating or not. In addition to the costs of setting up the vehicle, running costs should be budgeted for. For example, to be on the safe side, petrol consumption should be estimated at half a gallon per lesson. You will also need to make provision for cleaning, servicing, routine maintenance such as tyres, brakes and clutches and other repairs. You should also make provision for unforeseen circumstances such as the consequences of accidents, ie the payment of insurance excesses and hire car charges.

3. Being self-employed means that no-one else is going to provide for or pay your wages when you are on holiday. Set aside a sum to cover this and remember that the bills will still keep on coming in while you are away. Are you in good health? What provisions can you make for illness? There are specialist accident and sickness schemes available for driving instructors. Remember, too, that you will probably not wish to continue working until you can no longer do so – make provisions for your retirement.

Instructor Associations

At the present time, there are about 32000 Approved Driving Instructors registered with the Department of Transport. Many of these ADIs are represented by trade associations at both local and national level. There are also several 'umbrella' organisations to which most of the associations belong. However, despite the apparent choice of representation for the individual instructor, the fact remains that most ADIs do not belong to any association. It is also clear that, partly due to the lack of clear representation, the industry is fragmented in its approach to matters involving both business and technical expertise, including the need for training and retraining. The Department, for example, consults with six separate organisations on all matters relating to driving instruction. Information is then disseminated to instructors through those organisations.

The clear message to *all* instructors is, therefore, that they should join an association – or indeed, two or more associations in order to obtain the kind of representation required at local and national levels and to make their views known.

Ask different instructors what they want from an association and you will probably receive many different answers. Some will feel that associations should develop minimum standards of instruction and promote higher standards of road safety, while a few see them as bodies for setting standards of professional and ethical behaviour which may improve the status of the industry.

Others think the main benefit from membership is up-to-date information and an opportunity to exchange views and experiences relevant to instruction, and some see meetings more as social events. Employers may feel that associations should promote their personal business interests while the employee may want them to further minimum standards of employment.

Some self-employed or franchised instructors may want to prevent new schools starting up in competition; others may just want the provision of commercial services and marketing support.

A major problem for many self-employed instructors is that they choose to work in self-imposed isolation. In this respect the small local associations are potentially one of an instructor's greatest assets. Individuals can help to shape the future of the industry by becoming a member of a local association, especially if it is affiliated to one of the national organisations. It is estimated that there are well over 150 small local groups throughout the country.

They are formed to further the common interests of local instructors and to improve the quality of service to the public. There is little or no conflict between groups and they have much to offer instructors in the form of advice, local seminars, joint visits and various kinds of social function. Meetings tend to be rather enthusiastic and discursive, generally informative affairs. Members sometimes work together as co-operatives to provide additional facilities which they would otherwise find uneconomical.

These associations can bring pressure to bear locally at Traffic Area level and can express their views at national level through affiliated membership of the larger bodies such as the ADI National Joint Council and the Driving Instructor's Scottish Council.

ADI National Joint Council

The Approved Driving Instructors National Joint Council (NJC) is a consortium of national and local instructors associations. It was formed with the aim of unifying the industry by offering membership to associations and organisations rather than individuals. Membership at the present time consists of 28 instructor associations including three national organisations representing a total of some 6600 ADIs.

The Council meets usually quarterly, and holds a National Conference annually. Since its formation in 1973 the NJC has been actively involved in the training of instructors and particularly the training of 'tutors'.

Tutor training courses, developed with the assistance of the Department of Transport, comprehensively cover the whole of the examination syllabus and more besides. Instructor training is structured in modular form with built-in flexibility to cater for the individual trainee's needs. There are now NJC qualified tutors in many parts of the country, and ADI training courses are available in many areas.

Further information about the NJC and the courses is available from: General Secretary, ADI NJC, 41 Edinburgh Road, Cambridge CB4 1QR (telephone 0233-359079).

The Driving Instructors' Association

The DIA is the largest independent trade association for 'Road Safety Educationalists' in the world. It has full-time staff who are available to help driving instructors, potential instructors and all who are concerned with driver training, at any time. Advice on training, professional and business matters is always available.

Membership

Becoming a member of the DIA is vitally important to all concerned in the Driver Education Industry for the following reasons:

1. To enable the DIA to act on behalf of majority views with interested parties on important issues involving the industry.
2. To liaise with various bodies concerned with forming future legislation and policy pertaining to the industry.
3. To create a far higher level of dissemination of knowledge through the media to the general public on the subject of driver education.
4. To increase public awareness of legislation relating to driver education and its related training industry.
5. To promote and develop ideas and projects which will ultimately increase the social standing of the driver training educationalist in the UK.

Membership benefits
- Driving magazine
- Training car insurance
- Adverse weather insurance
- Safeguard with insurance
- Accountancy bureau
- Car purchase plan
- Legal services
- Technical services
- Mail order supplies

The DIA was founded in 1978 to represent the professional driving instructor. Since that time it has established itself as the largest independent organisation of its kind in the world. The DIA is a proprietary association, the proprietors being DIA (Int) Ltd and is officially consulted by both the British and European Parliament. DIA members are protected from any financial liability from the Association, and there is an Annual General Meeting at which the Association's General Purposes Committee is democratically elected from the floor. There are a number of other committees, each dealing with a particular aspect of the Association's work, including 'education', 'future legislation', 'technical matters', 'information services' and 'publicity'. The Association is concerned with the future of the professional instructor and over the years has offered a unique range of seminars, conferences and exhibitions for the profession. The Headquarters of the DIA is now Safety House, Beddington Farm Road, Croydon CR0 4X2 (telephone 01-665 5151).

The Driving Instructors' Association is an international organisation, designed to represent all those who are concerned with professional driver training and road safety education. Membership is open to all on an individual basis, and is important to everyone in the road safety environment. By ensuring that members come from all aspects of road user training a total representation of the industry is ensured. Membership offers many benefits to individual instructors, as well as to companies and government departments with a permanent two-way exchange of ideas, information and expertise.

DIAmond Advanced Instructor

Professional instructors who have gained the Diploma in Driving Instruction apply to take a practical module held at the Department of Transport Driving Establishment, Cardington. The stringent driving test ensures that a DIAmond Advanced Instructor can justly claim to be one of the highest qualified instructors in the world. DIAmond Advanced Instructors must sign a Certificate of Professional Competence and be an Approved Driving Instructor. Those driving instructors who are successful in achieving DIAmond Advanced Instructor status will be eligible to take advantage of the benefits of special, professional services.

Driving Instructors' Scottish Council (DISC)

The Council was formed on 6 October 1974 when the Scottish Region of the Motor Schools Association invited Scottish based associations to co-operate in the pursuit of their commonly held policies and to co-ordinate their efforts.

The Council comprises two representatives from each of its affiliated associations. It has two administrative officers who are appointed bi-annually and who do not represent any of the member associations.

The Council is consulted by the Department of Transport on all matters relating to driver testing, driver training and other road safety matters in Scotland.

The associations which currently hold seats on the Council are: Aberdeen & District; Dundee & District; Edinburgh; Approved Driving Instructors of Scotland; and the Motor Schools Association (Scottish Region).

For further information please contact the secretary of DISC at: 5 North Lodge Avenue, Motherwell ML1 2RP (telephone 0698 68711).

Addresses of the individual associations are given in Appendix III (page 360).

Motor Schools Association

The Motor Schools Association of Great Britain Limited (MSA) was formed on 31 March 1935 just before the driving test which also started in that year. The association's principal aim then, as now, was to set standards of professional and ethical behaviour for teachers of driving.

Originally run purely as a national body, with the governing council elected each year at a national AGM, it was decided in the mid 1950s to regionalise the organisation to improve its democracy and representation. In 1958 the association become incorporated under the title of the Motor Schools Association of Great Britain Ltd. Being a company limited by the guarantee of its members, this means that no dividends are paid and that every member is a part owner of the association.

The MSA is run on behalf of members by the Board of Management, and members are elected to the board from local elections held annually in each region. The board is therefore made up of one representative from each region together with a maximum of three co-opted members, usually brought on to the board to carry out specific tasks.

Voting at these elections as well as on matters of policy is restricted to full MSA members who must be qualified ADIs. There are various other classes of MSA membership but only full members are eligible to vote or to sit on the Board of Management.

As well as annual general meetings, meetings for members and non-members are held all over the country, and it is from these meetings that members' representatives can get to know the views of members. So if you have a point to make, make sure you are there.

In addition to setting professional standards (all members agree to abide by a code of conduct agreed with the Office of Fair Trading), the MSA also prides itself on the information and representation available to its members. Most of the information passed on to members is contained in the MSA's national and regional magazines. The MSA *News Journal*, published bi-monthly, is sent free to all members who also receive free copies of their local MSA Regional Instructor Magazine twice a year. Every member therefore receives eight magazines each year, plus the Annual Report and Year Book. In addition members are mailed directly with any important information, particularly when the MSA is contacted by the Department of Transport as a consultative body. On these occasions information usually goes direct to members. This keeps everyone right up to date on current issues and gives every member an opportunity to voice his or her opinion. A truly representative view can then be put forward to the DTp. The MSA is also involved in many other activities designed to benefit members including training courses, legal advice services, supply of training aids etc.

Over the past 50 years the Motor Schools Association has built an enviable reputation and tradition in the provision of training courses for its members. In keeping with this tradition the following courses are available to members:

Instructors Refresher Course – 5 Days
The aim of the course is to enable the ADI to evaluate his or her potential as a teacher of driving and to achieve it.

Approved Defensive Driving Assessor – 5 Days
This qualification is required for those seeking entry on to the joint MSA-RoSPA Register of Advanced Driving Instructors.

Motor Schools Association Tutors Qualification
This highly respected qualification is available to MSA members who wish to be recognised as a Tutor of Potential Driving Instructors. Members who wish to qualify will be required to undertake a three-part course and to pass searching final examinations at each stage, including a rigorous driving test at the DTp training establishment.

Part One – 5 days
Part Two – allow 1 day
Part Three – 5 days

The course ends with final examinations both in theory and practical ability as instructor and tutor.

The association is an organisation of driving instructors, owned by driving instructors, run by driving instructors for driving instructors. In fact – YOU!

There is no joining fee and special rates are offered for the first year's membership. Annual subscription thereafter is £25. Further details can be obtained from MSA, 182A Heaton Moor Road, Stockport, Cheshire SK4 4DU (telephone: 061-443 1611); Fax: 061-443 1699; Membership (November 1989) 6697.

The National Association of Approved Driving Instructors (NAADI)

The NAADI is controlled by executive committee members nominated from various regions. Membership is open to ADIs only. Its purpose is to represent the interests of driving instructors. It provides members with a bi-monthly newsletter and other commercial services. There is no joining fee and the annual subscription is £20. Further details can be obtained from the Membership Secretary, 90 Ash Lane, Hale Barns, Altrincham WA15 8PB. Membership – approximately 200.

The RAC Register of Instructors

This Register was formed by the Royal Automobile Club when driving tests started, in 1935, to establish the first impartially recognised qualification for professional driving instructors. Its aim, as then, is to serve the public and the driving instruction industry by promoting and providing high quality driving instruction combined with high standards of personal character and integrity. For ADIs the RAC Register provides an additional qualification to which they may aspire; to the public it is a register to which they may and do apply for details of recommended driving instructors.

Entry is subject to approval of references followed by passing a practical examination. Driving schools and driver training centres may also become RAC Registered, and instructors and such organisations may be described as RAC Registered if accepted. Promotional, training and administrative materials are available.

Members are kept fully briefed in DTp, road safety and other activities through a monthly newsletter and quarterly journal *Instructor*.

The RAC Register of Instructors comes under the jurisdiction of RAC Driver Training Division which also provides Defensive Driver Training Programmes for company drivers.

Driving has never been more demanding than in the present day, with more cars on the road, faster moving traffic and the ever increasing pressure on company drivers trying to get from A to B. With road accidents increasing in number and cost, and insurance premiums and repair bills escalating, RAC Defensive Driver Training provides a wide variety of 'hands-on' courses, run by skilled RAC instructors drawn from their Register, designed to improve performance.

For further details of the RAC Register of Instructors and Defensive Driver Training, please apply to: RAC Driver Training, RAC House, PO Box 100, South Croydon, Surrey CR2 6XW.

Chapter 2

Defensive Driving

Road Accidents – An Epidemic

Every year accidents kill over 5000 road users in the UK and seriously injure another 300 000. This is approximately equivalent to exploding a Hiroshima sized Atom bomb over a small town somewhere in Britain every year. The cost to the community is over £2500 million a year or £288 000.00 per hour. Every day 14 men, women and children die from road accidents caused by lack of attention, deficient driving skills or impairment. Every hour 30 people are seriously injured, many of them children.

Why Accidents Happen

TRRL Supplementary Report 567, 'The known risks we run: the highway' by Barbara E Sabey and H Taylor identifies the contributory factors involved in road accidents.

Vehicle defects contribute to about 8 per cent of all accidents.
This includes factors relating to:

> tyres (3.3%); brakes (3.2%); steering (.34%); lights (.49%); mechanical failure (1%); electrical failure (.2%); loads (.49%); windscreen (.2); bad visibility (.2%); overall poor condition (.25%); unsuitable design (.44%).

Adverse road environment contributes to about 28 per cent of accidents.
This category includes factors relating to:

Adverse Road Design (15.5%) ie:
- unsuitable layout or junction design
- poor visibility due to layout

Adverse Environment (13.8%) ie:
- slippery road or flooded surface
- lack of maintenance
- weather conditions or dazzle

Inadequate Furniture or Markings (7.7%) ie:
- inadequate signs, worn road markings
- street lighting

Obstructions (6.3%) ie:
- road works
- parked vehicles or other objects

Human error contributes to about 95% of all road accidents.
It includes factors relating to:

Perceptive errors (56%) ie:
- lack of concentration
- failure to see or recognise the risk
- misjudgement of speed or distance

Lack of skill (22%) ie:
- inexperience
- lack of judgement
- incorrect actions or decisions

Manner of execution (66%) ie:
- excessive speed
- unsafe overtaking
- failure to look
- following too closely
- irresponsible reckless, frustrated or aggressive behaviour

Impairment (31%) ie:
- alcohol
- fatigue
- drugs
- illness
- emotional distress.

An Introduction to Defensive Driving

In Britain we used to have one of the best road safety records in the world, and to some extent still do. But, while many other nations are forging ahead with improvements in learner driver training and education, we are beginning to fall further behind. The traditional approach to driver training in the UK is based on altruism. This implies that safe drivers require an attitude of mind that embodies consideration for the rights and *safety of others.*

While no-one would seriously argue the desirability of these qualities, the OECD (Organisation for Economic Co-operation and Development) Road Research Report 1981 'Guidelines for Driver Instruction' points out that the behaviour of individuals is seldom governed by altruistic motives and suggests that training should prepare drivers with an attitude to preserve *their own safety.*

As human behaviour is generally motivated more powerfully by self preservation, the report suggests that training should be founded on the driver's natural instincts to survive and aim to make 'reduced risk driving strategies' a personal motivation for survival. Defensive driver training carried out in other countries clearly shows that reduced risk driving strategies offer an exciting new hope for the future. It has already shown it can reduce the risk of accident involvement of qualified drivers by up to 50 per cent. The strategy places greater emphasis on the perception of risk, increasing hazard awareness and influencing more favourable and safer attitudes by linking risk to accident potential.

Current UK practice is that most practical skill training is carried out in a vehicle on the road and that most theory is learnt at home with the Highway Code. During in-car lessons, partly because of commercial pressures, there tends to be an over-emphasis on the superficial acquisition of simple skills and routine procedures in preparation for the driving test.

A common misconception in driving instruction seems to be that all in-class tuition is theory and all in-car training practical. New drivers are unlikely to obtain all the knowledge they need, or generate safe attitudes, or fully develop their perceptual-motor skills from in-car practice alone; equally they cannot learn to effectively manipulate the car controls at home from the Highway Code or in a classroom. A real life emergency confrontation in a dangerous situation is not the best place to be introduced to the rules and responses required. Nor is it always possible to create high-risk situations during practical in-car on-road lessons because of the danger caused, and because of the unreliable occurrence and inconsistent nature of learning experiences. Many aspects of theory are better learnt in the car, and many aspects of perceptual-motor skills are better learnt away from the fuss and buzz of busy traffic.

It is argued by many that the cost of more comprehensive and fully integrated courses on driving would make learning prohibitively expensive. This argument presupposes that traditional teaching methods will be retained. Systematic techniques can reduce the cost of training or obtain higher levels of achievement for the same cost. In-car and in-class training must be integrated in a way which will complement and reinforce each other. The classroom and organised 'home study' programme present instructors with alternatives and a challenge and opportunity to present a wider variety of experiences to new drivers. Systematic 'home study' of Highway Code rules related to current lessons is one way to add more practical meaning to the theory. More effective methods of training new drivers, and of improving the skills of full licence holders, must be tried alongside traditional methods if we are to reduce accidents without increasing the cost.

Influences on Driver Behaviour

Attitude-related Factors

Attitudes reflect the manner in which a person responds to people, things, situations and problems. They are formed from total personal experiences from birth interacting with the emerging personality. Attitude is assumed to influence the behaviour of drivers and reckless or unsafe actions are often attributed to negative attitudes. When making a judgement on another person, driver or traffic situation, opinions can rarely be objective. Judgements are influenced by attitudes assumed in advance towards the matter in question. Attitude tends to make drivers see things not as they actually are, but as they imagine them to be.

Knowledge is thought to generate favourable attitudes. In driver instruction, as in education in general, there is an implied suggestion that the acquisition of knowledge is sufficient to generate attitudes which in turn determine driver behaviour. Reliable scientific data supporting this theory is lacking and the hypothesis may be questioned because attitudes also contain powerful motivational and emotional influences. The OECD suggest that a reasonable hypothesis is that 'systematic training in strenuous traffic situations and in emergencies (for instance braking and steering on slippery surfaces) may, in addition to improving skill, also have an effect on the driver's apprehension of risks and self-criticism'.

The development of favourable attitudes and the changing of negative attitudes is a central purpose for driving instructors, and of vital importance. This may be attempted by education, persuasion and personal example. When faced with influences which affect their attitudes, drivers may characteristically react by being rigid and unresponsive, flexible and objective, or suggestible and over-responsive.

The design of the road environment permits a certain degree of road user error without incurring accidents. This can negatively reinforce erroneous actions simply because drivers get away with the deficient behaviour. This tends to develop a feeling of immunity and influence the individual's attitude as to the degree of risk they think they are taking. Attempts to encourage favourable attitudes may be more successful if directed to emphasise the consequences of unsafe behaviour rather than simply aimed towards altruistic ideals.

Various teaching methods may be used to develop safe driver attitudes. These should involve a combination of formal lectures, lesson demonstrations and discussion exercises which link the individual's survival to defensive driving behaviour. After completing the course new drivers should be able to:

(a) recognise the features of road design where accidents are most likely to occur;
(b) identify the causes of road accidents and correctly assess their personal risk of becoming involved in one;
(c) correctly estimate their own driving capabilities and limitations;
(d) apply defensive techniques that minimise the level of potential risk of becoming involved in an accident.

It should be remembered that:

1. Favourable attitudes do not automatically result from the acquisition of knowledge.
2. The behaviour of an individual is rarely governed by altruistic motives.
3. The development of safe driving attitudes is thought to be linked to the individual's perception and assessment of the potential risks for their personal involvement in an accident.
4. As attitudes are formed from the 'total learning experience', instructors should *always* set a good example. (Particular mention

should be made of situations where instructors may be off guard, for example between lessons and when conveying learners to and from training areas and after a driving test.)

5. Due to motivational and emotional characteristics, a driver's attitude can suddenly change from consideration to hostility.

Motivation describes the personal needs and drives of the individual and a simplistic view of it suggests that these are directed to survival, wellbeing and achieving fulfilment of personal desires. These sometimes manifest themselves in unusual and seemingly illogical ways. For example, a driver may take risks that he might otherwise find unacceptable:

    (a) if late for work or an important appointment;

    (b) to get the better of the driver of the sports car that just passed him;

    (c) to demonstrate the superiority of skills and/or to gain the admiration of friends of the opposite sex, or peers, or self.

Emotion is the term used to describe states of feeling such as love, hate or fear. Intense emotions like anger, frustration and grief tend to focus the attention of the mind upon itself. This lowers the attention on the driving task and limits the perceptive abilities of the mind. Anger may result from an argument with a wife or husband, frustration may result from being held up behind a slow-moving vehicle, anxiety may be the result of worries about work or an important appointment. Inexperienced drivers lacking in confidence, may suffer from their own ill-founded fears that they cannot cope. Driving is, in itself, a stressful activity. Deficient knowledge or skills can result in frustration and generate destructive emotions.

Personality is described as the outcome of inherited potentialities modified by experience. The individual's perception of oneself is different from that personality as it is perceived by others. The overt personality which an individual displays is rarely the same as that perceived within one's own personal consciousness. Personality tends to be inconsistent; faced with different circumstances the same driver may display different sides of his make-up. There is evidence to suggest that extrovert drivers are more likely to be involved in accidents than introverts. This may be linked to the driver's ability to attend to the driving task for long periods of time.

Knowledge-Related Factors

Knowledge is assumed to influence attitudes and assist in the acquisition of driving skills.

In driving, objectives are used to describe what new drivers are expected to do at the end of a course of lessons. They are stated in observable behaviour terms and attempt to communicate the sought-for changes in the learner toward others. Success or failure in the driving test is measured in terms of whether the objectives contained on the test application form and in the DL68 have been achieved.

There are a number of recognised classifications or taxonomies of educational objectives which relate to the affective, cognitive or psychomotor domains of the mental life (referring to attitude, knowledge and skill respectively). These include the Krathwohl taxonomy in the affective domain; the Bloom taxonomy in the cognitive domain (intellectual skills); and the Simpson/Harrow taxonomy in the psychomotor domain.

Bloom's taxonomy and classifications in the cognitive domain are concerned with the measurement of knowledge. Despite criticisms that the distinctions between the levels are unclear and the hierarchy questionable, it is the most widely used taxonomy. There are six ascending levels or classes of knowledge in Bloom's taxonomy. These are knowledge, comprehension, application, analysis, synthesis and evaluation. It is essential that learning drivers are taught at least to comprehend and apply, otherwise their knowledge will remain more or less useless. It is generally accepted that knowledge helps to generate favourable attitudes; conversely, inadequate or incorrect knowledge might result in the development of negative attitudes leading to unsafe driver behaviour.

The following are examples of objectives in the cognitive domain (knowledge) of the mental life.

At the end of a course of lessons new drivers should be able to:

1. Comprehend the numbers of road users killed and injured; the distribution of fatal/serious injury accidents among groups of drivers, passengers, cyclists and pedestrians; the distribution of accident involvement relating to sex/age/experience; the cause/consequence/cure of road accidents (see DTp Road Accidents Great Britain HMSO).

2. Recognise road, traffic and environmental risk factors (see *Learn to Drive* by Margaret and Nigel Stacey, published by Kogan Page).

3. Recognise the driver's legal responsibility for roadworthiness and the need for daily and weekly vehicle checks; regular servicing in accordance with the manufacturer's recommendations; and particularly the safety implications of the brakes/lights/steering/tyres/loads (see Appendix II, page 352).

4. Comprehend the principles relating to the control and stability of a vehicle in motion and those to do with maintaining road surface adhesion (see Chapter 3, page 48).

5. Comprehend the principles of attending, perceiving and responding to the road, traffic and vehicle environment, and recognise the limitations of human attention capacity.

6. Recognise the effects of impairment caused by alcohol, fatigue, drugs, illness and emotional stress (see page 27 of this chapter).

7. Comprehend and apply the rules and procedures outlined in the Highway Code and comprehend the regulations contained at the rear of the Highway Code booklet together with understanding the need for them.

8. Recognise that defensive driving strategies provide an effective way of responding to the demands placed upon drivers by recommended procedures and legislation.

Perceptual Motor Skills

Driving involves activities relating to the effective, cognitive and psycho-motor domains. The psychomotor domain is the most important of these due to the fact that driving mainly involves the perceptual-motor sub-processes. These are a complex set of interacting perceptive and manipulative skills which are executed partly consciously and partly subconsciously.

The driving task involves *attending, perceiving* and *responding* safely to driving relevant stimulae. The driver must obtain relevant information from the environment, process it and respond with decisions and the appropriate car control skills. The perceptual-motor skills include:

- paying *attention* to the driving task
- applying *systematic visual search* procedures
- *identifying and awarding priorities* for/to driving relevant cues
- *assessing* the potential risk of accidents
- *anticipating* possible and subsequent events
- *deciding* upon appropriate action
- *responding* in a restrained manner, by communicating with others and by executing controlled changes in speed and/or position with continual re-assessment.

At the end of a course of lessons, a new driver should be able to:

(a) concentrate on the driving task by applying an effective visual search system, allocating priorities and distributing attention over the whole road, traffic and vehicle situation;

(b) perceive related information concerning road geometry, surface conditions, advance warning and other signs and road markings, signals by other road users, obstructions to intended path, view restrictions, and the position, movement and potential movement of other road users;

(c) draw upon previous experience and learned habits and relate these to the information collected; anticipate subsequent and possible events; assess the levels of risk involved and decide upon the appropriate actions;

(d) communicate intentions and/or indicate presence to other road users by correct use of signals, position, speed, warning devices, eye contact;

(e) adjust speeds to maintain safety margins relating to: following distances, distances seen and known to be clear, perceptual workload and personal driving ability;

(f) cross/emerge/meet/overtake/others safely and permit others to overtake/cross/emerge/meet safely;

(g) maintain adequate clearances from other vehicles and road users allowing additional space for pedestrians and other road users hidden from view;

(h) demonstrate a knowledge of maintaining directional control during emergency braking; the actions required in emergencies such as aquaplaning, skidding, blowouts and brake failure; the value of seatbelts when involved in a collision; accident and first aid procedures.

Attention to the Driving Task

Driving skills are executed part consciously and part subconsciously, depending upon the level of attention the driver places on the task the demands being made by the vehicle, road and traffic conditions. Attention occurs at both conscious and subconscious levels; and the amount allocated to particular situations fluctuates according to priorities awarded, the task demands and the driver's personal level of arousal and apprehension.

Attention can either be divided over the whole traffic scene or focussed selectively on specific areas or objects of particular interest. Selective attention requires more effort and can only be sustained for short periods. New drivers find it particularly difficult to concentrate for long periods although this will normally improve with practice. High levels of conscious attention are difficult for anyone to sustain for periods in excess of 20 minutes. This suggests that in training, drivers would benefit from imposed breaks and changes in activity, particularly during the early stages of learning.

Experienced drivers learn how to allocate and distribute their attention to maximise the useful information they obtain about road and traffic hazards. A hazard is anything containing an element of risk or potential risk that causes the driver concern or makes him consider changes in direction and/or speed. For example:

- physical features such as bends, junctions and hillcrests
- blind areas of road, footpath or relevant nearby areas
- movement or potential movement of others into or across the path of the car
- road surface condition and other factors affecting stability/ adhesion.

Actual hazards contain risk factors which are easily seen and identified. Most drivers are prepared to act when they recognise, for example, a pedestrian running across the road. Potential hazards tend to be more difficult for the untrained eye to recognise. They hold risk factors which are less easily seen, difficult to identify and sometimes hard for inexperienced minds to even accept. They include the potential for movement across their path, restricted sightlines behind parked vehicles and factors affecting vehicle stability.

Commonsense is not inherited. It has to be learnt from practical experience

New drivers should not be expected to recognise hazards until they have actual practical experience of what to look for and why. What may be obvious to an experienced driver may not warrant a second thought to an untrained eye. Not only should drivers recognise the obvious risk caused by the child running out into the road, but also the less obvious risk that a child standing on the pavement may run out or the even less obvious risk of the unseen child who may run out from behind a parked vehicle.

To experienced professionals, hazard recognition is almost instantaneous with little conscious effort and the response is an instinctive and skilled reaction. To the novice, hazard recognition is much slower and the process requires tremendous conscious effort. Furthermore, traffic hazards rarely occur in isolation. This means the new driver must attend to and identify other risk factors in different parts of the road. Priorities must be allocated, decisions taken and action executed. The perceptive capacities of new drivers are particularly limited and if exceeded a 'perceptive overload' may occur. This means the driver is likely to attend to only one of the risk factors, ignoring or rejecting the others. Such pressures can be reduced by appropriate reductions in speed.

Perception

Perception is the brain's interpretation of information provided by the eyes, ears and other senses. The perception of a particular traffic hazard involves the primary information-processing functions of the brain. These appear to involve comparisons with existing knowledge and previous experience. Hazard recognition requires an active and rapid assessment of the potential risks involved in a particular situation. The driver must anticipate events before they occur. This relies heavily on stored memories of previous learning or similar experiences. Other relevant factors include the driver's personality and levels of arousal, motivation and attitude. Perception is the driver's visual and mental awareness! It provides information on speed, position and timing.

Numerous studies show that drivers have limited perceptual capacities but are frequently faced with an overload of information from the vehicle and the road and traffic environment. A decision must be made to attend to some of the available information and reject, ignore or fail to attend to other aspects of it. New drivers should be encouraged to recognise this discrepancy between the task demands and their own personal capabilities. Such an acknowledgement may serve to motivate the application of defensive driving techniques as a means to bridge the gap between the task demands and ability.

Visual Search Skills

Passive observation of the road and traffic scene is unlikely to provide the level of awareness required to drive safely. The driver is unlikely to obtain sufficient advance information, resulting in late, uncoordinated use of the controls. Passive observation is also likely to create additional stress which further reduces the driver's attention on relevant aspects. There seems to be a connection between passive observation and the failure of some new drivers to recognise themselves as an active part of the road and traffic situation. Encouragement in the use and development of an active visual road scan will not only provide more information earlier but will help to promote a more positive and active response to the environment.

The eye movements of experienced drivers are very rapid, moving quickly from one point of interest to another, checking and re-checking areas of risk. New drivers should be encouraged to practise an effective visual search system. The Smith-Cumming-Sherman system is widely recognised and taught by many experts throughout the world. An adaptation of these five rules is outlined below:

1. Look ahead to steer. It is more important for new drivers to concentrate on where they are going than on what their hands are doing on the wheel. Encourage learners to steer with their eyes and let their hands be guided by them. Emphasise the importance of steering accuracy over method.

   Drivers should look and plan well ahead in order to steer a safe and smooth line and make early adjustments to speeds in response to possible obstructions, road geometry and traffic signs.

2. Keep the eyes moving. Experiments carried out at the Transport and Road Research Laboratory relating to the eye movements of drivers shows that an experienced driver's eyes flit about, focussing upon one object after another in rapid succession. This seems to help drivers build up a more complete picture and improve awareness. Novice drivers tend to stare at fewer objects for longer periods of time. This may deprive the driver of essential information. A possible explanation for 'staring' is probably that the learner requires more time to assimilate traffic information, recognise risk factors, allocate priorities, assess risks and decide on an action.

   New drivers should be encouraged not to stare for long periods at one aspect of the traffic environment as this will probably result in steering off-course and important information about the road ahead being missed completely.

   New drivers should be encouraged to continually look for situations containing a potential for other road users to move into or turn across their course, and for areas of restricted vision which may be hiding other road users moving into or turning across their path.

   The eyes are naturally attracted to movement, bright colours and unusual happenings. Not all will be relevant to particular road and traffic situations and driving therefore requires an effective system of visual scanning which maximises the input of useful information.

3. Get the big picture. Encourage new drivers to apply the less sensitive periphery vision to sense the lateral position of the vehicle. They should learn to rely on it to detect movement of nearby objects. Research suggests that periphery vision, in experienced drivers, serves as a detection area for subsequent forveal fixations. Periphery vision also assists the driver in the judgement of speed.

4. Make others see you. Encourage new drivers to position themselves where they can see and be seen by other road users. Use the lights and horn where necessary and make proper use of the direction indicators and other signals. Encourage them to check that other road users are responding to their presence, signals and intentions.

5. Always look for alternatives. Encourage new drivers to look for and work out the alternative courses of action which may be required if events within the existing traffic situation change. Pre-decide the

actions and responses necessary in the event of a change. This enables drivers to keep alternative options for as long as possible right up to the 'point of no return'.

Assessing Risk

Driving is a continuous process of attending to, perceiving and responding to constantly changing needs involving the vehicle, the road layout and traffic conditions. Drivers must continually check, assess and re-assess the hazards and the responses they are making to them. Responses involve the

MIRROR/SIGNAL/MANOEUVRE and POSITION/SPEED/LOOK routines.

Within the individual elements of these routines new drivers must learn to:

- look, assess, and decide what action can safely be taken relating to information received from the *mirrors* and decide if a *signal* is necessary
- look, assess, and decide whether a *signal* is having the required effect on the actions of following traffic
- look, assess, and decide what effect any changes in *position and speed* are likely to have or are having on other road users; and decide what further *looks* may be required.

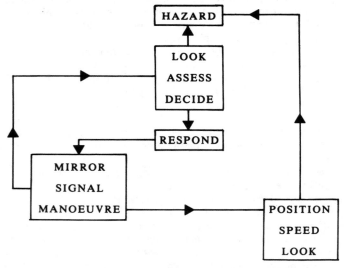

It seems probable that there is a connection between safe behaviour and a driver's personal assessment of the potential accident risk he attaches to individual hazards. On the other hand, it is suggested that some drivers, especially the young, deliberately seek risk and that the majority of new drivers require several years of experience to become relatively safe. This characteristic may be linked to lack of 'hazard awareness'. Risk assessment is influenced by a driver's knowledge and previous experiences and may either be learnt on a trial and error basis or from contrived experiences. It should not be assumed that because a driver recognises a hazard, for example a bend, that he will automatically assess the risk of accident potential with the possibility of vehicles hidden from view around the bend. Accident research suggests that most collisions result from deficiencies in the information processing task and not from deficient car control skills, and that a large proportion of collisions could be avoided if drivers were more aware of the risks involved and knew what to look for and expect.

New drivers should be taught to assess their role as an active part of the changing road and traffic environment. For example, they must not only respond to developing situations, but must see themselves as an active part of those developments, often contributing to them. The driver has a choice! The stresses generated and the risks taken together with unmanageable task demands can be reduced by the learners if they *choose* to do so by driving more slowly.

Assessing the risks and deciding on an appropriate response to a traffic hazard involves a continuous re-circulating chain of checking, re-checking, assessing and re-assessing a constantly changing environment. It involves:

1. Assessing the degree of risk involved in the hazard.
2. Awarding priorities to the hazard in relation to the whole traffic scene.
3. Directing further attention to it.
4. Deciding on a specific course of action.
5. Responding by signalling intentions and/or maintaining or changing speed and/or position to create time for the situation to change and/or to obtain additional information about the situation before re-assessing.

Anticipation is the driver's ability to predict the actions of other road users. The skill is related to risk assessment and they are often jointly called the hazard recognition skills. Anticipation is also closely linked to the visual search skills and involves attaching meaning to driving-relevant cues. Drivers must know:

- what to expect and the kind of things to look for
- why, where and when they must look most
- how to see effectively as opposed to just looking.

Risk assessment skills are linked to practical experience and the degree of accident potential the driver recognises in a particular situation. After introducing and encouraging the application of the basic rules, instructors should provide new drivers with plenty of practical experience in actively deciding between the possible and reasonable precautions required to reduce risk.

Making Decisions

This can be a difficult and inconsistent process for some. Many new drivers are indecisive and yet make rash decisions on the spur of the moment. One major problem seems to be that they make decisions before they have sufficient information on which to base them. Decisions frequently polarise between 'stop and go' where neither are correct, for example when a decision is required to initiate action which provides *time* to let the situation develop or to obtain more information. Inadequate information and hurried assessments appear to be a major cause of incorrect decisions. This stop/go, decision-making model is characteristic of those decisions which result in high accident risk. New drivers should be encouraged to make decisions early to initiate the actions needed to provide them with extra time and alternative choices of subsequent action. In difficult situations, reassure learners that feelings of doubt and uncertainty on the approach to many developing situations are quite normal and to be expected. For example, there are three possible choices when approaching a stationary car parked on the left 300 yards ahead with a stream of slow moving traffic approaching from the opposite direction:

1. It is safe to proceed or to carry out an intended manoeuvre.
2. It is unsafe at the moment to proceed or to execute an intended manoeuvre.
3. More information is needed to assess the situation or more time is required to permit development before a decision can be made.

Any decision to proceed, hold back, give way, wait or stop must be continually reassessed. For choices 2 and 3, the response is nearly always the same – to delay the ultimate manoeuvre, either until circumstances permit or until sufficient information has been obtained to make a decision to proceed. Explain also that the responses to 2 and 3 are virtually the same. They are:

- slow down and make time for the situation to develop
- slow down to obtain more information about the potential movement of pedestrians
- obtain more information about the presence or potential presence of any oncoming vehicles
- review the changed situation after and as a result of slowing down
- improve the view by changes in lateral position and/or 'feeling' the way forward cautiously.

Encourage learners to work things out in advance! For example, approaching a green traffic light, get them to anticipate the possibility of the lights changing and to be ready with the decision to stop. At some point on the approach, however, the learner will be too close to pull up safely. Once they have reached and crossed this point the only decision they can make is to continue. Encourage learners to continually re-assess what they will do if the lights change. The decisions can be made in advance leaving the response to be triggered by the event.

Lack of confidence sometimes prevents new drivers from making decisions. They may be frightened of doing wrong. This will result in inaction in traffic situations that require a response. Reassure them and provide them with plenty of encouragement to discuss the problem and plenty of opportunity to make decisions without fear of rebuke.

Hazard Recognition Skills

As they proceed along a road, the natural inclination of most drivers is to keep going unless it is unsafe. To assist the development of the hazard recognition skills, new drivers will require encouragement to actively search the road ahead and assess the safety of proceeding. They must also be made to recognise the consequences of their own actions or inaction. There is a tendency amongst new drivers to attend to the driving task in a very passive way. Because they are not actively establishing the safety of proceeding they tend not to respond when unsafe.

New drivers do not instinctively know what they are looking for and how to respond. They will require instruction on what to expect and how to predict the actions and mistakes of others. One of an instructor's primary aims is to encourage new drivers to obtain as much relevant information about the road and traffic environment as they can. For example:

1. To steer accurately and adjust to safe speeds before reaching a hazard they should be persuaded to look well (10 seconds) ahead for:

    physical features such as bends, gradients, road signs, road junctions;
    obstructions such as parked cars, roadworks and traffic holdups.

2. To maintain tyre and road surface friction, encourage them to:

    drive smoothly and approach hazards at suitable speeds for conditions;
    consider the temperature and weather conditions;
    consider the type and condition of the road surface;
    consider the effect of adverse camber on bends;
    maintain their vehicles properly, check tyre wear, condition and pressures.

3. To anticipate the actions, and act on the mistakes, of other road users, they must be encouraged to scan the road about four seconds ahead for anything with a potential for moving into or across their path such as:

    an approaching driver signalling right and who is nearing the turn;
    a pedestrian walking toward the junction they intend turning into;
    a cyclist ahead approaching a parked vehicle;
    the driver approaching the end of a side road;
    the child playing near the road;
    the dog off its lead;
    the car door opening.

4. To stop well within the distance they can see to be clear, new drivers must scan the road about four seconds ahead. They must identify any blind areas in their field of vision and adjust their speed according to the risk. They must fully understand the risk of road

users hidden from view or crossing into or across their path and must demonstrate this understanding by responding properly to features and conditions such as:

    parked vehicles and other obstructions in or near the roadway;
    building lines, walls and hedges approaching side roads and entrances;
    bends, hillcrests and 'dead ground';
    stationary traffic queues;
    heavy rain, shadows at night, fog and dazzle from sunlight/ headlights.

5. To avoid collisions with road users at the sides and rear, new drivers must be encouraged to make full use of their mirrors and periphery vision. They must understand the principles of communicating with other road users and of lane discipline and will demonstrate this understanding by responding safely to situations at the rear and sides such as:

    the vehicle driving in the blindspot or in the lane at the side;
    the vehicle waiting to overtake or coming up fast from behind;
    the cyclist passing on the left when setting off at traffic lights;
    the driver trying to overtake when the learner is turning right;
    the pedestrian dashing across the road through a queue of traffic.

6. Self-control is an important driving skill and emotions such as anger, frustration and depression can affect a driver's ability to think, reason and make rational judgements. Defensive driving requires the ability to recognise risk factors caused by these emotions. Instructors can assist new drivers to control their emotions by:

    identifying situations that can lead to upsets and pointing out that people often get emotional when faced with threatening situations;
    emphasising the need to leave sufficient time for journeys, pointing out that everyday traffic holdups are extremely frustrating when one is late;
    pointing out and tolerating the mistakes of other road users, emphasising the point that all drivers make them (compare the mistake to previous errors which may have been committed by the new driver). Suggest that emotions are directed to the driving errors of the person and not the person committing the error. Discuss areas of conflict and the different goals of those involved;
    emphasising that most emotional upsets are fairly temporary. Stress the need to allow time for 'cooling off' before driving. Depression and other emotional upsets such as grief and anxiety may last for several days. Persons in this state of mind should be advised not to drive;
    stopping for a short time if learners become upset either by their own performance or the behaviour of others.

7. Observance of traffic rules. The purpose of traffic legislation is to reduce the risks to all road users. However, new drivers must be left in no doubt that rights of way, rules of the road and speed limits do not guarantee the safe behaviour of other road users. They should be given tasks to learn the Highway Code rules and traffic procedures which relate to current lessons and practice. A Highway Code self learning programme which organises home study exercises for learners and relates to their practical lessons is set out in *Learn to Drive*, published by Kogan Page. Route finding is another skill which instructors should encourage drivers to develop. It not only involves their ability to read a road map but also their skill in reading signs and following directions without causing danger to other road users or impeding the flow of traffic.

Response and Car Control Skills

After carrying out the Look/Assess/Decide routine and starting a course of action to proceed, wait, or to delay progress to obtain more information before making a commitment, the new driver will respond with the routine procedures:

This is the Mirror/Signal/Manoeuvre/Position/Speed/Look routine

Mirror

Apply the Look/Assess/Decide routine to the mirror and consider how the information obtained from it will affect the intended actions.

Signals and Communication

Methods of communication between road users are complex and much broader than traditional signals such as direction indicators, arm signals to other road users, stop light signals, arm signals to traffic controllers, horn, flashing headlights and the hazard warning flasher. The communications system also involves:

- the speed of a vehicle
- the lateral position of a vehicle along the road
- implied signals of intent (linked to movement/position of pedestrians)
- eye contact with other road users
- courtesy signals and acknowledgements to other road users.

Little needs to be said about the use of direction indicators, arm signals and the other commonly recognised signals except perhaps to quote from a Ministry of Transport (as it then was) ADI News Bulletin dated April 1969.

'DO tell your pupil the facts about signals generally:

(i) Signals should be given only when the driver considers that they will be helpful to some other road user (including pedestrians), ie when they are *necessary*.

(ii) A candidate in the test is expected to be able to discriminate between a situation in which a signal is necessary and one in which it is not. It takes *time* and *practice* to learn discrimination; but there is no short cut.

DON'T let your pupil give directional signals both by indicator *and* by arm. He's got enough to think about already, remembering the timing and sequence of the operations involved in negotiating a junction. Combinations of indicator and arm signals lead to a number of difficulties:

   (i)   Loss of steering control and incorrect road positioning.
  (ii)   The arm signal being too brief and the indicator signal too late.
 (iii)   Braking or gear-changing (or both) being left too late.

   – all this because the driver has too many things to do at once.

DO make sure your pupil knows the facts about arm signals in the test:

Indiscriminate 'hand-wagging' is not (and never has been) accepted by the Ministry's Examiners. It is the hall-mark of inadequate driving instruction.'

Signalling by position

It is said by some motoring experts that the driver who maintains the correct steering course and position does not need signals. Although such statements are not completely valid they do contain some truth.

Anticipating an intended act from a driver's position or steering line is an important means of communication which can only be ignored at the driver's peril.

Correct positioning helps to confirm a signal given by the direction indicators. Where the position does not confirm a direction signal, other drivers may become confused. For example, a vehicle ahead may be signalling left, but if the position is that usually taken for a right turn others may understandably become confused because they are receiving conflicting information.

Signalling by speed

Speed and changes in it are also used by other road users as evidence of intended actions. For example, where a vehicle is signalling to turn left, positioned to turn left and is seen to be appropriately slowing down for the turn, there is a combination of evidence to suggest a left turn will be made. Other drivers and road users are not relying upon one single factor.

Another example of where speed signals the driver's intention to other road users is when a car approaches a give way line/sign too fast to allow it to give way, or perhaps when a car accelerates when it should more appropriately be slowing down.

By slowing down well before a pedestrian crossing a driver can clearly signal his intentions to the pedestrians waiting to cross.

Defensive signals

These are the signals a driver might use to warn road users of his presence. They consist of flashing the headlights or sounding the horn.

Another warning signal is the hazard flasher – this should be used in an emergency situation only.

Implied signals, eye contact and courtesy signals

Not only must drivers learn to recognise and interpret speed and movement they must also be alert to the conditions of implied or potential movement such as the pedestrian standing at the edge of the pavement near a zebra crossing.

A vehicle waiting at the give way line in a minor road has the potential to move into the path of a vehicle travelling on the main road and should be treated with concern.

Eye contact is another valid form of communication. For example, when slowing down on the approach to, or waiting at, a pedestrian crossing it helps to reassure pedestrians they have been seen. When waiting to pull into a line of slow-moving traffic it often persuades others to wait long enough for you to move out into the traffic stream.

Manoeuvre

The manoeuvre consists of the Position, Speed, Look routine. Suffice it to say it is anything involving change in speed or direction. It is normally always preceded and followed by an ongoing process of Looking, Assessing and Deciding.

Position and Speed

The senses used in the judgement of speed are: sight, hearing, balance and touch.

The interpretation of speed can be very misleading at times, particularly in a modern car with sound-insulated interiors. In the absence of vibration and noise on a smooth road with no nearby side features such as buildings, fencing or hedges, speed can seem deceptively slow.

Speed seems to be assessed from a combination of factors which appears to involve an established speed 'norm' learnt through previous experience.

The speed is judged from:

1. The rate at which visual images disappear to the sides.
2. Road, wind and engine noise.
3. The sense of balance when changing speeds and direction.
4. The general 'feel' of the vehicle on the road.
5. Comparisons with established 'speed norms'.
   (These speed norms can be very misleading, for example after travelling for a long distance at high speeds on a motorway when approaching the intersection at the end of the slip road.)

Adjusting speeds

Speed adjustments are required to maintain sufficient safety margins with respect to being able to stop in accordance with traffic conditions, visibility and regulations. These adjustments must take into account the critical perceptual/attention overload limitations of the driver in dealing with the traffic workload.

As speed is increased, the focus point for drivers is further ahead with a corresponding reduction in their field of vision or periphery vision. Where drivers need to attend to foreground detail, speed must be reduced. Periphery vision also assists drivers to judge their speed and position. Failure to reduce speed will result in important risk factors being ignored and reduced awareness of lateral positions and safety margins.

Awareness of position and direction is a perceptive skill developed by practice and experience.

Awareness is achieved mainly through an active visual scanning process observing the road and traffic environment in its entirety. The driver steers and positions along a safe course by observing the road geometry, features, signs and markings while visually searching for the movement or potential movement of other road users in order to compensate for them.

Maintaining a correct and safe position not only involves steering, but the driver's awareness and ability to control the speed.

Positioning involves adjusting speeds to maintain an adequate safety cushion between the vehicle ahead and in order that the driver can pull up under control in a precise position along the road as well as laterally when faced with an obstruction.

Positioning with safety and consideration involves:

1. The driving position in the road.
2. Driving in the centre of a lane.
3. Not changing lanes or lateral position unnecessarily, quickly or unexpectedly.
4. Allowing sufficient safety cushion between own vehicle and the one ahead.
5. Allowing sufficient safety margins when passing parked vehicles or other obstructions.
6. Allowing sufficient safety margins to allow for unexpected movement of other road users.
7. Selecting safe parking positions.
8. Manoeuvring into a suitable position at road junctions prior to, or in order to, take effective observations safely before emerging into a new road.
   (Too far back may mean the driver cannot see, too far forward may be dangerous.)
9. Positioning correctly when turning in order to cause the minimum of disruption to the flow of other traffic.

Other important aspects of positioning, concerned with maintaining good sightlines and visibility of the road ahead, are:

(a) Keeping too close to the left kerb prior to overtaking either stationary or moving vehicles, severely restricts visibility of the road ahead.
(b) Holdback position – when giving way to oncoming traffic before passing a parked vehicle, the driver should be prepared to wait well back from, and well out into the road to maintain the sightline beyond the obstruction. (Not too far out however as to impede the flow of oncoming traffic.)

Other considerations involve:

(c)   When waiting in a traffic queue, not blocking the access to side roads.

(d)   When waiting in a traffic queue, not pulling up so close to the vehicle ahead as to be unable to pull out should the need arise.

Final observations (Look)

This is precisely where the whole process of attending, assessing, deciding and responding started.

There is a tendency for many drivers to make commitments before they have sufficient information to reason properly through the problem. It is emphasised that driving is not a series of decisions to stop or go, and there is a particular need in traffic situations to slow down and see without making any definite commitment to stop or proceed whilst keeping both options open. This is an information-gathering exercise which serves two purposes:

(i)   It allows the traffic situation (hazard) to develop or clear.

(ii)   It allows the driver more time to reason through the information and choose the best possible moment to make the final commitment to either wait or proceed.

Precautionary measures

In some situations where there is doubt and where a positive response to slow down is necessary to provide more time and information, many novice drivers will react passively and do nothing until it becomes obvious, by which time it is often too late to take any kind of safe action at all. In most of these situations the driver should 'slow down and see'. Failing to take precautionary measures in doubtful situations can only result in extreme measures becoming critical.

These precautionary measures should be taken not only when the driver can see a potential threat, but anywhere when vision is restricted or where there may be an unseen hazard.

Holdback Procedure

There are varying degrees of holdback procedure. These range from momentarily easing of the accelerator to taking the more active measures necessary to maintain safe options through more positive braking control with a view to waiting or holding back from a traffic hazard.

Holdback procedure involves *actively* reducing speed and slowing down with a view to looking, deciding or waiting. Maintaining safe options in moments of uncertainty should almost always be met with some degree of *active* precautionary measure to create a 'safety cushion' relating to speeds, distances and safety margins.

Powered Progress

Whereas the holdback procedure involves slowing down with a view to looking, waiting or deciding what further action is required, powered progress involves the conclusion to proceed as a conscious decision after seeking and considering all the available information. This includes creeping forwards, using first gear/clutch control, in order to look round any obstruction before making a final commitment to proceed.

The appropriate gear should be selected just prior to making the decision to make 'powered progress'. It is emphasised that the gear is only selected with a view to proceeding and not as a result of slowing down. Whilst the gears may be used after reducing speed, it is important that the learner driver associates them with making progress and not slowing down.

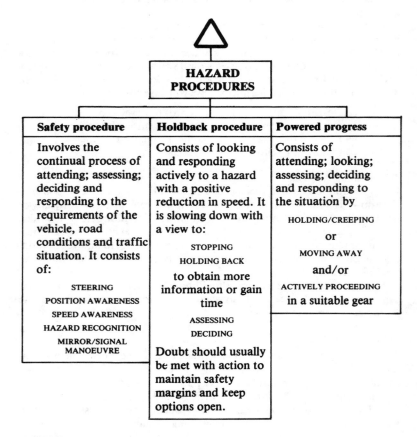

Safety procedure	Holdback procedure	Powered progress
Involves the continual process of attending; assessing; deciding and responding to the requirements of the vehicle, road conditions and traffic situation. It consists of: STEERING POSITION AWARENESS SPEED AWARENESS HAZARD RECOGNITION MIRROR/SIGNAL MANOEUVRE	Consists of looking and responding actively to a hazard with a positive reduction in speed. It is slowing down with a view to: STOPPING HOLDING BACK to obtain more information or gain time ASSESSING DECIDING **Doubt should usually be met with action to maintain safety margins and keep options open.**	Consists of attending; looking; assessing; deciding and responding to the situation by HOLDING/CREEPING or MOVING AWAY and/or ACTIVELY PROCEEDING in a suitable gear

Speed Control and Steering

The main car control skills involved in driving can be summarised as the ability to:

1. *Make powered progress*
   This involves moving off under control on all gradients, sometimes using sustained clutch control to hold or achieve low speed control. This is normally followed by making controlled rates of progress

with the accelerator and gears to take account of changing gradients.

2. *Holdback procedure*

This involves slowing down by use of deceleration and controlled rates of braking which takes account of varying gradients, possibly leading to stopping and finally securing the vehicle in a stationary condition.

These two procedures alternate according to the road and traffic environment, from one of making powered progress to one of holding back progress. This simplified version of car control is essential to the new driver who will otherwise see driving as an extremely complex and inconsistent series of isolated skills.

The new driver requires a thorough knowledge of the skills involved in speed control. In addition to this he needs an understanding of the safe use of speed, both from the acceleration, braking and cornering limitations of the vehicle, to the qualities of adhesion between the tyres and road surface. The new driver should be aware of the overall stopping distances both in good and poor driving conditions and should be able to relate to these distances in practice.

A driver should be familiar with the various speed limits applicable to both the road he is travelling along and the type of vehicle he is using. Speeds used should also be such that the driver is, at all times, able to pull up under control well within the distance seen to be actually clear.

The driver should also be able to recognise the need to maintain a reasonable legal speed according to the general traffic flow and should realise the inconvenience and dangers caused by driving too slowly.

The new driver should also be aware that all speed changes should be preceded by mirror checks.

Chapter 3

Factors Affecting Vehicle Stability

Factors Affecting the Stability of Vehicles in Motion

Friction provides the only control a driver has over the direction and speed of his vehicle. If the driver allows the forces acting on the vehicle in motion to exceed the friction between the tyre and road surface, it will go out of control.

The importance of friction and other factors which affect the stability of a vehicle are not always properly understood by many drivers. They include:

(a) adhesive characteristics of tyres such as:

- state of wear;
- design factors;
- pressure;
- rubber compounds used;

(b) grip coefficient of the road surface:

- state of repair and condition;
- presence of surface lubricants such as water, oil, rubber-dust, melting rubber, mud and loose grit;

(c) inertia – the natural resistance of a moving mass to changes in its state of rest or uniform motion;

(d) gravity – holding the vehicle on the road and keeping the tyres in contact with the surface:

- applying acceleration and braking forces on hills;
- deflecting vehicle direction on cambered roads;
- particularly at speed on curves with adverse cambers;

(e) efficiency of the suspension system in coping with the effects of inertia:

- over uneven surfaces;
- on curved paths;
- when braking or accelerating;
- and in preventing the tyres becoming airborne;
- over bumps and hollows;
- when cornering;
- when changing speed;

(f) the speed of the vehicle and the lift forces being generated.

Partial or complete contact may be lost between the tyres and road surface due to a combination of excess speed on an uneven or bumpy road or a faulty or inadequate suspension system.

Adhesion may be lost due to the tyres riding above the surface on a cushion of water, oil or other unstable material or excessive acceleration, braking or cornering forces exerted, causing the rubber compound of the tyre to melt and form a thin film of lubricant on top of the road surface.

Vehicle Steering Characteristics

Centrifugal force and other factors contribute to reducing the stability of a vehicle when it is negotiating a curved path. The tyres and suspension system are designed to optimise the grip on the road surface and control the natural effect of these forces. The weight distribution of loads and passengers in a car and the layout of the engine and transmission affect the steering. Due to the position of the engine and transmission, front wheel drive vehicles carry the weight at the front and consequently tend to under-steer with the natural stability of a dart. Vehicles with their engine/transmission systems at the rear tend to over-steer and they are naturally unstable.

Under-steer handling characteristics are designed into most modern cars to improve stability when cornering and driving at speed in crosswinds. Under-steer describes the tendency for the vehicle to run wide on a curved path. It is countered by a slight increase in the degree of steering lock needed to negotiate the bend. Mild understeer provides good directional stability and is less demanding. Excessive understeer makes a vehicle unresponsive to the driver's efforts with the wheel. This can make driving hard work in towns and on winding country roads. Neutral steering characteristics or mild over-steer makes the steering more responsive.

Over-steer reduces a vehicle's stability particularly when driving at higher speeds and when cornering. Oversteering vehicles are directionally unstable and require frequent steering corrections, particularly in strong crosswinds,· when driving at speed and on roads with pronounced changes in camber. Over-steer is the tendency for the vehicle to point itself into a bend more than anticipated from the steering wheel movement. It is countered by slight decreases in the degree of steering used.

The over- and under-steer characteristics may change as speed is increased. For example: a car which normally understeers can, as the speed increases, develop neutral steer and then over-steer. To be controllable these changes must be progressive and predictable otherwise they can catch a driver unawares and prove very dangerous.

The steering characteristics of a vehicle can change according to accelerator pressures. Releasing the accelerator of a front-wheel drive car transfers weight onto the front and increases the cornering force the front wheels exert on the road surface. A naturally oversteering vehicle can snake about quite violently if hard acceleration is used on a corner or bend.

Slip Angles

When steering round bends, the tyres are pointing in a slightly different direction to the path followed by the vehicle. The slip angle is the difference between the direction of tyre travel and the plane of the wheel. Where the slip angles of the front tyres are greater than those at the rear the vehicle understeers. Conversely, where the slip angles at the rear are greater than those at the front then the vehicle oversteers. Radial tyres have smaller slip angles than crossply. It is illegal to fit radial tyres to the front wheels when crossply are fitted to the rear because this creates an oversteer characteristic which causes directional instability.

Roadholding and Handling characteristics

The purpose of any suspension system is to insulate the vehicle body and its occupants from road shocks, maintain tyre and road surface adhesion and improve the roadholding and handling characteristics when cornering, braking and accelerating. A vehicle with excessively hard springing will give a poor ride and contact between the tyre and road surface will be lost when driven over bumps and hollows. This reduces stability and road surface adhesion. A more comfortable ride requires softer springs to give plenty of suspension travel. Unfortunately this reduces the resistance to body roll when cornering. Excess roll means poor handling on corners and soft suspension means excessive front end dip on braking and lift under acceleration.

The roadholding and handling characteristics of any vehicle are usually a compromise between the comfort of the ride and handling characteristics. The ride describes the smoothed out motion experienced by the occupants after the insulating effect of the tyres, seats and suspension. The handling describes the manner in which the vehicle behaves and responds to the steering, brakes and accelerator. Roadholding describes the grip between the tyres and road surface when executing braking, accelerating and cornering manoeuvres.

The roadholding and handling qualities of a vehicle can be modified by the suspension camber angles and differentials between the front and rear tyre pressures. Due to the weight transfer generated by centrifugal force, the outer wheel on a curve exerts more cornering force than the inside tyre. This means that a vehicle with negative camber will apply an increased cornering force to the road surface. This will reduce its tendency to under-steer. Conversely, a vehicle with positive camber will reduce the tendency to oversteer.

Aerodynamic Instability

Drag increases fuel consumption and holds a car back, particularly at higher speed. Modern cars are aerodynamically shaped to reduce the drag factors and improve fuel consumption. The shape also helps them slide through the air cleanly, causing little air turbulance. The wedge shape of a modern car can be compared with that of an aircraft wing. The wing section is flat at the bottom to let the air travel unrestricted directly underneath. Air travelling over the top has to travel further over the curved surface, making it warmer and less dense. The denser air underneath the wing pushes it up.

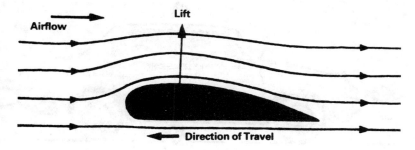

Diagram 1: *Airflow over aircraft wing*

As the air passes over a motor vehicle it creates a low pressure area over the top and produces a lift force. (It is worth remembering that some four-seater aircraft have take-off speeds of around 55 mph!)

Lift forces make a vehicle lighter and reduce the road surface adhesion, particularly at motorway speeds. Although the smoother ride and lighter steering may give an illusion of greater safety and a false sense of security, the vehicle is considerably less stable. The diagram below shows the forces acting on a vehicle when it is travelling in a straight line and under light acceleration.

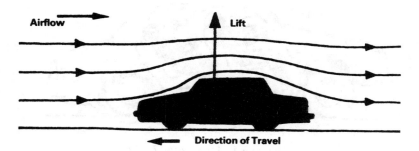

Diagram 2: *Aerodynamic forces*

A motor vehicle passing through an airstream has a *centre of pressure* through which the aerodynamic forces (lift, drag and crosswind thrust) act. This can be compared with the way that weight and centrifugal force act through the *centre of gravity*. The aerodynamic stability of a vehicle is related to the relative positions of the centre of pressure and the centre of gravity. If the centre of pressure is ahead of the centre of gravity the vehicle will become unstable when driven in crosswinds.

Airflow over the body of the car can also produce a significant lift force at the front of the vehicle equivalent to putting additional weight in the boot. This can result in severe oversteer, or at least a reduction in the more stable understeer characteristics designed into many cars.

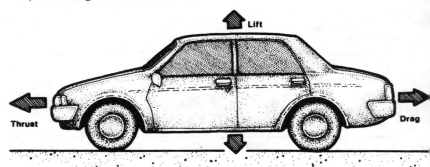

Diagram 3: *Centre of Aerodynamic Pressure*

Vehicle Instability

Inertia is the natural tendency of any mass, such as a motor car, to maintain its state of rest or uniform motion. Newton's Laws of Motion state that a moving mass will retain its velocity at a constant speed in a straight line until an external force is applied to it. Inertia will offer a resistance to the efforts of drivers to change speed or direction. The effect of inertia is readily experienced by occupants as a vehicle moves off, stops and corners.

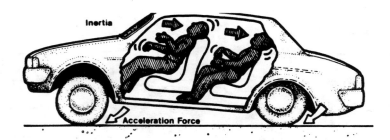

Diagram 4: *Acceleration Forces*

Diagram 5: *Braking Forces*

A moving vehicle is most stable when travelling straight on a level road at a constant speed. To change speed and/or direction, drivers apply an external force through tyre and road surface adhesion. These acceleration, braking and cornering forces reduce vehicle stability.

Centrifugal Force is the natural reaction to a centripetal force. Centripetal force is the proper subject for consideration since it is the cause of the phenomenon. For example: a person standing on a bus as it swerved round a bend at high speed would say that he/she was flung outwards or experienced a centrifugal force. What really happened was that a centripetal force was exerted on his/her feet by the floor of the bus.

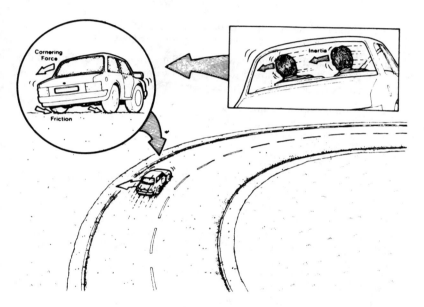

Diagram 6: *Cornering Force*

Centrifugal force is only an expression of the resistance offered by inertia to the centripetal force (cornering force) being applied to the vehicle through the adhesion of the tyres to the road surface. The vehicle wants to go straight on and inertia will resist the centripetal force (cornering force) applied at the tyres. Newton's Third Law states that the forces occur in equal and opposite pairs. Thus the cornering force (centripetal force) of the tyres on the vehicle is equal and opposite to the outward thrust (centrifugal force) of the vehicle on the tyres.

Kinetic energy is that possessed by a moving body such as a motor vehicle. There is sufficient stored energy in a one-ton vehicle travelling at 60 mph to boil two pints of ice in about four seconds. Kinetic energy is related to the vehicle weight and its speed. Any increase in vehicle speed is accompanied by a disproportionate increase in kinetic energy. For example, if you double the speed the kinetic energy is four times greater. On a dry road, the braking distance of a car travelling at 40 mph with good brakes, sound tyres and a skilled driver is about 80 feet. At 80 mph the braking distance is about 320 feet (four times greater).

The formula is:

$$\tfrac{1}{2}MV^2 \text{ where } M = \text{the Mass and } V = \text{its velocity}$$

A one-ton vehicle (2240 lbs) travelling at 20 mph (approx 30 ft per second) has a kinetic energy value of about 1 000 000 lbs/ft.

$$(\tfrac{1}{2} \times 2240) \times (30^2) = 1\,008\,000$$

At 40 mph the kinetic energy value is over 4 000 000 lbs/ft.
At 80 mph the kinetic energy value is well over 16 000 000 lbs/ft.

There is a direct relationship between these figures and those outlined in the Highway Code for braking distances. Every time the speed doubles the braking distance becomes four times greater. For example at:

20 mph the braking distance is 20 ft
40 mph the braking distance is 80 ft
80 mph the braking distance is 320 ft

Forces Induced by the Driver

A moving vehicle is in its most stable condition when travelling straight on a level road at a constant speed. It will remain stable until an external force is applied. Driving requires frequent changes in speed and direction. Drivers execute these changes through the application of the acceleration, braking and cornering forces. Whenever these forces are applied to the tyres, there is a natural resistance to the change they are trying to bring about which makes the vehicle less stable.

A driver's control of a motor vehicle relies totally upon the friction between the tyres and road surface. Conversely, it is the driver and the manner in which a vehicle is driven that is the most important single factor affecting the level of tyre and road surface friction. To maintain friction, drivers must control the effects of inertia by cornering at appropriate speeds and by braking and accelerating smoothly and progressively. Harsh acceleration, late heavy braking and sudden changes in direction are the hallmarks of bad driving.

Acceleration force is limited by the power of an engine, the driver's skill with the accelerator, clutch and gears and the adhesion of the driving tyres to the road surface. Instability occurs when the driver applies too much force too quickly. The resistance of inertia shifts weight from the front to the rear of the vehicle and reduces the efficiency of the steering.

In extremes, the natural resistance of the vehicle to accelerate may result in the driving wheels skidding on the road surface. Drivers should avoid harsh acceleration and deceleration, particularly in the lower gears and on slippery roads.

Once a cruising speed is reached, throttle openings can be reduced slightly to maintain a constant speed more economically. Remember the natural state of a moving mass is to continue travelling at a constant speed and power is needed only to overcome the effects of gravity, drag, tyre rolling resistance and friction losses in the transmission system. To further reduce fuel consumption, avoid unnecessary or fidgety movements on the accelerator pedal.

Braking force is limited by the efficiency of the brakes, the driver's skill in using them and tyre and road surface adhesion. Engine compression provides a slight braking force when in a high gear and a significantly more pronounced effect when a low gear is engaged.

Instability occurs because the vehicle resists the applied force. The result is a shift in weight from the rear to the front of the vehicle. This makes the steering heavier to handle and reduces the adhesion of the rear tyres on the road surface.

Drivers should look well ahead for signs or obstructions and be prepared to slow down early. They should keep both hands on the wheel and try to do most of the braking while travelling in a straight line. An initial light braking pressure should normally be followed by a firm but progressive increase until the vehicle is pulling up short with a margin for error. This provides early warning to those behind and permits a gradual reduction in pedal pressure as the vehicle loses speed. It provides more time to assess the situation and execute gear changes. Progressive braking also maximises the comfort of passengers and their confidence in the driver. The final stage of braking is a gradual easing of the pressure to let the car roll on a little. This also reduces the risk of rear-end collisions.

A common error, even with experienced drivers, is to apply the brakes either too late or too lightly in the intermediate stage. This often results in a harsh, uncontrolled last-minute application ending in frequent and unnecessary stops.

Cornering force is limited by the tyre and road surface adhesion, the efficiency of the suspension system and the driver's skill with the steering wheel. Instability occurs due to the resistance of the centrifugal force to the centripetal force applied by the tyre. The result is a shift in weight to the wheels on the outside of the corner. This reduces the adhesion of the inside tyres on the road surface.

The effect of combining the cornering force with braking or acceleration forces will cause additional imbalance to stability when the tyre adhesion and other factors may be stretched to their limit. Drivers should try to minimise the need for sudden changes in speed and direction. Braking and acceleration should be smooth and drivers should try to keep both hands on the steering wheel when the vehicle is subjected to these forces.

Try to maintain a constant speed on bends and when cornering. Try to keep two hands on the steering wheel at all times when not using other controls. Drive at lower speeds in windy weather and when contact between the tyre and the road surface is reduced in wet or icy conditions.

Drivers should slow down, or power down, before reaching bends and corners. 'Power down' means easing slightly off the accelerator. Do this while on the straightest course possible. The approach speed should be low enough to permit the vehicle to be driven round the bend under slight power. Except when going downhill, use a light pressure on the accelerator to maintain a constant speed. This maximises stability. Drivers should avoid sudden changes in direction and keep both hands on the wheel when cornering. Combinations of harsh acceleration or braking with cornering should also be avoided.

When approaching bends with an adverse camber, drivers should be taught to slow down more than normally, as gravity will cause the vehicle to become less stable.

Factors Influencing Stopping Distances

Stopping distances are affected by the driver's reactions, health and state of mind; the size and weight of the vehicle; the effectiveness of its braking system; the type of tyres, their pressures and depth of tread; and the condition of the road surface. Stopping distances will be greater when travelling downhill and will increase considerably on wet and slippery roads.

On a dry road, a car with good brakes and tyres can stop within the distances shown below, providing the driver is fit and alert. When the speed is doubled the braking distance will be quadrupled.

	Thinking Distance	Braking Distance		Overall Stopping Distance
20 mph	20 ft +	20 ft	=	40 ft
30 mph	30 ft +	45 ft	=	75 ft
40 mph	40 ft +	80 ft	=	120 ft
50 mph	50 ft +	120 ft	=	175 ft
60 mph	60 ft +	180 ft	=	240 ft
70 mph	70 ft +	245 ft	=	315 ft

The Cause and Correction of Skidding

Although the vehicle and road surface condition may contribute to a skid, the main cause is without doubt the driver. There are three different types of skid and they are all caused by:

(a) excessive speed for the road conditions and/or traffic situation; or
(b) excessive acceleration, braking and/or cornering forces applied to the tyres; or
(c) combinations of both.

The rear-wheel skid occurs when the rear wheels lose their grip. It is usually the result of excessive speeds and cornering forces. These may be in association with acceleration or more usually excessive braking force. It is easily and instantly recognised because the rear of the car slides away from the centre of the corner. Uncorrected the vehicle may turn completely round. It is essential to eliminate the cause, eg release the accelerator and/or footbrake and compensate with the steering. Because the vehicle is pointing in the wrong direction, the driver's natural reaction is normally to steer back on course. There is a danger however, particularly with the quick response of radial tyres, for drivers to over react and steer back too far.

The front-wheel skid occurs when the front wheels lose their grip, leaving the driver with no directional control. It is usually the result of turning sharply into a corner or bend at excessive speed and/or under hard acceleration or braking. It is recognised when the vehicle fails to go where it is steered. Eliminate the cause and regain steering control by momentarily straightening the wheels and/or reducing pressure on the accelerator or brake.

The four-wheel skid occurs when all four wheels lose their grip. It is usually due to excessive speed for the road conditions or traffic situation, resulting in uncontrolled overbraking. On a wet or slippery surface drivers may even feel they are increasing speed. They are left with no control over direction and the result may be a combination of turning broadside and no response to steering corrections. Steering control can be partially restored by momentarily releasing the brake to allow wheel rotation to recover and then quickly re-applying the brake in a rapid on-off action.

The prevention of skids is better than the cure!
It is important to recognise the danger signs early and act on them. For example, slowing down early upon sighting a group of children playing near the road will mean that less braking pressure is needed if one of them dashes out. Concentration, planning and the early anticipation of the possible actions of others is essential. In snow and ice, slow down early with light braking pressure. Gentle braking is less likely to cause skidding than changing into a lower gear. Use gradual acceleration and keep in the highest gear possible without distressing the engine. When going uphill in snow try to maintain a steady momentum by staying well back from the vehicle ahead.

Drive at safe speeds for the road surface conditions. Accelerate, brake and corner gently. Drive slower on wet, icy and slippery surfaces. Watch out for loose gravel, fallen leaves and damp patches under trees. Make sure your tyres are correctly inflated and that they have a minimum of 2 mm of tread all around. Never mix crossply and radial tyres on the same axle.

Keep off soft verges! Read the surface conditions and slow down well before reaching any bumpy parts of the road. Also slow down if the edges are rough and broken. Avoid heavy braking on loose gravel and muddy surfaces and on damp patches under trees. The combination of oil, rubber dust and water can make the surface very slippery after a light summer shower following a long dry spell. In freezing temperatures, remember that black ice forms on exposed bridges first.

Emergency Braking

Drivers should be realistic about the distance it takes to stop, particularly in wet conditions. Pivot promptly to the brake and apply it progressively and firmly. Keep both hands on the wheel and try to keep the vehicle on a straight course. Maximum braking force is applied to the vehicle just before the wheels lock; it is most important to avoid braking so hard that the wheels lock, as this will considerably lengthen the stopping distance. Pushing the clutch down too soon will increase the risk of locking the wheels and lengthen the stopping distance. If the wheels do lock, the brake should be released and quickly re-applied.

Particularly in wet slippery conditions where the driver has applied too much pressure and locked the wheels, the brake should be momentarily released, to allow the tyres to regain their grip, and quickly re-applied. This method of rapid on-off braking can be likened to the very rapid on-off action of automatic braking systems. It gives the driver greater braking efficiency and increased directional control in emergency situations where the natural reaction is to lock the wheels.

This braking technique, sometimes known as 'cadence braking', relies in part on the fact that as the brakes are applied some weight is transferred to the front wheels. The brakes are then released, ensuring that the wheels do not lock.

System of Car Control

The natural phenomenon and forces that affect the stability of vehicles in motion are scientific facts of which any system of car control must take proper account. The early development of an efficient system helps to provide new drivers with a firm foundation on which to link other skills. It also gives them more time to look for and recognise 'high risk' situations, and to correctly assess their responses to the road and traffic conditions.

Any system taught to new drivers should have a built-in set of safety margins which help compensate for human error, deficient skills, minor lapses in concentration and mistakes made by other road users. An efficient system will ensure drivers have time to control their vehicles in a proper and sympathetic manner.

Many driving instructors incorporate the following tried and tested principles as an integrated part of the system of car control they teach.

1. Vehicle speed should never exceed that which permits the driver to bring the vehicle to a properly controlled stop well within the distance that can be seen to be clear. Drivers should look for and respond to:

    (a) actual obstructions to the intended course;
    (b) the potential of other road users to move out of blind areas behind obstructions, into or across the intended course;
    (c) restrictions to the driver's sightlines caused by road features such as bends, hillcrests and hollows (dead ground);
    (d) potential obstructions which may be hidden by restricted sightlines.

2. Vehicle control and speed should take account of the natural phenomenon and forces that affect the stability of a vehicle in motion. Drivers should be made aware of:

(a) the physical roadholding and handling limitations of their vehicles;

(b) the tyre and road surface adhesion and increased stopping distances resulting from wet and icy conditions;

(c) the effects of camber and gravity on hills;

(d) aerodynamic forces acting on the vehicle.

3. To minimise the effects of the natural phenomenon and forces that affect the stability of a vehicle in motion, drivers should:

(a) apply and remove acceleration, braking and cornering forces smoothly;

(b) avoid excessive acceleration and/or braking forces when negotiating a curved path;

(c) avoid changing gear when negotiating severe changes in direction;

(d) avoid unnecessary gear changing. Be selective when changing down for example: keep both hands on the wheel whilst braking; after slowing down to less than 10 mph and as the braking pressure is being gradually reduced and/or released, change direct from fourth gear to second. Gears enable drivers to maintain efficient engine speeds through a wide range of road speeds and different power requirements. Although, in some circumstances gears can be legitimately used as a braking source, the practice is no longer, generally considered good driving practice;

(e) keep both hands on the steering wheel when braking and cornering;

(f) keep both hands on the steering wheel when accelerating hard;

(g) use gentle controlled power when negotiating a curved path. When stationary for more than the time it takes to comfortably apply and then release the handbrake, it should be applied, even on a level road. For example a one- to two-second pause will normally involve the use of the handbrake. Having said this, it should also be stated that experienced drivers rarely come to complete stops for this length of time. By planning their approach to situations likely to require stops, they creep at very slow speeds on the final two or three yards before the stop is required. This often gives the situation time to clear, enabling them to move off again before stopping completely. In such circumstances using the handbrake is inappropriate.

4. Drivers who are sympathetic to the needs of their vehicle not only prolong its working life but make more efficient use of fuel. Drivers should:

(a) avoid unnecessary or fidgety movements on the accelerator;

(b) use the accelerator and/or footbrake early/smoothly;

(c) avoid excessive clutch slip, drag and unnecessary coasting;

(d) avoid excessive tyre wear by cornering at lower speeds;

(e) avoid using gears unnecessarily to reduce speed;

(f) switch off engine while stationary for prolonged periods;
(g) avoid switching the car's interior heating system on before the engine is hot;
(h) avoid additional drag caused by roof signs;
(i) avoid unnecessary loads in the boot;
(j) keep engines properly tuned;
(k) check tyres regularly for uneven wear and pressure;
(l) have brakes and vehicle services regularly;
(m) keep a regular eye on the bodywork for corrosion.

Gear-Assisted Braking

Changing down to reduce speed is unsympathetic to the vehicle, wastes petrol and is not normally acceptable as good driving practice. However, a lower gear can be engaged to offset the effects of gravity on downhill gradients. The brakes should be used first, however, to bring the speed under control before selecting an appropriate lower gear. This provides increased engine braking and reduces the risk of brake failure from overheating due to their continuous use down long hills.

Selective Gear Changing

To slow down, keep two hands on the wheel and use the footbrake to reduce speed. After slowing down change down, if necessary, before reaching the hazard, eg:

Approaching a simple left turn in fourth gear, use the brake to slow down to less than 10 mph and change direct to second as you are easing the pressure from the brake or after it is fully released.

Approaching the end of a road in third or fourth gear where your view is restricted; use the brake to slow down until you have almost stopped. Push the clutch down and gradually ease the braking pressure to let the vehicle roll. Just before it stops, change into first gear, ready for moving away.

The Power Change

This technique permits lower gears to be selected smoothly when travelling at higher than normal speeds. It matches the engine speed to the lower gear and lets them be engaged quickly without the loss of road speed or power. It is beneficial when extra power is needed for overtaking or climbing a hill.

To change, hand on the gear lever and cover the clutch; clutch down quickly, depress the accelerator, release it immediately and select the lower gear; raise the clutch and accelerate as appropriate.

Double De-Clutch

This specialised gear-changing technique is generally only necessary in some heavy goods vehicles. Although it is still recommended in some advanced driving manuals, it is inappropriate in a modern vehicle with synchromesh gears. It also increases unnecessary wear on the transmission system.

To change up: hand on gear lever and cover the clutch; clutch down, off the accelerator and move the gear lever to neutral; clutch up quickly and then down again; engage the higher gear; finally raise the clutch and accelerate.

To change down: hand on gear lever and cover the clutch; clutch down, off the accelerator and move the gear lever to neutral; clutch up and depress the accelerator quickly, releasing it immediately; clutch down quickly and engage the lower gear; finally raise the clutch; continue braking/accelerating.

Heel and Toe

This specialised technique is used in high performance driving and is unsuited to on-road use. It permits the driver to make a power change into a lower gear by blipping the accelerator with the heel or side of the right foot whilst braking with the ball of the foot.

Chapter 4
The Learning Process

Some Theoretical Considerations

The Sensory System

What is this magic ability or set of abilities which evolution has provided and which we call learning?

Learning can be thought of as nature's way of enabling us to adapt and survive in a fast-changing and complicated environment. It is a continuous, but peculiarly inconsistent, process over which there is little reliable control.

Learning is sometimes the result of a deliberate and directed effort (this is particularly true of the learner driver under instruction) or it may be the unintentional result of a chance experience – (this of course also occurs during the learner driver's tuition, through unexpected or unforeseen circumstances arising).

It is our senses which provide us with the information about the environment in which we live and it is from the sensations they provide that we learn.

These sensations are personal to the individual and will be in some way different from those felt by other individuals perceiving the same experience.

The amount or quality of learning appears to depend partly upon how much attention the individual gives to the actual experience, but also to the individual ability of the learner to cope with the learning situation. Thus an elderly learner driver may show less clutch control after hours of concentration and practice than her/his youthful counterpart whose abilities are much greater but whose attention may be mediocre.

Elements of the Learning Experience Within the Individual

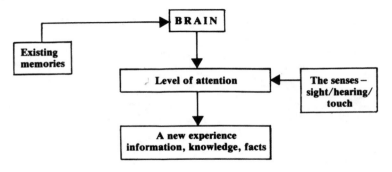

The Importance of Sight

Most learning is the result of attention and information from the senses. The principal ones are sight, hearing, touch, taste and smell. Others include: cold, thirst, hunger, pressure, pain and kinaesthesis which involves a sense of muscular movement. Sight is the most powerful and important of the senses.

Sight is the single most powerful factor involved in the learning process and the one sense most difficult for learners to ignore. As instructors we ignore it to the risk and detriment of the lessons we give.

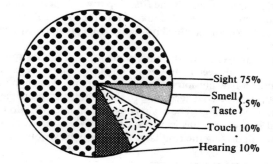

Sight 75%
Smell ⎱ 5%
Taste ⎰
Touch 10%
Hearing 10%

The proportions in which our senses gather information

Perception

The next step in learning is the process of interpreting and adding some kind of meaning to the incoming sensations. This process is called perception. What an individual student actually perceives during any adventure or involvement in a learning experience not only depends upon the actual sensations, but also upon existing knowledge gained from previous experiences and how that particular individual has learnt to see and view things.

The incoming sensations are instantly compared with the existing knowledge stored in the memory from previous experiences. The nature of these memories can either help or hinder the learning of new material. Where the new information is compatible with existing knowledge and thoughts, the established memories will be reinforced. The ability of the brain to establish these connections is amazingly high. Establishing a few thousand of these memory connections will need time, repetition and patience on the part of the instructor.

Where the new information is not compatible with established knowledge, the new information may be totally rejected.

Perception appears to occur within the conscious decision-making part of the mind with the power to direct the attention of the appropriate senses to whatever task or purpose it chooses. Attention, however, is not always under completely conscious control and the mind has a tendency to be easily distracted and wander off in an unrelated direction.

The physical responses we make to the incoming sensations are also initiated within this area of the mind.

Awareness

Awareness involves the perception and interpretation of one's own vehicle speeds, position and direction in addition to the recognition of traffic hazards in time to act safely upon them.

Perception is the interpretation and meaning the brain attaches to the information it receives from the senses. It is the inner awareness we experience of the external environment. Without it life as we know it is inconceivable.

Perception or awareness is the first step towards performing a skill.

Awareness involves not only looking with the eyes; it also entails using the mind and calling upon existing knowledge from previous experiences to 'see' with the mind.

This inner awareness of the environment is not always totally objective and what is actually seen by the eyes is not always the same as that perceived by the brain. Optical illusions offer evidence of this. What happens is that the visual image is perceived according to the established principles of how we have learnt to see things. The brain adds its own interpretation to the visual image and sees what it has learnt to expect. When this kind of perceptual error occurs in driving the results can obviously be serious.

Endless Stairway
This is an endless stairway. No matter how far you climb up the steps, you end up in the same position. On the contrary, once you start descending, you will keep going down. That's why it is called an endless stairway.

How Many Matches?
Do you see three matches
or four?

A Strange Jar
This is a jar with a shape like the
outline of two faces facing each
other. One can only visualise
either the jar, or the outline of the
faces, at one time, but not both.

If three equal size images of a person are lined up, they look larger
and larger according to the perspective.

Memory

Research suggests that we have two kinds of memory. One of these appears to be of a short-term nature while the other is a more permanent long-term store of information. The total capacity to retain information in the memory is so vast it is actually beyond our comprehension.

The brain is made up of about ten thousand million separate cells which combine to give the possible number of memory inter-connections as the figure of ten with 800 noughts after it.

Although the total capacity of the brain is extremely large, the input capacity is very limited by comparison. One reason put forward for this is that the environment in which we live contains vast amounts of irrelevant information. The eyes alone provide the brain with up to four million pieces of information every second and, besieged with new information at this rate, it is not difficult to understand why we need some biological method of controlling and selecting material to be retained.

Information about the environment is transmitted from the eyes, ears and other senses to the short-term memory where it is analysed and processed prior to being filed in the long-term memory banks. How the brain actually selects and remembers information appears to depend upon existing memories.

Where the new information seems irrelevant or where it does not relate to, or agree with, existing knowledge, it appears to be forgotten. Where the new information is considered relevant or where it fits into the existing network of associated knowledge it is usually remembered or incorporated as a permanent modification to the existing knowledge store.

Remembering and Forgetting

New information which is not actually used tends not to be remembered. Existing memories which are not reinforced by use tend to recede from consciousness. These memories are never completely lost however and evidence shows they can be relearnt more quickly than if no previous memory had existed.

Although we *all* have a high capacity for retaining information, recalling it back to consciousness is sometimes another matter. Memories sometimes prove very elusive. Recall requires some kind of cue which brings back a whole string of associated knowledge. A string of events experienced together or subsequently modified, tend to be recorded as an inter-connected pattern. The recall of any part may bring associated memories flooding back to consciousness.

Memory might also be deceptive on occasions, because a single cue may tap more than one store of information. This can lead to confusion and conflict and what is remembered may be totally different from what actually occurred.

Recall can be facilitated or blocked by emotional factors associated with the memory. High levels of emotion produce more vivid memories of the experience than an indifferent learning situation. Feelings of pleasure and satisfaction help to reinforce learning in a positive manner which will help these feelings to occur again. Unpleasant emotions such as fear also help retain memories but in a negative way. Negative memories will inhibit the kind of action which caused the unpleasant feelings whereas positive memories will encourage the kind of action which caused the satisfaction to be repeated.

Methods of Learning

The basic requirements of learning are attention, activity and involvement in the task.

Attention – is not a completely conscious activity and long periods of undivided concentration are difficult to maintain without a break or change in the type of activity concerned.

Activity and involvement – learning is the result of being actively involved in a learning experience. Activity should not only be thought of as physical. For example, learning to drive a car involves some degree of physical activity, but it is the process of mental involvement which initiates the physical responses.

The more active and involved the novice is in the learning experiences, the more he will normally remember. Physical activity alone is not sufficient. Make the learner think!

What I hear – I FORGET
What I see – I REMEMBER
What I do – I KNOW.

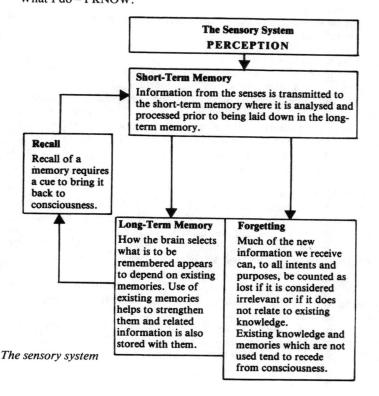

The sensory system

Two essentially different approaches to learning can be described as:

1. *Rote* – This is the traditional approach to learning and consists of nothing more than memorising lists, numbers, facts and formulae etc, in a manner which requires no understanding.
2. *Gestalt* – This is the progressive approach to learning and is based on understanding and the ability we have of making connections and comparing new information with what we already know.

Learning by habit (rote)

We all have the ability to memorise information 'parrot fashion'. Material and information stored in this manner, in precise order, can usually only be recalled in the order it was learnt. We are sure you can remember learning your multiplication tables in this manner: 2 x 2 = 4, 3 x 2 = 6 and so on. The alphabet is also learnt by rote. Can you say what follows the letter R? You were probably able to answer this straight away.

Now, what comes before the letter R? You probably found you had to break into the alphabet a few letters before the R and then run through. We learn telephone numbers in this manner because they have no meaning in themselves.

Rote learning is useful as a basis or foundation upon which more information can subsequently be added to give it more meaning, but it is the lowest form of learning.

Some car driving control skills can be learnt by rote if correct drill procedures are followed.

Learning to understand (Gestalt)

Understanding can be defined broadly as the ability of the learner to attach meaning to new information. This is an important part of the learning process and can be explained as learning through recognising and/or making connections with previously established principles. This can include filling in gaps in existing memories and adding or attaching meaning to known material. Thus, controlled braking and smooth moving-off techniques may be correctly combined by able pupils who may not necessarily require formal instruction. (Though of course most will.)

The need for rote and Gestalt

Both methods of learning are important for retaining new information. You may need to teach some basic facts or skills in a rote (memorising) manner to help the 'L' driver to acquire the basic competence to move the car. In participating in the action of moving the car, however, the learner should be encouraged to extend his own knowledge by analysing the material and comparing and memorising the effects of it.

What started out as a memorised list of actions begins to take on some meaning. It is by no means certain however that this initial 'meaning' implies an understanding of how to apply this information and skill to a new situation. This kind of rote learning therefore must normally be followed by a more meaningful approach to the task of moving off if the 'L' driver is to be able to apply the new skill usefully to varying situations.

As an instructor, the difficulties you will experience should not be in whether you use rote or Gestalt methods, but in deciding upon the best mixture of the two. It is poor teaching to overemphasise the traditional rote learning method with little consideration given to understanding, and equally bad to overemphasise progressive learning methods and 'doing your own thing' without an adequate basis of essential rules and skills.

Transfer of learning

It is doubtful whether anyone actually presents himself for driving lessons without bringing some basic knowledge and/or some of the basic skills required.

Take the simple example of the pedestrian who is able to cross a busy main road successfully. This pedestrian is, in fact, showing skill in the judgement of speeds, distance and timing and these are some of the most essential skills involved in driving a car.

An instructor can help this student transfer those basic skills and apply them to driving a motor car. There are numerous other associations like this in which the instructor can help the learner relate or transfer other existing skills and knowledge to driving.

Interference in learning

Previous learning, however, can also work the other way around and interfere with learning new skills and knowledge. Take the person who has probably developed a partial 'sense of speed' as a car passenger – he will have subconsciously learnt an impression of speed norm gained whilst sitting next to a more experienced and competent driver. This can often be detrimental if the novice starts trying to emulate the experienced person and drive at what he considers the normal speed before the basic manipulative skills required to drive the car are developed. Unless strictly controlled, this 'previous learning' can severely interfere with the basic manipulative skills which initially need to be carried out at a slower than normal speed.

Interference of a different kind can be demonstrated in the following examples.

Two widely held, but false, conceptions are that it is good driving practice to:

1. Always change down progressively through the gears when slowing down or stopping.
2. Always signal for passing parked cars whether it is useful or not.

Where the novice has previously been indoctrinated with these views, it is likely to cause conflict with new information provided by the instructor. Even when actually giving lessons, the instructor must recognise that his pupil is not learning in a vacuum and is therefore subject to all kinds of conflicting pressures outside of their brief encounters on the driving lessons.

Where this type of interference occurs, the instructor must display considerable tolerance and understanding of the student's problems through the period of 'unlearning'.

For further reading in educational techniques: Stephens, Michael D. and Roderick, Gordon W. (eds), *Teaching Techniques in Adult Education*; Rogers, Jennifer (ed), *Adults in Education*; Winfield, Ian, *Learning to Teach Practical Skills*; Baddeley, Alan, *Your Memory, A User's Guide*; Walklin, L., *Instructional Techniques and Practice*.

Motivating Students

The fact that a student is prepared to pay for a course of lessons shows that he is motivated with a desire to learn. The student will normally be alert and keen at the start of the course with a willingness to follow instructions in eager anticipation of the next session. This initial enthusiasm however may not always be enough to maintain full interest and attention for the whole course.

An important part of your work as a teacher/instructor will be to help your pupils over any difficult periods with your own efforts and enthusiasm.

Interest can be stimulated by success. Even small successes are important to a pupil who is finding the learning hard work. By creating the correct conditions the instructor can do much to ensure success. He can do this by properly grading the tuition in *short, progressive steps*. He must then try to further this interest by giving suitable encouragement and approval for effort.

Traditional driver tuition in the car means the student is often learning in total isolation from other learners and this can frequently cause problems for both instructor and student. While 'individual' tuition does have obvious advantages over other forms of teaching it limits contact with other students.

Where deprived of the group learning situation, the student is unable to measure his progress against that of others. More importantly, if he has no means of assessing his own progress and improvement, he may easily feel he is getting nowhere — often because the instructor fails to indicate where and how he has improved.

If the student feels he is making slow progress, or none at all, encouragement alone from the teacher is not always sufficient to allay the student's fears of his own inability. An unsympathetic teacher may cause the student to feel so discouraged, isolated and incompetent, that he becomes completely and utterly demoralised. In this situation, revise the progress made; do not be excessively critical.

If you set up some easily attainable, intermediate targets, they will help to reinforce your feedback of progress. Intermediate targets also help to organise an otherwise haphazard learning situation. They also do much to prevent a pupil from being thrown in at the deep end before he can swim. Nor are these targets as formidable to the new client as the far-off driving test.

It is important to remember that many of the driving skills are conditioned responses. That is, they not only require the correct approach to the task to be learnt correctly, but they also need continual repetition to master them properly. Thus clutch control can be guided by the instructor in the early lessons, demonstrated on working models and visual aids, but in the final analysis it is only by practice that the skill becomes 'second nature' and an established part of the skilled driver's expertise.

The balance between explanation and activity must be carefully controlled for best effect. How well the pupil learns depends largely upon his understanding.

Teaching and Learning

You will know from experience that learning is an inconsistent process over which there is little reliable control. The teacher has no mystical power whereby he is able to pour knowledge into the mind of the learner, so whatever the student learns (be it mental or physical) he must do so for himself!

The teacher provides the situation and circumstances from which learning *may* occur. These are the learning conditions. These may be the activities and instruction of a practical driving lesson, a lecture or discussion or one of the many other teaching or instructional methods used.

The teacher's role is essentially one of establishing the quality and of planning and organising the conditions of this learning situation.

The teacher is the manager of the learning experience:

1. Preparing, and
2. Organising the material.
3. Presenting the experience to the student.
4. Observation of the student's reactions.

No matter how carefully prepared and presented, the success can only be judged by how much of the intended knowledge or skill the learner takes away with him.

*   *   *

The complete experience involves the car, the classroom or other location and the personality and teaching methods of the instructor. It also involves existing attitudes, knowledge and the skills of the student.

Whatever the natural abilities and aptitude, what the student learns he must achieve for himself through attention and active involvement in the learning experience.

The student's motivation is vital to his willingness to learn. The teacher must motivate the student and create situations and an environment for students to learn from.

The driving instructor should think of himself as a manager of the learning experience, with responsibilities extending far beyond the act of teaching. He must always be aware that what he is teaching – or neglecting to teach – could at some time in the future be a matter of life or death to the student.

Apart from the quality or content of lessons, the instructor's responsibilities range from the organisation of the course to the final assessments prior to the driving test.

The key to the successful *management of learning* for the instructor is the ability to present, adapt and adjust the same basic knowledge and skills for the wide range of *learning abilities* of different pupils. The instructor must not only be master of his craft and skills, he must also have an infinitely variable range of instructional techniques at his command and be able to call on these as the situation and responses of the learner require. This is a challenging task demanding careful preparatory training for the instructor.

The Learner's Needs

The most successful instructors are those concerned with their students as learners and who are most sensitive to their learning requirements.

These needs are as varied and complex as the differences between the students themselves. Avoid grouping people into preconceived categories such as young, old, indifferent, difficult, quick or slow to learn, etc. Pre-judging the learner in this manner tends to prevent you from looking at him as an individual and prohibits you from seeing him with 'open' and 'more sensitive' eyes.

One of your first priorities is to create a good working relationship with your student. A good test of this is the rapport which exists between you, but perhaps more significantly, the level of communication from the student to you, for example does he readily admit his mistakes? How freely does he talk about his fears and anxieties? How often do you laugh together about a silly mistake?

Learning should be founded upon mutual co-operation to develop the learner's abilities and confidence in himself. You can develop this confidence by structuring the learning in such a way that he is exposed only to the tasks he can successfully achieve.

Points to Remember about Learning

1. Start with what the learner knows, or can do, and build upon it.
2. Structure the learning into short progressive steps.
3. Be consistent with your instructions and terminology.
4. Does the learner really understand the technical terms you may use?
5. Explanations should be short and to the point.
6. Emphasise the key points.
7. Tell the learner what he should do rather than what he should not do.
8. Explain the purpose of a demonstration before carrying it out.
9. Demonstration should be at the correct level according to the ability of the learner.
10. Too many variables confuse – keep it simple.
11. Demonstration commentaries should be restricted to key aspects.
12. People learn by doing things for themselves.
13. The demonstration should be immediately followed by practice.
14. The learner must not be in any doubt about what is expected of him.
15. Initial practice should be successful.
16. Failure saps confidence and inhibits future progress.
17. Interest and involvement can be stimulated by success.
18. Praise and encouragement will help further the learner's progress.
19. Criticism is less effective in motivating the learner than praise.

20. Excessive criticism destroys confidence and the desire to learn.
21. Provide the learner with continuous feedback of progress.
22. Correct initial errors before they become habitual.
23. Criticise only in a constructive manner intended to improve the learner's performance.
24. Even small successes are important to the learner who finds the going difficult.
25. Where a learner feels he is making no progress, an unsympathetic teacher may cause him to become completely demoralised.
26. Reassure him that periods of slow learning are quite natural and common.
27. Avoid comparing the learner with other students.
28. Shorter, easier steps will help to promote progress.
29. Let the student learn at his own pace.
30. Excessive repetition can be boring – a change in activity will help sustain interest.
31. Older students can benefit from longer periods of practice.
32. Fear of failure or feeling silly are prime causes of anxiety.
33. Reassure the learner and provide him with emotional encouragement.
34. Ensure, as far as possible, that learning conditions are within the student's ability to cope, particularly with route and traffic conditions.
35. Be prepared to vary methods of instruction if at first unsuccessful.
36. Avoid attempting to expand on variables before the student has grasped the key points.

Chapter 5

Learning Aids

A learning aid is any medium the driving instructor might devise and/or use to enable him to present his own personal ideas, knowledge and skills in a manner which can be more easily understood by the learner.

Learning aids can assist the learning process by helping to hold the learner's attention. They can also be used to generate an interest which stimulates the student's desire to learn.

It has been said that, 'The purpose of a learning aid is to liberate the teacher from the limitations of his own speech.' Whilst learning aids may help to make a good instructor better, they will not compensate for bad teaching.

Learning aids range from a simple notepad and pencil to sophisticated driving simulators. Between these two extremes there is a vast range of aids available to the instructor. Many of these can be adapted in some form to in-car tuition.

For example, while it may be impractical to use a slide projector in a car, a photograph is a perfect substitute. A well thought-out folder of diagrams is the ideal alternative to the overhead projector.

Text and Reference Books

Instructors should offer learners some form of written guide outlining the course content and exercises. This provides them with an opportunity to study the routines and procedures before practising them and develop a cognitive strategy which will enhance the efficiency of subsequent skill training.

Textbook guides should be structured according to the natural step-by-step organisation of practical lessons. They should be well illustrated and written in simple everyday language. They should support professional tuition by stating clearly and positively what learners are expected to do on lessons.

There is a plethora of publications on learning to drive. Many are unclear, inaccurate and over emphasise 'what not to do'. Others contain so much padding that the point gets completely lost. Although familiar with many of them, ADIs often find it difficult to recommend specific texts because they are unable to find one conforming to their own course structure. Text and reference books most recommended as ADI teaching support materials are listed below.

The Highway Code, published by HMSO, is the 'Road User's bible'. It should be kept in the car and used regularly to reinforce the points under instruction.

Unfortunately, even with considerable coaxing from instructors, many learners fail to seriously study the Highway Code until two or three weeks before their test. Short projects can help stimulate interest in it and learners can be further motivated by relating the exercises to practical lessons.

The DL68 outlines the driving test syllabus and explains to the candidates how it is conducted and what is expected from them. Use it to reinforce points under instruction.

Driving, Department of Transport manual, published by HMSO. It is an essential reference book for all professional driving instructors. More comprehensive than the Highway Code and DL68, and useful on lessons to support and reinforce finer points under instruction.

Roadcraft, police drivers manual, published by HMSO. A useful reference text for ADIs. Clearly written and full of sound advice.

Learn to Drive is a structured learning guide for provisional licence holders. Published by Kogan Page, it has been specially written to support professional instruction by ADIs. Simple common sense advice written in easy-to-understand terms. (Approved by the Motor Schools Association.)

The Advanced Drivers' Handbook provides ADIs with a structured outline teaching programme for a course in defensive driving techniques. Published by Kogan Page, it forms an important element in a comprehensive series of complementary driving guides. (Approved by RoSPA, Royal Society for Prevention of Accidents.)

Visual Aids

The eyes transmit 75 per cent of the information received by a driver's brain. Visual teaching aids can be used to stimulate interest, simplify difficult concepts, focus attention, increase awareness and emphasise key learning points. They can help achieve up to 30 per cent more comprehension and 40 per cent more retention.

Visual Teaching Systems
A simple visual teaching system is available from Autodriva Training Systems, 53 Heanor Road, Ilkeston, Derbyshire DE7 8DY (0602 324499). Graphically literate illustrations are used to emphasise the key learning points. They are filed in a loose leaf A5 folder for use in the car. A4 OHP transparencies are available for in-class use.

Identi-sign
A visual aid booklet for testing recognition of traffic signs, R Smith, 28 Beech Grove, Higham, Rochester, Kent ME3 7AZ.

The Note Pad and Blackboard
A simple note pad is the ADIs equivalent of the blackboard. Used to develop simple drawings or lists of key learning points step by step, it can focus attention, generate interest and be one of the ADIs most effective aids. The technique can help to sustain interest and enhance the whole process of

communication between instructors and learners.

In addition there are:

Printed matter
Many articles appearing in both local and national press or magazines from time to time which are of interest to the 'L' driver and/or of road safety value. There are specialist magazines published by driving instructor organisations, the Institute of Advanced Motorists, RoSPA and other road safety organisations.

In addition, and of particular interest to the instructor, there are many special relevant reports published by the Transport and Road Research Laboratory.

Apart from keeping instructors up to date with new information, an organised file of such material can prove an invaluable asset and teaching aid. Controversial material can stimulate interest in an otherwise routine topic and can be particularly helpful in setting in motion a very lively discussion.

Some of the best aids the instructor uses may well be those he can make for himself. Pre-printed notes for supplementary homework or study, or printed diagrams, can easily be produced by the instructor. You might like to produce a set of diagrams which you can use to assist with explanations on various aspects of road procedure. Choose a topic where a visual aid will be of most use to the learner.

We offer you the following advice in making these aids:

Imagination	–	do not be frightened to use your imagination but organise it to help the learner.
Factual	–	avoid mistakes and get any spelling correct. It is also important to get the scale correct.
Clarity	–	for the sake of clarity avoid unnecessary detail. Keep it simple, tidy and professional. If necessary use one diagram for each idea.
Emphasis	–	emphasise the main points by making them more obvious.

Photographs
These can make the ideal learning aid for the in-car instructor. They can be just as effective as the slide projector. The same basic rules apply to making photographs as to diagrams.

Tuition vehicle
The car is the learner driver's main classroom and it must be in first-class mechanical condition. There is nothing that shows up vehicle faults more than the driving of a novice and there is nothing more disheartening for the learner, or frustrating for the instructor, than a car which refuses to respond correctly and sympathetically to the manner in which it is driven.

The car interior should be kept warm or cool enough for the student's comfort and have sufficient ventilation. The windows should be clean and free from stickers or mascots which both restrict visibility and/or cause distractions. The wipers should be in good condition and the washer bottle topped up. It is a good idea to keep a damp window leather in the vehicle to deal with any problems.

Driving Simulators

There are two main types of existing simulator. Both fail to provide learners with a true simulation of the driving task. However they may be useful for learning some basic skills, routines and simple procedures. The time which can usefully be spent training in simulators is limited. It must be recognised as supplementary and not as a substitute for on-road instruction. Simulators may sometimes be useful in helping nervous people to get started and for providing 'contrived practical' experiences for students on pre-driver courses.

The film simulator presents the road and traffic environment on a single large screen in front of as many as 20 to 30 students each in their own simulator unit. This type gives a reasonable visual reproduction of the real traffic environment with partial sensations of being involved in it and may have applications in basic skill training and the possible development of hazard recognition skills. The simulator units are linked to a computer which records deviations from the correct procedure. These are assessed after the session by an instructor and feedback given to the students. This lack of immediate feedback and reinforcement seriously limits the application of this type of simulator. Training on this kind of machine should not be considered as being more effective than viewing a well presented film.

The instant feedback simulator presents a visual image which responds more or less accurately to the 'drivers' actions on the accelerator, brakes, clutch, gear and steering controls. Compared with film simulators, however, the visual images are indifferent and unrealistic. Other serious limitations include the inability to reproduce interactive traffic situations. However, with advances being made in microtechnology and computerised simulators, great advances in realism and the response to the controls are anticipated in this type of simulator.

Slides and Slide Projectors

A simple 35mm slide projector is a very effective teaching aid. Slides can be viewed singly or in a progressive sequence to illustrate numerous situations. Synchronised programmes can be made up using special cassette recorders which electronically change the slide at the appropriate time. It is interesting to note that research suggests the human brain learns in a series of 'stills' not unlike slides.

Film slides can stimulate the learners interest, focus their attention and add more reality and meaning to in-class tuition. Slides freeze movement and time and enable instructors to present a wider range of traffic situations and road conditions than otherwise possible. Short slide sequences can be taken and shown in rapid succession to provide movement. Instructors can create their own semi-professional presentations of synchronised slide/sound productions relatively easily with modern equipment. A common error in the use of slides is to show large numbers of slides in rapid succession, each containing different learning points.

Models and Mechanical Aids

Models are simplified versions of the real thing. They should be reasonably accurate in detail and scale and may either show cross-sections of components or have cutaways to display the interior of them. A model junction layout with electric traffic lights is another example. If learners are able to operate aspects of the models for themselves it will increase the instructional value of them.

Magnetic road layouts are available to instructors. One very sophisticated system includes many different types of roads and junctions. One version of this system includes working traffic lights.

Simplified models can be used to emphasise important aspects of the real thing through the removal of irrelevant detail. This helps to improve clarity and assist understanding. Various types of mechanical models are available from continental suppliers which illustrate basic mechanical principles. These tend to be more appropriate to car maintenance courses, however, than they are to learning to drive.

A model steerable driving school car, available from most good toy shops, makes an exceptionally simple and effective aid for demonstrating manoeuvres and the principles of driving in reverse gear.

OHP Transparencies and the Overhead Projector

The overhead projector is one of the most versatile training aids in use today. Large transparencies can either be pre-prepared or used as a blackboard with special acetate markers to build up lists, pictures or diagrams step by step. A high-intensity light projects the image, which can be clearly seen in daylight, onto an angled overhead screen. There are various processes whereby printed matter can be copied quickly onto the acetate transparencies.

Transparencies can be used to develop concepts and procedures one step at a time by showing a simple outline and using overlays to build up a complete picture. Alternatively, by starting with the complete picture and removing one element at a time, situations can be analysed, for example: a road situation as seen by the eyes of a driver intending to turn right at a busy crossroads with a large oncoming vehicle turning right at the same time. Removing a separate overlay containing the large vehicle exposes a car approaching in the far lane.

Films and Videos

Films can contribute to driving instruction by stimulating interest, focusing attention and adding reality and meaning through movement. They can be used to freeze, slow down and speed up movement and time. They can enhance classroom instruction through presenting a wider range of traffic situations and road conditions than would be otherwise possible. Video can provide an instant record of developing traffic situations and reveal important clues about the critical events leading up to incidents. Films and videos can be used to influence and change attitudes. They may also leave learners with wrong time and size concepts and with distorted impressions and incorrect conclusions.

16mm film projector: there are many useful films available for the 'L' driver, most of which are available on loan, from the Central Film Library.

For a film to be used to its greatest effect, it should be preceded by a short introduction outlining its purpose and/or content with a guide of what to look for. It should be concluded with a summary immediately following the showing. Where permanent classroom facilities are not available, rooms and equipment can normally be hired at reasonable costs.

Before showing a film, study those available with the object of the lesson in mind. Arrange to see the film first and take notes on the content. Is it to the point and up to date? Impact will be lost if shown too soon before or too long after related practical sessions. The content will determine whether the film is better shown before or after instruction on that particular topic. Films should be introduced before viewing by the students and they should be given the key learning points to look out for. After showing the film, instructors should summarise the key points again and answer questions.

More and more films are becoming available on video tape. The quality of some productions is very amateurish and the clarity of the sound and pictures sometimes leaves a lot to be desired.

Instant playback television has been usefully installed in some driving school cars and HGV training vehicles. Used sensibly this type of equipment should prove very useful to provide instant feedback to more advanced students of developing traffic situations. They should help learners to 'see' after an incident how the critical events leading up to it could have been recognised earlier. The biggest problem appears to be securing the camera safely and in a position which does not impede movement or intrude upon the driver's view.

A portable video system combining six hours of video tape is available for in-car use. The idea seems to be that instead of instructors explaining the topic under instruction, they locate relevant parts of the relevant tape and let learners view it on a six-inch television screen. The concept of learners paying professional instructors for this type of in-car instruction is, to put it mildly, badly conceived.

Some training films are listed below together with a brief description.

Key	Available from:
TRRL	Transport & Road Research Laboratory, Crowthorne, Berkshire RG11 6AU.
Conoco	Conoco Limited, Conoco House, 230 Blackfriars Road, London SE1 8NR.
Shell	Shell Film Library, 25 The Burroughs, Hendon, London NW4 4AT.
CFL	Central Film Library, Chalfont Grove, Gerrards Cross, Buckinghamshire SL9 8TN.

Key	*Available from:*
RoSPA	Film Library, RoSPA, Cannon House, The Priory, Queensway, Birmingham.
BIA	British Insurance Association, Aldermary House, Queen Street, London.
GSV	Guide Sound and Vision Ltd, Woodston House, Cundle Road, Peterborough.

SP114 Thinking Ahead Sound. Colour. 30 mins, 16 mm film (TRRL)
Shows a driver using 'commentary driving' to think ahead and improve driving.

SP118 Overtaking Behaviour (IDBRA) 16 mm film (TRRL)
A study to determine if overtaking accidents could be reduced.

Collision Course 16 mm film (Conoco)
A film to help experienced drivers examine their attitudes and behaviour.

Car Maintenance at Home 42 mins, 16 mm film and VHS (AA Service/ Motorcraft Centre)
Weekly/monthly vehicle checks and engine care.

A Matter of Attitude Colour. 26 mins VHS and 16 mm film (Shell)
A look at the varied attitudes of different groups of road user.

The Engine Colour. 17 mins, 16 mm film (Shell)
Demonstrates engine and ignition working principles.

Engine Lubrication Colour. 10 mins, 16 mm film (Shell)
Shows oil circulation and damage resulting from incorrect oil.

UK2881 Driving Test 24 mins, 16 mm film (CFL)
Explains the test and how candidates are marked.

L for Logic 14 mins VHS and 16 mm film (CFL)
Comparisons between test items and skills used by an experienced driver.

UK2740 Drive Carefully Darling 17 mins, 16 mm film (CFL)
Action set in a science fiction control room in the driver's mind shows the consequences of ignoring rules.

UK2879 Room to Manoeuvre VHS (CFL)
Problems facing road users and the dangers of insufficient margins for error.

UK2848 After Dark VHS and 16 mm film (CFL)
Shows importance of maintenance and how shadows and silhouettes hide danger.

UK2773 Driver's Eye View 5 mins, 16 mm film (CFL)
Demonstrates what drivers look at.

UK2748 The Motorway File 33 mins VHS and 16 mm film (CFL)
A story of four drivers showing the events leading up to an accident.

UK2796 Night Call 27 mins VHS and 16 mm film (CFL)
Shows aspects of motorway driving, lane discipline, separation and signalling.

D.54 Drivers – Turning Right 7 mins, 16 mm film (RoSPA)
Shows driver involvement in right-turn accidents.

D.76 Turn to Better Driving 9 mins, 16 mm film (RoSPA)
Dick Emery demonstrates the right and wrong way of dealing with hazards.
D.FL Motoring Practice 21 mins, 16 mm film (RoSPA)
Demonstrates a wide range of driving techniques.
D.59 None for the Road 12 mins, 16 mm film (RoSPA)
An emotional and thought-provoking approach to the social drinking driver.
D.92 Under the Influence 27 mins, 16 mm film (RoSPA)
Shows deterioration in driving skill as the alcohol/blood level creeps up.
D.60 The Anatomy of an Accident 17 mins, 16 mm film (RoSPA)
Shows how a lifetime of training can result in tragedy because of impatience.
D.21 Motor Mania Walt Disney 7 mins, 16 mm film (RoSPA)
Illustrates how many people become selfish and thoughtless when driving.
D.66 Freewayphobia Walt Disney 15 mins, 16 mm film (RoSPA)
Animated characters illustrate errors and techniques to avoid accidents.
Candles for Katie 22 mins, 16 mm and VHS (BIA)
How to reduce and avoid accidents. It illustrates the dangers that lead to someone's death or injury every two minutes.
You Can Save Lives Colour. 20 mins, 16 mm film (GSV)
How people with no specialist knowledge can save lives in an accident.

Chapter 6
Teaching in a Classroom

In-class training should be generally considered as being complementary to and not a substitute for practical in-car instruction.

Traditionally most driving instruction is given in the car on the road. While there is much to commend this practical approach to a practical subject, some aspects of driving are more effectively learnt in a group or classroom environment. This can be achieved at lower cost to the student with expenses and facilities being shared with the rest of the class.

While demand for this kind of driver education has not been particularly strong in the past, the general idea is becoming more acceptable as learning to drive by traditional methods becomes more and more expensive. The demand for this type of driver education will grow as more schools begin to look at the possibilities of introducing traffic education into the curriculum.

Although this area of driver education does have its limitations, there are some real savings to be made on the cost of practical tuition and considerable additional economies can be made by producing safer, more informed and considerate drivers. This type of course ought not to be sold only as an alternative to practical tuition but rather as supplementary to it.

One of the biggest advantages of classroom tuition over the in-car situation can be the opportunity to influence and develop the right attitudes. Under the combined power of the group, the individual is far more likely to conform by modifying his own attitudes than through contact with the instructor alone.

Another obvious advantage of group training is that it is more economical to pass on facts and information to a number of people than it is to an individual while parked at the kerbside.

There are also many important aspects of motoring which are rarely, if ever, covered in the normal course of driving tuition because of the expense.

Reduce nerves by planning and preparing the lesson thoroughly. Decide what you want the students to know, be able to do or how you want them to think at the end of the lesson, and collate as much information on the topic as you can. Keep the students active, interested and comfortable and appeal to their visual sense. Let them discuss and decide things for themselves.

Students should be encouraged to learn from each other. Instructors should provide opportunity for free expression. Remember that favourable attitudes are influenced by case studies, discussions, tutorials, role play and simulation. Provide students with adequate background information from which they draw their own conclusions with additional guidance provided where necessary. Make eye contact with students, one at a time. Speak to them as individuals. Avoid looking away or down at your feet and don't speak over their heads. Accept long periods of silence: these can be quite useful. Take your time! When asking questions, pause deliberately to give all the students time to think about the answer. Only then select one to respond!

Instructors should also ensure that:

- they have an adequately lit, ventilated and heated classroom
- there is adequate seating
- they are of clean and smart appearance
- the students know your name
- they are punctual and have proper notes to refer to
- they introduce the topic of the lesson before they start
- they speak clearly and at a natural speed
- they avoid sarcasm and bad language
- they are friendly, confident and fair
- they are aware of the time
- they allow time for questions from students
- they ask questions and get student feedback
- the lesson is finished with students wanting more
- they summarise the main points
- they tell students what they will be doing on their next session.

Rules for the Use of Learning Aids

A = Accuracy – keep them factual
B = Brevity – avoid unnecessary detail
C = Clarity – keep them simple
D = Deletion – when finished with aids, move them out of sight
E = Emphasis – stress the main points
F = Feedback – are the aids serving the intended purpose?

Choosing a Teaching Method

Instructors use a number of teaching methods in their efforts to teach skills, impart knowledge and influence the attitudes of their pupils. When selecting the method it is important to consider the type of learning desired. If you are wishing to: teach a *psychomotor skill*, select a method from column 1; impart *knowledge* select from column 2; influence *attitude* select from column 3.

Column 1 (Skills)	Column 2 (Knowledge)	Column 3 (Attitude)
Lesson demonstrations	Private study (reading)	Tutorials
Individual practice	Programmed instruction	Discussions
Demonstrations	Homework exercises	Case studies
Discovery method	Lesson demonstrations	Simulation
Simulation	Case Studies	Games
Home practice with	Lectures	Role play
workbooks or cards	Tutorials	
	Discussions	

No single technique is better than all the others at all things and it would be as inappropriate to attempt to teach car control through a case study or driver maintenance through simulation as it would to change the learner's attitude through home study. Although most of the methods listed are usually associated with group teaching, the chart provides a 'rule of thumb' guide to the appropriateness of a particular teaching method.

Simulation provides practical experience in controlled conditions where the real life situation is impractical or too dangerous. In driving instruction the technique has fallen out of favour, perhaps because of unfulfilled and exaggerated claims made in the infancy of the driving simulator.

Demonstrations must be immediately consolidated with practice to be of any use. Demonstrating how an expert performs the skill enables the student to copy. They should be simple and easy to follow and avoid unnecessary variables until main points have been grasped. Students should be briefed beforehand about the key learning points to look for.

Discussions enable students to learn from the vast amount of knowledge and experience they possess as a group. A well run discussion is a valuable learning experience. To gain something from it however students must be able to contribute. A poorly run discussion can easily miss the point. Instructors should try to ensure that all students participate and encourage them to express their views freely. The amount of teacher participation in the discussion will probably depend on the level of knowledge and experience of the students participating. Advanced students can be left to their own devices with the teacher listening in or visiting separate groups in turn and involving himself only where useful or to encourage silent students to take part.

Projects and Homework Exercises These help to maintain interest and motivate students. They involve the student in what can be best described as a self-learning exercise through investigation and research. Projects may be individual or group activities. They should be capable of completion within the time scale allowed and should be fairly simple and straightforward. The end result must be beneficial to the course objectives. Projects of this nature appeal to most students and enable them to exercise their own abilities and imagination.

Lectures are the most formal of all teaching methods. Illustrated or not, they tend to be one-way expositions of facts and information with little student participation. The advantage is that efficient use is made of the teacher's time, for example where a visiting specialist has only a limited amount of time available. They are generally inappropriate for driving or pre-driver courses, except when given by visiting specialists.

Case Studies of real life experiences are given to the student. This provides full background information and encourages them to form their own conclusions. It is a 'what went wrong?' analysis leading to how the consequences can be repeated or avoided.

Role Play is one of the most powerful teaching methods. Students play the roles of others as they see them. Those not wishing to participate in such exercises should not be pressured into doing so however. The technique is very effective in getting students to see things from another's point of view.

Lesson Demonstrations contain a number of different teaching methods. This is the method of group teaching most parallel to traditional driving instruction and consists of an introductory talk, questions and answers, demonstration and practice, followed by a summary given by the instructor. This method of teaching falls somewhere between a lecture and a discussion. Favourable attitudes can be influenced by case studies, discussions, tutorials, role play and simulation.

Discovery Learning is a term used to describe general teaching strategies which cut across the other teaching methods. Students are guided to discover the facts, form sympathetic opinions and experience new skills for themselves. The term is used by Dr R M Belbin to describe his very controlled method of discovery learning. The method, derived from programmed learning, presents learners with a series of carefully and progressively graded problems. For example, instead of being told how electricity flows round a circuit, students were invited to build a simple circuit and following worksheet instructions, to make changes, observe and record the result. The record produced by the students turned out to be an accurate account of the rules of electricity which the students 'discovered for themselves'. The method took half as long and nearly doubled the pass rates at the end of the course.

Teacher and Student Centred Learning In teacher-centred instruction the instructor plays a dominant role. Although useful during the early lessons, it will not permit students to achieve their full potential. In learner-centred instruction the teacher places the student into a more dominant role. The instructor then acts as adviser rather than as teacher. The students become more involved and develop increased responsibility for their own learning. Students are allowed to make up their own minds. This improves the learning processes and increases understanding.

Natural Teaching Styles An individual instructor's preferences and skills, a student's preferences and abilities, and the teaching conditions and instructor to student ratio will, to a large extent, also help to determine the choice of teaching method. Some instructors who may be absolute masters at giving practical in-car instruction may be temperamentally unsuited to delivering formal lectures in a classroom. Their nature may dictate an informal, self-effacing classroom style while others may feel completely at home delivering lectures. The technique used should also take those factors which affect the learning processes into consideration. These include factors such as:

- 75 per cent of the brain's input is received from the eyes
- Verbal information is the hardest to learn
- Students learn at different rates and learn best with some personal control
- They are anxious about possible failure, so they need to experience successes and receive continual reassurance of them
- They require immediate feedback of their performance
- Students learn by being involved and doing things for themselves
- They learn by practising skills, using knowledge and experiencing attitudes
- Student limitations in ability to attend to specific tasks
- Involuntary breaks in the student's concentration; which recur at more frequent intervals with the passage of time
- Students are unable to recall everything learnt on a lesson.

Chapter 7
Driver Training

Route Planning

Route planning is an essential element of lesson preparation. It requires a thorough knowledge of the local geography and traffic conditions and must take into consideration any specific driving skill or procedure to be learnt.

An unsympathetic route can have disastrous consequences when the learner is unnecessarily exposed to conditions with which he is unable to cope. In severe cases, and with particularly nervous pupils, it may even make them give up the idea of learning to drive at all.

Ideally a fairly wide selection of planned routes containing various types of traffic hazards and conditions will be required. These need not be considered as rigidly fixed routes from which there must be no deviation. Flexibility is in fact an important consideration when planning a route because it allows for changes to be made midway through a lesson. This may be necessary to allow more time to be spent on an area of driving which may be proving unexpectedly troublesome, and still complete the lesson on time for the instructor's next appointment.

Excessive repetition over the same routes will often prove counter-productive because frequently it reduces interest, resulting in boredom and slow progress. Some repetition can be helpful at times when it is carried out deliberately for a specific purpose relevant to the lesson.

Training routes and areas loosely fall into three groups:

1. Nursery routes.
2. Intermediate.
3. Advanced.

There is no hard and fast division between these groups and there may frequently be considerable overlap between them. On occasions there is justification for incorporating all kinds on one lesson, for instance when making an initial assessment of a new client with previous driving experience.

Starting with the nursery routes, new traffic situations should be introduced at a controlled rate which is both sensitive to the needs of the pupil and sympathetic to his ability.

In practice, the nature of traffic conditions can be very erratic and even the most carefully planned route might suddenly prove unsuitable, with the pupil finding himself having to deal with new situations with which he cannot cope. Route preparation will however help keep these incidents down to a fairly isolated and acceptable level.

Training routes are often a compromise between the ideal and the reality of the local geography and traffic conditions. In general, instructors working near the centre of a large city may experience difficulty in finding suitable nursery routes, while their counterparts operating in isolated rural areas may experience problems in finding suitably varied conditions for the advanced routes. Extending the length of some lessons may be a satisfactory answer in both instances by allowing more travelling time to better suited areas.

Nursery routes
Various kinds of roads are required on these routes but in general they should avoid areas containing many turns or junctions. As far as possible avoid other traffic and initially, in the very early stages, parked vehicles. These routes should not include pedestrian crossings, traffic lights or roundabouts.

Routes required will progressively incorporate:

1. Fairly straight, wide roads, long enough to allow uninterrupted progression through all the gears and preferably free from parked vehicles.
2. Quiet, fairly wide roads on up/down/level gradients, suitable for practising manipulative skills and allowing unimpeded passage for other traffic.
3. Roads containing right/left hand bends and allowing for use of the gears on hills.
4. Simple left turns from main into side roads.
5. Simple left turns into main roads.
6. Right turns from main into side roads and right turns into main roads.
7. Some routes containing parked vehicles will also be necessary.

Intermediate routes

1. There will be overlap between some of these routes and the more advanced nursery routes.
2. Include all types of basic rule crossroads and junctions with the various give way and stop controls.
3. A route with an abundance of uphill give way junctions should be included for practising first gear hold and control.
4. Some routes should include traffic lights and roundabouts which conform to basic rules.
5. Roads selected for the initial practice of the 'turn in the road' and reversing exercises should be free from other traffic and obstructions on the footpaths. Driving test routes should also be avoided – certainly for basic training.

These routes should specifically avoid dual carriageways, multi-laned roads and one-way streets. Junctions which do not conform to basic rules should also be excluded. Right turns on to very busy main roads and any other particularly difficult situations should not normally be incorporated into these routes.

Advanced routes

These routes will incorporate most of the intermediate routes and progressively extend them to include as many variations to the basic rules as possible. They will include dual carriageways, multi-laned roads, one-way streets, level crossings (where possible), busy shopping streets and rural roads providing an opportunity to practise overtaking.

These routes will also include properly prepared 'mock test' routes similar to those used by the Department of Transport (do however try to avoid actual test routes).

1. Pedestrian crossings (zebra, pelican, traffic light controlled).
2. Level crossings.
3. Dual carriageways.
4. Multi-laned roads and lane discipline.
5. One-way streets.
6. Motorway class dual carriageways (where possible).
7. Rural roads.

Points to Remember

When planning and selecting routes consideration should be given to the following:

(a) The standard and ability of the pupil.
(b) The specific skills you wish to impart.
(c) What particular hazards are to be included or avoided.
(d) How much time is available.
(e) What danger or inconvenience might be caused to other road users.
(f) Is any excessive nuisance likely to be caused to local residents?
(g) Excessive repetition of routes is boring for the learner.
(h) Avoid using Department of Transport test routes for early training and do not use corners or roads used by the driving examiners for manoeuvre exercises during the normal testing hours (9 am to 5 pm).
(i) Other traffic can be a severe distraction to learning the basic skills, particularly in early lessons.

Giving Route Directions

The quality of a driving performance can be totally destroyed by late or unclear directions. The learner must be given sufficient time to both interpret and respond to any request. The instructor must also remember that inexperienced students often take longer to react.

The direction must be clear and precise, stating the action required and identifying the location where the action is to take place. The manner in which the direction is phrased should also alert the learner to the forthcoming change of course.

Most instructions concerning the route contain three necessary ingredients; these are:

1. *Alert* – draw the learner's attention to the imminent request.
2. *Direct* – the instruction to turn or pull up.
3. *Identify* – confirm where the instruction is to be carried out.

Examples:

Alert	– I would like you to
Direct	– turn left
Identify	– at the junction ahead.

Alert	– I want you to
Direct	– take the second road on the right
Identify	– this one being the first.

Alert	– At the roundabout I want you to
Direct	– take the road leading off to the right
Identify	– that is, the third exit.

Alert	– At the roundabout I want you to
Direct	– follow the road ahead
Identify	– that is the second exit.

Alert	– At the roundabout I want you to
Direct	– take the first road leading off to your left
Identify	– that is the first exit.

Alert	– I want you to
Direct	– take the next road
Identify	– on the left please.

(Confirmation should be given where required by adding further information such as:

It's just out of sight around the bend.

Just before the telephone box, bus stop, etc.)

Special Instructions

1. General route brief

I want you to follow the road ahead unless otherwise directed by road signs or markings. When I want you to turn I will ask you in good time. Drive on when you are ready please.

2. Stopping – parking – angled start – moving off

I want you to pull up and park on the left at the next convenient place please. I want you to pull up just behind the stationary vehicle, but leaving yourself sufficient room to move out again.

Drive on when you are ready.

3. Emergency stop

Shortly I will ask you to stop the vehicle as in an emergency. The signal will be

'Stop'. When I give this signal, stop immediately and under full control, as though a child has run off the pavement. Drive on when you are ready please.

After the exercise:
Thank you! I won't/will be asking you to do that exercise again. Drive on when you are ready please.

4. Left/right hand reverse exercise

Left – The road on the left is the one I want you to reverse into. Drive past it and stop, reverse in and continue back for some distance into the side road. Keep reasonably close to the kerb.

Right – The road on the right is the one I want you to reverse into. Drive on the left side until you have passed it, then move across to the right and stop. Reverse in and continue back for some distance down the side road keeping reasonably close to the right-hand kerb.

5. Turn in the road

I want you to turn the car round by means of forward and reverse gears. Try not to touch the kerb while turning.

6. Following direction signs

An interesting and valuable exercise for the advanced learner is to provide him with an opportunity to follow a clearly signed route by means of the direction signs, rather than following instructions.

7. Lane selection

Wherever possible the learner should be allowed and encouraged to make lane selection decisions for himself, but on early practice and in some complex situations, assistance may be required, for example:

(a) Approach in and maintain the left-hand lane through the roundabout.
(b) Select and maintain the centre/right lane.

8. Route confirmation

When confirming a straight ahead direction use the term, 'Follow the road ahead', at a junction or roundabout.

Avoid 'Go straight on', or, 'Carry straight on', as these terms may be taken literally by the learner and cause him to ignore any traffic signs, markings or give way rules.

Mistakes

Giving clear directions in good time will not always guarantee the correct response. Some students get momentarily confused between left and right, particularly where they are under stress and this can be embarrassing for them. Providing no danger or inconvenience is caused to other road users, do not overemphasise the problem and make them feel even more foolish. Although the learner will not be tested on his ability to distinguish between left and right, excessive errors of this nature on a driving test could prove very difficult for the examiner.

These faults only become classed as driving errors if, for example, the left-hand signal is given where the learner intends to turn right. Obviously it is a problem which should be cured as soon as possible and one way of helping the student who is right handed is by saying, 'I write with my right and what's left is my left.' Almost all people wear their watches on the left wrist, similarly wedding and engagement rings are worn on the left so this should be a guide also.

Driver Assessments

When giving directions to students approaching driving test standard, it is important that those instructions be as neutral as the circumstances allow. While the directions should always be clear and precise, guard against giving the pupil too many verbal reminders of what he should be observing for himself.

Telling an advanced pupil to 'Turn left at the traffic lights,' provides the information 'traffic lights' which the pupil should discover for himself. Such information, however, can be justified in certain circumstances on a particularly complex part of a route. Also in certain areas it is virtually impossible to distinguish which lane will subsequently be required without previous knowledge of the area; under such circumstances the pupil should be told which lane to select.

Points to Remember

1. Late instructions are likely to cause:

    (a)   Rash, hurried decisions.
    (b)   Poor control.
    (c)   Poor observations.
    (d)   Erratic steering.
    (e)   Lack of confidence.

2. Avoid the word 'Stop' except in an emergency.
3. Avoid starting an instruction with the words 'Turn' or 'Pull up'.
4. Avoid using the word 'right' for anything other than a directional change. For example, 'Right! Turn left at the crossroads,' can cause obvious confusion, or, 'That's right!' when in fact you mean, 'That's correct!'

The Use of Instructions and Terminology

Any instruction given to the learner while the vehicle is in motion should be firm, concise and clearly understood. The terminology used should be consistent, particularly in the early stages of tuition. For example, if, after mostly referring to the 'holding point' the instruction is suddenly changed to 'biting point', there is chance of causing confusion. Similarly, if after giving frequent instructions to 'signal' right or left, the terminology is changed to 'indicate' this could lead to momentary hesitation on the part of the learner, which in turn might lead to serious consequences if driving in traffic.

The pupil must be able to recognise and interpret the terminology if the instruction is to instigate the correct response immediately.

The need for most instructional jargon is at its highest during the early stages of tuition when, unfortunately, your pupil will be least familiar with it.

A new client will, in time, become accustomed to your style of terminology. Pupils from other driving schools however may be used to a completely different style of instructional language. In order to make life easier for the pupil it may help if the instructor can adapt to the difference rather than expecting the pupil to learn new vocabulary. This is not easy, nor always successful, but it will certainly help the instructor appreciate the difficulties caused by unfamiliar phraseology.

KOPLINGS – BREMSE – GIRKASSE

Unless you are Norwegian, the above words are strange and unfamiliar titles for three vehicle controls. When talking to an absolute novice about the clutch, brake, or gearbox, you might as well be speaking in a foreign language.

When introducing a new client to these controls and to the function and use of each, he must be given sufficient time to assimilate what might be new and strange words. Wherever possible, terminology should be in simple English which will be easily recognised and clearly understood.

Basic Instructions

The following are lists of example instructions which can be used to instigate set responses from the learner, providing he has received adequate explanation and practice at using the terms beforehand. In most cases the basic responses can be practised in a stationary vehicle. The tone of the voice should be varied according to the personality of the learner and the nature or speed of the response required. For example a short firm 'Brake harder' is far more likely to achieve a positive effect than a quietly spoken 'Brake harder'. Get to know your client and adjust your voice *to suit the urgency of the situation*.

Make sure the learner can understand and carry out the following instructions before attempting to move off:

The Instruction	*What it means*
Handbrake ready.	Hand on the handbrake ready to release it.
Set the gas.	Increase the engine speed to a fast tickover.
Find the holding point.	Clutch up until engine slows down a little. Often called the biting point.
Cover the clutch.	Foot over the clutch pedal.
Cover the brake.	Foot over the brake pedal.

Instructions Used for Moving Off and Increasing Speed
Initial check to the front and rear;
Clutch down: hand on gearlever palm towards . . . and select first gear;
Set the gas: and then . . . handbrake ready;
Find the holding point: and . . . keep your feet still;
Check interior and door mirrors . . . look over shoulder in blind spots;
Signal if helpful to warn or inform others;
Handbrake off . . . increase the gas . . . slowly raise the clutch;
Cancel signal (if used).

Instructions Used to Change Up the Gears
Hold the wheel firmly with your right hand . . . cover the clutch;
Hand on gearlever palm towards . . . ;
Push the clutch down . . . off the gas together;
Move the gear lever into . . . ;
Clutch up smoothly . . . increase the gas;
Return your hand to the wheel (and rest your left foot . . .).

Instructions Used to Change Down the Gears
Keep both hands on the wheel . . . off the gas . . . cover the brake;
Brake gently . . . off the brake but keep it covered;
Hold the wheel firmly with your right hand . . . cover the clutch;
Hand on the gearlever palm towards . . . ;
Push the clutch down;
Move the gear lever into . . . ;
Clutch up smoothly . . . keep brake/clutch covered/increase the gas . . . ;
Return your hand to the wheel.

Instructions Used in Normal Driving
Hold the wheel firmly;
Look well ahead . . . look where you want to steer;
Prepare to turn the wheel left/right;
Check the mirrors;
Signal left/right;
Increase the gas . . . off the gas;
Brake gently . . . brake harder . . . ease off the brake;
Clutch down;
Handbrake on . . . select neutral.

Instructions and Prompts Used to Alert Drivers to Risks and Hazards
Look for pedestrians/cyclists/animals/vehicles moving into/across your
    path;
Look for and act on things which restrict your view;
Look for and act on signs/signals/roadmarking;
Look for and act on bends/junctions/obstructions;
Look both ways.

Instructions to Reduce Speed
Hold back for . . . ;

Once explained and demonstrated, 'hold back' provides a useful abbreviated expression which can be used to replace a lot of abstract instructions relating to braking pressure. It involves judgement of speed and timing and requires considerable practice. It leaves the learners with more freedom and responsibility for their own actions. It involves slowing down early enough and in a manner which gives traffic situations more time to clear and reduces the likelihood of the need to come to a complete stop.

The holdback position describes the position in which drivers should normally:
— wait behind parked vehicles or other obstructions for oncoming traffic;
— follow behind cyclists when waiting for oncoming traffic.

Slow down for...; give way to...;
Both are positive commands which should leave the driver in no doubt as to the required action. Both leave the learner with more freedom and responsibility for their own actions to 'stop'.

Stop...
Only use in an emergency! It is almost the verbal equivalent to using the dual controls. The tone of command will affect the learner's response and used in a careless manner it could result in an emergency stop particularly if the learner is under stress.

Instructions and Prompts Used to Stimulate Thought

New drivers fail to recognise or anticipate danger in many common 'high risk' situations. Short comments or questions directed to drawing their attention to the danger can help to improve their anticipation and responses. Provided it is used in plenty of time for them to respond, the technique helps to make the learners think and consider the consequences of their own inaction. For example:

I would approach much slower than this...
I would give way to the oncoming driver...
Are you ready to move away if...?
What's happening behind?
Is it safe to proceed?
Can you see...?
Is it clear?
Do you need to signal?

Approaching a row of parked vehicles at an excessive speed ask:

'What will you do if a child runs out?'
'What will you do if a car moves out?'
'What will you do if a car door opens?'
'What will you do if the cyclist pulls out?'
'What will you do if the oncoming car keeps coming?'

Approaching a pedestrian crossing at excessive speed ask:

'What will you do if the pedestrian steps onto the crossing?'

Driving too close to the vehicle ahead ask:

'What will you do if the car in front has to stop quickly?'

Approaching a bend or corner at excessive speed ask:

'What will you do if there is a car parked just round the bend?'
'What will you do if there is a pedestrian crossing the sideroad?'

Corrections Made on the Move

Under normal circumstances, detailed explanations should be avoided whilst the vehicle is in motion or while the learner is concentrating on something else, such as emerging from a junction or when waiting at red traffic lights.

However, most incidents involving minor errors will not be recognised by the learner at the time and, ten minutes later, most of those recognised will have been forgotten anyway. Except when conducting mock tests therefore, give the learner some feedback on any errors committed at the time, or as soon after as possible. This draws attention to them, making incidents easier to recall when later referred to.

It is useful however to make short comments as cues to help learners deal with difficult situations, or as minor rebukes for errors which may have been committed. Where corrections are made, they should be of a positive nature and ideally state the action required to cure the error. For example it is better to say 'hold the clutch still' rather than: 'don't let the clutch up' or 'drive about two or three feet from the kerb' rather than 'don't drive in the gutter.'

Serious errors, or repeated minor ones, which appear to involve misunderstandings, should be corrected as soon as is reasonably possible after they have occurred, but only when a suitable parking place has been found.

Using the Dual Controls

New drivers lack anticipation and fail to recognise or respond to potentially dangerous traffic situations. Instructors should never completely trust them to follow instructions or do the right thing. They should always keep in mind their legal responsibilities and remember they can be prosecuted for aiding and abetting offences committed by the learner.

Instructors must be firm and take whatever action necessary to protect the student, the vehicle and others. Look, think and plan well ahead. Get to know individual students and watch them. Predict how they are likely to respond in given situations. Anticipate changes in the traffic situation and give firm instructions early enough for the student to react. Uncorrected errors will lead to the development of potentially dangerous and frightening situations. Avoid these through verbal commands or action with the dual controls.

There are four reasons why the instructor should intervene:

1. To prevent risk of injury or damage to persons or property.
2. To prevent an offence against the law.
3. To prevent excessive stress to the learner in certain unplanned circumstances.
4. To prevent mechanical damage to the vehicle.

A verbal command is often sufficient if given in time. If the instruction is not carried out by the learner however, you will need to act. For example you may sound the horn, turn the wheel, switch the engine off, select a missed gear, release a partially engaged handbrake or prevent an unsympathetic gear change by covering the lever. If necessary use the dual controls, but these should not be used as a matter of routine and the student should be told afterwards that they have been used and why. Continual steering corrections and excessive use of the duals does little to build the student's faith in an instructor. Generally students harbour various degrees of resentment at such action, particularly if they do not understand why the controls were used. Even where the use of dual controls is totally justified, some students will be upset by such action.

There are various methods through which instructors maintain a safe learning environment. These include verbal and physical prompting or intervention with the dual controls, steering or use of other controls such as the ignition switch, horn, direction indicators and gear lever etc.

Verbal intervention

The verbal command is the most common form of intervention used by the driving instructor and is nearly always successful in dealing with most traffic situations or driver errors, provided sufficient concentration is applied to the task. These commands range from the mild memory prompt, to a more positive command for a specific and immediate action.

The prompt is usually associated more with the earlier lessons but may be extended to more positive instructions such as:

Use the mirror *before* changing direction.
Brake harder, or, Ease the brake off.
Clutch down, or, Hold the clutch still.
Increase the gas, or, Off the gas.

The more positive commands required to relieve potentially dangerous traffic situations are usually those requiring the learner to slow down earlier when approaching hazards.

'Hold back,' or, 'Give way,' are positive commands requiring a specific reaction from the learner but without depriving the student of some freedom of judgement.

'Stop' is the final and absolute command and should generally only be used in a situation which is fast getting out of control and/or where other instructions have not been followed or are unlikely to achieve any response.

Physical intervention

Physical intervention should normally be restricted to those situations where it is considered essential and where verbal intervention does not work, or when there is insufficient time to give verbal instruction.

The main methods of physical intervention are the use of the dual control footbrake and steering corrections from the passenger seat.

In any traffic situation the instructor should consider the method of intervention best suited to correcting the error. There are occasions when both steering and braking may be required together. For example, it may be essential to hold the steering wheel while using the dual footbrake. This is to resist the tendency the pupil may have of swinging the wheel. In order to generate more time for the instructor to intervene and turn the wheel from the passenger seat, it may be necessary to reduce and control the speed with the dual brake, particularly if the pupil has 'frozen' on the accelerator.

The Dual Footbrake

1. Keep your foot readily accessible for the brake with the minimum amount of movement.
2. If any potential cause arises for use of the brake – sight it ready.
3. Avoid fidgeting with the brake – this is likely to unnerve the pupil.
4. If the learner is frozen on the accelerator, it is generally inadvisable to use the dual clutch as complementary to the brake as this could result in a 'blown' engine.
5. Where the pupil sees a sudden movement towards the pedal, or where he feels a pressure change on his pedal, he may react instinctively by braking harder. This double pressure can be dangerous to following traffic or may possibly lock the wheels. Be ready for this possible reaction.
6. Before the brake is used, check the dual control mirror.
7. After using the dual control explain to the pupil why it was necessary.
8. Reducing the speed with the dual brake will allow the learner more time to turn the wheel in circumstances which he might otherwise find impossible.

The Steering Wheel

1. Turning the wheel from the passenger seat is generally more difficult than using the dual footbrake.
2. In certain circumstances it may be the only safe or practical method of intervention.
3. The need for this kind of intervention can be kept to an acceptable minimum by ensuring the route and conditions are commensurate with the ability of the driver.
4. Other than for minor corrections to the course, if you intend turning the wheel left, go for an initially high position on the wheel which will give more leverage to the left, and for turning right – go for a lower position suitable for pushing the wheel.
5. When turning the wheel avoid physical contact with the pupil, though circumstances may make contact with the hands or arms inevitable.
6. Where 'frozen' to the wheel, even a very frail person becomes immensely strong and may resist any attempt you make to turn it.
7. Minor corrections to the steering course and positioning are frequently more practical and safer alternatives to the footbrake, for example where the pupil is steering loosely towards the kerb or too close to oncoming traffic, parked vehicles, cyclists or pedestrians.

8. There is sometimes a slight resentment by pupils against physical intervention with the steering wheel, particularly when they fail to recognise the reason.

The Dual Clutch and Accelerator

Assisting the learner by using the dual clutch is usually unnecessary. It should be avoided in all but the most exceptional and isolated of instances. Dual accelerators are uncommon in Britain and must in any event be disconnected while the vehicle is being used for a driving test.

The Horn

This should be used sensibly where it is accessible to the instructor. It is better to remove a danger at source than to later find more drastic intervention is necessary.

Other forms of intervention

Engaging a missed gear at a critical time or place.

Damage can be prevented to a racing engine by switching it off, providing the switch is accessible.

Operating the indicator in critical circumstances may prevent a dangerous occurrence where the learner is unable to attend to it.

Rectifying a mistake in the use of the handbrake.

Preventing an unsympathetic gear change by covering the lever until the speed has been increased/reduced.

Wherever any form of physical intervention has been used, the pupil should be told why, even where it may be obvious.

Where much verbal or physical intervention is required for learners approaching the driving test, it is extremely doubtful that, independent of such help, they would achieve a satisfactory standard on test.

Dual Eye Mirrors

These help the instructor to keep in constant touch with the all-round traffic situation, and at the same time to check that the pupil is using the mirrors sufficiently. An additional small dual eye mirror, strategically placed and focused on the pupil's eyes, will greatly assist.

Using the Dual Control Mirrors

The importance of the instructor's dual mirror is obvious so it is not intended to dwell on it long here except perhaps to remind new instructors that mirrors should be placed fairly high on the screen so as not to impede the learner's view in any way. However they should be low enough to provide an adequate view of the rear distance. Dual mirrors should be correctly adjusted and perfectly directed toward the instructor's eyes as he is seated in his normal position.

Some instructors are reported to be using nearside door mirrors for their own convenience on the grounds that they are not a legal requirement. This can be counter-productive and defeats the commonsense purpose of encouraging rear vision. It is pointed out that in the absence of nearside mirrors there are certain circumstances when drivers must turn their heads to check blindspots prior to executing some manoeuvres. Looking round unnecessarily in this manner when driving forward sometimes at speed is an unnecessary risk factor being introduced artificially. Driving instructors wishing to verify the safety on the nearside have more time to look round than the driver and can more easily turn in their seats than the learner.

Avoiding Common Driving School Accidents

Safety is no accident and instructors maintain a safe learning environment for students by:

- (a) Planning routes commensurate with ability.
- (b) Forward planning and concentration on the traffic situation – front and rear.
- (c) Alertness and anticipation of the learner's action.
- (d) Giving clear directions in good time for the learner to respond.

Contrary to popular belief, the novice driver is far less likely to be involved in an accident than the experienced motorist, providing he is learning in a dual controlled car under professional supervision.

Where the driving school car is involved in an accident it is most likely to be a 'rear end shunt' from the vehicle behind. There are two main reasons for this:

1. Most learners show a tendency of being reluctant to slow down, give way or stop. This initial reluctance to deal with a traffic hazard may subsequently develop into an emergency. Where the situation is allowed to reach this critical level, there are two possible unwanted reactions from the learner:

    (a) Do nothing and remain frozen at the controls on a collision course.

    (b) Over-react – resulting in a harsh unregulated braking pressure which will usually bring the car to an uncontrolled and abrupt stop yards before it is necessary.

    Whether it is the instructor or the pupil who stops the car in these situations, the result is likely to be the same if the driver behind is also not concentrating or is following too closely.

2. The 'false start' or 'stall' when moving off into a roundabout or when pulling out of an 'open' junction is the other main cause of the 'rear end shunt.' What usually happens is that, as the learner starts to pull out, the driver behind looks to the right, moving into the space he thinks has been vacated. Unfortunately, and, unknown to him since he was not paying attention, the learner has stalled half-way out into the space (or the instructor has stopped the car because of approaching traffic). This emphasises the need for proper route selection according to the student's abilities.

How to Avoid Rear End Collisions

1. Keep your distance, slow down earlier and allow the car to run gently to a halt.
2. Act promptly to correct a learner attempting to move off at the wrong time. To allow the pupil to move off in a false start, necessitating a stop within a few feet, is potentially dangerous because the driver following is also encouraged to move.

Other Accident-prone Situations

Special alertness is required from the instructor when approaching traffic lights. Some learners are apt to do emergency stops when the lights change, even if they have already crossed the stop line.

The right turn at traffic lights is a particularly dangerous manoeuvre and great care should be exercised in the supervision of its execution. In addition, great care should be taken over observations when emerging from a blind junction or one where visibility is restricted by parked vehicles or other obstructions.

Consideration should also be given to the fact that the 'L' driver is not usually as quick off the mark as an experienced driver. This can make turns on to busy roads and large roundabouts potentially dangerous manoeuvres.

The instructor should be ready to compensate for any sudden movement of the car on a low speed manoeuvre exercise where a slight slip on the part of the learner might have disastrous consequences.

When moving off from junctions, the instructor should pay particular attention to the blind area behind the learner's head, being careful at the same time to keep his own head out of the pupil's line of observation.

Structuring a Course of Driving Instruction

The nine principles of structuring a course of driving lessons are largely common sense and good instructors tend to follow them intuitively. The general principles are:

Principle 1   The aims and objectives of a course of lessons and each part of the course should be clearly specified in advance in terms of observable behaviour.

Principle 2   The material to be learned and routes used should be appropriate to achieving the specified aims and objectives.

Principle 3   The content of the course and individual lessons should be organised in short progressive steps which follow a logical sequence.

Principle 4   The content of lesson and routes should be graded in difficulty so that the learner makes as few mistakes as possible.

Principle 5   Learners should be introduced to new materials and skills at a level of difficulty which is commensurate with their ability, previous experience and current attainments.

Principle 6   Learners should be allowed to proceed through the course at their own pace.

Principle 7   Learners should be 'actively' involved in the process of learning.

Principle 8   Learners should receive continuous feedback of how they are progressing through the course of lessons.

Principle 9   A learner should master each skill and section of the course before moving on to the next.

Principle 1: The aims and objectives of a course of lessons and each part of the course should be clearly specified in advance in terms of observable behaviour.

Objectives are written statements used to describe what learners are expected to know, do or think at the end of a lesson or course of lessons. They should be stated in observable behaviour, and attempt to communicate to others the sought for changes in the learner.

Driving instructors have little control over the 'superficial' procedures and other aspects of driving they teach because they are mainly decided by driving test criteria. However, it is obviously useful for instructors to decide beforehand what changes they want to bring about in the learner's behaviour in particular concerning those important aspects of driving which are not effectively assessed on the driving test such as knowledge, attitudes and some vital aspects of hazard recognition skills.

Chapter 2 in this book contains objectives relating to the affective, cognitive or psychomotor domains of the mental life (referring to attitude, knowledge and skill respectively).

Objectives in the affective domain are concerned with stating what the learner should think and how he should behave. Those in the cognitive domain are concerned with intellectual skills and state what the learner should know, while those in the psychomotor domain are concerned with stating what the learner should be able to do.

Bloom's taxonomy and classification in the cognitive domain are concerned with the measurement of knowledge and despite criticisms, it is the most widely used. There are six ascending levels or classes of knowledge. These are: knowledge; comprehension; application; analysis; synthesis; and evaluation. It is essential that learner drivers are taught at least to comprehend and apply, otherwise their knowledge will remain more or less useless. It is generally accepted that knowledge helps to generate favourable attitudes, conversely inadequate or incorrect knowledge might result in the development of negative attitudes and result in unsafe driver behaviour.

Success or failure in the driving test is measured by the objectives contained on the test application form and in the DL68. Instructors may wish to extend these or write their own set of intermediate or structured 'short term' objectives.

The following are examples of structured or short term objectives relating to the psychomotor domain which are specifically concerned with the use of the gear lever on a first lesson.

On completing this stage of the lesson the learner will be able to:

Stage 1   Carry out instructions to move the gear lever to specified positions while stationary and looking at the gear lever.

Stage 2   Carry out instructions to move the gear lever to specified positions while stationary and without looking at the gear lever.

Stage 3   Carry out instructions on the move, which enable the learner to select specified gears on command while steering and without looking at the gear lever.

Stage 4   Execute specified gear changes on command while steering and without looking at the gear lever.

Principle 2: The material to be learned and routes used should be appropriate to achieving the specified aims and objectives.

The content of the lesson, support materials and routes used should be appropriate to achieving the specified aims and objectives. Research into the causes of road accidents shows that deficiencies in perceptive abilities, personality and other psychological characteristics are more significant in accident involvement than deficiencies in car control skills.

Instructors should classify material in order of importance. For example:

Essential material is what the learner *must* cover in order to achieve the course objectives.

Desirable material is what the learner *should* cover but which is not essential in order to achieve the course objectives.

Useful material is what the learner *could* cover but which is not completely relevant to the course objectives.

For example, how to check the fan belt tension is probably more suited to a course on car maintenance than it is on a course in learning to drive.

The facts, skills and techniques selected for learning should not only be relevant to the course objectives, but they must also be accurate and reliable. There is a vast source of learning material available to the 'L' driver in books and films.

Some of this material is useful to the 'L' driver, but sometimes discrepancies occur. For example the Department of Transport states, 'Slow down and keep to the left approaching a left-hand bend.' The police and Institute of Advanced Motorists state, 'To improve visibility round a left-hand bend you should approach in a more central road position.'

Check the source of your information. The Department of Transport is the highest authority on driving in Britain and its advice is sought and respected worldwide. What you teach the 'L' driver must be compatible with road safety principles, and it should always be borne in mind that the learner will be finally assessed on the driving test to Department of Transport criteria.

Principle 3: The content of the course and individual lessons should be organised in short progressive steps which follow a logical sequence.

Intermediate targets will help to stimulate interest and progress. They can help to reinforce learning by providing positive evidence of progress through each section and also to organise an otherwise totally haphazard learning situation.

The driving task should be analysed and organised into short progressive units of instruction. Considered in its totality, driving is a complex task. It is made up of many sub-skills such as moving off, steering, stopping etc. These sub-skills are each made up of several sub-divisions.

A course of driving lessons should normally be structured to proceed from:

the known to the unknown
the simple to the complex
the basic rules to the variations
concrete observations to abstract reasoning

Once the learner has grasped the basic rules and concepts it is an easier matter to develop new skills and understand the variables.

Principle 4: The content of lessons and routes should be graded in difficulty so that the learner makes as few mistakes as possible.

Make sure the student is able to experience success during the early stages of the course. Avoid setting standards too high during the early stages. Be prepared to accept some technical inaccuracies and deficiencies until the learner has developed more confidence in his own driving ability.

Initial failure may deter the learner and inhibit future progress. Build confidence and understanding upon a firm foundation of practical skills. Progress from what the student knows and can do to the unknown and the new. Progress from a simple task to a more detailed procedure. Simple skills must be taught before the more complex ones; for example – it would be unreasonable to expect a learner to deal with a right turn at a busy traffic light controlled junction before he has proper control over the movement of the vehicle.

Principle 5: Learners should be introduced to new material and skills at a level of difficulty which is commensurate with their ability, previous experience and attainments.

There are considerable variations in the rate at which different students learn. This should cause few problems when giving individual tuition because the course can be tailored to suit the needs of each student. The student should be allowed to work through each unit of learning at his own pace, with new skills and techniques being introduced at a level commensurate with current ability, knowledge and previous achievement.

One of the first tasks, when meeting a new student, is to find out what previous experience he has had and also how much he knows and can do. In order to plan the level of training it is necessary to establish the student's current knowledge and skills. Students should be consulted about their own learning and encouraged to take some responsibility for the decisions involved.

As skills develop, and mastery of the controls is applied, students should be kept informed of what they are doing and why. They should never be left confused or in doubt. It is important, however, that many basic skills are taught as simple conditioned reflex procedures. It is more important that a student *responds correctly* to an emergency than that he understands *why* he should respond in that way.

Principle 6: Learners should be allowed to proceed through the course at their own pace.

Learning is more efficient when students are allowed to proceed at their own pace, either as quickly or slowly as the instructor feels they are able.

Principle 7: Learners should be 'actively' involved in the process of learning.

The student should be kept physically and/or mentally involved with the learning experience. Whatever the student learns he can only achieve by *thinking* and *doing* things, for himself. Activity will help to capture the student's attention. Where a student is passively sitting in a classroom, supposedly listening to a necessary, but boring, lecture on matters he possibly does not consider relevant or important to his needs, it is easy to see how he may 'switch off'. You may think driving a car at 40 mph along a quiet road with little happening is a far cry from a boring lecture! In some ways that is correct, but it requires little physical activity other than steering. The problem in this situation is that there is very little to occupy the mind which may not be actively involved in the driving at all. These situations provide ideal opportunities for developing the pupil's visual search and observational skills together with the reasoning powers of a skilled driver.

Observing the physical activity of the student is relatively easy for the instructor; observation of what the pupil is thinking, however, is a far more difficult problem. An active mind is essential to learning and an extremely important part of driving.

In the early stages of the learning task keep the student's mind active – ask questions about relevant road features or his intended actions. (However – do not distract the learner when busy.)

There will be many instances where, once the learning experience has been set up, the teacher/driving instructor will take a back seat and play a passive role observing the quality of the student's work.

Principle 8: Learners should receive continuous feedback as to how they are progressing through the course of lessons.

Learning should be reinforced with feedback of progress, helpful comments, constructive criticism and encouragement.

Active involvement facilitates learning but it does not ensure that the learning is of the right kind and that the student is making progress towards the final performance as stated in the objectives. Make sure that the student is not just perfecting his faults. To reinforce learning and to improve the driver's performance, the student should be given continual information on his progress and performance. This feedback should occur as soon as possible after the event or between each step in an exercise or manoeuvre, thereby helping to prevent further faults appearing.

Comments such as 'good' or 'very good' may be useful as an indication of progress where there is insufficient time to give the student more detailed information, but they do not tell him anything about the actual performance. Comments such as, 'Our position was slightly too close to the kerb on the approach to the turn,' or, 'The gear change was left a little too late,' or, 'The approach speed is still a little too fast,' are all of more use because they give information on the actual performance.

Better still are comments which state the action required to rectify the error such as: position about three feet from the kerb when turning left; change down to second a little earlier next time; or slow down more before reaching the corner.

Short comments and corrections made on the move such as those outlined above will be of great value in improving the learner's performance. Detailed verbal corrections should however be avoided when the vehicle is in motion. Where these are required they should be given as soon as is practicable after the incident when a suitable parking position is found.

Principle 9: A learner should master each skill and section of the course before moving on to the next.

There is sometimes confusion over what is meant by complete mastery and some instructors argue that complete mastery cannot be attained until a very advanced stage. Complete mastery at intermediate stages of training should not require 'total mastery of the full task demands'. The demands on students can be reduced by properly structured objectives and a careful choice of routes.

If a course is correctly structured, complete mastery can and should be attained in each sub-skill, technique or procedure before introducing new and progressively more complicated variables.

Consistency is an essential feature of good driving. To achieve this each skill or task should be 'over-learnt'.

Full mastery of each unit or stage of learning should be achieved before proceeding to the next. Progress based on mastery of each phase of learning will do much to develop a sense of achievement and confidence.

Staging a long course into a number of progressive learning units also helps to increase motivation to learn by sustaining a continuous sense of urgency.

A Structured Programme for Learner Drivers

Learn to Drive published by Kogan Page, is a systematic course programme to support the professional instruction provided by ADIs. Each lesson identifies key learning points and shows learners what they will be doing in the car.

The guide contains a revision chart, linked to the Department of Transport Driving Test Syllabus and which instructors can use to identify areas of weakness and organise revision exercises. The page references give learners rapid access to the relevant text and Highway Code rules needing most revision. Cross-referenced to the Highway Code, it encourages learners to read the rules and complete the appropriate checkpoint before practical on-road lessons.

The guide supports professional driving instruction and is linked to a special appointment card used by thousands of instructors around the UK. These give instant feedback to learners of their progress throughout the course and serve as reminders to instructors.

The guide follows the principles outlined in the previous section and is structured on the four phases of skill development described below. It contains ten basic lessons concerned with:

1. Driving lessons, schools instructors and private practice.
2. Vehicle Familiarisation (Part 1) Explanation of use of controls.
3. Vehicle Familiarisation (Part 2) Practice in a moving car.
4. Special exercises to develop car control skills.
5. Systematic control and procedures approaching junctions and hazards.
6. Structured development of manoeuvering and reversing skills.
7. Further development of car control and perceptive skills.
8. Defensive attitudes towards avoiding conflict and accidents.
9. The final preparation for the driving test.
10. Driving after the test.

The Four Phases of Skill Development

Starting from a complete novice, new drivers pass through four phases of learning before they reach a competent standard. These are: Dissociated Passive — Dissociated Active — Injudicious — Safe.

Phase 1 – Dissociated Passive

This level is very superficial and learners are only passively attending to the driving task. The instructor plays the dominant role in talking learners through the routines and procedures. (For future reference this is referred to as 'controlled practice'.) Learners are: visually inactive; slow to respond and often with 'near misses'; slow and hesitant and with a tendency to make sudden 'unusual manoeuvres.'

'Controlled Practice' –

During this phase instruct learners fully through each routine or skill. Restrict the initial stages of training to helping them develop their car control skills. Although routines are superficial, try to develop good habits such as the MSM sequence.

The first lesson should familiarise learners with the controls of the vehicle and give them an opportunity to get a feel for them by practising some simple exercises before moving away. Make sure learners can understand and are able to carry out basic instructions before moving away such as: handbrake ready; set the gas; find the holding point; cover the clutch; and cover the brake.

Talk students through the routines and allow them to practice and develop their car control and steering skills on routes which avoid busy roads, junctions and traffic. Instructors should tell learners what to do when they want it done. This helps get things right first time and builds confidence.

Keep to quiet routes and use the step-by-step exercises to get the learners doing more for themselves. Let them practice each step of each exercise separately until they have completely mastered it.

Phase 2 – Dissociated Active

At this stage learners are becoming more 'active' in the manipulative skills but still visually inactive and with slow perceptive responses. The instructor needs to frequently prompt them into action. (For future reference this is referred to as 'prompted practice'.) Near misses, sudden unusual manoeuvres, late overreactions tend to be the norm and learners actively take risks.

'Prompted Practice' –

The student will require considerable prompting at the beginning of this phase. Progression through the phase should be structured within the learners' capabilities. First teach them to deal with static hazards. The circumstances of routes and movement of pedestrians and traffic however, will sometimes create unforeseen situations with which learners are unable to cope. Under these circumstances, reassure the students and talk them through fully.

To develop the learners' skills, use a quiet estate with wide roads, rounded corners and few parked cars. Practise simple MSM routines, turning left and right into side roads. Once they have mastered these practise the system approaching the end of roads. At first, only practise on junctions which provide a clear view into the main road.

Once learners can cope with the quiet estates, give them the opportunity to practise on sharper corners and major roads with more traffic. Avoid very busy junctions and those on uphill gradients.

Only when they have mastered the system of car control at junction routines and their confidence is beginning to increase should you practise on busier roads, uphill junctions and those with a restricted view. Introduce the parking and maneouvering exercises.

As learners improve towards the end of this phase, encourage them to assess situations, make decisions and take on more responsibility for themselves.

Phase 3 – Injudicious

Learners are becoming 'visually aware', developing a perceptive response and actively attending to driving the vehicle. They are becoming more responsible for their own actions. (For future reference this is referred to as 'transferred responsibility'.) They make false assumptions, are still prepared to take risks, have occasional misjudgements, near misses and still make some unusual manoeuvres.

'Transferred Responsibility' –

When learners have mastered the car control skills and the basic rules and routine procedures, give them some experience on busier roads and in traffic.

Try to keep them calm and build their confidence in these conditions by practising in them. Give them plenty of experience on a wide variety of roads and junctions. Practise in laned traffic and on one-way streets, turning on to and off dual carriageways, dealing with roundabouts and turning right at busy traffic light controlled crossroads.

Excessive criticism of students will destroy their confidence. A little praise will encourage them to do better next time. Tell students when they execute procedures well, commend them for making good decisions and flatter them for their concentration and effort.

Avoid heavy, fast-moving traffic and multi-lane roads containing combinations of parked vehicles, pedestrians and complex junctions until the final stages of training.

Phase 4 – Safe

Road accidents claim over 5000 lives, maim over 250 000 people and cost over £2 000 000 000 every year. Fourteen lives are lost and 685 people are seriously injured every day. The cost is £230 000 per hour. Proper training can reduce accidents by as much as 50 per cent. Newly qualified drivers are those most at risk.

By now learners should recognise that other road users make mistakes. Teach them how to avoid accidents by compensating for the mistakes of other people.

Learners are becoming visually active and aware. They have developed a fast perceptive response with unhurried and skilful reactions. There are no near misses or unusual reactions. They are prepared to respond to recognised risks.

'Safe' –

Assessments and mock tests should be constructive. They should help to provide the student with evidence of progress as well as any weaknesses. Before presenting students for the test, ensure as far as you possibly can that they are able to cope with busy road and traffic conditions. It is insufficient for students to merely satisfy the minimum standard required on the test.

Skill Training

The term skill describes an activity in which the performance is economical and effective in achieving a consistent and desired result. Although it is relatively easy to recognise the skilled performance of an expert driver, it is considerably more difficult to define what makes it so and even harder to explain and analyse the skill. While ADIs are usually very skilled drivers, many are unaware of the skills they possess and use when driving. The driver must obtain relative information from the environment, process it and respond by making decisions and executing appropriate car control skills.

The driving task involves *attending* to, *perceiving* and *responding* safely to driving-relevant stimulae and includes activities relating to the affective, cognitive and psycho-motor domains of the mental life.

The driver allocates attention by using his senses to gather information about the performance of the vehicle and the conditions of the road and traffic environment. He must then process the information by comparing it with existing knowledge, memories and previous experiences, assess its relevance, ignore it, or decide on a particular response or course of action or inaction.

Analysing the Learning Task
To assist learner drivers in the acquisition of new skills requires an ability to identify key learning points and isolate areas of weakness. To do this you will need to identify the elements of knowledge, attitude and skill involved in a particular learning task.

Knowledge: describes things that you know. It is assumed to influence attitudes and assist the acquisition of skills.

Safe driving involves considerable knowledge of the Highway Code, traffic law and the principles of road safety procedures. Certain aspects of this can be learnt more effectively in a classroom or in the peace and quiet of one's home than it can in the hurly-burly of modern road traffic conditions.

However, knowledge is only a basis for 'real' learning. Although it may influence our attitudes, in practice, it is not on its own sufficient to ensure we have the will or skill needed to behave in a certain way.

For example, although a driver knows he shouldn't drink and drive, it doesn't always prevent him from doing it! Legislation and the consequences of being caught however, place incentives on drivers not to drink and drive. Other incentives include the consequences of accident involvement. A knowledge of these consequences helps to influence our attitude towards alcohol and driving. On this basis, the more we know, the better equipped we are to decide.

Attitude: describes what we really think and it influences driver behaviour.

Attitudes are formed over a lifetime of experience and learning. They will not normally be changed overnight! Unsympathetic attitudes towards others and towards the established principles of road safety are a contributory factor in the cause of many road accidents. The student must therefore learn to develop safe attitudes towards others. These can be learnt from the constant persuasion and example provided by the instructor and the situations he creates.

In addition to knowledge, an attitude has powerful motivational and emotional elements which influence behaviour. These elements can be so powerful that we may sometimes lose control of our actions. Uncontrolled aggression and love are two extreme examples of this.

A skill: describes what we can do! There are two main types.

Manipulative skills describe physical actions such as turning the steering wheel, pressing the footbrake or operating the clutch pedal.

Perceptive skills are the most predominant in driving. They describe those associated with awareness, thinking, reasoning and making decisions. In driving they rely heavily on the visual sense and involve judgements of such things as the reduction in speed due to braking or of detecting changes in direction when steering or movement of the vehicle when controlling the clutch.

Driving skills include: *attention* (staying alert and concentrating); *visual search* (systematic scanning of the road and traffic scene); *awareness* (general state of mind involving comparison with previous experience and hazard recognition); *assessing and predicting risk, decision making* (to instigate a response in the use of *car control skills*).

Use the following test to help you break down any task into its various elements. At the start of a lesson or part of a lesson ask yourself these questions:

What precisely is it you want the student to do? What does the student need to know in order to do it?

For example: find the 'holding point' and keep the foot perfectly still! To do this efficiently and consistently, the student should know that only a small proportion of the total clutch pedal travel has any noticeable effect upon the behaviour of the vehicle; and that the first 'two or three' inches from the floor have no effect at all.

What senses will the learner need to use?

For example: many new drivers are taught to physically lean over and check the passenger door is properly closed; when most experienced drivers would use their ears to assess whether it was shut.

What does the student need to think if he is to take a particular action even when you are not about?

For example: learners need to recognise and accept the possibility of, and dangers associated with, cars emerging from side roads or crossroads and be prepared to act in the interests of their own survival.

After answering this kind of question, you should be able to decide what and how to set about teaching the student. Decide what you want them to be able to do at the end of the lesson. Be realistic about what they can achieve in the time available. Don't attempt too much. Organise lessons into short progressive steps and let the student work through them at his own pace. Aptitudes and abilities vary so adapt the pace of your instruction to the ability of individuals. Build on what the student already knows and can do and move on one step at a time.

Before executing a new skill the learner will require some basic knowledge upon which to build. Each physical action has a 'get set' position from which the actual skill commences. This involves preliminary movements and positioning of the hands and/or feet in anticipation of carrying out the skill or sub-skill. This 'get set' position is important for ensuring the smooth and controlled movement of the skill itself. It involves being poised and ready for action. For example, selecting a new gear requires the hand to be on the gear lever and the foot to be poised over the pedal; prior to signalling, the fingers touch and feel the indicator arm; just before turning the steering wheel there should be a slight raising of the appropriate hand and a flexing of the muscles in anticipation of the action.

Teaching a Skill

Decide on the present standard and abilities of the learner. Decide on the level at which the skill will be introduced, demonstrated and practised and *be* prepared to adjust this level up or down, depending upon the learner's responses and overall performance.

Make sure the learners clearly understand what they are going to do and why. They should clearly understand how the skill is to be performed and what is expected of them. If necessary break the skill down into its individual actions and components.

The generally accepted pattern of skill training is:

explanation → demonstration → practice

The Explanation

Introduce the topic for instruction.

Any explanation should be short, to the point and appropriate to the ability of the students and their level of attainment. For example: it is virtually useless to go into lengthy explanations about how a clutch works and how to operate it on busy uphill junctions until the learner has achieved reasonable levels of skill and comprehension adequate to relate to and understand what is being said.

During the early stages of learning to drive, it might sometimes be better to skate lightly over the finer points in order to establish and consolidate the main principles. Once these are firmly established, it will be easier for the learner to understand and retain any additional information given at a later date.

There are three main constituent parts to the majority of explanations. These include details and information concerning:

Control – of vehicle speed.
Observations – of hazards and general attitudes towards them.
Positioning – and steering of the vehicle.

Control – most explanations need to cover the general control of the vehicle and speed approaching or dealing with hazards. This part is mainly concerned with the manipulative aspects of driving, for example control and co-ordination when moving off, low speed clutch control, smooth, progressive use of accelerator and gears, smooth, progressive or positive use of the brake when slowing down or stopping and securing the vehicle when stationary.

Observations – this part will contain necessary information on the visual search required to deal safely with any manoeuvre or hazard and any signal which may be necessary, together with any special danger cues the learner should look for. This section of the explanation will also cover information on perceptive skills and safety margins together with general attitudes towards the various aspects of the skill or procedure and of the decision-making process required to instigate a physical response.

Positioning – this section will cover aspects of positioning, steering and general accuracy of the required course and of lane discipline where appropriate.

Points to Remember

A good guide for most lessons is to say what you want the students to do, explain how and then let them do it. Get straight to the point and say what you mean. Use visual aids wherever possible to reduce misunderstandings.

Use published material to support the points under instruction. Emphasise the key learning points, leaving the detail until these have been grasped. It's a waste of time to teach complex procedures before the car control skills are properly developed.

The Demonstration

The demonstration has a number of applications in the training of a driver. It can be used effectively to show the learner exactly how an expert would carry out a procedure or it might be used to emphasise and reinforce specific parts of a skill. The demonstration might also be used to provide the learner with a basis of information in order that a subsequent explanation might be more readily understood.

To obtain the maximum effect from the demonstration it must be preceded by a briefing, outlining the key points and/or they should be emphasised as an integral part of the demonstration in the form of an abbreviated commentary. The demonstration should be concluded with a summary of key points which might then lead to a more in-depth explanation.

Points learnt from the demonstration need to be consolidated immediately with practice under controlled conditions.

A learner driver is often genuinely blind to a mistake. A demonstration may help him to see. This is particularly true of safety margins, hangback positions and also in the use of speed when approaching hazards.

You might talk about slowing down before the corner and get no result whatsoever if the pupil's understanding of the word 'slow' is different from your own. Under these circumstances a demonstration can be an invaluable aid to your explanation. It should however be used as part of the explanation and not simply as a substitute.

Points to Remember

1. The demonstration should be at the correct level for the competence of the learner.
2. Explain beforehand what the demonstration is about.
3. The demonstration should be a perfect example of the skill or procedure carried out at near normal speed. (Slightly less than normal may be advantageous at times, but it should not be so slow as to become unreal.)
4. Commentary should be restricted to the key points using key words (too many variables may confuse).
5. The demonstration must be consolidated with practical experience using the skill or procedure in controlled conditions.

Practice

Practice is the most important element in learning a new skill. New skills can only be learnt by doing! Put students at ease and explain what you want them to do.

Controlled Practice and the Talk-through

Explain what you want the learner to do, demonstrate the skill if necessary and let students practise. As far as possible try to ensure they get it right the first time. To do this talk the learners through each action and stage of the operation, skill or exercise until they develop the skill and confidence to do it for themselves. The learner simply follows verbal instructions to carry out each sub-skill, element of a skill or procedure.

This 'talk through' technique enables the initial practice of new skills or procedures to take place realistically and in relative safety. It also helps to prevent vehicle abuse and interference caused to other road users. The need for the 'talk through' is greatest in the early stages when learners are least familiar with the terminology used and therefore more likely to misunderstand the instructions given.

Make sure learners are familiar with the terminology and can execute the instructions before moving away. Instructions should be clear and given early enough for the learner to interpret and execute the instruction.

An important consideration is that the initial practice should be successful. The 'talk through' ensures, as far as possible, that nothing goes wrong at this early stage.

While this method is usually successful for introducing the learner to the basic new skills, it is not entirely without its problems. Due to the limitations of speech, the timing of some skills is slightly artificial. We can only speak, or give instructions, in a specific order – one at a time. Some skills require perfectly co-ordinated movements at the *same* time and it is therefore impossible to give instructions verbally exactly as they should be carried out. Another problem lies in the learner's speed of interpreting and obeying the instruction. There will always be a delay of varying lengths for different students. The learner may also temporarily become confused over an instruction.

There are no real alternatives to using this method in the initial stages of training. The driving simulator is perhaps a safe alternative, but it falls a long way short of being ideal because it provides no sensation of movement, direction or change of speed.

The skill will normally begin to develop after two or three of these talk-through exercises, after which the pupil should be encouraged to take some personal responsibility for his own actions.

There are a number of ways in which development of this responsibility can be encouraged:

1. Ask the pupil to talk himself through the sequence. This gives him responsibility but, doing it in this manner, it will also give the instructor forewarning of any errors, which can then be verbally rectified before they are actually committed.
2. Break the full sequence into three shorter parts (ie preparation, observations, motivation) and get the learner verbally to talk you through each part separately before physically carrying it out.

The pupil may become confused with the unfamiliar terminology. This is not important as long as he knows what he means. Don't be too particular about making the pupil use the precise phrasing; it may discourage the performance of the skill.

If the pupil 'dries up' with the sequence, give him a cue or prompt and then let him continue if he can. Practise until the learner can consistently complete the whole sequence unaided.

Always insist that previously learnt routines are carried out correctly. Errors must be corrected before they become habitual. Excessive criticism and pettiness must be avoided as it can destroy confidence. Encourage improvement by pointing out progress. Identify any weakness and help the student overcome it. Devise simple exercises to help with any problems. Experiment and be prepared to vary the methods of instruction if problems persist. Make students feel they can approach you without feeling foolish or incompetent. If the problems persist, try something new for a while. Reassure students who find things hard. Let them know that periods of slow progress are quite common. At the end of practice sessions decide if the objectives have been achieved. Observe the student's performance and ask questions to be sure things are clearly understood before you move on. Practice sessions should finish with a review of what has been achieved and what skills will be covered on the next. *Before practising new skills on a new lesson first revise and let the learner practice and reinforce those learnt on the previous one.*

Prompted Practice

Some learners may become very good at following instructions, but when left to carry out the skill unaided they are unable to do so. Others who find it more difficult to follow individual instructions, are often found to be far more advanced when allowed to work on their own initiative.

While controlled practice is an essential part of basic training in the skill, it should be gradually phased out as soon as the learner can cope for himself. Some will require a lot of encouragement to act and think for themselves.

Prompting where required is perhaps the natural progression from the controlled practice or talk-through. The amount of prompting required will largely depend on the ability and willingness of the learner to make decisions for himself. The type of decisions required is also significant because, if the conditions become too busy for his ability, there will be a tendency for him to withdraw from making any decisions at all. Where these situations arise, the instructor must be prepared to prompt as required.

The ultimate objective is to get the learner to carry out each skill under *all* normal traffic conditions without any prompting at all.

Revision is an important aspect which requires continuous consideration, particularly in the early stages of establishing a new skill. A true and wholly accurate assessment cannot be made of the driving skill where it is still necessary to prompt the learner. Prompting should not be necessary in any form where a client is driving at Department of Transport driving test standard.

As the ability of the student improves, the use of detailed instructions should decrease. For example, a young lady pupil hesitates and shows minor signs of distress at the beginning of a lesson after you have asked her to move off. Your experience and knowledge of the client tell you she is perfectly capable of moving off without any instruction. All you may need to do is give her a simple cue such as, 'Select first gear'. Normally she should make all the other associations for herself as the correct sequence comes back to her. Try not to help her by telling her everything. If she is capable she needs the opportunity of achieving some success on her own. Remember that a simple cue like this is often sufficient to bring back a whole sequence of complicated actions without further instruction.

Further practice will be required to build consistency, stamina and to reduce the time taken to complete the sequence. When the skill becomes consistent and is carried out in a reasonable length of time, other important aspects of it can be introduced with more emphasis on the visual search and timing. Progressively the skill must be applied and practised in various traffic situations, eg moving off from junctions and traffic lights, moving off and maintaining low speed control in conjunction with steering.

Transferred Responsibility

This is when the learners take over the responsibility for their own decisions and actions.

As the control skills develop and the student's confidence grows, instructors should place more emphasis on the full development of the perceptive and hazard recognition skills. Point out what students should look for and where to expect it. Explain the dangers involved and why a particular response is called for.

Encourage students to think and make decisions for themselves. Get them to *look* for the information and encourage them to use their own knowledge of rules and previous experiences to *assess* it. Build the confidence needed to *decide* and act for themselves.

Distributed Practice

No matter what skills are being learnt, there is no substitute for practice. Practice should be organised sensibly. Massing it all into a few marathon learning sessions is not an efficient way of learning. Little and often is a more efficient strategy. Carefully spaced driving practice divided evenly over four or five weeks is more efficient than having the same amount of hours during an intensive one-week course.

For example, one hour of training a day is considerably more efficient than:

   One hour of training twice a day
   Two hours training once a day
   Two hours training twice a day

The General Learning Curve

While the manipulative aspects of the driving task can be observed by the students executing them, they will still require prompts and verbal guidance during the early stages of learning. This should be followed by hints and reassurance once the skill has developed. A student's progress varies depending upon the type of skill being learnt. When learning many skills students reach a stage, called the plateau, at which little progress is made. This is not necessarily the limit of performance and most students will subsequently progress to their personal ceiling.

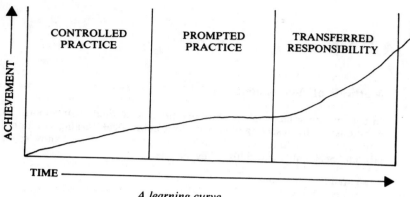

A learning curve

Chapter 8

Assessments and Standards

Methods of Assessment

Instructors assess learners' standard and progress through their response to questions and by observing their behaviour in practical learning situations. Tests can be devised to assess the different aspects of learning, knowledge, attitude, personality and skills. They include:

Written Examinations
Objective Tests
Aptitude Tests
Interviews
Oral Assessments
Practical Tests and Assessments.

Driving instructors are primarily concerned with practical tests of driving skills and oral assessments of the learner's knowledge of the Highway Code and other motoring matters. However, during the initial meeting with a learner, instructors may be using a mixture of interview technique and aptitude testing to assess the learning status of the student.

Initial Assessments

Use this first lesson to find out what the students know and can do. Get to know them, reassure them and gain their confidence. Give learners the opportunity to tell you of any handicaps or disabilities they may have but do not cause any embarrassment.

In many ways this lesson is a little different to subsequent training sessions. Little or nothing may be known about the client and before conducting the lesson it will be necessary to establish certain basic information.

The instructor should not rely entirely on information about previous driving experience volunteered by the client. Some pupils, perhaps unintentionally, give the impression that they are at a very advanced level of learning when in fact they are at a very basic stage. Some, usually those who are very self-critical, give the initial impression they have only a very basic knowledge and then immediately prove themselves to be at an advanced level of competence during a short assessment drive.

Except where the new clients have had very little or no previous experience, it will be necessary to verify the standard personally. This should be carried out as soon as the initial introduction to the vehicle is completed. This introduction can in itself provide valuable information about the general knowledge of the client and may result in a change of plans, for example to shorten or increase the length and depth of the explanation of the controls.

Where clients are felt to have very little knowledge of the motor car it may be advisable to tactfully disregard previous experience and proceed with a full vehicle familiarisation lesson. Where it is decided to make an initial assessment of the learner's standard this should normally start on a nursery route and gradually progress to more difficult situations until a standard is firmly established.

The following is a guide to the general pattern of a first lesson:

Initial introductions

First impressions go a long way towards building the client's confidence in you the instructor. Try to remember his name without having to refer to your appointment diary.

Your manner should be professional and confident. Your attitude should be one of interest and caring. The client should be encouraged to feel he can speak to you at any time on any relevant matter, regardless of how trivial it may seem to him.

The car should be clean, roadworthy and tanked up with petrol. Learning how to fill up at the garage may be an important aspect of driving, but this first lesson is definitely not the time for it.

Licence and Eyesight Check

Unless you have previously checked the driving licence, it should be inspected now and details recorded on to the appointment/progress card. Where the licence is not available, an absolute assurance must be obtained from the client that he is in possession of one (subject to current regulations) and that it will be brought to the next lesson. If there is any doubt the lesson should be postponed.

Where a client is unable to read a number plate at the prescribed distance, the lesson must be postponed. Where the number is read but with difficulty, or where some minor mistakes are made on some similar letters or numbers, the lesson may proceed but the client should be politely requested to seek professional advice.

Establish previous experience and other details

The time spent with the instructor, driving to a suitable location to commence this first lesson, can normally be utilised to gather some, if not all, of this information. Long periods of silence en route should be avoided as these tend to add to an already tense and nervous situation for the client. A friendly and informal chat on the way can be used unobtrusively to serve three main purposes:

(a) To help break the ice by relieving any initial tensions which may exist between two strangers.

(b) The new learner is frequently afraid of making a fool of himself — talking will keep his mind off the forthcoming lesson.

(c) Light conversation will provide a basis of information which may help the instructor to assist the learner in achieving his final goal.

Where clients are reluctant to talk about themselves they should not be pressed too hard as other opportunities will present themselves. Some clients may attempt to cover up their nervousness by talking all the time – in any event the conversation should be professional but with a sympathetic ear.

Specific questions should be restricted to those involving the gathering of relevant information. These may include:

(a) Is the client still at school or college?
(b) What kind of work does he/she do?
(c) What interests and hobbies does he have?
(d) Has he any physical disabilities which the instructor may be able to compensate for?
(e) Does he need to drive for his job?
(f) General details of previous driving experience on any vehicle, motorcycle, cycle etc.
(g) Has he any particular fears about learning to drive – outline the stages of learning for him.

Drive client to a suitable route
The initial route must consider the following needs:

(a) It must be as perfectly suited for the absolute novice as possible.
(b) It must be flexible enough to allow for progression to intermediate routes for those whose ability to cope proves satisfactory.
(c) For those clients with considerable previous experience, the route should start quietly and allow sufficient time to adjust to the strange vehicle and then progressively get more difficult. It must also be possible to pull out of these more difficult areas if the client is unable to manage.

Oral Questions and Answers

It is an instructor's responsibility to find out what a pupil already knows so that a lesson can start from what he does know and progress to that which he does not. It is also important to ensure instructions are understood and that information is retained at the level of comprehension intended. In addition the driving test includes an oral test of the Highway Code and other motoring matters.

Questions should be short and to the point and elicit the intended response. Begin each question with how; why; what; when; where; or which. Ask the question so that it has only the one correct answer you want. For example:

Do you know the main causes of skidding? A correct response could be 'Yes' or 'No'. What do you know about correcting skids? A correct response could be 'Nothing'. It is doubtful whether either of these two responses were wanted by the instructor.

Better questions would have been 'What are the main causes of skidding' and 'How should you correct a skid where the rear of the car is sliding to your left'.

After asking more open-ended questions, such as: 'What kind of things should you look for about four seconds ahead'; allow students time to answer. Don't be afraid of the silence while students interpret the question, search for the answer and the words to express themselves. If the student is having obvious difficulty ask the question in another way or give some clues about your desired answer. For example, you might add 'Think about the movement of other road users' or 'What about restrictions to your sight-lines.'

Listen to what the student is trying to say and make the most out of incorrect answers! Of course you must point out that they are not correct but give a little praise for partially correct or thoughtful answers.

Instructors should avoid questioning beyond the point that students obviously are unable to supply reasonable answers.

The timing of when questions are put to the students can be as important as the wording of the question itself. Each stage of development should be concluded with a few questions to ensure the student has grasped the main points. Recapitulation at the end of each lesson is probably most effectively done by using the question and answer technique. The same technique is also useful as revision exercises on subsequent lessons.

Answering Questions with Questions

Students should be encouraged and given the opportunity to ask questions which are relevant to the points under instruction. Irrelevant questions should be stated irrelevant. Genuine questions however, must not be snubbed even if they are not totally relevant to a particular lesson.

Socrates the Greek philosopher is famous for his inductive technique of answering questions with questions to reach new definitions. This Socratic 'method' is probably one of the most effective methods of teaching. It puts students into the position of acquiring knowledge through their own personal involvement and effort.

Highway Code and Driving Related Questions

Learners generally require some kind of motivation to develop their interest in learning the Highway Code rules. Words of encouragement and a few simple oral questions asked from time to time generally help to arouse a degree of interest in the Code. Organise between-lesson projects and provide self-test exercises consisting of multiple choice objective questions. These are ideal for short Highway Code projects. Providing an answer code enables students to check their own scores. Continually emphasise the importance of the Code and its relevance to practical lessons.

There are various different types of test questions which instructors can devise to reinforce learning and/or assess the learner's knowledge of the Highway Code and driving related matters.

Objective Questions

These are designed so the learner has to select the correct response from the several alternative answers which are provided. For example:

1. Triangular signs usually give:

   (a) orders;
   (b) warnings;
   (c) information.

2. Tyres must have a minimum legal tread depth of:

   (a) 1 mm;
   (b) 2 mm;
   (c) 3 mm.

Short-Answer Questions

These are questions which require a specific answer and which can also be used to reinforce specific learning points. For example:

3. Give reasons for each of the following:

   (a) Drivers must allow adequate clearance for parked cars.
   (b) Drivers should reduce speeds in busy shopping areas.
   (c) Drivers should take extra care on country roads without footpaths.

Examples of those more commonly used in driving instruction and testing are given below.

4. What is the minimum legal tread depth of a tyre?

5. Give six examples of places unsuitable for parking.

6. What are the characteristics of a safe parking position?

Designing Highway Code Questions

Asking appropriate questions at suitable intervals can do much to change attitudes towards learning the Highway Code rules.

'What must you not do before turning right?'

After considering the above question you should find two basic flaws in it which could prove counter-productive if put to a novice driver:

1. Because the question asks what not to do, the learner will probably go up a number of 'blind alleys' prior to reaching the correct answer. There are literally dozens of correct and sensible answers to this negative question. While occasionally there may be justification in this negative type of question, it is normally far better to ask in a manner which requires a positive and constructive response.

2. Changing the question to, 'What must you do when turning right?' narrows down the field of correct answers. Whilst this has improved the question, the word 'what' implies it requires a specific answer.

However there is not one specific answer to this question as the full procedure for turning right requires many considerations. If you require a short, exact response then more information should be included in the question.

Examples:

  (a) Q. What must you check before signalling to turn right?

or

  (b) Q. When turning right into a side road what must you particularly look out for just before turning?

If a more general answer is required the question will be better phrased in the following manner:

  Outline the basic procedure for turning right into a side road.

While this kind of general question may frequently be necessary, one of the problems is that it also tests the pupil's ability to communicate. He may know the procedure very well but have difficulty in explaining the details. Patience and understanding should be given and where necessary help by asking further questions of a more specific nature.

Practical Assessments

The driving instructor assesses the 'L' driver's progress by finding the traffic conditions appropriate to the learner's previous experience and practice and then by observing the learner's behaviour in those situations.

  The assessment is mostly visual and consists of watching the learner's actions within the car, ie use of the controls, ancillary equipment, instrumentation and the use of mirrors, etc, in addition to how he is behaving towards the external traffic situations as they arise.

  The instructor must guard against:

1. watching the pupil too intently; he may miss important changes in the traffic situation with which the learner is dealing;
2. reading the road too intently the instructor may miss faults of a physical nature inside the car, such as an incorrect signal, riding the clutch, poor mirror use, engaging reverse gear without the clutch being disengaged etc.

The instructor must spread his attention over a wide area of the driver's performance in fairly rapid succession. The need to read the road and traffic conditions at all times should be, in the interest of safety, fairly obvious. There are some occasions, however, where prolonged observations of the pupil are required in order to make a thorough assessment. These are:

  (i) Observations of the pupil's mirror checks.
  (ii) Assessing the pupil's pattern of observations on the approach and emerging from road junctions, crossroads, etc.

The problems caused by the instructor's requiring excessive time to observe the pupil's mirror checks, whilst himself keeping in constant touch with the situation, and to some extent when checking for observations on the approach to road junctions, can be alleviated by the use of an additional dual mirror discreetly focused onto the pupil's eyes.

Another problem experienced by the new instructor while making an entirely objective assessment is that of giving the learner subconscious signals, for example looking directly at the driver for a mirror check can be a sufficient prompt for the pupil to use the mirror when it may otherwise have been forgotten. The same applies when the instructor is checking the road before emerging from junctions and when carrying out the 'turn in the road' or reverse exercise etc. These observations must be carried out very discreetly unless they are intended to be used as a prompt to the pupil.

Driving examiners are trained to be very discreet with these observations and the pupil is unlikely to get the same kind of prompt on the driving test which an unknowing instructor may be giving.

Examinations and intermediate assessments of a student's knowledge and ability are an integral part of a teacher's work; a considerable amount of an instructor's time is involved directly in, or as a result of, them.

The driving instructor will be involved in two different forms of practical driver assessments. The first of these is a practical test, similar to that used by the Department of Transport on the driving test. This is the type of assessment the instructor will use when conducting a 'mock test'. These objective assessments are also useful for keeping accurate records of progress made by the intermediate and advanced learners, but, because of the 'pass or fail' nature of this kind of assessment, it is unsuited for the basic training sessions.

The second form of practical appraisal is called *continuous assessment*. This is more sensitive to the learner's needs and is particularly concerned with improving the driving performance of the student.

Mock Tests

An objective assessment is one which measures the learner's actual performance against a pre-fixed standard. This pre-fixed standard is the 'perfect driver'. This is a satisfactory yardstick by which any level of driving can be measured.

The perfect driver can be defined as one who is in perfect tune with the vehicle and traffic conditions. He is always in the correct position on the road, travelling at a safe speed for the conditions and visibility, and with the ideal gear engaged to suit varying speed and power requirements. He is totally aware of his surroundings and shows consideration for the rights of other road users.

Technically anything which detracts from this perfection is an error. Perfection to this level however is rare, even in an experienced driver. Therefore it will be unrealistic to expect the inexperienced 'L' driver to achieve this standard consistently.

To overcome these problems, it is necessary to devise some means of grading faults in a manner which attaches significantly more importance to serious and dangerous faults than is given to those of a minor nature.

Grading of errors

The driving instructor must not view driving errors as black or white. There are many shades of grey, and, when assessing the seriousness of a fault, the instructor needs to reflect upon the following points:

1. There are various degrees of the same error.
2. Some errors are of a more serious nature involving more severe consequences than others.

Department of Transport fault categories

On the driving test the Department of Transport assesses faults under the following, progressively more serious, headings:

(i) *Minor faults* – faults assessed in this category, either singly or in combination with any number of others, will not result in failure. A minor fault is one which does not involve a serious or dangerous situation. No other road user is involved.

(ii) *Serious faults* – a single fault falling into this category will result in failure. A serious fault is one which is assessed to involve *potential danger.*

(iii) *Dangerous faults* – a single fault assessed within this category will result in failure. A dangerous fault is one which is assessed to involve an *actual danger. Intervention faults* fall into this category. These are faults where the examiner has been forced to intervene with either a verbal command or by physical action and they will result automatically in test failure.

There is an obvious need for a degree of standardisation between the consistency of assessments made in training and those used for the driving test. It is essential therefore that the driving instructor is familiar with this grading system.

In addition to the foregoing grading system, and because there is a distinct difference between training the 'L' driver and examining him, the instructor must also provide for another group of faults. These may not be of sufficient significance to warrant even a minor error on the driving test, but they may well develop into a subsequent problem by causing a more serious error either on or after the test. We will call this group of faults *marginal errors.*

Within themselves these errors do not affect road safety. Some of them may be of a fairly subjective, or even doubtful, nature even to justify the term error in its true sense. However, they may be of real concern to the instructor who should give them due attention in relation to any more serious errors he may also need to cure.

This group of faults should include slight errors in co-ordination, inefficient or uneconomic driving style, and other errors which do not fall into the Department of Transport grading system.

In order to help you differentiate more clearly between the various groups of faults we have defined, study carefully the following:

Example 1. Marginal error

The learner is approaching an intended right turn into a fairly wide side road.

Visibility into the road is good and, after making all the necessary safety checks, the learner makes the turn. Whilst he does not actually cut the corner it is getting near to a borderline case and although no fault would be recorded on a driving test, the instructor's responsibilities go further than the examiner's. It may have been a 'one off' type of error in which case the instructor may decide not to mention it unless it occurs again. If it has occurred previously, or if the learner has a past record of this particular fault, then it should be mentioned rather than recorded.

Example 2. Minor fault
The learner is approaching the same right turn as in example 1. Visibility into the road is good and after ensuring it is safe to turn and that the side road is free of traffic movement, the learner turns into the side road cutting the corner very slightly as he does so. No potential danger was caused to other road users because the learner had checked before turning. On a driving test this would be recorded as a minor fault, but it would not result in failure.

Example 3. Serious fault
Again the learner is approaching the same right turn, but this time visibility is severely restricted into the side road by parked vehicles, making it impossible for the driver to see whether the junction to the right is clear of approaching traffic. The learner blatantly cuts the corner into this unknown situation. No actual danger occurred because no other road user appeared from the side road. This however was purely good luck and not an assessed judgement. The incident involved *potential danger* and the learner would fail the test.

Example 4. Dangerous fault
In exactly the same circumstances as example 3, above, the learner cuts the corner. This time, another vehicle does appear from the side road, the driver of which has to brake to avoid a collision. This incident involved *actual danger* and, of course, the learner would fail the test.

Minor, serious or dangerous?
The driving instructor often feels he must assess and grade errors exactly to Department of Transport driving test standards. While some degree of standardisation is desirable, it is not absolutely essential to get it right all the time and instructors need not worry unduly over this matter. In any event, the difference between serious and dangerous is purely academic, because in both instances the result is the same – failure.

The difference bet ween minor and serious faults however is the difference between pass and fail. Again, using examples 2 and 3 for comparison, we will define the difference once more.

The essential difference between the two incidents is that the driver committing the minor fault in example 2 was able to see the road was clear, while the driver in example 3 committed the serious fault when unable to see whether the road was clear, yet he was prepared to take a risk. The fault really is not the difference between the two people cutting the corner and one of them getting away with it, but one of them was able to see and might well have acted differently had the visibility been restricted – the other proved himself totally unaware of the danger.

It is only possible to assess the actions of a driver in the light of the *prevailing situation*.

Continuous assessment

This type of assessment is more sensitive to the needs of the learner than the more decisive objective assessments previously discussed. Particularly in the early stages of learning, it would be unreasonable to compare the performance of the novice with the 'perfect driver'. Although this type of assessment should still be objective it will take into account previous experience, practice and general progress, as well as the ability of the learner.

The assessments should sympathetically look for reasons why the faults are occurring and for ways in which the performance can be improved.

When an 'L' driver makes a mistake there is usually a valid reason for it. If the instructor is to prevent the same, or similar, error recurring, then he must look to the cause and cure it at source rather than superficially treat the symptoms.

There are literally hundreds of different errors waiting to be committed by the 'L' driver. Their causes are relatively few. If the instructor concentrates primarily on curing the cause of an error improvements will occur in other areas where similar mistakes may be occurring.

The 'halo' effect

It is not possible to remove the human element from driver assessments and, when an instructor has a particular regard for a pupil with whom he gets on well, it is possible to ignore minor errors subconsciously, or even gloss over those of a more serious nature. He may perhaps even find an easier route for him/her by missing out some of the significantly more difficult traffic situations. Acceptance that this phenomenon, known as the 'halo effect', exists is, in most cases, sufficient to guard against it.

The opposite can also occur with the not too popular client, and, in this case the instructor may subconsciously treat relatively minor errors as more serious and perhaps fail to notice improvements in performance.

Assessment Records

At any one time most instructors will probably have about 30 to 40 pupils on their books who will all be at different stages of learning and even those at similar stages will not have covered identical aspects of driving in exact order.

The students will be of a wide range of abilities and aptitude and will all have their own personal likes and dislikes.

For teaching purposes alone this information is of vital importance in helping the instructor create suitable and effective learning experiences for the student.

Without some form of record it is impossible for the instructor to carry this detailed information around in his head from week to week for so many students.

Apart from obvious information such as name and address, records could usefully contain some of the following details:

1. *General —*

   (a) Licence.
   (b) Result of eyesight test.
   (c) Date of test application.
   (d) Details of test fees.
   (e) Details of driving test — centre, time, etc.

2. *Basic tuition record —* some form of simple record is required of skills and procedures upon which basic tuition has been covered by the instructor and which the learner has had the opportunity to practise.

3. *Assessment and progress report —* this should cover all main aspects of driving skills and procedures.

4. *Route record —* it is useful to keep a record of routes covered, particularly by intermediate and advanced learners in order to avoid too much duplication of the same area.

A suggested marking system to record severity of faults is outlined below, but it is emphasised that this is only an example and schemes should be designed to suit your own personal choice:

Marginal error   —   ·
Minor fault   —   /
Serious fault   —   X
Dangerous fault — O

Patterns of Errors

A properly kept progress record will sometimes show a distinct pattern of errors which might otherwise not be obvious to the instructor and which might be the difference between a pass or fail on the driving test.

Oral and Written Assessment Reports

These reports are often required by close relatives, employers or others who may be paying for novices' lessons. Generally they should not necessarily include detailed information of faults but they should give a clear and honest outline or the driver's performance. In certain cases an employer may require a complete driver assessment before employment.

The following general headings may assist in devising your format for these reports.

1. General knowledge of the Highway Code rules.
2. General attitude to speed and safety of other road users.
3. General attitude to lessons and the driving test.
4. General ability in vehicle control.
5. General visual and perceptive ability.

Assessment Records

On this page and the next are examples of some types of assessment records.

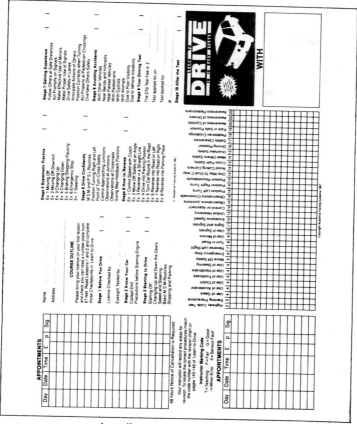

A pupil assessment progress record

'L' Driver Errors

Driving errors range from those with sometimes very simple causes, such as unsuitable shoes being worn or an incorrect seating position, which can make good control of the pedals extremely difficult, to those caused by the complex pressures and stresses built up by the traffic conditions. Such tensions can sometimes result in unusual and possibly dangerous actions or decisions by the learner.

Poorly developed perceptive skills frequently result in the learner using excessive speed approaching hazards. The outcome of this is rushed movements carrying out the manipulative skills and thereby producing errors in control of the vehicle.

The type of errors committed by the 'L' driver vary considerably according to the particular stage of learning reached. The aptitude and attitudes of

DRIVING ASSESSMENT RECORD

Name: . . . . Date: . . . .

		Minor : Serious			Minor : Serious
1	Comply with eyesight requirements.	I I I I	**11**	Take prompt and appropriate action on: traffic signs; road markings; traffic light signals; signals by traffic controllers; signals by other road users.	I I I I I I I I I I I I I I I I I I I I
2	Know the Highway Code.	I I I I			
3	Take precautions before starting the engine.	I I I I	**12**	Exercise care in the use of speed.	I I I I
4	Make proper use of the: accelerator; clutch; gears; footbrake; handbrake; steering.	I I I I I I I I I I I I I I I I I I I I I I I I	**13**	Make safe progress by: driving at appropriate speeds; avoiding undue hesitancy.	I I I I I I I I
			14	Act properly at junctions/crossroads: regulate speed approaching; control of brakes and gears; look properly before emerging; position before turning right; position before turning left; avoid cutting corners.	I I I I I I I I I I I I I I I I I I I I I I I I
5	Move away safely: with due regard for others; under control.	I I I I I I I I			
6	Stop vehicle in an emergency: promptly; under control.	I I I I I I I I	**15**	Overtake other vehicles safely. Meet other vehicles safely. Cross path of others safely.	I I I I I I I I I I I I
7	Reverse to left/right: under proper control; with due regard for others.	I I I I I I I I	**16**	Position your vehicle correctly: during normal driving; when driving in lanes.	I I I I I I I I
8	Turn in road using forward/reverse gears: under control; with due regard for others.	I I I I I I I I	**17**	Allow adequate clearance to stationary vehicles.	I I I I
9	Make effective use of mirrors before: signalling; changing direction; slowing down; stopping.	I I I I I I I I I I I I I I I I	**18**	Take appropriate action at and approaching pedestrian crossings.	I I I I
			19	Select safe stopping positions.	I I I I
10	Give signals: where necessary; correctly; in good time.	I I I I I I I I I I I I	**20**	Be aware and anticipate the actions of: pedestrians; cyclists; other drivers.	I I I I I I I I I I I I

Remarks: . . . .

. . . . Assessor's Signature: . . . .

A driver assessment form

the learner also influence the mistakes made. Most errors in the early stages of learning cannot seriously be considered driving faults at all but unless they are rectified now they will almost certainly develop into them.

Many errors committed during the early stages of learning are substantially caused by lack of knowledge and experience. This is possibly coupled with misunderstanding new information provided by the instructor. Many such problems are intensified by insufficient practice at the basic control skills carried out in relatively safe surroundings on suitable routes.

Particularly during the initial stages of teaching the novice, the instructor must remain acutely alert for any unusual or sudden and excessive movements or reactions with the steering or other controls. No matter how good your instructions may be, you should not take it for granted that the pupil will carry them out. Initially most learners have difficulty in co-ordinating their hands, feet, steering and observations.

Some of the main *causes* of error are listed below:

1. Lack of correct knowledge.

2. Conflicting knowledge.
3. Underdeveloped perceptive skills.
4. Lack of or inadequate observations and/or misinterpretation of visual information.
5. Deficiencies in the basic manipulative skills.
6. Deficiencies in behaviour caused by timidity or irresponsible attitudes.
7. Poor health, fatigue, drink, drugs, emotional stress.

Note: The learner driver is subject to considerable pressure in interpreting oral directions and attempting to assimilate other information and instructions while on the move.

General Errors

Poor car control – inadequate car control can usually be traced to insufficient practice at a basic skill, incorrect training and interference, lack of knowledge, poor co-ordination of body movements, hurried movements and excessive speeds.

Persistent excess of speed – excessive speed is often attributable to incorrect attitudes, poor control of the footbrake, lack of awareness of potential or actual danger, poor perception of speed owing to the novice being a regular passenger in a fast-driven vehicle.

Lack of awareness – lack of awareness of potential or actual dangers – these faults are very common and are caused through lack of experience, knowledge, imagination and visual scanning.
    Passively observing a traffic scene does not imply active participation and attention to a developing traffic hazard.

Indecision – can be associated with lack of confidence, poor control skills, lack of knowledge, timidity and conditions too busy for the ability. Indecision and/or an unwillingness to give way, slow down or stop is often caused because the learner lacks confidence and/or efficiency in his ability to move off again after the hazard has cleared. The learner fails to recognise that slowing down early relieves the situation by giving more time and actually reduces the need to stop.

Common Errors

1. *Starting and stopping*
    Failure to take precautions before starting engine.
    Failure to recognise the engine has/has not started.
    Failure to depress clutch before attempting to engage gear.
    Failure to select the correct gear.
    Difficulty in selecting correct engine speed setting prior to moving off.
    Failure to assess clutch free play.

Failure to recognise and/or hold clutch at holding/biting/driving point.

Failure to control clutch whilst releasing handbrake.

Removal of foot from clutch as the car moves away (provoked and assisted by movement of car).

Failure to release handbrake.

Releasing the accelerator as the car moves away.

Excessive braking pressure when stopping.

Stopping without declutching.

Releasing feet from pedals before handbrake engaged and neutral selected.

Failure to recognise engine has stalled.

Failure to take proper observations before moving off.

Taking observations but moving off when unsafe.

Incorrect signal given.

Failure to use mirror/s before stopping.

Stopping without consideration for following traffic.

Unwilling to stop or give way. (Sometimes associated with difficulty over moving away again.)

2. *Speed control*

Late, excessive movement of pedals.

Freezing on the brake or accelerator.

Non-progressive application of footbrake.

Sudden release of braking pressure.

Non-progressive application/release of accelerator.

Fierce uncontrolled use of clutch.

Clutch held down unnecessarily.

Riding the clutch.

Failure to recognise the effect of hills.

Failure to secure vehicle when stationary.

Unnecessarily sluggish build up of speed.

Non-preparation for a gear change.

Poor co-ordination of controls when changing gear.

Clutch depressed sluggishly or held down too long after changing gear.

Accelerator not released when changing gear and/or re-applied too early/fiercely.

Incorrect gear selected or inadvertent pressure against reverse gear, or missed gear.

Staying in low gears too long.

Causing engines to labour/over-rev.

Unsympathetic changing down.

Mirror/s not used before changing speed.

Poor steering control and accuracy may be attributed to some of the following:

3. *Physical steering control*

Poor seating position.

Incorrect position and/or grip of hands on wheel.
Loose/fidgety/rigid grip of wheel.
Shoulders or arms held rigid.
Inefficient or a forced unnatural steering method.
Body movement when changing gear.
Excessive speed which is severely detrimental to steering accuracy.

Observations and steering accuracy
Looking at the feet, gear lever or instructor.
Looking intently at the road just ahead of the bonnet of the car.
Staring at a *fixed* point in the far distance.
Staring intently at the mirror.
Lack of an active visual search system.
Looking at the kerb or centre line in an attempt to follow it.
Looking intently at, and following, the approach of oncoming
   traffic.
Looking intently at an obstruction on the left side of the road, such
   as a parked vehicle.

Left and right turns
Failure to respond to the instruction to turn.
Failure to use the mirror/s.
Failure to act sensibly on information from mirror/s.
Incorrect signal given.
Failure to re-operate self-cancelled signal where it has operated
   prematurely.
Late/incorrect positioning of vehicle and/or course steering.
Failure to reduce speed approaching turn.
Attempting to select low gear at excessive speed.
Missing the gear or selecting incorrect one.
Poor co-ordination between the brake and gear change.
Late change and proceeding round the corner with clutch held
   down.
Preparedness to attempt corner at excessive speed and poor steering
   control.
Failure to secure the vehicle while waiting to turn.

4. *Position – turning left*
Failure to maintain correct steering course.
Approaching turn too close to the kerb, resulting in swinging out
   before turn, striking kerb on the turn and thus resulting in a
   dangerously wide position after the turn.
Turning wheel too slowly/late/early.
Failure/or slow to straighten up after the turn.

5. *Position – turning right*
Failure to maintain correct steering course.
Drifting back to the left before the turn.

Drifting over the centre of the road before the turn.
Cutting the corner.
Failure to take correct line out of the turn.
Continuing to move forward past the turning point resulting in a 'swan's neck' turn.

6. *Observations before turning*
    Failure to use or act on information from the mirrors when approaching the turn and particularly just before turning.
    Reluctance to slow down and give way.
    Turning across fast or closely approaching traffic.
    Failure to appreciate a possible flow of oncoming traffic/cyclist/ motorcyclist in the left lane or left side where the right lane or main flow is stationary.
    Preparedness to overtake cyclists when closely approaching a left turn.
    Lack of observations into side road prior to turn.
    Commencing turn before realising side road is blocked.
    Failure to give pedestrians precedence when turning.

7. *Junctions and crossroads*
    Failure to comply with 'Stop' or 'Give Way' signs and/or road markings.
    Failure to observe and/or give way to pedestrians on the approach to junctions.
    Failure to anticipate traffic turning into road.
    Failure to anticipate larger turning circle of bigger vehicles.
    Failure to take effective observations before emerging and/or emerging when unsafe.
    Failure to recognise visibility is restricted by parked vehicles.
    Taking effective observations but failing to consider the consequences of a subsequent delay in moving off through poor co-ordination of controls etc.
    Turning left without observations in that direction and while looking right.
    Position wide on left turn or striking left kerb for reasons stated above.

8. *Minor crossroads and side roads*
    Failure to observe the crossroad or side road.
    Failure to recognise or accept such roads are potentially dangerous to priority traffic.
    Failure to look on the approach.
    Excessive speed.
    Looking intently but too late to be useful.
    Failure to look both ways when turning.

9. *Traffic lights and busy junctions*
    Failure to show any caution approaching and/or emerging through a green light.

Unusual changes in lane.

Failure to observe/act upon a parked car at the other side of the crossroads.

Failure to observe and comply with direction signs and road markings when choosing a suitable lane.

Failure to anticipate the actions of any oncoming and right turning traffic.

Failure to observe or act upon a green filter arrow.

Failure to take suitable precautions prior to filtering on a green arrow.

Failure to take the correct action in relation to colours/sequence and traffic conditions (including flashing amber).

10. *Roundabouts*

Failure to recognise 'give way to traffic from right' rule.

Failure to anticipate traffic moving round the roundabout and moving off into an 'apparent' space.

Failure to build up speed after emerging.

Sudden or unusual lane changes in the roundabout.

Sudden lane changes to leave roundabout by incorrect exit.

Failure to check left lane (where appropriate) before leaving.

Failure to maintain signal in roundabout and/or changing to left signal for leaving it.

11. *Road and traffic hazards*

Failure to observe and/or act upon warning signs or road markings or plan ahead.

Failure to take suitable precautions on the approach to areas containing restrictions to visibility.

Driving too fast past parked cars/cyclists/pedestrians.

Driving too close to parked cars/cyclists/pedestrians.

Failure to anticipate the actions of pedestrians in the vicinity of pedestrian crossings.

Failure to take suitable precautions approaching a pedestrian crossing where any part of the crossing or pavement near it is restricted from view.

Failure to give way to a pedestrian at a crossing.

Failure to give way to oncoming traffic when approaching a parked vehicle on the left side of the road.

Crossing give way line at a pedestrian crossing too early before pedestrian is safely clear.

Failure to use mirror well before signalling and changing speed or direction.

Failure to act sensibly upon information from the mirror.

Unusual sudden or late change of lane.

Failure to recognise a dual carriageway or one-way street.

Poor low speed control.

Slow turning steering wheel.

Not changing lock to conclude each movement.
Lack of suitable observations immediately prior to commencing each movement.
Lack of attention to other traffic during each movement.
Lack of observation of and consideration for pedestrians and other obstructions on the pavement, particularly on the reversing movement.
Lack of emotional control when exercise is being observed by other drivers.

12. *Reversing and parking*
Poor low speed control.
Lack of observation of and consideration for other traffic prior to and during the exercise.
Lack of observation of and consideration for pedestrians.
Failure to ensure good visibility through the centre of the rear window when attempting to drive backwards in a straight line.

Chapter 9

Disabilities, Minor Handicaps and Other Impairments

Teaching People with Disabilities

Many thousands of disabled people have passed the driving test and are regular, safe and competent drivers. Many will need no more than automatic transmission and a steering ball on the wheel to enable them to control the car. Others, with more severe disabilities, may need a range of more complex adaptations. Recent developments in technology mean that even those with no movement or strength are now able to control cars safely by use of joy stick steering and infra-red or voice control for other functions.

People with a severe disability will need advice on the right vehicle and adaptations to meet their needs before they can start to learn to drive. There are specialist assessment centres around the country, whose function is to give such advice. A list of these centres is shown in Appendix III on page 362.

Teaching disabled people is essentially the same as teaching anyone else. You must be particularly sensitive to the individual's needs and be prepared to adapt normal techniques where necessary in order to build on the learner's strengths and abilities. He may also need to allow more time for the process of getting in and out of the vehicle and for finding the most comfortable and convenient driving position.

No disabled person should ever be told that they will be unable to learn to drive without first being given the opportunity to visit an assessment centre for specialist advice. Adaptations are now available to compensate for the effects of most disabilities. Commonly available adaptations include:

1. Simple hand controls for accelerating and braking, either a push pull type or rotary, ie up and down, for either right or left hand use.
2. Steering spinners, grips or pegs.
3. Left footed accelerator pedals.
4. Easy release handbrake and gear selector attachments.
5. Vacuum assistance for braking and for accelerating.
6. Infra-red remote control to operate the secondary controls, ie indicator, wipers, lights, horn, etc.

There are also many ways in which minor disabilities can be overcome with simple adaptations, for example pedal extensions can be used for people with short legs or small feet. Where a person is unable to turn their body or neck, additional mirrors can be used to cover the blind areas when reversing.

Where a person is hard of hearing or profoundly deaf, the instructor will need to be guided by them on the most effective means of communication. For profoundly deaf pupils the use of diagrams, writing and demonstration can be helpful. The pupil's advice should always be sought about the best means of communication.

Other Handicaps

Visual acuity is the ability to see clearly. If a client fails to read a number plate at the prescribed distance when attending a first driving lesson, the lesson must be postponed. If the number plate is read but with difficulty, or if minor mistakes are made on similar letters or numbers, the lesson may proceed but the client should be politely requested to seek the professional advice of a qualified optician. Eyesight is known to deteriorate with fatigue, when under stress and more permanently after the age of about 40.

Field of vision describes the extent of the areas to the left and right that the driver can see without turning the head. Most people can see or detect motion at right angles on both sides of them giving them a field of vision of 180°. Drivers with less than 120° field of vision can be considered to have an impairment. Their periphery vision is less sensitive and they may have greater difficulty in detecting movement at their sides and perhaps in the judgement of speed. For those with restricted head movement, supplementary mirrors may help.

Tunnel vision is a condition where the sufferer has a severely restricted field of vision. The condition is not, in itself, a bar to driving, but applicants for a driving licence are recommended to see an opthalmic optician to obtain a report and where the field of vision is less than 120° a licence will not normally be granted. Instruction should encourage greater use of head movements both when driving along and checking to the sides.

Judgement of distances
An accurate judgement requires that both eyes are working together. The assessment of distances is more difficult when in motion. The perception of depth and distance is particularly difficult if one eye is impaired. Practice at comparing the size of vehicles and pedestrians etc at different angles and distances will help to improve the skill.

Adjustment to changes in light intensity
The ability of the eyes to adjust to changes in light intensity varies from one individual to another. So does the ability to see in the dark. Some people will find night driving particularly difficult. Some will experience considerable glare from streetlights and headlights. The recovery rate from glare due to bright sunlight or headlights may be such that some drivers will be blinded for a considerable time.

A full conversion of disability adaptations for a manual transmission car

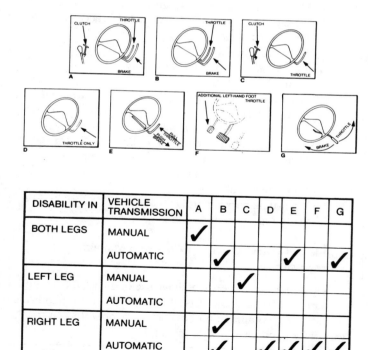

DISABILITY IN	VEHICLE TRANSMISSION	A	B	C	D	E	F	G
BOTH LEGS	MANUAL	✓						
	AUTOMATIC		✓			✓		✓
LEFT LEG	MANUAL			✓				
	AUTOMATIC							
RIGHT LEG	MANUAL		✓					
	AUTOMATIC		✓		✓	✓	✓	✓

Uses of adaptations relative to disability

Single-lever Control System for Cars with Automatic Transmission

This system, for drivers with disability in both legs, uses a combined control lever which is fitted to the steering wheel. This operates the brake and the accelerator.

The simple action of pulling upwards on the lever activates the accelerator, while pushing down on the lever operates the brake. This system is also available with two-lever control, if required.

Examples of controls available:

- *For total disability in both legs*
  - Combined manual brake and accelerator and steering wheel knob
  - Accelerator pedal guard or detachable accelerator pedal
  - Brake pedal guard.
- *For total disability in right leg only*
  - Manual brake and accelerator
  - Accelerator pedal guard or detachable accelerator pedal
  - Brake pedal guard
  - Steering wheel knob.
- *For partial disability in right leg only*
  - Manual accelerator
  - Accelerator pedal or detachable accelerator guard
  - Steering wheel knob.
- *Other modifications available*
  - Completely detachable and replaceable foot pedals
  - Brake pedal mounted on steering column
  - Trigger release handbrake
  - Steering wheel knob
  - Cam-type parking brake
  - Rotating car seats.

Two-lever Control System for Cars with Manual Transmission

This system is for drivers who have use of their left leg for clutch operation. The accelerator is situated on the right-hand side of the steering column, and the brake is operated by pushing forward a hand lever beside the left leg.

Based on material used with the permission of Ashley Health Care.

Hearing Disabilities

Sound provides important information about other vehicles and the operating condition of the one being driven. It gives information concerning the proximity of other vehicles and alerts drivers to danger and emergency vehicles. Identifying the source of sound can be difficult in a moving vehicle for people with normal hearing.

When a learner suffers from reduced hearing, instructors should compensate by speaking clearly and distinctly. In heavy traffic noise some learners with normal hearing may easily miss or misunderstand some instructions if an instructor speaks very quietly. This can lead to a number of problems, increase anxiety and reduce confidence.

Pupils who are completely deaf will need reassurance and the method of communication chosen can also be adopted with the Department of Transport examiner during the driving test. The method can be agreed with the examiner before the beginning of the test. Many deaf persons will be able to lip read your instructions while they are stationary at the kerbside. Alternatively, complicated instructions should be written down and passed to them.

Giving directions and instructions on the move requires an effective system of hand or finger signals with which to communicate easily with the driver. For example: point with *one* finger for directing the student to the *first* road on the left or right; point with *two* fingers for a *second* road on the left or right; hold the hand pointing up for give way, slow down or pull in and park and so on.

Communicating directions to dumb candidates should present no real problems. Highway Code questions can be answered in writing but when students are deaf and dumb, it may sometimes be advisable to obtain the services of someone they know who is able to relay your instructions and the student responses.

Make greater use of visual aids, flash cards, route cards and give more demonstrations. Stop more frequently to give instructions and give extra Highway Code homework.

Illiteracy, Dyslexia and Non-English-Speaking Students

Some pupils have difficulty in reading and some cannot read at all. This does not mean they are mentally sub-normal, or that they are likely to experience any particular difficulty in learning to drive.

If a student suffers from dyslexia (word blindness) or is illiterate (can't read or write), try to enlist the help of the student's family or friends to assist with Highway Code studies. During lessons place more emphasis on the use of visual aids and communicating concepts and procedures through pictures and diagrams.

Where a student's command of English is inadequate for training and testing purposes, try to develop some comprehension of the 'key word' instructions outlined on pages 93-94. It is probably advisable to obtain the services of someone they know to act as interpreter. You will not be permitted to act as an interpreter on the driving test but interpreters are permitted as long as they have no connection with your driving school.

On no account must these groups of people be embarrassed by their handicaps or made to feel inadequate. Spend more time going over the Highway Code and get relatives and friends to assist where possible. *Learn to Drive* is ideal for helping with the organisation of learning and testing the Highway Code rules and the graphically literate illustration is ideal for people with reading or language difficulties.

Discomfort, Physical stature and Ill Health

Physical discomfort such as toothache, cramp and natural functions can distract drivers. The performance of even the most skilful of drivers can deteriorate when they are feeling unwell. Alcohol and drugs affect every aspect of the driver's physical and perceptive processes and some simple cold cures contain drugs which affect driving performance. Some common drugs to be avoided while driving are:

Sleeping pills	Tranquilisers	Antihistamines
Anti-depressants	Pain killers	Opiates
Amphetomines	Belladonna	

Drivers suffering from the following may be taking the above drugs:

Anxiety	Depression	Insomnia
Toothache	Indigestion	Headaches
Colds/flu	Hay fever	Asthma
Period pains and pre-menstrual tension		

One of the difficulties in helping clients with some of the less obvious handicaps is that they can often go unnoticed for a long time, throughout which period the learners simply struggle on as best they can. Another problem is that some people suffering from a minor handicap may be embarrassed by it and so do not mention it. Others may even deny a handicap through ill-founded fears that the instructors may be reluctant to teach them if they knew about it. Tact and understanding must be the order of the day in dealing with these problems. In some cases *a properly secured* cushion may be all that is required. Pedal extensions can be used for people with short legs or small feet. The floor of the car can be easily raised by placing a board (or similar object) under the carpet or mat.

Where a person is unable to turn the body or neck, special additional mirrors can be used to cover the blind areas and for use when reversing.

None of us feel well all of the time and your pupils will be no exception. Women in particular may feel less well one week in every four due to the menstrual cycle.

Mothers-to-be are not invalids and most of them will not appreciate being treated as such. However, they must be given some consideration particularly with regard to ensuring the happy event does not occur during the driving test (or, for that matter during a lesson!). Plan the lessons and test sensibly – opinions in this respect vary considerably and the final discretion must be exercised jointly by the instructor and pupil in relation to both lessons and test. Where there is any doubt the client should seek her doctor's advice.

Impairments and Distractions

Alcohol

Alcohol is a drug and is a contributory factor in over 30 per cent of road accidents. After just one drink a driver is less able to make decisions quickly or react promptly in an emergency.

After the second drink a driver will become more relaxed with less concern for normal restraint and attention to detail. There is a further deterioration in mental responses and physical reactions, combined with a slight degeneration in co-ordination and the execution of manipulative skills.

After the third drink a driver's emotions become more extreme and behaviour exaggerated. The driver becomes more confident, talkative, noisy or morose and there is a further deterioration in reactions, co-ordination and manipulative skill. Perceptive responses become slower and impossible feats are far more likely to be attempted.

After the fourth drink there is still further deterioration in co-ordination to the point of clumsiness. Confidence continues to increase while perceptive skills are unknowingly deteriorating. The driver's levels of attention and powers of discrimination and normal restraint are rapidly disappearing. Impossible feats are even more likely to be attempted.

After the fifth drink normal perception of moving and static objects becomes blurred. It takes longer for the eyes to focus: and speeds and distances are severely misjudged. The driver's ability to make sensible decisions, and react promptly, is totally unreliable, resulting in high accident risk manoeuvres being unknowingly attempted.

Non-Alcoholic Drugs

Drugs impair driving ability by reducing attention levels, the perception of risk, and the ability to make sound decisions quickly and respond promptly to the road and traffic scene. Studies in the USA show that about 10 per cent of drivers involved in accidents take non-alcoholic drugs of some kind.

Instructors should be particularly cautious when new drivers are suffering from some temporary illness for which they may be taking drugs. New drivers should be advised to ask their doctors whether any prescribed drug will affect driving ability and also read instructions on the labels of non-prescribed drugs. It may also be appropriate to offer advice on the use of illegal drugs and their effect on driving.

Amphetamines speed up the nervous system and help users to 'keep going'. While taking this type of drug, users may feel more alert and confident but when the effect wears off, they are likely to feel very tired and depressed.

Barbiturates are used to calm the nerves. They have an effect similar to that of alcohol, but when the effect wears off depression may follow. A combination of barbiturates and alcohol can cause severe depression. Tranquilisers are used by people with nervous and emotional conditions. They cause drowsiness and the people who take them often combine their use with alcohol with the likelihood of severe or even fatal consequences.

Marijuana is an hallucinogen which can act as either a stimulant or depressant. It slows mental responses and physical reactions, affects the judgement of time and space and limits the ability to concentrate on more than one thing at a time.

Fatigue

Fatigue is a temporary condition that impairs the ability of all drivers. It reduces the ability to concentrate, impairs vision and the other senses, makes decisions more difficult and makes drivers more irritable and so less tolerant with other road users.

It can be caused by hard work, lack of rest, emotional stress, boredom or carbon monoxide poisoning. Contributory factors may include illness, overeating, an overheated car, driving for long distances without rest, bright sunlight or glare from oncoming headlights.

Carbon monoxide is discharged by the car's exhaust system. If this is leaking, or if boot seals are not effective, or if the tailgate of an estate or hatchback car is not fully closed, carbon monoxide may find its way into the passenger compartment. It is colourless, odourless, tasteless and poisonous. Keep plenty of fresh air circulating through the car.

The effects of fatigue on driving performance are not always obvious to the driver. They are:

– concentration becoming more difficult;
– the eyes becoming inactive;
– increased thinking time;
– a slowing of physical reactions;
– it becomes harder to make decisions.

Emotions and Stress

Extremes of emotions, such as fear or anger, affect attention levels, perception and response to everyday traffic situations. They limit the driver's ability to reason quickly and logically.

Driving is in itself a stressful activity. High levels of frustration or stress are created by the vehicle and traffic environment. Stress can cause excessive over-reaction which add even more fuel to the fire. On the other hand these over-reactions may (particularly in the case of new drivers in situations they are not yet competent to deal with) be associated with poorly developed hazard recognition skills, resulting in additional stresses due to late reactions and lack of confidence due to deficient car control skills.

Aggression is characterised by the hostile feelings or behaviour which some drivers display towards others. Normal mentally healthy people are able to tolerate a degree of aggression towards themselves without retaliation. Some experts claim aggression is linked to an individual's desire to dominate another and to compensate for feelings of inferiority or inadequacy. Others describe it as a surge of destructive feeling provoked by frustration. It is unlikely that aggression can be completely suppressed and when it manifests itself in new drivers, instructors should direct it towards the driver error rather than the person committing it.

Young people are generally more at risk because they are less able to control hostile feelings. However, aggressive behaviour is not restricted to any particular age, group or gender if drivers are pushed beyond their limits.

Anxiety

Most normal people get upset and anxious from time to time, particularly when faced with a threat of some kind. Anxiety describes the psychological disturbance characterised by feelings of apprehension. Some people are more susceptible to anxiety than others. This may be due to feeling helpless and alone or experiencing a deep sense of inadequacy. These feelings are all normal in themselves but they have become over-obtrusive. Anxiety ranges in intensity from a vague restlessness to extreme uneasiness and is usually accompanied by some kind of physical distress such as a tightness of the chest, dryness of the throat, sweating, trembling or tears. It can be caused by financial or business difficulties, uncertainty about how to behave in some circumstances, fear of failure or fear of the consequences of an action. Intense anxiety can also be caused by seemingly insignificant matters such as meeting a stranger or having dirt on one's shirt or blouse. Such exaggerated cases may indicate some subconscious cause relating to forgotten experiences.

Anxiety makes it difficult for learners to think, reason or make judgements. It reduces their level of awareness and makes it difficult for them to concentrate on driving or any point under instruction. It results in a low level of retention of new information and skills, panic, reduced physical co-ordination, forced errors and a high degree of risk taking (to flee the situation).

Instructors can assist over-anxious students by creating a confident but relaxed and caring atmosphere, giving more reassurance and encouragement. Common sense over the task demands will help to build confidence. For example, let them drive slower on routes with reduced task demands until confidence grows. Shorter training periods and frequent breaks may help. Make sure students understand. Follow the structure outlined on pages 98-99, demonstrate and present information as graphically as possible.

Illness

Everyone suffers from temporary minor illnesses from time to time, such as colds, toothache, headache, tummy upsets. These can reduce attention, impair vision and upset judgements, timing and co-ordination.

Ageing

Ageing can reduce perception and impair manipulative co-ordination. Older people are more set in their ways and will generally find learning to drive more difficult. They tend to be more anxious and their reactions are generally slower. Instructors should not place them under too much pressure, nor compare their progress with younger learners.

Distractions

The growing use of microphones, car telephones and CB radios is of serious concern. They are serious distractions and drivers should not use hand-held microphones or telephone handsets while the vehicle is moving, except in an emergency. Drivers should only use fixed, neckslung or clipped on microphones when it will not distract their attention from the road and traffic situation. (Any serious conversation is a distraction.) The problems can be alleviated by the sensible use of the equipment and it is safest when the vehicle is standing. It is advisable that calls are not answered or put out when in motion and that serious conversations are suspended until a suitable parking place can be found.

There are many other similar activities which reduce the driver's attention on the road and traffic scene. For example, when drivers are carrying out unrelated physical actions such as lighting a cigarette, tuning the car radio, looking for maps, cassette tapes or papers, winding the window down, having serious conversation or arguments with passengers, or looking for a street name or house number, their attention to driving is reduced.

Chapter 10

The 'L' Test

Nearly two million driving tests are carried out each year and more than 90 per cent of the drivers taking the test have had at least *some* driving lessons with a professional instructor.

This section is written with the assumption that you, the instructor, will not only be teaching your pupils to drive but also preparing them for the test and accompanying them to the test.

Frequent references will be made to the main documents which are used in relation to the driving tests and driving applications. A complete list of documents, numbers and explanations is given below.

(a) DL68 'Your Driving Test'

This booklet is issued by the Department of Transport to drivers when they apply for their *first* provisional licence. It describes in detail the requirements of the test, including the different types of vehicle suitable for driving tests, and the special needs of different categories of driver – disabled, deaf and dumb. The various set manoeuvres to be carried out are explained in detail, together with an explanation of the examiner's job and the routes on which tests are conducted.

Driving instructors should ensure that they hold a stock of the booklet and that each pupil is in possession of a copy. Driving test examiners normally issue a copy when a candidate fails the test.

(b) DL26 – Application for a driving test appointment

Copies are available from Post Offices or the Department of Transport. As well as being an application form the document gives considerable information regarding licence groups and test requirements, together with a list of Driving Test Centres and Traffic Area Offices.

(c) DL25 – Examiner's marking sheet

During the test an examiner uses this sheet for recording the candidate's driving faults. Other information regarding the conduct of the test is also itemised. The details of individual markings are not normally disclosed by the Department of Transport to the candidate or instructor, but the use of the form is discussed in some detail during practical training courses for instructors.

(d) D10 – Certificate of competence to drive
The document is issued by a driving test examiner to the successful candidate. Used in conjunction with a current, valid provisional licence, it entitles the person to drive without 'L' plates and without a supervising driver.

(e) DL24 – Statement of failure
The full title of this document is 'A statement of failure to pass the test of fitness or competence to drive' and it is issued by a driving test examiner to the candidate who is unsuccessful in the test. The examiner cannot and will not discuss details of the test with your pupil or with you; he will simply give the pupil a copy of the DL24 on which he has marked some of the items of driving which require special attention.

The form lists the main headings of the paragraphs 1 to 20 in the DL68 and can be used as a guide for pupil and instructor. However, the fact that an item is not marked does *not* indicate the candidate's performance was faultless.

The object of the test is to see if the candidate – your pupil – is competent to drive. After he has passed the test and gained a full licence he is free of an 'L' driver's restrictions and may now drive without an accompanying driver and on the motorway. It is essential therefore that the instructor prepares his pupil correctly for this vital examination.

As the driving test has traditionally been the subject of many myths, rumours and half truths, we shall deal here with the detailed facts regarding driving test procedures including application, the test itself, the role of the examiner and the role of the instructor.

Application for the Test
Sooner or later every driving instructor must advise a client when to make an application for a driving test.

This is one of the most difficult and subjective decisions the instructor has to make for a number of reasons:

1. From a business point of view, an instructor often feels under pressure to apply for a test at the earliest possible date.
2. The clients themselves often put the instructor under pressure to apply for an early appointment.
3. These pressures almost always affect the instructor's decision to advise on application, especially where there is a long waiting list and the end of the list seems to be a long way away.
4. Where no pressure of the above kind exists to any significant degree, it is still not as easy as it may sound. The instructor must be fair to a client and not impose standards so high as to guarantee a 'pass' absolutely before applying, because this perfection is not economically practical from the client's point of view. That is not to say that an instructor should not strive, and indeed expect, a standard higher than that of the Department.
5. Different clients make different rates of progress at different levels of instruction. For example, some make very rapid progress for

DTp driving test application

General Notes

Filling in this form

- Please make sure that you answer **all** the questions. Write in the white boxes using black ink and in CAPITAL LETTERS.
- If you find that you need more information to help you fill in this form, the booklet, DL68 'Your Driving test,' provides helpful advice. Copies of this pamphlet are given out with provisional licences, you can also get a copy free from your Traffic Area Office.
- You can only make **one** application at a time.

Penalty

- If you deliberately give false information on this form you may be fined up to £1000.

Your driving test

- You should ensure that you are ready for the test. You can do this by seeking advice and tuition from an Approved Driving Instructor. Also make sure that you read the booklet DL68, 'Your Driving Test,' before taking the test.
- You must be legally entitled to drive and if you have got your driving licence (provisional or other) you should bring it with you.
- You must supply a suitable vehicle for your test:
  - It must not be loaded or partially loaded;
  - The examiner must be able to see through the rear windscreen;
  - It must be properly insured.
- If you cannot speak English or are deaf, you may bring along an interpreter.

Motor cycle test

- Part 1 motorcycle tests take place at Heavy Goods Vehicle driving test centres, these are given on the back of this form.
- If you are applying for Part 2 please make sure you enclose your certificate of passing Part 1 (form DL23). If you have lost your certificate you can get a duplicate from either the appointed training body or the Traffic Area Office to whom you applied for your test.

Table of vehicle groups

Group	Description of vehicles in the group
A	A vehicle without automatic transmission (e.g. a motor car with manual gear shift)
B	A vehicle with automatic transmission
C	Motor tricycle weighing not more than 450kg unladen
D	A motor bicycle (with or without side car)
E	Moped of maximum engine capacity 50cc.

- If you want to drive a vehicle not included in this table, see form D100 for advice. You can get this from the Post Office.

Checklist

- Have you answered **all** the questions and included your Driver Number?
- Have you filled in your name and address at the bottom of the form?
- Have you **signed** and dated the form?
- Have you enclosed the fee?

Where to send this form

- When you have answered all the questions, please tear the form in half down the dotted line. Send the part of the form which you have filled in to the Clerk at the Traffic Area Office responsible for the area where you want to be tested. You will find the address on the back of this form. **Do Not** send this form to DVLC.

Important

- If you have not received an appointment card within 21 days please inform the Traffic Area Office where you sent this form immediately.
- Please enclose either a cheque or postal order, made payable to, 'Department of Transport' and crossed /&Co./. If you send a cheque, write your name, address and choice of test centre on the back. If you send a postal order, fill in and retain the counterfoil until you have received your appointment card.

Driver number You must fill this in

- You will find this at the **top** of your licence

Name

- For title give Mr. Mrs. Miss or Ms.
- Give your surname and first name in full.
- For your other names give your initials only.
- Do not forget to **sign** and date the form.

Address

- If you change your address please tell the Traffic Area Office immediately so that we can contact you if your appointment has to be changed for any reason.

Test centre

- A list of centres is shown on the back of this form.
- For tests within the Metropolitan Traffic Area please write in the code shown (eg. Barnet — BT).

Motor cycle test

- If you are applying for Part 2 please enclose your certificate of passing Part 1, unless you are taking a test with a side-car.

Type of vehicle

- See the table of vehicle groups and tick one box or give details of group in 'other' box.

Previous test

- Tick 'Yes' if you have taken a test before in the same vehicle group. If you have, you may not take another for one calendar month unless you are applying for a Part 1 motorcycle test.

Date

- Say when you will be ready to take your test.
- Tick any of the boxes to show any days when you cannot take your test.
- Please write down any periods (such as holidays) when you will be unable to take a test.
- Please tick 'Yes' if you could accept a test with less than a week's notice if one becomes available, otherwise tick 'No'.

Disabilities

- If you have any disabilities please state what they are.
- If you have none, please state 'none'.

Driving school

- Please give the name and telephone No. of your driving school. And ask your instructor to fill in the code boxes on the right hand side if necessary.

Fee Do not send bank notes or coins.

- The fee for a test appointment is displayed in all test centres and Traffic Area Offices.
- An ansaphone giving fee information operates in some Traffic Area Offices (see back page for details). These operate using an automatic calling system. A ringing tone means that calls are being answered in turn please wait for a reply.

DTp driving test application (continued)

Please write in block ink and in CAPITAL LETTERS

Driver No.	

Title		Surname	

First name & initials		Date of Birth	day month year

Signed		Dated	

Address	

	Postcode	

☎	Home	STD code		Work	STD code	

First choice centre		Second choice centre	

DL23MC noted

Cert. No. _____

ATB _____

Date returned to candidate

_____

Tick one box	Motorcycle test Part 1		Motorcycle test Part 2	

Type of Vehicle	A	B	C	D with side-car
	D without side-car	E	Other group	

8   V/T   P

Previous test	Yes	No	Centre		Date	day month year

9   D   M

Earliest date	day month year

10

Unacceptable days	Monday		Tuesday		Wednesday		Thursday		Friday	
	am	pm	am	pm	am	pm	am	pm	am	pm
	1	2	3	4	5	6	7	8	9	0

11 Ind   D   M   D   M

Unacceptable dates	

Short notice test	Yes	No	

12 S/N

Disabilities	

Dis

13   Driving school code

Driving school		Telephone No.	

14   D   M   P

Fee enclosed	£	Cheque or postal order number	

Name	

Address	

☞ *Please fill in this box so that your appointment card can be sent to you:*

Postcode	

DTp driving test application (continued)

SCOTTISH TRAFFIC AREA
83 Princes Street
Edinburgh EH2 2ER
(Tel. No. 031 225 5418)

Fee enquiry message
(Tel. No. 031 225 1257)

Aberdeen, -Albert Street, -Clunie Place, Aberfeldy, Alloa, Arbroath, Ayr, Ballachulish, Ballater, Banff, Bathgate, Bettyhill, Blairgowrie, Brechin, Buckie, Callander, Campbeltown, Castle Douglas, Coatbridge, Crieff, Cupar, Cumnock

Dingwall, Dumbarton, Dumfries, Dundee, Dunfermline, Dunoon, Duns, Edinburgh, -Joppa, -Newington, -Parkhead, Elgin, Falkirk, Forfar, Fort Augustus, Fort William, Fraserburgh, Gairloch, Galashiels, Girvan, Glasgow, -Anniesland

-Riddrie, -Rutherglen, -Shawlands, -Shettleston, Golspie, Grantown-on-spey, Greenock, Haddington, Hamilton, Hawick, Helmsdale, Huntly, Inveraray, Inverness, Inverurie, Keith, Kelso, Kilmarnock, Kingussie, Kinross, Kirkcaldy, Kyle of Lochalsh

Lairg, Lanark, Lochgilphead, Lochinver, Mallaig, Montrose, Newton Stewart, Oban, Paisley, Peebles, Perth, Peterhead, Pitlochry, Rothesay, Saltcoats, Stirling, Stonehaven, Stranraer, Strontian, Tain, Thurso, Turriff

Ullapool, Wick, Wishaw, ISLANDS, Barra, Benbecula, Brodick, Harris, Islay, Lewis, Millport, Mull, North Uist, Orkney, Shetland, Skye, South Uist, Tiree

Test centres: Aberdeen, Bishopbriggs (Glasgow), Dumfries, Elgin (Keith), Galashiels, Inverness, Kilmarnock, Kirkwall, Livingston (Edinburgh), Oban, Perth, Stornoway, Wick

---

NORTH EASTERN TRAFFIC AREA
(Newcastle)
Westgate House, Westgate Road
Newcastle-upon-Tyne NE1 1TW
(Tel. No. 091 261 0031)

Alnwick, Berwick-on-Tweed, Bishop Auckland, Blyth, Darlington

Durham, Gateshead, Gosforth, Hartlepool, Hexham

Jarrow, Kenton Bar, Longbenton, Middlesbrough, Northallerton

North Shields, Redcar, Sunderland, Thornaby

Test centres: Berwick, Darlington, Newcastle

NORTH EASTERN TRAFFIC AREA
(Leeds)
Hillcrest House
386 Harehills Lane
Leeds LS9 6NF
(Tel. No. 0532 495661)

Barnsley, Bradford, -Eccleshill, -Heaton, -Wibsey, Bridlington, Cleethorpes, Doncaster

Goole, Halifax, Harrogate, Heckmondwike, Hessle, Horsforth, Huddersfield

Hull, -Chamberlain Road, -Salisbury Street, Keighley, Leeds, -Harehills, -Crossgates

Malton, Pontefract, Rotherham, Scarborough, Scunthorpe, Sheffield, -Handsworth, -Middlewood Road

-Manor Top, Skipton, Wakefield, Whitby, York

Test centres: Beverley, Grimsby, Keighley, Leeds, Sheffield, Wetherby

---

NORTH WESTERN TRAFFIC AREA
Portcullis House, Seymour Grove
Stretford, Manchester M16 ONE
(Tel. No. 061 872 5077)
Driving Test Appointments
061 872 2333
24 Hour fees and waiting times
message only
061 848 0361

Bala, Bangor, Barrow, Birkenhead, Blackburn, Blackpool, Bolton, Bury, Buxton, Carlisle

Chester, Chorley, Congleton, Crewe, Ellesmere Port, Failsworth, Heysham, Holyhead, Hyde, Kendal

Liverpool, -Bootle, -Crosby, -Garston, -Norris Green, Llandudno, Macclesfield, Manchester, -Cheetham Hill, -Didsbury

-Whalley Range, -Withington, Mold, Northwich, Nelson, Preston, Pwllheli, Reddish, Rhyl, Rochdale

Sale, Southport, St Helens, Wallasey, Warrington, Widnes, Wigan, Wilmslow, Workington, Wrexham

Test centres: Bredbury (Manchester), Carlisle, Caernarfon, Heywood (Manchester), Kirkham (Preston), Simonswood (Liverpool), Upton (Wirral), Wrexham

---

WEST MIDLAND TRAFFIC AREA
Cumberland House
200 Broad Street
Birmingham B15 1TD
(Tel. No. 021 631 5300)

Bilston, Birmingham Area, -Kings Heath, -Kingstanding, -Quinton, -Sheldon, - Shirley, - Sutton Coldfield, -Washwood Heath

Bromsgrove, Burton-on-Trent, Cannock, Cobridge, Coventry, -Mason Road, -Holyhead Road, Evesham, Fenton

Hereford, Kidderminster, Leamington, Leek, Lichfield, Lower Gornal, Ludlow, Malvern, Newcastle-under-Lyme

Nuneaton, Oswestry, Redditch, Rugby, Shrewsbury, Stafford, Stratford-upon-Avon, Walsall, Bloxwich

Wednesbury, Wellington, Whitchurch, Wolverhampton, Worcester

Test centres: Featherstone (Wolverhampton), Garretts Green (Birmingham), Shrewsbury, Swynnerton (Stoke-on-Trent)

EASTERN TRAFFIC AREA
(Nottingham)
Birkbeck House
14 – 16 Trinity Square
Nottingham NG1 4BA
(Tel. No. 0602 475511)

Ashbourne, Boston, Chesterfield, Derby, -Sinfin Lane, -London Road, Gainsborough

Grantham, Hinckley, Kettering, Leicester, -Gipsy Lane, -Narborough Road, -Welford Road

Lincoln, Loughborough, Louth, Melton Mowbray, Newark, Northampton

Nottingham, -Arnold, -Beeston, -Chalfont Drive, -West Bridgford, Skegness, Spalding

Stamford, Sutton-in-Ashfield, Wellingborough, Worksop

Test centres: Alvaston (Derby), Leicester, Watnall (Nottingham), Weedon

---

EASTERN TRAFFIC AREA
(Cambridge)
Terrington House, 13-15 Hills Road
Cambridge CB2 1NP
(Tel. No. 0223 358922)

Bedford, Bury St Edmunds, Cambridge, -Brooklands Avenue, -Chesterton Road, Chelmsford

Clacton, Colchester, Ipswich, King's Lynn, Leighton Buzzard, Lowestoft

Luton, Norwich, -Jupiter Road, -Earlham House, Peterborough, Southend-on-Sea

Wisbech

Test centres: Chelmsford, Ipswich, Leighton Buzzard, Norwich, Peterborough, Waterbeach (Cambridge)

SOUTH WALES TRAFFIC AREA
Caradog House
1-6 St Andrew's Place
Cardiff, Glamorgan CF1 5PW
(Tel. 0222-25186 & 373400)
* 0222-395638

Abergavenny, Aberystwyth, Ammanford, Barry, Brecon, Bridgend

Cardiff, -Cathays Terrace, -Norbury Road, Cardigan, Carmarthen, Cwmbran

Haverfordwest, Lampeter, Llandrindod Wells, Llanelli, Machynlleth, Merthyr Tydfil

Milford Haven, Monmouth, Newport, Newtown, Pembroke Dock, Pontypridd

Swansea, Treorchy

Test centres: Llantrisant, Neath, Pontypool, Templeton (Haverfordwest)

WESTERN TRAFFIC AREA
The Gaunts' House
Denmark Street
Bristol BS1 5DR
(Tel. No. 0272 297221 /
From 1.4.1988 - 0272-221066)

Barnstaple, Bath, -Foxhill, -Sydney Road, Bodmin, Bournemouth, Bridgwater

Bristol, -Clifton Down, -Southmead, -St George, Cheltenham, Chippenham, Devonport, Dorchester

Exeter, Exmouth, Gloucester, Launceston, Minehead, Newton Abbot, Penzance, Plymouth

Poole, Salisbury, Scilly Isles, Swindon, Taunton, Tiverton, Trowbridge, Truro

Wells, Weston-super-Mare, Yeovil

Test centres: Bristol, Camborne, Chiseldon (Swindon), Exeter, Gloucester, Plymouth, Poole, Taunton

---

SOUTH EASTERN TRAFFIC AREA
Ivy House, 3 Ivy Terrace
Eastbourne BN21 4QT
(Tel. No. 0323 21471)
24 Hour fees & waiting times message
Kent / Sussex
0323 647994
Oxfordshire / Hampshire /
Buckinghamshire / Berkshire
0323 647955

Aldershot, Ashford (Kent), Aylesbury, Banbury, Basingstoke, Bletchley, Brighton, Broadstairs, Canterbury

Caversham, Chichester, Crawley, Eastbourne, Farnborough, Folkestone, Gillingham, Gosport

Gravesend, Hastings, Henley-on-Thames, Herne Bay, High Wycombe, Hove, Maidstone

Newbury, Newport (IOW), Oxford, -Headington, -Marston Road, Portsmouth, Reading

Slough, Southampton, -Forest Hills Drive, -Maybush, Tunbridge Wells, Winchester, Worthing

Test centres: Canterbury, Culham, Gillingham, Hastings, Isle of Wight, Lancing, Reading, Southampton

---

METROPOLITAN TRAFFIC AREA
PO Box 643
Government Buildings
Bromyard Avenue
The Vale, Acton W3 7AY
(Enquiries 01 743 5522)
24 Hour fees & waiting times message
01 743 2087

* Fees, waiting times & cancellation message

Ashford (Surrey) AS, Barking BG, Barnet BT, Belvedere BE, Berkhamstead BD, Bexleyheath BX, Bishops Stortford BS, Brentwood BW, Burnt Oak BK, Chertsey CS, Chingford CG, Croydon CD

East Ham EH, Grays GY, Greenford, -Horsenden Lane GN, -Ruislip Road GR, Guildford GF, Hayes (Middx) HA, Hendon HE, Hither Green HN, Hornchurch RL, Ilford IL

Isleworth IS, Lee LE, Letchworth LC, Loughton LO, Mill Hill MH, Morden MO, Norwood ND, Palmers Green PG, Pinner PI, Redhill RL, Ruislip RP, St Albans SA

Sevenoaks SV, Sidcup SP, Southall SX, Southfields SF, Southgate SG, Stevenage ST, Surbiton SB, Sutton SN, Teddington TD, Wallington, -Wallington Court WL, -Old Town Hall WO

Wanstead WS, Watford WR, Wealdstone WE, West Wickham WW, Weybridge WY, Winchmore Hill WH, Wood Green, -Bounds Green Road WG, -Lordship Lane WN

Test centres: Croydon, Enfield, Guildford, Purfleet, Yeading

various reasons in the early stages and later when a higher degree of understanding is required, progress may sometimes grind to a halt. Others make very slow progress at first, then make very rapid headway after a better 'understanding' is achieved.

6. The test waiting list is sometimes unpredictable in its length and care should be taken to write in the appropriate place on the application form the earliest date required.

It is as well to remember that if an instructor applies for a client's test too early that:

(a) It will have to be subsequently postponed and this means extra expense, time and possible ill feeling because pupils generally do not like having a test deferred.

(b) The client will fail, and that may be considered a reflection on the instructor who is in effect saying, 'I consider that this person is ready for the test.'

When advising a client to apply for a test at some distant point in the future it is desirable that the instructor should emphasise that the booking is made on the assumption that the pupil's driving will have reached a suitable standard. If the driving does not reach that minimum standard, the client should be advised four weeks prior to the test appointment and certainly not less than two weeks. On no account should the instructor attempt to postpone the test without the candidate's express permission. He can only 'advise' the pupil rather than take the responsibility for cancelling. Where the candidate insists on taking the test then all the instructor is entitled to do is withhold the use of the school car.

It is inevitable that there will be times when an instructor must be firm about the non-use of the car. In these cases he should remember (and if necessary emphasise to the pupil) that it is in the interests of safety that the advice has been given:

1. The pupil's own safety.
2. The safety of other road users, including the driving test examiner.

It should be noted that driving test examiners do not necessarily use the dual controls to avoid an accident unless there is danger to life or limb, and then only as a last-second decision. The tuition vehicle may then be at risk in this situation. The school car is a basic 'tool of the trade' for the instructor. It is imperative, therefore, that it is not off the road for unnecessary repairs.

Pupils should also appreciate that in presenting themselves for the test too early they are depriving other candidates who may have been waiting for some time. Very occasionally the pupil will offer heavy resistance to the suggestion of a deferment. Be sympathetic, tactful, but firm. Be logical, and give the pupil a realistic 'mock test'. This will usually convince all but the most adamant.

When the pupil is ready to make the application for test it is usually better for the instructor to help him or her to complete the application form (DL26) thus eliminating the risk of errors and a subsequent delay. You should ensure, therefore, that you are completely familiar with the form. Make sure that you are aware of the general waiting period for your local area – the waiting time may vary considerably from one centre to another, depending on the demand for tests at that time. It should be noted that, with computerisation of test bookings, the Department will in future normally return the test appointment card to the individual candidate at the address as shown on the application form. This arrangement can only be altered at the special request of the candidate. The instructor then takes on a responsibility for that test appointment. The following points should be noted:

1. If the appointment card is to be returned to the school, an accurate record should be kept of all applications made; the returned appointment cards should be filed in a functional system; the customer should be advised at the earliest possible opportunity that a date has been arranged; the appointment time and date should be recorded in the work diary and on the pupil record card; the appointment card *must* be handed over to the pupil on request.
2. If the card is to be sent to the pupil a note should be made of the application date. In this way, the pupil may be reminded to book the school car at an early date, or to check with the Department of Transport in the event of a delay in returning the card.

Whichever system is used there are certain basic rules which should be applied. These include:

1. In section 13 on the driving test application form you should write the name of the driving school and the reference in the appropriate boxes in order to avoid any unnecessary double booking of test appointments on the same car.
2. It is advisable to accept only cheques and postal orders payable to the Department of Transport rather than cash. This ensures that there is no misunderstanding over the fees paid to the Department on behalf of pupils.
3. Disabled drivers and people who are new residents in this country are given priority when booking tests. An application supported by a letter from the applicant's employer may also be given priority.
4. When the test appointment card is received from either the Department of Transport or client, a booking for the school car will be made – probably for a lesson as well as for use of the school car for the test. The payment for this booking should be agreed at the earliest possible time, as some pupils imagine that the payment of the test application fee *includes* the instructor's time on the day of the test.

Cancellation of the Test

We have already discussed the possibility of the test appointment being cancelled by the pupil. In this event he should give at least ten clear working days' notice of cancellation to the Department of Transport. 'Ten clear days' means that there must be an interval of ten whole days not counting the day the Traffic Area Office receives the notification, the day of the test appointment, nor Saturdays, Sundays and public holidays.

If this amount of notice is not given your pupil will be required to make a further application and send a further fee if he wants another appointment.

So long as an adequate amount of notice is given the application fee may be refunded or another test appointment may be made, or the test may be transferred to another area, depending on the instructions which the candidate gives to the Traffic Area Office.

There are, of course, other reasons for the cancellation of a test. The first of these is the cancellation by the driving school for reasons of instructor sickness or vehicle breakdown. In these cases the responsibility rests with the driving school to either reimburse the pupil, or to pay for another application fee and supply a vehicle for the subsequent test. The same moral obligation exists in the event of a test not taken owing to a school vehicle not being in a roadworthy condition and not acceptable to the examiner.

The normal business rules of a driving school require the pupil to give a minimum period of notice when cancelling appointments. If a driving test is cancelled at short notice by the Department of Transport, the pupil may be faced with unavoidable expenses, even though the Department will allocate an alternative date for the test. In this case the customer may apply to the Department for payment of the out-of-pocket expenses, and would be advised to support his application with the driving school receipt and a copy of the business conditions. In the normal way the Department will make a payment to cover the hire of the car for test and the pre-test lesson, but payment is regarded by it as *ex gratia*, indicating that payment is not a legal obligation!

From time to time a driving test may be cancelled by the department owing to poor weather conditions such as fog, ice, snow. In this event the Department will offer an alternative date for the test, but will not allow a claim for expenses from the candidate. The payment of the driving school fees for the cancelled test is, therefore, a matter for negotiation between the the client and the school. The school may decide that it would be good business practice to transfer a proportion of the fee to the rearranged test in order to maintain goodwill.

Attendance for the Test

Check list

1. Ensure that the client arrives at the centre in good time and is familiar with the location of the nearest toilets.
2. Ensure that the client can read a number plate at the required distance (do not leave this until five minutes before the test).
3. Ensure where possible that the client is in possession of a signed valid licence.
4. Have you checked the car for fuel, tyres, lights, seatbelts?
5. Have you got the appointment card in case the Department of Transport has made an error?

6. Have you arrived at the correct centre, if you use more than one?
7. Does the client know how to operate the wipers, lights, horn, etc?
8. Are the windows clean – are they likely to mist up during the test? Keep at least one window partly open and the demister on if necessary.
9. Has the client got the ignition key and does he know how to insert it and use the steering lock?
10. Five minutes before the test outside the centre is not the time to find out that the client cannot answer questions on the Highway Code.

The vehicle used for the test must:

- be roadworthy, suitable and constructed to enable the examiner to conduct the test in an orthodox manner. It must have a secure forward facing seat for the examiner
- not have controls, seating nor any articles or equipment which will interfere with the test
- not be fitted with any means of operating the accelerator pedal from the passenger side. (Dual control accelerator pedals must be disconnected.)
- be properly registered, licensed and insured
- normally be fitted with clean seat belts in proper working order
- display 'L' plates clearly where driven by a provisional licenceholder
- not carry animals, children or loads
- not exceed 7.5 tonnes maximum permissible weight
- have its engine properly adjusted at normal tickover speed.

The Driving Test

An examiner is trained to look for a 'perfect driver' (it is not too important that he/she will be unlikely to find one). At the outset of a test every candidate is 'perfect' at the point of getting into the vehicle. Deviations from perfection are graded into three categories of fault: minor, serious, or dangerous.

Candidates do not normally fail for a minor fault. Faults are graded by the examiner at the time they occur; they are then marked and graded onto the examiner's marking sheet (DL25). Before a deviation from perfect is even marked onto this sheet as a minor fault, it should be of a significant nature and not simply a difference in style.

In theory a test candidate could have, say, 27 minor faults marked and still pass. In practice this would be unlikely as anyone making that amount of minor errors would almost certainly make a potentially dangerous error during the period of the test.

The examiner will be sympathetic to the test candidate and will understand about nerves. An instructor should realise however that while nerves are frequently used as an excuse for failing, they are rarely a cause, provided the candidate is properly prepared and knows what to expect. A realistic 'mock' test conducted by the instructor can do much to prevent this problem.

The examiner must be satisfied on various aspects of driving. These are:

1. The candidate is fully conversant with the contents of the Highway Code.
2. The candidate must show that he/she is capable of driving safely showing due consideration for other road users.

The candidate must also fulfil the following specific requirements:

1. Read a number plate in good daylight at the prescribed distance (67 feet for 3⅛ inch letters).
2. Start the engine safely.
3. Move away safely.
4. Bring the vehicle to a stop safely and in an appropriate part of the road.
5. Turn right and left hand corners correctly.
6. Stop the vehicle in a simulated emergency.
7. Reverse into a limited opening to the left or right.
8. Turn the vehicle around between two kerbs and cause it to face the opposite way using forward and reverse gears.
9. Give signals where appropriate at the correct times and in a clear and unmistakable manner.
10. Take the correct action according to traffic signs, traffic controllers and upon signals given by other road users.

Forty minutes are allowed for the completion of each driving test. In practice the candidate is generally driving for just over half an hour of this time and is then required to answer questions on the Highway Code. Questions may also relate to conditions which arose during the test and about which the examiner has doubts regarding the candidate's actions.

Note: The eyesight test is conducted at the beginning of the test and if the candidate fails this the test *will not* continue.

At the end of the test the instructor will normally drive the car away from the test centre without too much delay. Whether the pupil has passed or failed there are several good reasons for this basic rule:

1. By moving away, the test centre car parking area is vacated for candidates arriving for the following test.
2. A pupil who has failed may be so annoyed or dejected that he is not fit to drive properly. Similarly, the pupil who has passed is often so elated that he is completely carefree and not concentrating on his driving.
3. The Driving Test Centre car park is not the place to carry out an 'inquest' on the result of the test.

If the pupil passes the test, he will be issued with a 'pass certificate' (D10). This entitles him to drive without 'L' plates or a supervising driver, but he should be advised to apply for a full licence as soon as possible. It should also be pointed out to him that a full licence must be obtained before (a) accompanying a learner driver, or, (b) driving abroad.

The Department makes special provision for testing disabled drivers. The examiner has to decide whether a restriction must be imposed on the type of vehicle which can be safely driven or whether the licence should restrict the candidate to driving an adapted car, and if so, the type of adaptation required.

If the candidate is not successful, the examiner will give him a 'statement of failure' (DL24) which shows the aspects of driving which require special attention. The items marked will be the main faults which caused the failure, but there may have been other relatively minor faults which are not marked. Examiners are not allowed to discuss the test either with the candidate or with a third party; neither are they permitted to advise that the candidate should take professional instruction. However, the issue of the form DL24 enables the pupil and instructor to discuss the matter at a later date with a view to correcting the faults.

Application for another test may be made immediately after the test – the only restriction is that the applicant is prohibited from taking a further test on the same type of vehicle for one calendar month.

As soon as possible after failing a test the pupil should have a lesson in which it is possible to analyse the test faults by reference to the DL24 (and DL68) and to plan the series of lessons required in order to prepare for the next test.

Driving Test Syllabus and Standards

Form D10 is the one which every candidate is seeking at the end of the driving test. Officially it is called the D10 but is more affectionately known as the pass certificate. Providing the candidate has had sufficient tuition of the right quality it should, in theory anyway, be within the reach of everyone.

In practice unfortunately not all test candidates do pass. In fact only about 45 per cent of those taking the test succeed. There are many reasons for this but an overriding cause must be that instructors present clients for the test before they are able to drive to a satisfactory standard.

Although this may not always be solely the fault of the instructor (often under pressure from his client), many of these failures could be avoided if the standards applied by the Department of Transport were properly related to the candidate's driving standard prior to the test appointment, and proper advice given to the learner, including temporary postponement of the test if necessary.

Where a candidate does fail, the instructor should be able to offer some constructive advice based on his interpretation of marked items listed on the 'failure form' (DL24). This is the form which the examiner completes after the test where the required standard has not been reached.

This form is not intended to be a detailed analysis of the candidate's performance and only the *most* serious faults are listed on it. Its main purpose is to provide an indication of the cause of the main errors for which the candidate has failed. it is not intended to be precise about the specific nature or exact location of the faults.

Some instructors complain that this form does not provide sufficient information to guarantee accurate interpretation. While this may be true, a form requiring specific detailing of faults would be impractical and in any

Certificate of passing of a test of competence to drive

ROAD TRAFFIC ACT 1972

Department of Transport

D10

D 283126

Driver Number of candidate | 2

If the Driver Number is not known, please state date of birth — Day _____ Month _____ Year _____

If candidate is holder of a licence issued outside Great Britain, tick here _____ Date of test

Month | Year | 3

Current Name _____

Current Address _____

Postcode _____

has been examined and has passed the test of competence to drive motor vehicles of group | 4

prescribed for the purposes of Section 85 of the Road Traffic Act 1972

Authorised by the Secretary of State to conduct tests

Signature

Test Centre _____

Signature of Candidate _____
To be signed in the presence of the Examiner

D 283126 | & | 5

CANCELLED

DTp driving test – pass certificate

Specimen copy. (Crown copyright, reproduced with the permission of the Controller of Her Majesty's Stationery Office)

Department of Transport

ROAD TRAFFIC ACT 1972

Test Centre:

Statement of Failure to Pass Test of Competence to Drive

W 0853053

CANCELLED

Name ....

has this day been examined and has failed to pass the test of competence to drive prescribed for the purposes of section 85 of the Road Traffic Act 1972.

Date ....

Authorised by the Secretary of State to conduct tests

Examiners have regard to the items listed below in deciding whether a candidate is competent to drive. The matters needing special attention are marked for your information and assistance and should be studied in detail. (See Note 1 overleaf)

1. ☐ Comply with the requirements of the eyesight test.
2. ☐ Know the Highway Code.
3. ☐ Take proper precautions before starting the engine.
4. ☐ Make proper use of/accelerator/clutch/gears/footbrake/handbrake/steering.
5. ☐ Move away/safely/under control.
6. ☐ Stop the vehicle in an emergency/promptly/under control/making proper use of front brake.
7. ☐ Reverse into a limited opening either to the right or left/under control/with due regard for other road users.
8. ☐ Turn round by means of forward and reverse gears/under control/with due regard for other road users.
9. ☐ Make effective use of mirror(s) well before ⎰ signalling/changing direction/slowing down or stopping.
       Take effective rear observation well before ⎱
10. ☐ Give signals/where necessary/correctly/in good time.
11. ☐ Take prompt and appropriate action on all/traffic signs/road markings/traffic lights/ signals given by traffic controllers/other road users.
12. ☐ Exercise proper care in the use of speed.
13. ☐ Make progress by/driving at a speed appropriate to the road and traffic conditions/ avoiding undue hesitancy.
14. ☐ Act properly at road junctions:–
       — regulate speed correctly on approach;
       — take effective observation before emerging;
       — position the vehicle correctly/before turning right/before turning left;
       — avoid cutting right hand corners.
15. ☐ Overtake/meet/cross the path of/other vehicles safely.
16. ☐ Position the vehicle correctly during normal driving.
17. ☐ Allow adequate clearance to stationary vehicles.
18. ☐ Take appropriate action at pedestrian crossings.
19. ☐ Select a safe position for normal stops.
20. ☐ Show awareness and anticipation of the actions of/pedestrians/cyclists/drivers.

DRIVING EXAMINERS ARE NOT PERMITTED
TO DISCUSS DETAILS OF THE TEST

SEE GUIDANCE NOTES OVERLEAF

56 1662 320 T8 B n9 81

DL 24
9/81

DTp driving test – failure certificate

event a professional instructor should not need a test report to tell him what is wrong with a client's driving.

The form upon which the examiner records the actual performance of the driver is called the DL25. This form is closely related to the failure form (DL24) and with reference to the codings on the latter it should be easy to work out the meaning of the abbreviations on the DL25. It should also be noted that the DL68 'Your Driving Test' is also useful in helping the instructor to interpret the failure form and relates directly to it.

In order to pass a Department of Transport driving test a candidate must satisfy the examiner that he/she is:

- Fully conversant with the Highway Code
- Competent to drive with consideration and without danger to other road users, a vehicle of the class or description as that on which he is being tested
- Able to read (with glasses if worn) a registration mark fixed to a stationary motor vehicle at the required distance
- Able to start the engine of the vehicle
- Able to move straight ahead – at an angle and on a gradient
- Able to overtake, meet or cross the path of other vehicles and take an appropriate course
- Able to turn left and right hand corners correctly
- Able to stop the vehicle normally in a suitable part of the road; and stop as in an emergency
- Able to drive the vehicle backwards into a limited opening either to the right or the left
- Able to turn the vehicle round in the road by using forward and reverse gears
- Able to act correctly and promptly on all signals given by traffic signs and traffic controllers. Take appropriate action on signals given by other road users.

The candidate must:

1. Comply with the requirements of the eyesight test
The candidate will be asked to read the number plate of a stationary vehicle in normal daylight at the required distance of 75 feet with 3½ inch letters and numbers, or 67 feet with 3⅛ inch letters and numbers. Normal daylight means the prevailing light conditions at the time of the test. Inability to comply will result in failure of the test and the candidate will be asked to sign a statement to the effect that he could not read the number plate. A point to consider is that the requirement for the eyesight test is only 50 per cent of perfect vision.

2. Know the Highway Code
Test candidates must obey the Highway Code rules when driving and at the end of the test the examiner will ask a number of questions relating to it and other motoring matters. He will also ask the candidate to identify the mean-

ing of several road signs from pictures. Unsatisfactory answers could result in test failure.

3. Take proper precautions before starting the engine

Care should be taken when entering the car to ensure that the handbrake is properly applied and the gear is in neutral before starting the engine. In the event of stalling the engine, apply the handbrake if necessary and disengage the engine before re-starting.

4. Make proper use of accelerator/clutch/gears/footbrake/handbrake/steering

Accelerator – the candidate must be able to regulate the speed of the engine smoothly and consistently when moving off, controlling the speed and changing gear. Uncontrolled or excessive use of the pedal might result in failure.

Clutch – should be used correctly and smoothly and at appropriate times. The candidate should be able to find the holding/driving points quickly and should then be able to co-ordinate its use with the accelerator and handbrake. Uncontrolled or fierce engaging of the clutch or poor co-ordination with the accelerator might result in failure.

Gears – should be used to maintain an efficient engine speed for the road and traffic conditions. Gear changes should be smooth and engaged in good time, particularly when approaching hazards and junctions. The vehicle should not be allowed to run for any distance in neutral or with the clutch disengaged, except in the normal course of changing gear and controlling the vehicle prior to stopping. In addition to driving in neutral, coasting can be defined as travelling with the clutch unnecessarily disengaged. Where the vehicle is properly restrained, holding the clutch down at very low speed is not coasting.

Looking down at the gear lever or other controls when changing gear should be avoided.

Footbrake – should be used in good time. It should be used *progressively* with a light pressure gradually building up and gradually decreased. Late braking usually leads to sudden, excessive pressure changes on the pedal and this could result in test failure.

Handbrake – its purpose is to safely secure the vehicle when it is stopped. It should be used when parking and when the vehicle is brought to rest in normal driving conditions where it is to be held stationary for more than a moment.

A 'moment' can in this context be defined as a very brief stop which would not allow sufficient time for the handbrake to be normally applied and then released without it causing delay.

Excessive use of the handbrake in situations where it is not essential to secure the vehicle on the one hand, and slipping the clutch excessively on those occasions when the handbrake would be more appropriate, might result in test failure.

Steering – two hands should be kept on the wheel except when changing gear, operating another control or giving an arm signal. Two hands should be kept on the steering wheel particularly when braking or cornering. Avoid letting the wheel spin between the fingers. When manoeuvring and cornering avoid excessive speed.

Look, think and plan ahead to steer a progressive, accurate and safe course for the conditions. Avoid fidgety movements with the wheel and use a safe steering method. Inaccurate judgement of the steering course or turning points on a corner can result in failure.

Note: Control faults which occur during moving off, the reverse or the turn in the road exercise will not be marked under section 4 but in the appropriate section relating to the particular manoeuvre.

5. Move away/safely/under control
Before moving away from the kerb either on up/down/level ground or even moving out from behind a parked vehicle, use the mirror/s and take appropriate observations to check the blind spots. Allow for the presence or movement of other road users when moving away and give an appropriate signal *if* it will help to warn or inform others of the intended action. Do not endanger or inconvenience any other road user, including pedestrians, when moving out. Careful co-ordination of the accelerator/clutch/handbrake and steering will also be required. Take particular care in the timing of necessary signals.

6. Stop the vehicle in an emergency – promptly/under control
The candidate must be able to stop *quickly but under control.*

Both hands should be kept firmly on the steering wheel until *after* the car has stopped. Braking pressure should be firm but progressive and not so hard as to cause the wheels to lock. (This will cause a skid and must be avoided.) In the event of the wheels locking the brake should be momentarily released and then re-applied. The clutch should *not* be pushed down until the car has nearly stopped. Reactions must be quick and efficient. When the vehicle has come to rest, and not before, secure the vehicle and select neutral.

7. Reverse into a limited opening either to the right or left – under control/ with due regard for other road users
Careful co-ordination of the controls must be maintained throughout the exercise to ensure proper control of the vehicle on an accurate course. Do not rush. Particular attention should be given to the appropriate observations before and during the manoeuvre, and the correct action taken in view of the movement of other road users, including pedestrians.

8. Turn the car round by means of forward and reverse gears – under control/with due regard for other road users
Careful co-ordination of the controls must be maintained throughout the exercise to ensure proper control of the vehicle on an accurate course. Do not rush. Particular attention should be given to the appropriate observations before and during the exercise and correct action taken in view of the movement of other road users. Care should be taken to ensure pedestrians are not inconvenienced or endangered by any kerb overhang. Observations of any obstructions on the pavement are essential. Do not bump the kerb. Be prepared to wait for other traffic.

9. Make effective use of mirror(s) well before – signalling/changing direction/slowing down/stopping
The mirror should be adjusted so as to avoid excessive or exaggerated head movement. The mirror should be used early enough to determine and correctly interpret the following traffic situation. Any subsequent action decided upon must allow for the movement of other traffic or pedestrians.

A single mirror check may not be adequate. For the safe execution of most manoeuvres, confirmation checks may be required.

10. Give signals – where necessary/correctly/in good time
Signals should be given where they will help to warn or inform other road users of an intended action. Signals do not give the driver the right to carry out an otherwise unsafe action. Signals should be correct, clear and cancelled after use. Special care may be required in the timing of some signals.

Signals should be given in good time for other road users to act upon them. Do not beckon pedestrians to cross the road or give other unauthorised signals.

11. Take prompt and appropriate action on all traffic signs/road markings/traffic lights/signals given by traffic controllers/other road users
A test candidate is expected to see and act for himself upon the information provided by road signs and markings. A candidate who does not comply with a stop sign or a turn or keep left sign will fail. Appropriate action is also expected on road markings for example 'No crossing' or 'lane markings'. The correct lane selection should be made fairly early and the candidate should avoid unnecessary lane changes. Traffic light changes should be anticipated and the candidate should act correctly in accordance with the lights shown, including filter arrows, taking into consideration the general traffic conditions.

Signals given by the police, traffic wardens and school crossing patrols must be recognised and obeyed.

Signals given by other road users include direction indicators, brake lights and hand signals. These must be acted upon correctly and interpreted in accordance with the overall traffic situation which will also involve the position and speeds of the signalling vehicles.

12. Exercise proper care in the use of speed

Drive within the legal limit for both road and vehicle type. Never drive too fast for the road or traffic conditions. Drive at a speed at which it is possible to pull up well within the distance actually seen to be clear and allow for the movement of other road users. Do not drive too close to the vehicle ahead. Adverse weather conditions necessitate increased stopping distances.

13. Make progress by driving at a speed appropriate to the road and traffic conditions/avoiding undue hesitancy

A candidate cannot expect to pass the test by driving unnecessarily slowly for the road and traffic conditions. The candidate who stops when it is safe and correct to proceed or waits needlessly at road junctions, when it is obviously safe to proceed will fail the test. Avoid slowing down too early on the approach to junctions.

14. Act properly at road juinctions, including roundabouts

Speed – must be regulated correctly on the approach. Slow down to a speed which allows the junction to be dealt with safely. Be prepared to stop if it is unsafe to proceed.

Observations – the candidate must look and be able to judge effectively the way is clear before moving into/out of/or across any junction. Special care must be shown where visibility is blocked or restricted. The driver must not inconvenience or disrupt the flow of traffic in the major road. Special consideration should be given to the movement of cyclists, motorcyclists and pedestrians.

Position – right – the candidate will be expected to position the vehicle correctly just left of centre and steer a safe course to the point of turn. Cutting right hand corners is a dangerous practice and should be avoided; overshooting the point of turn might also result in test failure.

If turning right from the end of a narrow road, keep well to the left to allow room for vehicles turning in.

Position in the right hand lane of dual carriageways and one-way streets. Take up the position in good time allowing for the movement of other road users.

Position – left – keep to the left on the approach before turning. Avoid swinging out before the turn or getting too close to the kerb on the approach. Do not swing wide after the turn.

15. Overtake/meet/cross the path of other vehicles safely

Overtake – do not overtake where it is, or may be, unsafe. Steer a suitably safe course past, allowing appropriate clearance, and do not cut in.

Meet – the candidate must be prepared to give way or hold back in the face of oncoming traffic where the circumstances merit this.

Cross – avoid turning right across the path of closely approaching oncoming traffic. Particular care is required in looking for cyclists and motorcyclists where visibility may be blocked by other vehicles.

16. Position the vehicle correctly during normal driving

The candidate should maintain a suitable position for normal driving which takes into account markings, signs and the road and traffic conditions prevailing at the time.

Normal – can be defined as taking account of the road and traffic conditions, but otherwise not hugging the kerb or hogging the road.

17. Allow adequate clearance to stationary vehicles

Candidates must take an appropriate and safe course past parked vehicles, allowing sufficient clearance to allow for margins of error. The driver should not drive at a speed or in a position which ignores possible danger to and around stationary vehicles.

18. Take appropriate action at pedestrian crossings

Pedestrian crossings must be approached with care and suitable caution. The candidate must approach at a proper speed, attentive to the potential movement of pedestrians and stop when and where required. At the flashing amber light of a pelican crossing the driver may proceed only if no pedestrians are crossing and providing it is otherwise safe.

19. Select a safe position for normal stops

Park close to the kerb. Avoid stopping over private driveways or near junctions. Select a safe and suitable place which will cause the least possible inconvenience or danger to other road users.

20. Show awareness and anticipation of the action of pedestrians/ cyclists/drivers

Actively look, think and plan ahead allowing for the movement or potential movement of other road users. Be prepared to compensate for any sudden or unusual movement by others, particularly cyclists and pedestrians. Be prepared to give way to pedestrians where appropriate near road junctions.

Driving Errors

The form on which the examiner records the actual performance of the driver is the DL25. This form is closely related to the failure form (DL24) and with reference to the latter it is relatively easy to interpret the abbreviations used on the DL25. Further details of errors are provided in the booklet 'Your Driving Test' (DL68).

Summary of some driving test errors

1. Eyesight test
   Unable to read a vehicle number plate at 67/75 feet.

2. Highway Code

   Knowledge of the Highway Code (and application of it during the drive) weak or wrong.

3. Precautions before starting engine

   Handbrake not applied, neutral not selected, when starting or re-starting the engine.

4. Make proper use of accelerator

   Erratic, fierce or jerky use: poor co-ordination with clutch.

   Clutch

   Not depressed far enough, causing noisy changing, or stalling; poor co-ordination with accelerator.

   Foot-brake

   Not used when needed; used late, harshly or erraticly.

   Gears

   Incorrect selection, coasting, not in neutral when needed.
   Harsh control of the gear lever, looking at lever, reluctant to change, incorrect use of selector on automatic.

   Hand-brake

   Not applied when required, not released when moving, used before stopping.

   Steering (Pos)

   Position of hands on wheel: one hand off, both hands off:
   hands on spokes, rim or centre: hands crossed unnecessarily, elbow on window ledge.

   Steering (Os)

   (Oversteer) Erratic control of steering, wandering on wheel; late correction, over or under steering; jerky or fiddling movements.

5. Moving off – angle, hill, level, straight

   Not done smoothly: not safe, not controlled. Causing inconvenience or danger to others: not using mirrors, looking round or acting sensibly on what is seen. Not signalling when needed, incorrect gear, lack of co-ordination of controls.

6. Emergency stop

   Slow reactions: like a normal stop: footbrake/clutch used in a manner likely to cause a skid: handbrake used before stopping.
   Both hands off the wheel.

7. Reverse: left/right

   Rushed; stalling; poor co-ordination of accelerator and clutch; incorrect course; mounting kerb; steering wrong way; too wide, or close (not realised); not looking around before/during reverse; not acting on what is seen.

8. Turning in road

   Rushed; stalling; poor co-ordination of accelerator and clutch; not using handbrake; incorrect steering, mounting or bouncing off kerb; uncontrolled footbrake or accelerator; more moves than

Department of Transport

Driving Test Report

Centre

Date / /

Candidate's full name

Name of School (where known)

Particulars of vehicle P C S

Make

Type

Reg Mark

Year 19

Group

FET			1
HC			2
PRE			3
ACC			4
CL			4
G			4
F.BR			4
H.BR			4
ST			4
MO	PRE		5
	CON		5
ES			6
	FR.BR		6
RV	CON		7
	OBS		7
TR	CON		8
	OBS		8

MIR	SIG		9
	DIR		9
	ST		9
ROB	SIG		9
	DIR		9
	ST		9
SIG	O		10
	W		10
	L		10
SNS	ST		11
	DIR		11
	NE		11
	RM		11
TRA	L		11
	CON		11
SIG	ORU		11
PRO	+		12
PRO	–		13

J	SP +		14
	OBS		14
	POSR		14
	POSL		14
	RCC		'14
OT			15
MAT			15
CAT			15
POSN			16
SH.V			17
PX			18
NS			19
AA	PED		20
	CYC		20
	DRI		20
ETA	V		
	P		

DL25 (1980)

DTp driving test examiner's marking sheet

Weather conditions		Route Number
Brief description of candidate		
REMARKS		

D 10 No	Examiner's Signature
DL 24 No	

Disability tests — including eyesight failure

Driver Number																
Description of any adaptation fitted																

Printed in the U.K. for HMSO. Dd 8840205 9/84 Aquaprint Ltd. 52132   DL25 (1980)

DTp driving test examiner's marking sheet (continued)

needed; lack of observation before or during manoeuvre; danger or inconvenience to others; looking but not acting sensibly on what is seen.

9. Effective use of mirrors

   Not looking in good time, not acting on what is seen. Omitted or used too late; used as or after movement is commenced. Not used effectively before signalling, changing direction, slowing or stopping. Omitting final look when necessary.

10. Give signals correctly

    Signals omitted, given wrongly, or given late. Too short to be of value, not cancelled after use; not repeated when needed. Arm signal not given when needed.

11. Prompt action on signals

    Failing to comply with signals or signs: Stop, Keep Left, No Entry, Traffic lights; Police signals, School Crossing wardens, Signals given by other road users.

12. Use of speed

    Not exercising proper care in use of speed; too fast for conditions or speed limits. Too close to vehicle in front, in view of speed, weather, road conditions.

13. Making progress

    Not making normal progress, too low speed for conditions crawling in low gear, no speed build up between gears, speed not maintained; undue hesitation at junctions, over cautious to point of being a nuisance.

14. Crossroads and junctions

    (i) Incorrect regulation of speed on approach; late appreciation of, or reaction to, junctions or crossroads.

    (ii) Not taking effective observation before emerging at a crossroad or junction. Not being sure it is safe to emerge, before doing so. Incorrect assessment of speed and distance of other vehicles, including cyclists.

    (iii) Incorrect positioning for right turns, at or on approach; position taken late, too far from centre; wrong position out of narrow road, or from one way street, wandering; wrong position at end of right turn. Incorrect positioning for left turns, at or on approach; too far from near kerb; swinging out before turning; striking or running over kerb; swinging out after turn.

    (iv) Cutting right turns when entering or leaving.

15. Overtaking/meeting/crossing other traffic

    Overtaking unsafely, wrong time or place, causing danger or inconvenience to others; too close or cutting in afterwards. Inadequate clearance for oncoming traffic; causing vehicles to swerve or brake.

    Turning right across oncoming traffic unsafely.

16. Normal position

    Unnecessarily far out from kerb.

17. Adequate clearance
   Passing too close to cyclists, pedestrians or stationary vehicles.
18. Pedestrian crossings
   Approaching pedestrian crossings too fast, not stopping when necessary, or preparing to stop if pedestrian waiting; overtaking on approach; not signalling (by arm if necessary) when needed. Giving dangerous signals to pedestrians.
19. Normal stops
   Stopping unsafely or in inconvenient place.
   Not parallel to kerb, too close to other vehicles or hazards; compounding hazards.
20. Awareness and anticipation
   Lack of awareness or anticipation of others' actions.
   (This is marked when the result of bad planning or lack of foresight involves the test candidate in a situation resulting in late, hurried or muddled decisions.)

Driving Examiners

The duty of an examiner is to test learner drivers to see whether they are fit to hold a licence to drive a motor vehicle. Tests are conducted on cars, motorcycles, tractors and other vehicles at more than 300 test centres throughout the country. Examiners have the sole responsibility for deciding the success or failure of candidates, and normally conduct some eight or nine tests on each working day. After successfully completing a training period, an examiner is usually allocated to a particular test centre and works as part of a team of examiners under a senior driving examiner.

Applicants for the post of examiner must have at least six years' driving experience with a variety of vehicles and are expected to show evidence of an active interest in motoring, traffic and road safety problems. Preference is often given to candidates who have experience of driving heavy goods and public service vehicles and/or riding motorcycles, and who have a knowledge of various vehicles. Some preference is also given to candidates who have experience of working with the public and who are accustomed to working without supervision.

Candidates are expected to have reached a standard of education which enables them to write accurate reports and to conduct oral examinations. Candidates convicted of certain serious motoring offences are not eligible to compete.

Driving examiners are drawn from all walks of life. They are carefully selected and trained in their own driving and their judgement of other people's driving ability. The very strict process of selection is followed by a period of intensive training at the Department of Transport training establishment at Cardington.

Examiners are selected for their general personalities and attitudes as well as for their driving experience and standards.

Before, during and at the end of the training course, examiners must pass a very stiff driving test themselves. These tests are set at such a high level of efficiency that it is almost impossible for the 'average' driver to appreciate the standard involved.

During the training course the Department of Transport makes sure that all trainees know exactly what they are expected to look for during a driving test. In some respects an ex-instructor may find some initial difficulty in the examiner training school because an instructor instinctively wants to help the novice driver rather than simply assess. No matter how much an examiner may sympathise with a test candidate he cannot normally assist because, by doing so, he is not examining objectively. Is it really fair to the test candidate or to other road users if an examiner helps the person with a potentially dangerous driving flaw? Of course it is not, and as professional instructors we can hardly expect an examiner to do our job for us.

An examiner is expected to be polite and pleasant to the candidate while he is conducting a test. He does not indulge in small talk nor discuss the driving or the test. He is, therefore, restricting his comments to a series of instructions and directions. This is taken by some pupils as an indication of impoliteness, rudeness or bad temper. This is not the case – he is simply doing his job correctly.

Some instructors who feel that they have achieved a certain level of attainment within the driving profession may decide to apply for one of the many vacancies as a driving examiner with the Department of Transport. They are often attracted by the security, the pension and the working hours available to examiners. The department has its own rigorous selection process and a purpose-built training centre at Cardington, Bedfordshire. The selection process involves a fairly lengthy procedure of application forms, references, interviews and driving tests, while the training consists of several weeks of concentrated instruction at Cardington, with a continuous programme of in-car and in-class work.

There are many disadvantages which the instructor should consider before embarking on a possible new career in this way. Initially, the department will expect the instructor to sever his connections with driving instruction before being accepted for a course. Acceptance for training does not necessarily mean that the applicant will be offered a job, and may be rejected either at the end of the training course or during the first year of work when the new examiner is 'on probation'. During this time he will be working at a centre some distance away from his home and will be faced with the decision of whether to move house or whether to travel on a daily basis. In either event, the department does not normally assist with expenses.

Experience has shown that many new examiners decide not to continue in their new profession under these conditions. They are then faced with the additional problem of reconstituting their original business or obtaining alternative employment. For an ex-instructor the job of examiner does not provide the same level of job satisfaction compared with teaching. Perhaps it is not surprising that the department appears to have regular shortages of staff and vacancies in various parts of the country.

Chapter 11

The HGV and PSV Tests

The HGV Driving Test

Application for the test is made on form DLG26 obtainable from Area Traffic Offices of the Department of Transport or from an HGV training organisation. Alternatively, bookings may be made by authorised training organisations using 'block booking' forms. This system enables an instructor to provisionally pre-book the tests and to confirm the candidate's name and vehicle details at a later date. The current fee for a Heavy Goods Vehicle test is £42.

HGV tests are conducted at special centres by experienced examiners who are specially trained for the requirements of heavy goods vehicles. A list of test centres is provided on the test application form.

The candidate has to provide a suitable vehicle for the test and it must comply with the following requirements:

(a) The vehicle must be unladen and of the class for which a licence is required.

(b) It must display approved HGV 'L' plates on the front and rear (and ordinary 'L' plates if the candidate holds a provisional ordinary licence).

(c) It must have sufficient fuel for the test lasting up to 1½ hours.

(d) It must be in a thoroughly roadworthy condition with all stop lamps and direction indicators working properly.

(e) Seating accommodation must be provided for the examiner.

(f) It must not be working on trade licence plates.

(g) The vehicle must not exceed 60 ft in length.

The booklet DLG68 'HGV driving test' explains what the test involves and how to prepare for it. The pamphlet DL68 'Your Driving Test' gives advice on correct control and driving procedures which should be followed by all drivers whether taking the ordinary test or the HGV test. The two booklets should be studied together.

In order to pass the HGV test you must:

Demonstrate to the examiner that you can handle the vehicle safely and competently in both town and country conditions.

Show courtesy and consideration for other road users, no matter what the situations.

Show that you have complete control of the vehicle throughout the test, whatever the weather or road conditions.

Department of Transport

Application for a Heavy Goods
Vehicle Driving Test Appointment

*Please read the notes overleaf before
completing the form. Delay will
occur if questions are answered
incorrectly or if any question is not
answered.*

For Official Use Only

Date	Month	Year	Date	Month	Year	Date	Month	Year	FTA Code
....			....			....			
Time.......................			Time.......................			Time.......................			

Before taking the test read pamphlets DLG68 "Heavy Goods Vehicle Driving Test" and DL68 "Your Driving Test and How to Pass". They will help you. Copies can be obtained free from your Traffic Area Office.
AT THE TIME OF THE TEST YOU MUST HOLD A CURRENT HGV DRIVER'S LICENCE AND A CURRENT
ORDINARY DRIVING LICENCE.
I APPLY for a Heavy Goods Vehicle Driving Test Appointment and enclose a *PO/Cheque (No. ....)

Date.................... Signature..

If you have not received a card notifying you of details of your appointment within 21 days of applying for your test,
you should inform as soon as possible the Clerk to the Traffic Commissioners at the address to which you sent the application form.

1.   Details of Applicant (Answer in BLOCK CAPITALS)

Surname (*Mr, Mrs, Miss, Ms)

First, Christian or other names

Home
Telephone Number

Employer's or Office
Telephone Number

Type of ordinary driver's licence held *FULL / PROVISIONAL
DRIVER NUMBER | | | | | | | | | | | | |

Details of physical disabilities, if any. If none, state NONE.

Address...
....
....
..............Postcode..

Type of HGV Driver's Licence held *FULL/PROVISIONAL
State serial number of licence...................................

Groups covered..

2.   Details of Test Appointment. See Note 3.

Centre at which you
wish to be tested   1. ....

If possible, give an
alternative   2. ....

Specific dates or periods when you will NOT be available for the test.

Particulars of last HGV Driving Test, if any.

Earliest date you will be ready for the test

Cross out days or parts of days when you will be UNABLE to
attend.
Monday   am/pm   Thursday   am/pm
Tuesday   am/pm   Friday   am/pm
Wednesday   am/pm

Date..
Place...

3.   Particulars of the vehicle to be used for the test — See Notes 4 and 5.

Class (Note 4)	Make	Seating capacity of the cab (including driver)	Type of body or semi-trailer (e.g. drop-side, tanker, box-van, etc.)
IF ARTICULATED, is unladen weight of tractive unit over 2 tons YES/NO*	IF RIGID, state: plated gross weight.................. kgs		Please write your name and full address including postcode using BLOCK CAPITALS
State train weight.................. kgs	unladen weight.................. kgs		....
Overall length. If articulated overall length of tractive unit and semi-trailer	Overall Width	Overall Height	....
.... *ft/mtrs .... in/cm	.... *ft/mtrs .... in/cm	.... *ft/mtrs .... in/cm	....

*Please delete as necessary

DLG 26
(Revised January 1987)

Printed in the UK for HMSO
D.8896574 65M 1/87 CTW&SL

DTp HGV test application form

Notes for Guidance

1 The fee for the heavy goods vehicle driving test should be remitted by cheque or Postal Order made payable to the 'Department of Transport' and crossed. NOTES OR COINS SHOULD NOT BE SENT. If you use a Postal Order you should fill in and retain the counterfoil until you have received your appointment card.

2 Send the completed form with the fee to the Clerk to the Traffic Commissioners. The addresses of the Traffic Area Offices and a list of the heavy goods vehicle driving test centres in each Area are shown below.

3 You are advised to cross out as few days as possible when answering question 2. The test will last approximately one and a half hours.

4 You must supply a suitable UNLADEN vehicle comprised in the class you wish to be tested for. The different classes of heavy goods vehicles and the vehicles comprised in each class are shown in the table below. The tractive unit of an articulated vehicle is NOT a suitable vehicle for a driving test in Classes 2, 2A, 3 and 3A. The train weight is that of the tractive unit and semi-trailer only. In the case of a rigid vehicle, the plated gross weight is either the "gross weight not to be exceeded in Great Britain" shown on the DOE (or MOT) plate, or, if the vehicle has not yet been plated by the Department, on the manufacturers' plate. If your vehicle is unplated, enter its unladen weight in the space provided. Where a vehicle is fitted with two wheels in line transversely and the distance between the centres of their respective areas of contact with the road is less than 18 inches (457 mm) they are regarded as only one wheel.

If you pass the heavy goods vehicle driving test you will be considered competent to drive vehicles in the same class as the vehicle on which you were tested. You will also be able to drive vehicles in any class or classes shown opposite that class in the third column of the table below. If, therefore you want to hold a licence to drive all types of heavy goods vehicles you will need to take a test on a Class 1 Vehicle.

Class	Vehicle	Additional Classes covered by the Licence
1	An articulated vehicle combination, not with automatic transmission.	1A, 2, 2A, 3 and 3A
1A	An articulated vehicle combination, with automatic transmission.	2A and 3A
2	A heavy goods vehicle not with automatic transmission, other than an articulated vehicle combination, designed and constructed to have more than four wheels in contact with the road surface.	2A, 3 and 3A
2A	A heavy goods vehicle with automatic transmission, other than an articulated vehicle combination, designed and constructed to have more than four wheels in contact with the road surface.	3A
3	A heavy goods vehicle not with automatic transmission, other than an articulated vehicle combination, designed and constructed to have not more than four wheels in contact with the road surface.	3A
3A	A heavy goods vehicle with automatic transmission, other than an articulated vehicle combination, designed and constructed to have not more than four wheels in contact with the road surface.	—

5 If you decide to bring a different vehicle to the centre from the one described in answer to question 3 you should inform the Traffic Area Office in good time. This will avoid any delay when you arrive for your test.

6 Notify the Traffic Area Office immediately if you change your address before your test.

Penalty—An applicant who for the purpose of obtaining a heavy goods vehicle driver's licence knowingly makes a false statement is liable to a fine not exceeding £1000.

Traffic Area Offices and Testing Centres

Traffic Area	Traffic Area Office Address	Heavy Goods Vehicle Driving Test Centre
North Eastern (Newcastle)	Westgate House, Westgate Road, Newcastle upon Tyne, NE1 1TW	Berwick, Darlington, Newcastle.
North Eastern (Leeds)	386 Harehills Lane, Leeds LS9 6NF.	Beverley, Grimsby, Keighley, Leeds, Sheffield, Walton (York).
North Western	Portcullis House, Seymour Grove, Stretford, Manchester M16 0NE	Bredbury (Manchester), Caernarfon, Carlisle, Heywood (Manchester), Kirkham (Preston), Simonswood (Liverpool), Wirral (Birkenhead), Wrexham.
West Midland	Cumberland House, 200 Broad Street, Birmingham B15 1TD	Featherstone (Wolverhampton), Garretts Green (Birmingham), Shrewsbury, Swynnerton (Stoke-on-Trent).
Eastern (Nottingham)	Birkbeck House, 14-16 Trinity Square, Nottingham NG1 4BA.	Alvaston (Derby), Leicester, Watnall (Nottingham), Weedon.
Eastern (Cambridge)	Terrington House, 13-15 Hills Road, Cambridge CB2 1NP.	Chelmsford, Ipswich, Leighton Buzzard, Norwich, Peterborough, Waterbeach (Cambridge).
South Wales	Caradog House, 1-6 St. Andrews Place, Cardiff, Glamorgan CF1 3PW.	Llantrisant, Neath, Pontypool, Templeton (Haverfordwest).
Western	The Gaunts' House, Denmark Street, Bristol BS1 5DR.	Bristol, Camborne, Chiseldon (Swindon), Exeter, Gloucester, Plymouth, Poole, Taunton.
South Eastern	Ivy House, 3 Ivy Terrace, Eastbourne, BN21 4QT.	Canterbury, Culham, Gillingham, Hastings, Isle of Wight, Lancing, Reading, Southampton.
Metropolitan	PO Box 643, Government Buildings, Bromyard Avenue, Acton, London W3.	Croydon, Enfield, Guildford, Purfleet, Yeading.
Scottish	83 Princes Street, Edinburgh EH2 2ER	Aberdeen, Bishopbriggs (Glasgow), Drem, Dumfries, Elgin (Keith), Galashiels, Inverness, Kilmarnock, Kirkwall, Lerwick, Livingstone (Edinburgh), Machrihanish (Kintyre), Oban, Perth, Port Ellen, Stornoway, Wick.

DTp HGV test application form (continued)

The test is in three parts:

1. A test of the driver's ability to control the vehicle in a confined space. This part of the test is conducted at the test centre on a special area of about 300 ft x 60 ft in size.
2. A drive over a route covering various road and traffic conditions. During this part of the test (which lasts about one hour) the examiner will ask the candidate to carry out several special exercises.
3. A test of the candidate's knowledge of the Highway Code, including questions about the traffic signs and road markings. The examiner will also ask questions relating to the mechanical operation of the vehicle and to the correct action to take in the event of a fault developing in components affecting the safe operation of the vehicle.

Manoeuvring Tests

Reversing – the candidate is expected to drive in reverse along a course marked out by cones, involving the use of right and left steering lock, finally finishing in a bay 1 ½ times the width of the vehicle. The object of the exercise is to complete the manoeuvre smoothly, without touching any of the cones and to stop with the extreme rear of the vehicle within a 3-ft marked area. Throughout the exercise the driver should maintain all-round observation.

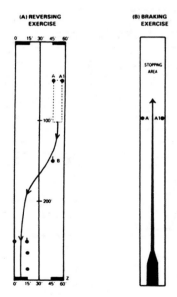

HGV driving test manoeuvres

Braking – the candidate drives forward over a distance of about 200 ft to a speed of about 20 mph. After passing the marker cones he applies the brakes, stopping the vehicle as quickly as possible, with safety, under full control.

On The Road

During the 'on road' section of the test the candidate will be asked to carry out various exercises together with normal driving over a route of approximately 25 miles. These include an uphill and downhill start and a gear change exercise. In order to show that *all* gears can be used when necessary the driver is required to demonstrate progressive downward gear changes until the lowest has been selected. During this exercise it is not necessary to use any auxillary transmission systems.

Depending on the size of the vehicle used for the test, some degree of tolerance in positioning before and after turning is permitted. However, care must be exercised so as not to endanger or inconvenience other road users.

For candidates who hold a full ordinary licence the test route may include a section of motorway driving.

Oral Test

The examiner tests the candidate's knowledge of the Highway Code by asking a series of questions and showing examples of road signs and markings.

Candidates are also tested on their knowledge of the correct action to be taken in the event of a fault developing which would affect the safe operation of the vehicle. The test includes questions on safe loading, load distribution and safety checks which should be carried out.

Drivers of articulated vehicles may be asked questions on the procedures for uncoupling and re-coupling a semi-trailer.

At the end of the test the successful candidate is given a DLG23 (Pass Certificate). The pass certificate and provisional HGV licence may then be exchanged for a full HGV licence for the appropriate class of vehicle. A driver who holds a provisional ordinary licence will also be issued with a D10 pass certificate which permits him to obtain a Group A licence without having to take an ordinary driving test.

The unsuccessful candidate is issued with a DLG24 (Statement of Failure Guidance Notes). On this form the examiner will have marked the points which require particular attention. An application for re-test may be made at once – unlike the car test there is no requirement to wait one calendar month before taking another test. However, if the test was for both an ordinary licence and an HGV licence the one-month rule would apply.

The PSV Driving Test

PSV driving tests are conducted at HGV test centres by HGV examiners. The purpose of the test is to assess the driver's competence to drive a public service vehicle in a manner which shows consideration for the safety and comfort of passengers and without danger to others. The safety and comfort of passengers should be reflected in the candidate's smooth use of the controls and steering. Candidates should not strike the kerb nor mount the pavement unless this is necessary due to the large size of the vehicle combined with a restricted space in which to manoeuvre. Under such circumstances it must be *safe* and executed sympathetically.

Department of Transport   DLG1 (08/88)

Application for a
Heavy Goods Vehicle
Driver's Licence –
Please tick the appropriate boxes

For office use only

■ **Personal information**

1 Surname.. Mr ☐ Mrs ☐ Miss ☐ Other title? ☐

  Forenames in full.. Date of birth ☐☐ 19☐☐

2 Permanent address in Great Britain ....
  ....
  ....
  ....Postcode...
  Telephone number (home)..................................(business)..........................

3 Are you applying through an Armed Forces unit, with a view to driving as a member of it?

  Yes ☐   No ☐

  If 'yes' what is the name of your unit? ....

  Its address? ....
  ....Postcode...

■ **Details of other licences**

4 Please enclose your ordinary driving licence and give following details:

  Driver number ☐☐☐☐☐ ☐☐☐☐☐ ☐☐☐☐ Issue No ☐☐

  Full ☐ or provisional ☐ Valid from .... to ....

  If full, groups you are licensed to drive ....

5 Have you held a British or Northern Ireland, hgv or psv, driver's licence before?

  Yes ☐   No ☐

  If 'yes', state for each type of licence

	hgv	psv
● in which Traffic Area		
● in what year granted		
● licence number, if known		

1

DTp HGV licence application form

6 Have you ever been refused a hgv or psv driver's licence or had such a licence suspended or revoked?

Yes ☐   No ☐

If 'yes', state for each type of licence

		hgv	psv
• in which Traffic Area(s)			
• in what year(s)			

■ **Licence applied for** *(see notes 2 — 5)*

7 What type of hgv driver's licence are you applying for?   provisional ☐   or full ☐

8 If applying for a full licence, and you have passed a hgv driving test since your last licence was granted, please tick this box ☐ and enclose the test pass certificate.

9 On what date do you want your hgv driver's licence to begin? ....

■ **Details of convictions** *(see note 9)*

10 In the space provided below, give details of any driving convictions:

    • in the last 4 years, for offences which involved the endorsement of your licence;

    • in the last 4 years*, for which you were fined or imprisoned for offences relating to drivers' hours and records or the roadworthiness or loading of vehicles;

    • which in the last 11 years involved the endorsement of your licence for driving or attempting to drive under the influence of drink or drugs or driving or attempting to drive with a blood/alcohol concentration above the prescribed limit;

    • for which you have been imprisoned for a period of more than 2½ years;

*2½ years if you were under 17 years of age at the time of conviction.

Date of conviction	Court	Offence	Sentence (including period of disqualification if any)
(a)			
(b)			
(c)			
(d)			

2

DTp HGV licence application form (continued)

■ **Medical Information** *(see note 7)*

11 Have you ever had:-	Yes No		Yes No
● any heart condition	☐ ☐	● any epileptic attack, stroke or loss of consciousness	☐ ☐
● loss of sight in one eye, cataract or double or tunnel vision	☐ ☐	● a drink problem or drug addiction	☐ ☐

12 Are you being treated for:-	Yes No		Yes No
● angina	☐ ☐	● diabetes, with insulin injections	☐ ☐
● mental or nervous disorder	☐ ☐		

13 If you answered YES in any of the boxes opposite questions 11 and 12, or if you have any other medical condition affecting your driving, please give particulars here —

....

....

....

and give the name and address of your present doctor or group practice:

....

....

....

■ **Application and declaration**

I apply for a heavy goods vehicle driver's licence and enclose (see notes overleaf) —

                                  tick

- ● my ordinary driving licence ☐
- ● my last British or Northern Ireland hgv driver's licence ☐
- ● hgv driving test pass certificate ☐
- ● completed medical report form ☐

- ● * † cheque/postal order no.   for £
  (crossed and made payable to Department of Transport)
*Do not enclose cash

† *If you are a member of the Armed Forces, and require the licence for driving in the service of the Crown, please delete these words and pass this application to your unit chief clerk, who will send it to the South Eastern Traffic Area Office.*

- ● I consent to my doctors and specialists giving confidential reports to the Medical Advisor, Department of Transport, if any matter affecting my fitness to drive arises in connection with this application or during the 3 years that this licence (when granted) will be in force; and to his advising the licensing authorities on my fitness to hold the ordinary, psv, or hgv driver's licence.

- ● I declare that I have checked my answers to the questions on this form, and that to the best of my knowledge and belief they are true.

Applicant's signature...

Date...

WARNING
You are liable to prosecution if you knowingly make a false statement to obtain a driving licence. So is anyone else who knowingly makes a false statement to help you obtain one.

■ **FINAL CHECK**

To avoid delay in the issue of your licence, make sure you have answered all the questions correctly and that you are sending all the required enclosures. Send your application to your local Traffic Area Office, not DVLC.

3

DTp HGV licence application form (continued)

■ Notes

1 When you have completed this form and obtained any other documents required for your application, send it (unless you are applying as a member of the Armed Forces through your unit) to the Traffic Commissioner for the Traffic Area in which you live. The counties and regions in each area are listed in leaflet DLG 100

2 Be sure to apply in good time for your licence — it cannot be back-dated. You may apply up to two months before you want it to begin.

3 If you are renewing a current licence be sure to apply before it expires. This will keep it in force until your application is dealt with.

4 You may apply for a full licence for the class of hgv for which

— you passed the British driving test in the past 5 years or
— you held a British or Northern Ireland licence within the past 5 years or
— you qualify under the European Community exchange provisions — see leaflet DLG 100

5 Six classes of hgv driver's licence are issued. Class 1 covers all hgvs. Class 2 is valid for all except articulated vehicles. Class 3 is valid for non-articulated hgvs with only two axles. Classes 1A, 2A and 3A are similar, but for vehicles with automatic transmission only. Full definitions are in leaflet DLG 100.

6 The minimum age for driving a hgv is 21, unless you are applying as a member of either the Armed Forces in order to drive for Crown purposes; or of the young hgv drivers' training scheme, in which case a special application form is obtainable through the registered employer.

7 You cannot obtain a licence if you have had any epileptic attack since you reached the age of 5. In other cases the Traffic Commissioner may need to make enquiries about your medical fitness.

8 A medical report, on form DTp 20003, must be submitted with your first application for a hgv driver's licence and with every renewal from the age of 60. A report must not be dated more than 3 months before the licence is to start.

9 Question 10 takes account of the provisions of the Rehabilitation of Offenders Act 1974. For further details, consult a legal advisory service or see Home Office leaflet Wiping the Slate Clean.

10 Information about the current fees for provisional, full and also for exchange and duplicate licences is obtainable from Traffic Area Offices. A full licence is valid for 3 years. A provisional licence is valid for 6 months. If a full licence is exchanged for one showing an additional group, this will run for the balance of the original licence period.

11 Further information about hgv drivers' licences is in leaflet DLG 100, obtainable from Traffic Area Offices of the Department of Transport.

DTp HGV licence application form (continued)

Public Service Vehicle Driver Licensing

For official use only

Application for a Public Service Vehicle (PSV) Driving Test Appointment

Please read the notes overleaf carefully before completing this form
Please tick the boxes below as appropriate

Date	Month	Year	Date	Month	Year	Date	Month	Year	FTA
Time			Time			Time			
Place			Place			Place			

1. Details of applicant *(BLOCK LETTERS)*

Surname (*Mr, Mrs, Miss)

Christian or other names

Telephone Numbers:
Home   Work

Address

_____ Postcode

2. Please state details of ORDINARY DRIVING LICENCE *(see note 1)*

Driver number: The Licence is   ☐ PROVISIONAL

                                  ☐ FULL for Group(s)

3. Details of the Test Appointment. *See Note 3.*

| Centre at which you wish to be tested | 1. |
| If possible, give an alternative | 2. |
| Specific dates or periods when you will NOT be available for the test. |

Earliest date you will be ready for the test

Cross out days or parts of days when you will be UNABLE to attend.

Monday   am/pm   Thursday   am/pm
Tuesday   am/pm   Friday   am/pm
Wednesday   am/pm

Particulars of last PSV Test, if any.   Date
                                             Place

4. Particulars of vehicle to be used for the test:

a. Category *(tick one box only after reading note 3 carefully):*

	Manual		Automatic
Double decker	1 ☐	1A ☐
Single decker longer than 8.5m	2 ☐	2A ☐
Single decker between 5.5m and 8.5m in length	3 ☐	3A ☐
Single decker no longer than 5.5m	4 ☐	4A ☐

b. Make and model
c. Overall dimensions: length   width   height

I enclose a *postal order/cheque for £_____ payable to the Department of Transport and crossed "A/C Payee" *(see note 4).*

Signature_____ Date_____

Please return the completed form to the address overleaf (NOT DVLC)

IMPORTANT
VEHICLE TO BE USED FOR THE TEST

Will the Examiner have a clear view through the rear of the test vehicle from the lower deck and at the same time be in a position to observe the driver?   YES ☐ NO ☐

Please delete as necessary

PSV 447
(Aug 1986)

(Please write your name and full address bellow including postcode using BLOCK CAPITALS)

Printed in the UK for HMSO

A PSV test application form

NOTES TO HELP YOU

1.   Question 2. If you do not hold a full "ordinary" driving licence in Group A or B (or if you hold one in Group B but wish to take your test on a manual vehicle) the test will be conducted as a "dual" test to qualify you for both the ordinary and the PSV licence. There is no extra fee for this. If your ordinary licence (full or provisional) is in your possession you should bring it to the test.

2.   Question 3. The test will last approximately 1½hrs. You are advised to cross out as few days as possible.

3.   Question 4. a. You should make sure the vehicle you bring is in the right category for the licence you want. The number of the box you tick for this question should be the same as the category number below:

		Manual and automatic	Automatic only
Any size of PSV	Category	1	1A
Single deck PSV of any length		2	2A
Single deck PSV no longer than 8.5m		3	3A
Single deck PSV no longer than 5.5m		4	4A

b.   Transmission is regarded as **automatic** if the driver is not provided with any means whereby he may, independently of the use of the accelerator or the brakes, vary gradually the proportion of the power being produced by the engine which is transmitted to the road wheels of the vehicle.

c.   If you have any doubts about the suitability of your vehicle for the test, particularly if it is not a PSV with a certificate of initial fitness, please get in touch with this office without delay. Your vehicle must be roadworthy, display a valid vehicle excise licence (road tax disc) and be insured against third-party risks.

4.   **Fees.** The current fee for the test is £............ It must be paid in advance by cheque or postal order made out to the Department of Transport and crossed "A/C Payee". It is refundable only if:

a.   The test does not take place, and the reason for this is not attributable either to yourself or to your vehicle.

b.   You cancel the test appointment giving this office at least 3 clear working days' notice (excluding Saturday, Sunday and bank or public holidays) between the day that this office receives the cancellation and the day of your test appointment.

If you need to take more than one test you must pay the fee at each attempt.

5.   Please contact this office if you have not received your PSV driving test appointment card within 21 days.

A PSV test application form (continued)

PSV 150 (8/87)

For office use only
Badge:

1 Surname .... Mr ☐ Mrs ☐ Miss ☐ Other title? ☐

   Forenames in full .... Date of birth ☐ | | 19, |

2 Permanent address in Great Britain ....

   ....

   .... Postcode ....

   Telephone number (home) .... (business) ....

3 Please enclose your British ordinary driving licence and give the following details:

   Driver number ☐ | | | | | | | | | | | | Issue No ☐

   Full ☐ or provisional ☐   Valid from................   to ....

   If full, groups you are licensed to drive ....

4 Do you currently hold a British psv driver's licence, or have you held one in the past 5 years?

   Yes ☐   No ☐ ▷ Go to question 8

   Go to question 5

5 State for your current psv driver's licence, or if you have no current licence, you last licence:

   ● the number with initial letter ....

   ● the date of expiry...

6 State the initial letter(s) and the number of your badge: ☐ ☐ | | | | | |

7 Do you wish to be licensed to drive any type or types of vehicles other than those you were previously licensed to drive?

   Yes ☐   No ☐

   If yes, please write the category required here ☐ —see note 7
   Now go to question 11

DTp PSV licence application form

New Application *(See notes 5 and 6)*

8　Write here the category of licence which you require (see note 7).

9　Have you held a psv or hgv licence before?　Yes ☐　No ☐

	psv	hgv
If yes, give details for the latest of each type ● in which Traffic Area...........		
● the licence number (if known)........		
● year when granted (if known).......		

10　Have you ever been refused a psv or hgv driver's licence or had such a licence suspended or revoked?

Yes ☐　No ☐

	psv	hgv
If 'yes', give details for each type ● in which Traffic Area..........		
● in what year it happened..........		

Now go to question 11.

11　In the space below, give details of any court sentences involving:
  ● licence endorsement for a driving offence related to drink or drugs in the last 11 years, or for any other driving offence in the last 4 years
  ● a sentence of imprisonment of more than 2½ years at any time, of between 6 and 30 months in the past 10* years, or of up to 6 months in the last 7* years
  ● a fine or community service order in the last 5* years

  * half these periods if you were under 17 at the time

Date of conviction	Court	Offence	Sentence (including period of disqualification if any)
(a)			
(b)			
(c)			
(d)			

DTp PSV licence application form (continued)

Medical Information *(See note 9)*

12 Have you ever had:	Yes	No		Yes	No
● any heart condition	☐	☐	● any epileptic attack, stroke or loss of consciousness	☐	☐
● loss of sight in one eye, cataract or double or tunnel vision	☐	☐	● a drink problem or drug addiction	☐	☐

13 Are you being treated for:	Yes	No		Yes	No
● angina	☐	☐	● diabetes, with insulin injections	☐	☐
● mental or nervous disorder	☐	☐			

14 If you answered YES in any of the boxes opposite questions 12 and 13, or if you have any other medical condition affecting your driving, please give particulars here —

....

....

....

and give the name and address of your present
doctor or group practice: ....

....

....

I apply for a public service vehicle driver's licence and enclose (see notes overleaf) —

tick

● my ordinary driving licence ☐

● my last British or Northern Ireland psv driver's licence ☐

● psv driving test application or pass certificate ☐

● completed medical report form ☐

● * cheque/postal order no.   for £
(crossed and made payable to the Traffic Commissioner)

* Do not enclose cash

I consent to my doctors and specialists giving confidential reports to the Medical Advisor, Department of Transport, if any matter affecting my fitness to drive arises in connection with this application or during the 5 years that this licence (when granted) will be in force; and to his advising the licensing authorities on my fitness to hold the ordinary, psv, or hgv driver's licence.

I declare that I have checked the answers to the questions on this form, and that to the best of my knowledge and belief they are true.

Applicant's signature ....

Date ....

WARNING

You are liable to prosecution if you knowingly make a false statement to obtain a driving licence. So is anyone who knowingly makes a false statement to help you obtain one.

FINAL CHECK

To avoid delay in the issue of your licence, make sure you have answered all the questions correctly and that you are sending all the required enclosures. Send you application to you local Traffic Area Office, not DVLC.

DTp PSV licence application form (continued)

▉ Notes

1. When you have completed your application form you should sent it to the Traffic Commissioner for the Traffic Area in which you live (see under Transport, Department of, in your telephone directory).

2. Be sure to apply in good time for your licence — it cannot be backdated. You may apply up to two months before you want it to begin.

3. If you are renewing a current licence be sure to apply before it expires. This will keep it in force until your application is dealt with.

4. You should apply for **renewal** if you have held a British psb driver's licence within the past 5 years.

5. You should make a new application if:

   • you have never held a British psv driver's licence

   • your last such licence expired more than 5 years ago.

6. You should also enclose an application for a psv driving test (form PSV 447) or test pass certificate unless:

   • You are **renewing** for the same categories as before or

   • you are making a **new** application and

      have held a Northern Ireland PSV 2,3 or 4 licence with in the last 5 years or

      have an exchangeable licence from another part of the European Community and can provide evidence of recent psv driving experience — ask you Traffic Area Office for details and form DTp 200048.

7. Nine categories of psv drivers' licences are issued. Category 1 covers all psvs. Categories 2, 3 and 4 are for single deckers only. Category 3 psvs are up to 8.5m (27ft 11 in), category 4 up to 5.5m (18ft) in length. Categories 1A, 2A, 3A and 4A are similar, but for vehicles with automatic transmission only. Category 4B licences carry other kinds of restriction.

8. Question 11 takes account of the provisions of the Rehabilitation of Offenders Act 1974. For further details, consult a legal advisory service or see Home Office leaflet Wiping the Slate Clean.

9. You cannot obtain a licence if you have had any epileptic attack since you reached the age of 5. In other cases the Traffic Commissioner may need to make enquiries about you medical fitness.

10. A medical report, on form DTp 20003, must be submitted with your first application for a psv driver's licence and with every renewal from the age of 46.

11. Normally, you must be at least 21 years old to drive vehicles adapted to carry more than 8 passengers. But a person who is 18 or over may hold a licence to drive a public service vehicle as follows:

    • when driving **without** passengers or

    • on a regular service where the route length does not exceed (31 miles) or

    • a vehicle constructed and equipped for not more than 14 passengers on journeys within the UK.

12. Information about current fees for licences is obtainable from Traffic Area Offices. A licence runs for 5 years from the date of first issue or subsequent renewal.

DTp PSV licence application form (continued)

Department of Transport

Medical Report

on an applicant for a Heavy Goods Vehicle or Public Service Vehicle Driver's Licence

Notes

- For the applicant (Part A): read the notes on the back of this form before you go to your doctor.

  This medical report cannot be issued free of charge as part of the National Health Service. The applicant must pay the medical practitioner's fee, unless other arrangements have been made. The Licensing Authority accepts no liability to pay it. If in doubt as to your fitness, talk to your doctor before the examination or write to Drivers Medical Branch, DVLC, Swansea SA1 1TU.

- For the medical practitioner. (Part B)

  (a) When completing this medical report, please have regard to the "Notes for Guidance" (1983 edition) published by the British Medical Association for doctors conducting these examinations, supplemented if necessary by the booklet "Medical Aspects of Fitness to Drive", published by the Medical Commission for Accident Prevention (1985 edition).

  (b) Please tick the answers that apply. Use the right hand margin if you want to add anything or write "see note attached" and use a separate sheet of paper.

  (c) This report is part of the application for a licence. The Traffic Area Office may ask the Department's medical adviser to make further enquiries if there is any doubt as to the applicant's fitness.

Part A — Information about the applicant.

1. Full name (in BLOCK CAPITALS)...

2. Address...

   ....

   Postcode.. Tel No (home).. (work)................................

3. Date of birth...(Day)..(Month)...........................(Year)

4. Name and address of your present general practitioner or of the group practice with which you have been registered for the last 12 months.

   Name..

   Address...

   ....

   .... Postcode..

5. I hereby give my consent to my doctors and specialists giving reports about my medical condition to the Medical Adviser to the Traffic Commissioner in connection with the licence I am applying for.

   Applicant's signature...
   (Please sign in the presence of the medical practitioner who signs the report (Part B)).

DTp 20003 (3/86)

DTp HGV/PSV medical form

Part B — Medical Report

1. Cardiovascular	Yes	No	Notes
(a) Is there any history of cardiac infarction (coronary thrombosis), any recurring anginal pain, or any current need of treatment for anginal pain?	☐	☐	
(b) Is there any other evidence of ischaemic heart disease?	☐	☐	
(c) Is there any history or evidence of arrhythmia (excluding extrasystoles rated as non-pathological by cardiologist)?	☐	☐	
(d) Is the systolic blood pressure over 200 or the diastolic over 110?	☐	☐	
(e) Is hypertension treated by medication other than a diuretic or beta blocker?	☐	☐	
(f) Is a cardiac pacemaker fitted?	☐	☐	
(g) Is there a history of current intermittent claudication?	☐	☐	
(h) Is there a history of open heart or arterial surgery?	☐	☐	

2. Endocrine System			
Is the applicant a diabetic requiring treatment by insulin injection?	☐	☐	

3. Epilepsy			
Has the applicant suffered any attack of epilepsy since attaining the age of 5 years?	☐	☐	

4. Nervous System			
(a) Is there any progressive disorder of the nervous system?	☐	☐	
(b) Is there any history of one or more transient ischaemic attacks or cerebrovascular accidents?	☐	☐	
(c) Is there a history of a severe head injury or craniotomy?	☐	☐	
(d) Is there any hearing defect to the extent of preventing communication by telephone?	☐	☐	

5. Psychiatric Illness			
(a) Is there a history of psychosis?	☐	☐	
(b) Is there abuse of alcohol or drugs?	☐	☐	
(c) Has the applicant suffered from any mental disorder requiring psychotropic medication during the last 6 months?	☐	☐	

DTp HGV/PSV medical form (continued)

		Yes	No	Notes

6. Vision*

(If you do not have the equipment to carry out these checks, then you should refer the applicant to an ophthalmic specialist or optician.) Please test each eye separately.

(a) ● Has the applicant had a cataract removed? ☐ ☐

    ● **Without correction**, is acuity **worse** than 6/60 in either eye?§ ☐ ☐

(b) Is the visual acuity, using corrective lenses if worn,†

    ● **worse** than 6/9 in the stronger or 6/12 in the weaker eye? ☐ ☐

    ● if 'Yes', is it **worse** than 6/12 or 6/36 respectively? ☐ ☐

(c) Is there double vision or a pathological field defect? ☐ ☐

* See also note 3 overleaf.
§ Please state if either eye has no vision.
† Please state if contact lenses are worn.

---

7. Musculoskeletal System

Has the applicant any deformity, loss of members, or physical disability (with special attention paid to the condition of the arms, legs, hands, and joints) which is likely to interfere with the efficient discharge of his or her duties as a vocational driver? ☐ ☐

If 'Yes', please specify.

---

8. Other Conditions

Does the applicant suffer from any disease or disability not mentioned above, which is likely to interfere with the efficient discharge of his or her duties as a driver, or to cause driving by him or her on a vocational licence to be a source of danger to the public? ☐ ☐

If 'Yes', please specify.

Signed.. Name...Date...................
Registered medical practitioner.   (in BLOCK CAPITALS)

Address...

....

.... Postcode...................... Telephone number....................................

DTp HGV/PSV medical form (continued)

NOTES FOR APPLICANTS (please read these before you go to your doctor)

1 **By law**:

— you cannot have a heavy goods or public service vehicle driver's licence if you have had even one epileptic attack since you reached the age of 5;

— the Traffic Commissioner has to be satisfied that you are fit to hold this licence, having regard to your health and any disability which you may suffer;

— you must tell the Drivers Medical Branch, DVLC, Swansea SA1 1TU, at once if you have any disability (this includes any physical or mental condition) that affects your fitness as a driver — or may do so in the future. (Conditions not expected to last more than three months do not count.)

2 **Medical standards for hgv and psv drivers** are higher than for those who hold only the ordinary driving licence. Hgv and psv drivers' licences may be refused if, for example:

— you have had a coronary thrombosis or heart surgery;

— you suffer problems with heart rhythm or have a disease of the heart or arteries;

— you are treated with certain drugs for high blood pressure;

— you need injections of insulin for diabetes;

— you have had a stroke, unexplained loss of consciousness, severe head injury with continuing after-effects, or major brain surgery;

— you suffer from Parkinson's disease or multiple sclerosis;

— you are being treated for mental or nervous problems;

— you have had drink or drug problems or suffered mental illness in recent years;

— your hearing is so bad that you cannot use the telephone in an emergency;

— you have any other condition which makes vocational driving inadvisable.

3. In addition,

— you should be able to see with both eyes and not suffer from double or tunnel vision or other eye trouble which might make you unfit to drive vocationally;

— **if you already held a hgv or psv driver's licence before 1 January 1983**, you should be able to read the sight chart as far as 6/12 with your better eye and 6/36 with your worse eye, with the help of glasses or contact lenses if worn; if you have had a cataract operation or wear contact lenses, you must be able to read at least as far as 6/60 with each eye without corrective lenses.

— **if your first hgv or psv driver's licence is dated on or after 1 January 1983**, you should be able to read the sight chart as far as 6/9 with your better eye and 6/12 with your worse eye, with the help of glasses or contact lenses if worn; and at least as far as 6/60 with each eye without any such correction.

DTp HGV/PSV medical form (continued)

Application for a PSV test must normally be accompanied by a medical report form and by an application for a full PSV licence. Before granting a licence the commissioners have to be satisfied not only that the applicant can drive to a sufficiently high standard but also that he is medically fit and of good character. For example, the applicant's previous driving history and offences related to drivers hours and/or loading of vehicles may be taken into account when considering the issue of a PSV or HGV licence.

Drivers applying for their first PSV licence should apply to the Traffic Commissioners for the area in which the applicant lives and must send:

1. PSV licence application form (PSV150) and the fee of £22.50.
2. Medical report form (DT20003).
3. PSV driving test application form (PSV447) and the fee of £42.
4. Ordinary driving licence (full or provisional).

Application should be made well in advance of the date required as a test appointment will only be allocated after all licence and medical details have been checked.

The applicant must hold an ordinary driving licence (either full or provisional). If the ordinary licence is a provisional the examiner will conduct a dual PSV and 'L' test.

When preparing for the test, the applicant should read the booklet DLP68 'The PSV Driving Test' as well as the DL68 and Highway Code. He will also need to know about:

The equipment which must by law be carried in a PSV.

The correct action to take in the event of a fault developing affecting the safe operation of the vehicle.

The conduct and responsibilities of a PSV driver (including knowledge of the regulations and the conduct of drivers, conductors and passengers).

The rules governing drivers hours and records.

The content of the PSV driving test is similar to the HGV test including the manoeuvring exercises but with several variations which are specific to PSVs. For example, a 'snatch' gear change may be needed after the uphill start. At bus stops the vehicle should be stopped with the platform or entrance positioned correctly in relation to the stopping place.

The candidate has to provide a suitable vehicle for the test and it must comply with the following requirements:

It must be thoroughly roadworthy with all stop lamps and direction indicators working correctly.

It must be properly insured and display a valid vehicle excise licence.

Seating accommodation must be provided for the examiner.

The examiner must have a clear view of the road behind without having to rely on mirrors.

The examiner must be able to speak to the driver while he is driving.

It must have enough fuel for the test of approximately 1½ hours.

Before taking the test the candidate should make sure that he knows the dimensions of the vehicle (height, width and weight) and the position of the fuel emergency cut off and fire extinguishers. He should ensure that all doors are properly closed and that any equipment carried is properly stowed and secured.

After completion of the 'on road' part of the test the examiner will ask the candidate a number of questions on:

Knowledge of the Highway Code.

Recognition of road signs and markings.

Matters which affect the safe working of the vehicle.

General theoretical knowledge of basic or special PSV subjects.

At the end of the test the examiner will tell the candidate the result and reports the result to the Traffic Commissioners who then have to decide whether to issue a licence. They take into account some of the factors discussed earlier. The successful candidate is issued with a DLP23 Pass Certificate. In the case of a 'dual' test ('L' and PSV) the examiner will issue a Certificate of Competence (D10) to drive vehicles of the group on which the test was taken.

A candidate who is unsuccessful is issued with form DLP24 (Guidance notes for unsuccessful candidates) and, if appropriate, DL24 (Statement of Failure). The examiner will mark on these forms the aspects of driving which require particular attention.

HGV/PSV Training

Training for HGV and PSV driving instructors is carried out by the Road Transport Industry Training Board at centres at High Ercall in Shropshire and at Livingstone in Scotland. Details of the facilities available may be obtained from the RTITB at Capitol House, Empire Way, Wembley, Middlesex. Tel: 01-902 8880.

The RTITB have several group training associations at centres in all areas around the country and there are many driving schools offering commercial vehicle driver training at various locations. For further information on the availability of HGV and PSV driver training facilities contact Mr J Ballantyne at Millers Transport Training, Goodwood Motor Circuit, Chichester, West Sussex; Tel: 0243 784715.

Chapter 12

Motorcycle Test

The driving test for solo motorcycle and scooter riders is in two parts. The first part is an off-road test of machine handling and the second part is carried out on the road by a Department of Transport examiner.

Motorcycle training organisations have been appointed as authorised training and testing centres. These organisations provide training courses of a standard designed to make the rider fully competent on the road. The courses offered at authorised centres prepare the rider for both parts of the test and should produce a safe and competent rider, fully aware of his responsibilities as a road user.

The Part I test can be taken at some stage during the training course and would normally be arranged by the training organisation, which has examiners as well as instructors. After passing the Part I, the rider may then apply to the Department of Transport for Part II.

Part I of the test can also be taken at one of the Department of Transport's Heavy Goods Vehicle driving test centres.

Part I

If the training is taken with an authorised centre, it will make the arrangements for Part I of the test and the fee will normally be included in the cost of the course.

If Part I of the test is to be taken with the Department of Transport the application is made on a driving test application form DL26. The fee for this application is currently £17.94 (£15.60 + VAT).

Candidates for the Part I test must show that they can control and manoeuvre a motorcycle to a satisfactory standard on an off-road area. The test comprises seven exercises. Riding faults are marked according to their degree of seriousness as single marking, double marking or serious. A total of more than seven fault marks or one or more serious faults will result in failure of the test. Seven or less marks and no serious faults means a pass.

During the first three exercises the candidate is expected to take rear observation, as when riding on the road, before moving off, before turning, and before stopping. Signals are not required during any of the exercises and, except when instructed to stop, the candidate should avoid putting a foot to the ground at any time during the test.

When the candidate has completed all the exercises the examiner asks questions relating to safe riding techniques.

After passing Part I the candidate may apply for Part II test which is conducted by DTp examiners at most driving test centres.

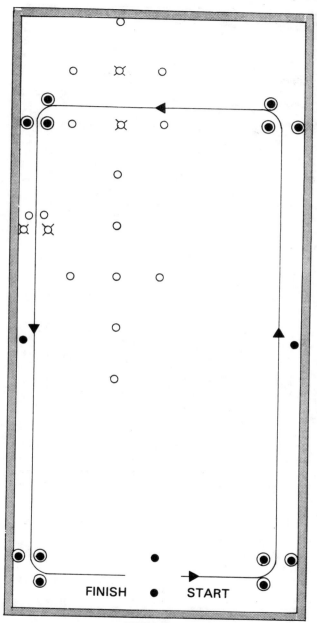

EXERCISE 1

The candidate is asked to ride around the circuit turning left between
the sets of three cones at each corner until the examiner asks him to stop.

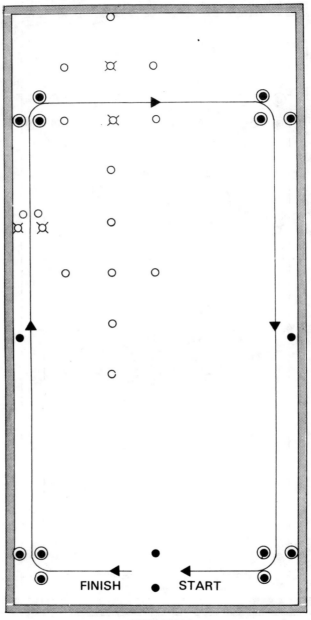

EXERCISE 2

The candidate is asked to ride around the circuit turning right between
the sets of three cones at each corner until the examiner asks him to stop.

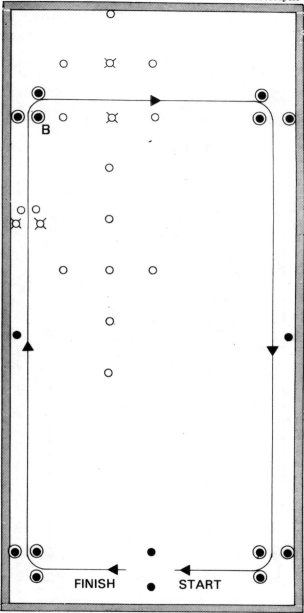

EXERCISE 3

This exercise is on the same circuit and in the same direction as Exercise 2, but the candidate is asked to stop each time at cone B as if at a junction, before riding on again.

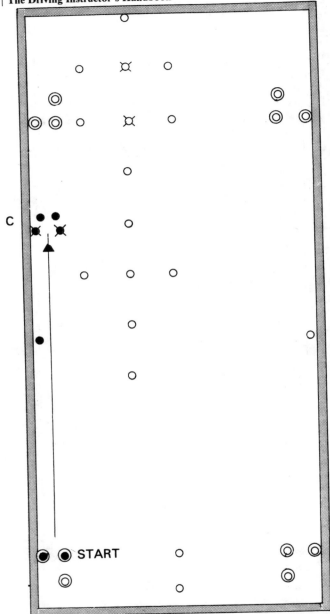

EXERCISE 4

To show that the motorcycle can be stopped under full control the candidate is asked to ride forward reaching about 15 mph and then brake, stopping with the front wheel within a box marked by four cones.

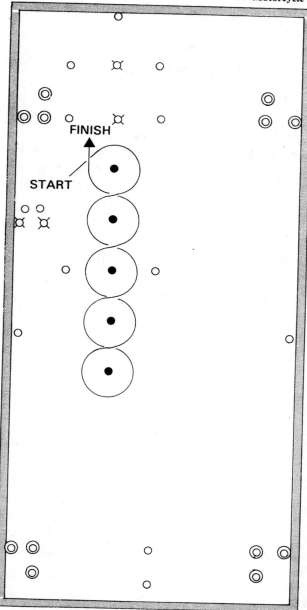

EXERCISE 5
The candidate is asked to ride in and out of a line of cones in both
directions without dismounting.

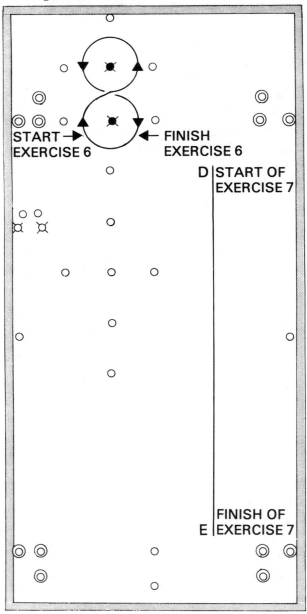

EXERCISE 6

The candidate is asked to ride in a figure of 8 around the two cones for up to three circuits without leaving the area bounded by six cones.

EXERCISE 7

This exercise simulates riding in slow moving traffic. The candidate is asked to ride alongside the examiner while he walks at a varying pace.

Department of Transport

Driving Test Report

MOTOR BICYCLE PART I

Test Centre

Date

Candidate's
full name

Name of Training Body
(if applicable)

Particulars of machine

Scooter   Motorcycle

Make

Model
or cc

Reg
Mark

Year   19

EXERCISE	1	2	3
MO PRE			
CON			
ROB			
TURNS CON			
ROB			
BAL			
STOPS CON			
ROB			
MAN ACC			

EXERCISE	4
CON	
FRONT BR	
REAR BR	
ACCURACY	

EXERCISE	5	6	7
CON			
BAL			
MAN ACC			

DL25MC

DTp motorcycle driving test (Part I)

Abbreviations used on form DL25 MC and marking of riding faults

PRE	Precautions before starting the engine	Exercises 1,2,3.
CON	Incorrect use of brakes (except exercise 4), clutch, throttle or steering	Exercises 1,2,3, 4,5,6 and 7.
	Partial loss of control	/
	Total loss of control	X
ROBS	Not taking rear observation prior to moving off, turning or stopping	/ Exercises 1,2 and 3 only.
BAL	Putting a foot down	/ Exercises 1,2, 3,5,6 and 7.
MAN ACC	Riding outside the manoeuvring area	/ Exercises 1,2 and 3.
	Not riding in a reasonably straight line	/ Exercise 7 only.
	Touching or diplacing a cone and keeping on its correct side	// Exercises 1,2, 3,5 and 6.
	Riding on the wrong side of a cone. (This may or may not entail touching or displacing the cone.)	X Exercises 1,2, 3,5 or 6.
FRONT BR	Not making effective use of front brake.	/ Exercise 4.
REAR BR	Not making effective use of rear brake	/ Exercise 4.
	Stopping by use of either front or rear brake only, or losing control	X Exercise 4.
ACCURACY	Stopping with the front wheel partially outside the stopping area	/ Exercise 4.
	Completely outside	X Exercise 4.

If the Part I test is failed the examiner issues a form detailing the reasons for failure. Unlike some other driving tests you do not have to wait a calendar month before taking the test again.

Part II Test

A new style on-road accompanied rider test was introduced in October 1989 and is now available at 240 centres. In most areas the test is conducted with the examiner accompanying the candidate on another motorcycle, although in areas of low demand the accompanying vehicle may be a motor car.

The examiner maintains contact with the candidate and gives directions by way of mobile radio communication equipment. Radios are worn by candidates on an adjustable waist belt, and earpieces are fitted into each rider's helmet on velcro pads. All equipment is fitted by the examiner and tested before each test is commenced. The radios allow one way communication only; the candidate is not able to talk back to the examiner. If a candidate does not understand an instruction or direction he should pull over to the side of the road.

Riders who have disabilities and those who are profoundly deaf should give full details on the application form. Riders who are unable to hear directions through an earpiece are asked by the examiner to stop from time to time and then given written route directions.

Candidates who do not speak English should ensure that this is made clear on the test application form. They should bring along an interpreter to relay instructions. The examiner will conduct the accompanied test from a car.

The test includes the same variety of road and traffic situations. There is provision for a slow ride to be included in the test if the candidate has not already demonstrated this ability during the Part I test. Candidates are also asked to complete a 'U' turn by turning the vehicle round in the road from kerb to kerb.

The Department of Transport are normally able to offer a Part II Test within four weeks of applying so that the training organisations can link training more closely to the on-road test. In the longer term, it is anticipated that a 'block booking' facility may be made available.

Moped Test

Mopeds are not included in the 'two part' test system. The moped test is conducted by Department of Transport examiners and includes a 'slow riding' exercise and an emergency stop.

Compulsory Basic Training

Provided that adequate training facilities exist throughout the country a new compulsory basic training scheme will be introduced by the middle of 1990. The new course will replace the existing Part I test and will be required as a validation of the provisional licence before the learner rider may ride on the road.

Provisional licence holders will need to complete a course of 'off- and on-' road basic training. The course will include three separate objectives:

(i) Practical on-site training – including vehicle familiarisation and basic preliminaries;

(ii) Practical on-site riding – practical instruction covering basic riding and manoeuvring exercises;

(iii) Practical on-road riding – supervised and controlled instruction including safety procedures.

Courses will also cover other important matters relating to equipment, visibility, vulnerability and speed.

Trainees will need to arrange for their motorcycles to be transported to training sites or, alternatively, will use a machine belonging to the training body.

A certificate of completion of training will be issued only when the trainee has satisfactorily completed the objectives and when the instructor is satisfied that the trainee is proficient to ride on the road unaccompanied.

Until the introduction of compulsory basic training, learner riders will need to pass Part I of the test before applying for Part II. When Part I is abolished riders will need to produce a certificate of Basic Training, or a Part I pass certificate in order to take the Accompanied Test.

Moped riders will be included in the compulsory training scheme.

Chapter 13

Advanced Driving Tests

The Institute of Advanced Motorists

The Institute was founded on 10 March 1956, for the purposes of raising driving standards and to establish an Advanced Driving Test. The Institute believes that a higher standard of behaviour by all road users, and drivers in particular, could reduce road accidents and their grim social consequences more effectively than any other method. The Advanced Driving Test offers to drivers of cars, trucks, and motorcycles an opportunity to check their own abilities under today's road conditions and membership of the Institute for those who achieve the Institute's standards then demands the responsibility that goes with proven skill.

The standard of the test is based on the police system of car control as taught in Home Office Approved Police Driving Schools. The examiners, all of whom are either serving or retired police officers, have to hold an Advanced Driving Certificate. This qualification has never been challenged by the public as it is the highest available – probably in the world. The 120 test routes are designed to provide all types of driving conditions and are about 35 miles long. The test takes one and a half hours which does not include the briefing and debriefing.

There are many books available on advanced driving, the main ones being the *Highway Code*, *Roadcraft*, the police drivers' text book and *Advanced Motoring*, the IAM's own driving manual, coupled with *Motor Cycle Roadcraft* and *Advanced Motorcycling*.

The advantages of taking an advanced test is that IAM members have a 50-75 per cent lower accident rate. Over 400 commercial concerns put their staff through the test in order to cut costs, so does the British Army. Many insurance companies grant a discount off normal motor insurance premiums of up to 20 per cent. The conviction rate among members appears to be five times lower than the public. Anyone with a full British driving licence can take the test and it is advisable to receive instruction from the ADI, preferably an IAM member, or contact the local IAM group who will give guidance in preparation for the test.

The Institute is a registered charity and receives full moral support from the Department of Transport, all UK police forces and the Ministry of Defence. The IAM motto is 'Skill with Responsibility'.

The Institute of Advanced Motorists Test

Application forms can be obtained from The Institute of Advanced Motorists, IAM House, 359 Chiswick High Road, London W4 4HS, or telephone 01-994 4403.

The cost of the test, including the first year's subscription, is £27.50. The test lasts for around 90 minutes on a route of about 35 to 40 miles covering a wide range of traffic conditions both in rural and urban roads. Candidates will be expected to make reasonable use of the vehicle's performance within the speed limits and normal parameters of safety with regard to the road, traffic and weather conditions. Candidates are expected to reverse into a side road and execute a hill start and will be assessed on their powers of observation.

The test is something which any driver with a reasonable amount of experience and skill should be able to pass without too much difficulty. Candidates do not fail for committing minor faults. Even those who do fail should learn some important lessons from the examiner conducting the test. Successful candidates may:

- display the Institute's badge on their car
- take advantage of special insurance terms
- receive 'Milestones', the motoring magazine especially written with a keen interest in driving
- join their local IAM group and participate in the road safety, driving and social events which they organise.

During the Test

Examiners look for the following points:

Acceleration – This should be smooth and progressive. It should be used at the right time and right place. Acceleration should not be excessive or insufficient.

Braking – This should be smooth and progressive. Brakes should be used in conjunction with the mirror and signals. They should not be used late or fiercely. Candidates will be expected to take account of the road conditions.

Clutch control – The engine and road speeds must be properly co-ordinated when changing gear. Candidates should not slip or ride the clutch, nor should they coast with the clutch disengaged.

Gear changing – Changes should be selected smoothly and fluently. If automatic transmission is fitted, candidates should make full use of it.

Use of gears – Candidates must make correct use of the gears. The correct gear should be selected before reaching a hazard.

Steering – The wheel should be held correctly with the hands at the quarter to three or ten to two position. The use of the crossed arm techniques, except when manoeuvring in a confined space, is not recommended by the Institute.

Seating position – Candidates should be alert and not slumped at the wheel. They should not rest an arm on the door while driving.

Observation – Candidates should read the road well ahead and anticipate the actions of other road users. They must be able to judge correctly the speeds and distances of other vehicles.

Concentration – Candidates should concentrate on the road and traffic situation and not allow themselves to be easily distracted.

Maintaining progress – With regard to the road, traffic and weather conditions, candidates should make use of their vehicle's performance by driving at a reasonable pace, maintaining good progress throughout.

Obstruction – Candidates should not obstruct other road users by driving too slowly, by positioning incorrectly on the road or by failing to anticipate and react correctly to the traffic situation ahead.

Positioning – Candidates should keep in the correct part of the road, especially when approaching and negotiating hazards.

Lane discipline – Candidates should drive in the appropriate lane and be careful not to straddle white lines.

Observation of surfaces – Candidates should continually assess the road surface, especially in poor weather, and look out for slippery conditions.

Traffic signals – Candidates must observe and respond correctly to signals, signs and road markings and extend proper courtesies at pedestrian crossings.

Speed limits and other legal requirements – Speed limits and other legal requirements must be observed at all times.

Overtaking – Candidates must overtake safely while maintaining a correct distance from other vehicles and using the mirrors, signals and gears correctly.

Hazard procedure and cornering – Candidates must have full control over their vehicle on the approach to a hazard. They must negotiate it in the correct position, driving at an appropriate speed with a suitable gear engaged.

Mirror – Candidates must use the mirrors frequently, especially before signalling and making changes to speed or course.

Signals – Signals given by direction indicator, or arm if required, should be given in the right place and in good time. The horn and headlight flasher should only be used in accordance with the Highway Code.

Restraint – Candidates should display reasonable restraint, without being indecisive.

Consideration – Candidates should extend consideration and courtesy to other road users.

Car sympathy – Candidates should not over-stress the vehicle, for example by revving the engine needlessly or by fierce braking.

Manoeuvring – This should be carried out smoothly and competently.

Reasons for Failure

78% *Hazard Procedure and Cornering:* incorrect assessment; poor safety margin; unsystematic procedure.

72% *Use of Gears:* late selection; intermediate gears not used to advantage.

70% *Positioning:* straddles lanes; incorrect for right and left turns.

60% *Braking:* late application; harsh handbrake application; braking and gearchanging simultaneous.

58% *Distance Observation:* late planning and assessment of traffic conditions.

48% *Method of Approach:* too fast; coasted to compulsory stop; off-side at 'keep left' sign.

48% *Clutch Control:* riding; slipping; coasting.

40% *Car Sympathy:* not expressed in use of clutch; brakes; gears.

38% *Gear Changing:* harsh selection; changed down with relaxed accelerator.

38% *Traffic Observation:* poor anticipation; late reaction.

38% *Overtaking:* too close prior to; on bends; in face of oncoming vehicles; cutting in after completing manoeuvre.

36% *Observation and Obedience:* failed to specify requested signs; failure to conform to stop sign/keep left signs and markings.

28% *Manoeuvring and Reversing:* lacked judgement and control.

26% *Correct Use of Speed:* excessive in country lanes; failed to make adequate progress in 70 mph areas.

22% *Speed Limits:* exceeding limit.

20% *Steering:* released wheel, crossed hands.

20% *Restraint:* insufficient demonstrated.

14% *Maintaining Adequate Progress:* not maintained when safe to make progress.

14% *Hand or Mechanical Signals:* late or misleading signals.

14% *Correct Use of the Horn:* non-use when required.

12% *Acceleration:* poor acceleration sense.

8% *Obstructing Other Vehicles:* loitering at minor hazards and cutting in.

IAM Fleet Training

As a result of many requests to the Institute of Advanced Motorists from commerce and industry to raise driving standards by professional driver improvement training, the IAM has now formed a subsidiary company known as 'IAM Fleet Training'.

IAM Fleet Training now has a nationwide team of about 60 ex-police driving instructors, all holders of Department of Transport Driving Instructor certificates, engaged in the training of company drivers on all types of vehicles. Their training is based on the techniques used by the police driving schools, who were able to reduce the accident rate among police drivers by some 89 per cent after commencing driver training programmes.

Among the services now available to companies by this experienced team are:

Presentations to groups of staff on road safety and advanced driver subjects.

Independent driver assessment (usually prior to or on appointment).

Individual driver training programmes to advanced level (with confidential reports, if required).

The advanced test conducted by the Institute's Examiners.

Courses are approved by the Road Transport Industry Training Board.

Further details are available from: IAM Fleet Training Ltd, 1A Marlborough Road, London W4 4EU. (Telephone 01-994 6783).

The RoSPA Advanced Driving Test

RoSPA advanced tests are conducted at locations all over the UK by police class 1 drivers and last about 1¼ hours. The cost is currently £24.95 and includes the first year's membership of the RoSPA Advanced Drivers Association. Subsequent annual subscriptions are £10.

RoSPA have a unique system of grading successful candidates into grades 1, 2 and 3, which seems to be a fairer way of assessing performance over a wider range of driving ability. It provides incentives for the less experienced seeking to improve on their standard continuously and, at the same time, gives a meaningful measure of attainment to the more skilful driver. Grade 1 is the highest and it is unlikely that anyone will achieve this without a thorough knowledge of *Roadcraft* the police drivers' manual, and the system of car control it advocates.

Applying For The Test

Application forms can be obtained from:

The Administrative Officer, RoSPA Advanced Drivers Association, Cannon House, The Priory, Queensway, Birmingham B4 6BS
Tel: 021-200 2461.

The Test

Cars used for the test must be in a roadworthy condition and the candidate's visibility must not be obscured by condensation or for other reasons. Examiners will take a serious view of candidates who, for example on a rainy day, attempt to drive whilst visibility is restricted by condensation on windows and mirrors. Proper use of the wipers, demisters and window winder are expected.

The Use of the Controls

At the start of the test examiners try to put candidates at ease.

Before starting off, candidates are required to carry out the cockpit drill followed by a brake test shortly after moving.

Candidates are expected to demonstrate their mechanical appreciation by controlling the vehicle smoothly. Examiners will assess the steering method and position of the hands and arms when turning the wheel. The clutch should be used smoothly. Single de-clutching is acceptable but examiners will be pleased to see double de-clutching where appropriate. Slipping and riding the clutch is frowned upon. Examiners will assess the position of the hand on the gear lever when executing selections, the matching of engine revolutions to road speed and the correct timing of gear changes. The intelligent use of intermediate gears will make a difference to the final grade achieved. The use of the brakes is assessed for smoothness, early braking in correct sequence relating to the 'system', skid avoidance through correct technique and progressive reduction in pedal pressure as the vehicle is brought to a smooth stop. The accelerator should be used firmly when needed, precisely and under control at all times. Acceleration sense in overtaking will be assessed along with anticipation and the smooth variation of speeds to meet changing road and traffic conditions without braking.

Candidates are expected to use the mirrors in the correct sequence and have an accurate and continuous knowledge of the traffic situation behind. Over-the-shoulder looks are expected at appropriate times. Candidates are also assessed in their use of the horn.

Driving Performance

Moving off and stopping should be smooth and carried out safely. Examiners will assess the correct application of the system of car control, whether candidates brake before or after changing gear and whether they signal too late or too early. Particular emphasis is placed on the way the vehicle is positioned at junctions, on the approach to roundabouts, on the open road and in lanes on the approach to hazards.

Candidates will be assessed on their course when cornering and whether the line taken optimises visibility and safety and that it allows for any tendency of the vehicle to over- or understeer to be compensated for. The use of speed and vehicle controls will be assessed whilst cornering.

Candidates will be assessed on whether necessary signals are omitted or wrongly timed and unnecessary ones used. The examiner will look for reinforcement of trafficators by an arm signal where necessary and assess reactions to traffic signs.

Candidates are required to perform a reversing exercise safely and accurately and in normal driving to make reasonable use of their vehicle's performance within legal limits and as safety allows according to the prevailing road and traffic conditions. Examiners will assess whether candidates are asking themselves the appropriate questions before executing an overtaking manoeuvre.

General Ability

Candidates who are slumped at the wheel or resting an elbow on the door will not be considered as advanced drivers. Consideration for others and self-control will be assessed. Temperament whilst driving should be calm, relaxed and decisive.

Candidates are not expected to abuse their vehicles by 'kerbing', etc.

Examiners will assess candidates' powers of observation, hazard recognition and planning. Candidates may, if they choose, elect to give a commentary drive if invited to 'think aloud' for a few minutes by the examiner. Candidates will also be assessed on their ability to judge their own speed and the speeds and distances of other vehicles. This will be linked to candidates' use of braking and acceleration.

The test is concluded with questions on the Highway Code and other motoring matters such as those contained in most vehicle handbooks.

After the Test

The examiner will discuss any points that have arisen and inform candidates whether they have passed and which grade they have achieved. Persons attaining grades 1 and 2 are expected to take a refresher test at three-yearly intervals. The fee for this is included in the yearly subscriptions. Grade 3 candidates are expected to take the test every year until they are upgraded. Candidates who fail the test are permitted to retake it after three months.

RoAD Association

The RoSPA Advanced Drivers Association currently has 29 local groups in various parts of the country. These groups offer training and free assessment drives to prospective test candidates as well as taking part in local road safety shows and organising social events for members. The group's main aim is to improve road safety by the raising of driving standards. Further information about membership (and the formation of new groups!) is available from Maria Perks, Group Development Officer, RoSPA Advanced Drivers Association, Cannon House, The Priory, Queensway, Birmingham B4 6BS (Telephone 021-200 2461 ext 228).

RoSPA Defensive Driving Courses

RoSPA development of defensive driving stems from the organised road accident prevention work which the Society has undertaken since 1918 and forms a significant element of its efforts to reduce the high level of deaths and injuries on the roads of Britain.

The importance of training drivers may be judged from current accident levels. Each year on our roads around 6 000 people are killed and a further 300 000 injured, at an estimated cost to the community of £2 000 million. In over 95 per cent of these accidents, human error has been shown to be the major factor. Given that the majority of road mileage is undertaken on business journeys, it is easy to see how helping the drivers of company vehicles to improve their performance can significantly improve the situation.

Cost-effectiveness is an important consideration whenever decisions are made on the expenditure of limited resources. In this context, it is important to remember the cost savings, particularly in the field of insurance premiums, which can be achieved by organisations which take serious steps to help their own staff secure improved standards in the driving task.

The RoSPA training service operates at two levels: in the classroom and in the vehicle. The classroom-based course, usually conducted as in-company training, is an intensive one-day session which will accommodate up to 15 students and aims to impart the basic theory of defensive driving. This session is aimed at increasing the driver's knowledge of advanced and defensive principles.

On-road training is achieved by taking groups of drivers out for the day in their company vehicle. In addition to observing a demonstration drive by the instructor, each student takes a turn at the wheel and all are encouraged to learn from each other's mistakes and the corrective tuition applied. In this way, drivers are helped with the difficult task of adapting their own driving technique in the light of the theoretical knowledge they have gained.

The course aims to increase awareness of accident potential and improve the driver's attitude to the task and includes a comprehensive defensive driving manual covering speed and overtaking, drink, drugs and driving, turning and cornering, night driving, observation, the law, aquaplaning and skidding, winter driving, roadcraft, the vehicle, signs and signals, stopping and parking, passenger safety, accidents, motorway driving, first aid, the heavy goods vehicle and a revision guide.

In addition to company training, RoSPA, in association with the Motor Schools Association, maintain a register of persons qualified to provide training linked to the advanced test syllabus. Instructors with their names on this register have all attended and passed a special three-day Diploma course in advanced driver instruction. Instructors requiring additional information about the register should either contact RoSPA direct or contact the Motor Schools Association.

The Society are also seeking to extend the availability of courses throughout the country and to this end have developed a Better Driving Course Syllabus Pack. This contains teaching notes, a master syllabus, a list of recommended resource materials and further guidance notes for use by road safety officers, police officers, approved driving instructors and others conducting better driving courses. The course consists of six two-hour sessions in the classroom with provision for an assessment drive with one of the local group associations. The Society also maintains a register of their local advanced driving groups from which these packs can be obtained. These groups can also offer associate membership and provide help and advice to candidates before they take the RoSPA Advanced Driving Test.

Chapter 14

The ADI Register

Department of Transport Approved Driving Instructor Register

The register was first introduced in 1964 under the name of the Ministry of Transport Approved Driving Instructors Register. Registration was voluntary until 1970, since which time all persons wishing to teach driving of motor cars for profit or reward have to register by law. The laws were introduced to ensure that all persons giving professional instruction are of the required standard. Persons giving professional instruction must be registered with the Department of Transport or possess a licence to give instruction. The Register and the licensing scheme are administered by the Registrar for Approved Driving Instructors, Department of Transport, 2 Marsham Street, London SW1P 3EB under the provisions of the Road Traffic Act 1972 and Road Traffic (Driving Instruction) Act 1984. Only persons with their name in the Register are permitted to use the title 'Department of Transport Approved Driving Instructor' or display the official certificate.

Registered and Licensed Instructors

Under Section 126 of the Road Traffic Act 1972, it is an offence for a person to teach another to drive a motor car for profit or reward (maximum penalty £1,000) unless the person:

    (a)   is on the Department of Transport Approved Driving Instructor Register; or

    (b)   holds a licence to give instruction issued by the Registrar.

Registered instructors (Department of Transport Approved Driving Instructors) are fully qualified. Licensed instructors are unqualified persons who have been granted a temporary licence to instruct after passing the first two parts of the examination.

Exemptions

Section 126 only applies to instruction in the driving of a motor car and does not apply to giving professional instruction in riding motorcycles or driving heavy goods vehicles etc.

Under Section 127 of the Act, police officers are exempted from Section 126 when giving driving instruction as part of their official duties and providing this is with the authority of the Chief Constable. Under Section 38 of the

Road Traffic Act, concerning the responsibilities of Local Authorities to provide 'traffic education', road safety officers are exempt from the ADI regulations while executing their official duties under the authority of the County Councils. These exemptions do not apply where police officers and road safety officers are giving instruction in driving a motor car outside their official duties.

The law does not apply to persons giving completely free tuition such as a person teaching her husband or friend to drive.

Qualifications to be Registered

Anyone who wants to become a Department of Transport Approved Driving Instructor must:

(a) be a fit and proper person to have their name entered in the Register, ie they must be of good character. (All motoring and non-motoring convictions, providing they are not 'spent' under the Rehabilitation of Offenders Act 1974, will be taken into account in assessing an applicant's suitability.);

(b) pass all three parts of the qualifying examination within a two-year period. (Subject to Section 84 of the Road Traffic Act 1972 (Driving Licences), persons wishing to take the Register examination before they satisfy the requirements under the Regulation outlined in (c) below, may do so.);

(c) have held a full car driving licence for periods totalling at least four years out of the six years preceding the date on which the application is made. (Any period after passing the driving test and during which a provisional licence is held may be counted as a full licence. A full licence to drive 'automatics' also counts towards the four-year period.); and

(d) not have been under a disqualification for driving at any time during the four years preceding the date on which the application is made.

Applicants should note that to accompany provisional licence holders, they must hold a full unrestricted driving licence. The only exception is for applicants with a leg disability.

The qualifying examination is in three parts: They are:

Part 1   Written Examination
Part 2   Practical Test of Driving Ability
Part 3   Practical Test of Instructional Ability.

The initial application for a person's name to be placed in the Register and the application for the Written Examination are made on the same form. Applicants must provide the name and address of their current employer (or last employer if unemployed) and give the name and address of a person, not a relative, who has known them for at least a year and is willing to provide them with a character reference.

Applicants must apply separately for and pass each part in the above sequence before they can apply for the next. To qualify for registration a

Department of Transport

Notes to help you apply to have your name in the Register of Approved Driving Instructors

General

◆ Please read these notes and booklet ADI14, "The Register of Approved Driving Instructors" **before** you fill in this form. You will be asked to declare that you have read it at the end of the form. If you have not already had a copy of the booklet you can get one from your local Traffic Area Office.

Licence Details

◆ On the form you will be asked to give details about your driving licence. You must have had a licence for periods totalling 4 out of the past 6 years. Any motor car driving licence issued outside the UK, and any unexpired part of a provisional licence **after** passing your driving test will count towards the 4 years. A full licence to drive 'automatics' (Group B) also counts towards the 4 years, but you must hold a full UK driving licence to drive vehicles in Group A before you can take the driving ability test (Part II) and before your name can be entered in the register. If your licence is marked 'restricted' the details of the restrictions listed on your licence must be sent with this application.

Character Details

◆ You will also be asked to give details of any motoring or non-motoring offences and these will be taken into account in assessing your suitability. The Rehabilitation of Offenders Act 1974 explains when a conviction becomes spent and when you do not have to declare it. You can get further information from the Citizen's Advice Bureau, public library, or your legal advisor.

Examination Details

◆ This form is also an application for the written part of the qualifying exam. When you have filled in the form tear it off and send it with the correct fee and a completed index card (ADI4) to your local Traffic Area Office.

Fees

◆ Please make cheques or postal orders payable to "The Accounting Officer -Department of Transport". **Please do not send cash.**

ADI 3
July 89

DTp ADI registration application form

Department of Transport - Traffic Area Offices

Scottish Traffic Area
83 Princes Street
Edinburgh
EH2 2ER

☎ 031-225-5494

North Eastern (Newcastle) Traffic Area
Westgate House
Westgate Road
Newcastle-upon-Tyne
NE1 ITW

☎ 091-261-0031

North Eastern (Leeds) Traffic Area
Hillcrest House
386 Harehills Lane
Leeds
LS9 6NF

☎ 0532-495661

Eastern (Cambridge) Traffic Area
Terrington House
13-15 Hills Road
Cambridge
CB2 1NP

☎ 0223-358922

Eastern (Nottingham) Traffic Area
Birkbeck House
14-16 Trinity Square
Nottingham
NG1 4BA

☎ 0602-475511

South Eastern Traffic Area
Ivy House
3 Ivy Terrace
Eastbourne
BN21 4QT

☎ 0323-21471

North Western Traffic Area
Portcullis House
Seymour Grove
Manchester
MI6 ONE

☎ 061-872-5077

West Midland Traffic Area
Cumberland House
200 Broad Street
Birmingham
B15 1TD

☎ 021-631-3300

South Wales Traffic Area
Caradog House
1-6 St. Andrews Place
Cardiff
CF1 3PW

☎ 0222-25188

Western Traffic Area
The Gaunts' House
Denmark Street
Bristol
BS1 5DR

☎ 0272-297221

Metropolitan Traffic Area
PO Box 643
Charles House
375 Kensington High Street
London
W14 8QU

☎ 01-276-6677

Fees

Written Examination	**£50.00**	Practical test of instructional ability	**£45.00**
Licence to give instruction	**£85.00**	Entry to the Register	**£100**
		From 01-09-89	**£110**
Practical test of driving ability	**£45.00**	Extension of Registration or Re-registration	**£100**
		From 01-09-89	**£110**

(Correct at time of printing)

DTp ADI registration application form (continued)

Department of Transport ADI3

Register of Approved Driving Instructors

Application for Registration

✐ in CAPITALS ✓ the boxes ◆ See the Notes sheet

1. Your Details

Title

Mr ☐ Mrs ☐ Miss ☐ Ms ☐

Surname

First name(s)

Home address & telephone No.

Postcode

☎ (including STD code)

Date of birth   Day   Month   Year

Have you ever applied for registration before?

Yes ☐   No ☐

2. Exam' Details

Please give your choice of centre where you wish
to take the written examination.

First Choice

Second Choice

Exam Centres

Aberdeen, Birmingham, Bristol, Cambridge, Cardiff,
Glasgow, Leeds, Leicester, London, Manchester,
Newcastle -upon-Tyne and Plymouth.

3. Licence Details

Please give your driver number below.

◆ If you have held a full UK or foreign licence for 4
out of the last 6 years please give details:

UK ☐ years

Foreign ☐ years ⟿ (ignore if not applicable)

◆ If your licence is marked 'restricted' give details of
the restrictions (use separate sheet if necessary)

Have you been convicted of a motoring offence
within the last 6 years?

Yes ☐   No ☐   If **'Yes'**, please give details

Offence(s) (use a separate sheet if necessary)

Name of Court

Exact date of conviction

Penalty imposed (including any penalty points)

Have you been disqualified from driving at any
time during the last 4 years?

Yes ☐   No ☐   If **'Yes'**, please give details

Offence

Exact date of conviction

Period of Disqualification

DTp ADI registration application form (continued)

4. Character Details

- Have you been convicted of a non-motoring offence? (See notes on spent convictions).

Yes ☐ No ☐ → If **'Yes'**, please give details

Offence(s) (use separate sheet if necessary)

Name of Court

Exact date of conviction

Penalty imposed

Are court proceedings of any kind pending against you?

Yes ☐ No ☐ → If **'Yes'**, please give details

Alleged offence(s) (use separate sheet if necessary)

Date of hearing (if known)

Name of court (if known)

Please give the name and address of either your current employer or last employer if you are unemployed.

Current ☐ Last ☐

Postcode

Please give the name and address of a person (not a relative) who has known you for at least a year and is willing to give a reference as to your character

Postcode

5. Declaration

I declare that:

The details given in this form are to the best of my knowledge true and correct;

I have read the Department's booklet ADI14;

I understand that once I am registered, and while seeking registration, I will inform the Registrar's office in writing within 7 days if I;

- change my home address or place of employment as an instuctor, and

- am convicted of any offence, including motoring offences;

I understand that the parts of the qualifying exams (and if approved for registration, tests of continued ability and fitness) will take place during the examiners normal working hours.

I apply for registration and for admission to the written part of the qualifying examination for which I enclose the fee of £ . . . . .

Signed

Dated

Warning

Any applicant who, for the purpose of securing registration, knowingly makes a false statement or gives instruction without being in possession of a licence, is liable to a fine of up to £1000.

Have you

- Signed the form?

- Enclosed the fee?

- Filled in and enclosed the index card?

- Given a choice of centre where you wish to take the written exam'?

DTp ADI registration application form (continued)

candidate must pass all three parts within a two-year period. Candidates who fail to do this must start at the beginning and pass them all again.

It is proposed by the Department to introduce in the near future a regulation restricting the number of attempts at the practical examinations.

Examination and training requirements are covered in Chapters 15 and 16.

Applications for Registration

All forms concerned with applications for names to be placed on the register, examination appointments and licence to instruct should be obtained from the appropriate Traffic Area Office (see Appendix II for addresses and telephone numbers).

Fees for examinations and registration are reviewed at regular intervals. Current fees are (January 1989):

Written Examination	£50.00
Practical Test of Driving Ability	£45.00
Practical Test of Ability to Instruct	£45.00

DTp ADI certificate

Registration Declaration

Applicants to the Register must sign a declaration that they will:

(i) notify the Registrar of any change of name, address and place of employment;

(ii) notify the Registrar if convicted of any offence;

(iii) return the certificate if the registration lapses or is revoked;

(iv) agree to periodic assessments of their instructional standards by Department of Transport staff.

After passing the qualifying examination the name of an applicant can be entered in the Register upon payment of the current fee.

Registration is normally for four years and subject to the payment of a fee.

DTp ADI certificate (reverse side)

Fees for registration or for licences issued are not refundable. Registration is normally renewable on application and payment of a further fee. It is not necessary to take the qualifying examination again unless there has been a lapse of at least a year since the expiry of the last registration.

Qualifying applicants are entitled to receive an official 'Certificate of Registration'. This incorporates the person's name, photograph and official title and must be displayed clearly on the nearside of the windscreen of vehicles in which driving tuition is being given. This certificate must be produced when requested by a police constable or any person authorised by the Secretary of State. Failure to produce the certificate when legally requested constitutes an offence.

If a registered instructor can satisfy the Registrar that the original certificate is lost, damaged or destroyed, a duplicate certificate can be issued upon payment of a fee.

Termination of Registration

A person's name may be removed from the Register if:

(i) the Registrar is not satisfied that he/she still possesses the necessary qualifications;

(ii) he/she refuses to take the test of continued ability;

(iii) he/she fails to reach an acceptable standard in the test of continued ability.

Appeals

Instructors who are aggrieved by the Registrar's refusal of their applications for registration have the right of appeal to the Secretary of State. Before refusing to renew, or deciding to terminate a registration, the Registrar should notify the instructor of the intention. Instructors are entitled to make representations to the Registrar with a view to reversing the decision. If the decision is confirmed, the instructor has the right of appeal to the Secretary of State.

An applicant for a Licence to Instruct can appeal to the Secretary of State against refusal. Before refusing to issue, renew or revoke a licence, the Registrar must notify the licensee of his intention. The applicant, or licensee, is entitled to make representations to the Registrar. If the Registrar confirms the decision, the applicant/licensee can appeal to the Secretary of State.

On receiving an appeal, the Secretary of State will appoint a board to hold an enquiry into the matter. The appeal is considered after the Board's recommendations. The Secretary of State also has the power to charge the appellant with the cost of the appeal.

An instructor can appeal to a magistrate's court (Sheriff in Scotland) if he thinks that any part of the examination was not conducted in accordance with the regulations.

Full details of the procedure for making a formal appeal are given in an official leaflet which can be obtained from the Registrar. Instructors affected by the Registrar's decisions, as described above, are automatically sent this leaflet. (See also 'The Right to Appeal', page 228.)

The Test of Continued Ability and Fitness

Instructors with their names in the Register have signed an undertaking that, when required by the Registrar, they will undergo a Test of Continued Ability and Fitness. The examiner assesses the instructor's performance while giving a driving lesson to a pupil.

Instructors who refuse to undergo the test, and those who fail to attain an acceptable standard on it, can be removed from the Register.

Instructors must provide both the vehicle and pupil for the purpose of this test. However, the car need not be dual-controlled nor the pupil a learner driver. It is also acceptable for instructors to be assessed in a classroom or simulator lesson if necessary.

When required, and in order that the statutory check may be conducted, the supervising examiner will contact the instructor by letter specifying a time, date and place for the test. Details are shown in the standard letter (page 223).

Test Requirements

The Test of Continued Ability and Fitness was upgraded in 1985 to include a more detailed analysis of the instructor's performance. The regulations allow for stricter control over the booking of the appointments and for more regular checks depending on the Department of Transport's grading of individual instructors. Supervising examiners look at various aspects of an instructor's performance during the test. These include:

(i) Characteristics such as patience, tact and firmness; whether the instructor inspires confidence, encourages the student or is petty and over-critical. There are various degrees of impatience, from sarcastic comments or tone of voice and impatient body movements, to total loss of self-control and open hostility towards the student. Instructors should be sympathetic and prepared to repeat themselves as many times as may be necessary without making the student feel inadequate. Physical contact should be avoided wherever possible. Instructors should try to create a professional but relaxed atmosphere in the vehicle, without becoming over-familiar. They should be alert and maintain a professional interest in the student continually looking for ways in which to help or improve performance. The enthusiasm of instructors is often reflected in the efforts made by their students who will not normally work as hard if the instructor appears to be bored and disinterested. Avoid smoking. The method of addressing students is always a difficult subject to define and depends on the background, personality, age and sex of both the instructor and student. The use of first names is becoming more socially acceptable and usually leads to a more relaxed atmosphere. In some cases however, the use of first names, particularly by younger instructors, may be classed as disrespectful by some social and professional classes and usually by older students.

Department of Transport

ADI40 (Rev. March 87)

Register of Approved Driving Instructors

ADI No. _____

Date _____

Dear

Tests of continued ability and fitness to give instruction (check tests)

1. You will know that it is a condition of your continued registration as an Approved Driving Instructor that you will undergo a check test when required to do so. I have therefore arranged to travel to your area to conduct a check test with you at the time and place set out below. Please arrange for a normal lesson of approximately one hour to begin at the time shown and attend with a car and pupil. You should allow up to 15 minutes for discussion at the end of this lesson.

It should not be a lesson which is immediately followed by a driving test.

2. I must make it clear that if you are unable to meet this request without good reason, it will not be possible for me to travel again to your area specifically to conduct your check test. It will then be necessary for you to bring a car and pupil to my office at a time and date to be arranged by the Department so that the check test - which is a statutory requirement on which your continued registration depends - may be carried out.

3. Please complete and return the detachable part of this letter to me, confirming that you will be able to attend for this appointment. This should reach me by Friday _____

4. If, due to unforeseen circumstances I am, at the last moment, prevented from attending the appointment, you should proceed with the lesson in the usual way. If this happens, I will contact you and make fresh arrangements. Should you be unable to keep this appointment, then please telephone me as soon as possible so that alternative arrangements can be made. I am usually in the office on Fridays, you can also leave messages on my answer phone, on _____

Yours Sincerely

Details of appointment

Date: _____ Time: _____

Supervising Examiner ADI

Place: _____

- -

The Supervising Examiner - **Register of Approved Driving Instructors**

I acknowledge receipt of your notice dated _____

ADI No. _____

and will be attending for the check test.

Details of appointment

Signature _____

Date: _____

Address _____

Time: _____

_____

Place: _____

Name of school _____ Vehicle to be used _____ Registration No _____

DTp ADI check test

(ii) Route directions should be clear and easy to follow and given in plenty of time for the student to respond. Instructions should be short and to the point. Explanations given should clearly express and emphasise the main concepts without losing them in excessive verbiage or needless repetition which may cloud the issue and cause confusion. The general level of instruction should be appropriate to students' ability. Over-instruction will inhibit the more able and suppress the initiative of the advanced student. Those students who are less able should not be expected to deal with situations they are unable to cope with unaided, or take in complex information and variables before they can deal with the basics. The lesson should be planned and delivered in an orderly manner and in the correct sequence for the task in hand.

Instructors who conduct lessons without any apparent purpose or briefing beforehand are not likely to raise students' performance or inspire confidence. Instructors should assess students' actions, probe their understanding and reasons for decisions. Instructors should ask questions which not only test student knowledge but also encourage them to think more about their actions and which ensure a greater mental/perceptive participation in the learning task. For example, where a student drives continually too close to parked vehicles ask: 'What kind of things should you expect and be looking for when approaching a row of parked cars?' Instructors must satisfactorily answer student's questions and assess the level of any related misunderstanding.

(iii) Instructors must make students aware of faults and identify the cause and consequences of them, together with the action required to prevent recurrence. Instructors who allow them to go unmentioned or uncorrected are simply reinforcing the faults. Corrections should state the actions required to remedy faults. It is not good enough to re-state the fault, for example, 'Don't drive in the middle of the road', when the instructor means 'Try to keep about two-to-three feet out from the kerb'. Instructors must isolate and treat the cause of an error rather than its effect. For example, students who continually drive excessively fast through minor crossroads with superficial observations, may show they do not appreciate the danger of emerging vehicles. In this example it is the lack of awareness which causes the excessive speed. Treating the lack of awareness should result in more meaningful observation thus solving the speed problem.

(iv) At the start of a lesson instructors should revise and/or refer to matters learnt previously. At the end of a lesson they should summarise and reinforce the points covered on it. This involves the re-stating, re-wording and general reinforcement of learned points.

(v) Instructors should demonstrate that they understand the importance of assessing and reinforcing progress during the course of the lesson. Instructors who only look for faults do not provide the same incentive to try harder as those who also give praise and encouragement for tasks carried out correctly, or when improvements are made.

(vi) Whether the instruction given is correct and whether instructors have taken account of technical content or other advice given previously by an examiner is also assessed.

Instructor Grading

During the check test the instructor is assessed on the method, clarity, adequacy and correctness of instruction; the observation and proper correction of pupils' errors; the instructor's manner, patience, tact, and his ability to inspire confidence.

As a result of these individual assessments the instructor is graded on a scale of 6 to 1. The grading system then allows the ADI Supervising Examiner to determine the date and timing of the next ADI check test.

A 'grade 6' instructor would be seen within 4 years;
A 'grade 5' instructor would be seen within 3 years;
A 'grade 4' instructor would be seen within 2 years;

Each of these grades is regarded as acceptable, with any grade below 4 requiring a more frequent re-test as shown:

Grade 3 would be seen in 3 months time, and must have improved;
Grade 2 would be seen in 2 months time, and also must improve;
Grade 1 is considered dangerous, and an urgent and immediate check test by an Assistant Chief Driving Examiner would follow. Failure on this would mean removal from the Register without any further chance.

Licence to Give Instruction

Under the provisions contained in the Road Traffic Act 1972 and the Road Traffic (Driving Instruction) Act 1984, a temporary six-month licence to give instruction can be issued by the Department of Transport to suitable applicants wishing to complete the final stages of their training under the close supervision of an ADI.

Persons studying or training and intending to pass all three parts of the examination before giving any professional tuition do not need to apply for this licence. To qualify for the Licence to Instruct applicants must:

(a) be a fit and proper person to have their name entered in the Register, ie be of good character. (All motoring and non-motoring convictions will, providing they are not 'spent' under the Rehabilitation of Offenders Act 1974, be taken into account in assessing an applicant's suitability.);

(b) have held a full car driving licence for periods totalling at least four years out of the six years preceding the date of *application*

DTp trainee licence

for the licence. (Any period after passing the driving test during which a provisional licence is held may be counted. A full licence to drive 'automatics' also counts towards the four-year period.);

(c) not have been under a disqualification for driving at any time in the four years preceding the date of application for the licence;

(d) have passed Parts 1 and 2 of the qualifying examination; and be eligible to take the test of ability to instruct within the statutory two-year period. This means that when the applicant takes the Part 3 test he/she will have passed the Tests of Theory and Practical Test of Driving Ability within the last two years.

Applicants must be sponsored by an ADI and the licence will only be granted to successful candidates in the Part 1 Test of Theory and the Part 2 Test of Driving Ability. The licence must be displayed on the nearside of the windscreen where it can be clearly seen by the student.

Qualifications to be licensed

The conditions under which a Licence to Instruct is granted are that:

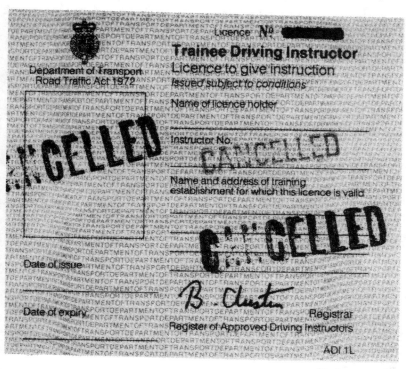

DTp trainee licence (reverse side)

(i)   the holder may only give professional instruction from the address specified on the licence;

(ii) there must be at least one ADI working at the address specified on the licence for every licence holder employed there;

(iii) for the first three months the licence is in force, the holder must be under the direct personal supervision of an ADI for at least one-fifth of the time spent giving instruction. This means the supervising ADI must accompany the licence holder on 20 per cent of all lessons conducted;

(iv) the licence holder must maintain a daily record of instruction given and supervision received during the first three months the licence is in force. The completed record must be signed by the holder and countersigned by the supervising ADI; records must be shown on demand to authorised officers of the Department of Transport and at the end of the three months, the completed record must be sent to the Registrar;

(v)   *in addition,* the holder must receive from an ADI at least 40 hours of practical in-car instructor training. 'Sitting-in' observing the supervising ADI giving instruction is not classed as part of the training. *Note:* All training must be received during the period starting 12 months before the date of issue of the licence and ending one month after the licence commences; the holder must receive some training in every one of the subjects set out under 'Curriculum of Training for Licence Holders' Chapter 16, page 267.

A record of training received must be signed by the licence holder and the ADI who gives the training. This must be sent to the department so that it is received by the Registrar not later than five weeks from the date the licence commences.

Special forms on which to record supervision and training are supplied with the licence. See Chapter 16, pages 268 and 270.

The licence may be revoked if:

(i) any of the conditions subject to which it was granted are not complied with;
(ii) at any time since it was granted, the holder no longer satisfies the entry requirements; eg is disqualified from driving or is no longer considered to be a fit and proper person;
(iii) it was issued by mistake or procured by fraud.

Applicants or licence holders have the same avenues of appeal as those already on the register. However, the time allowed for appeal is reduced to 14 days.

Refund of Fees

Where a candidate fails to keep an examination appointment, the fee will be forfeited unless ten clear days' notice are given. (The day the notice is received, the day of the examination, Saturdays, Sundays and public holidays are excluded.) The department will generally not refund a fee where less than this notice is given, or where the examination does not take place, or is not completed for reasons attributable to the candidate or any vehicle provided. Fees for licences issued are not refundable.

The Right to Appeal

Two types of appeal are established under Part V of the Road Traffic Act.

Test candidates who think an examination was not conducted in accordance with the Regulations can apply to have the matter considered by a Magistrate's Court, or by the Sheriff in Scotland.

Persons affected by the Registrar's decision to refuse or revoke registration or the licence to give instruction have the right of appeal to the Secretary of State.

Full details of the procedure for making a formal appeal are provided in an official leaflet (The Appeals Procedure, ADI 47), which can be obtained from the Registrar. Aggrieved persons who wish to appeal must follow the procedure laid down in this pamphlet. Persons affected by the Registrar's decisions to refuse or revoke registration or the licence to give instruction are sent the leaflet automatically.

Appeals to a Magistrate's Court and to the Sheriff in Scotland

Test candidates who think an examination was not conducted in accordance with the Regulations can apply to have the matter considered by a Magistrate's Court, or by the Sheriff in Scotland.

Although courts have no jurisdiction or power to reverse the result of an ADI examination, if the court is satisfied that the examination was not conducted in accordance with the regulations it may order the examination to be taken again and may order the refund of the fee.

Appeals to the Secretary of State for Transport

The Registrar decides whether applicants for licences, registration or renewal of registration possess the necessary qualifications set out earlier in this chapter. The Registrar has no power or discretion to vary the qualifications and if an applicant fails to satisfy the requirements of the Act, then the application must be refused. Where a person thinks the Registrar is wrong to refuse an application or terminate an existing licence or registration, there exists the right to appeal to the Secretary of State.

Existing instructors and applicants for licences and registration who are considering an appeal should also consider that the Secretary of State has no power to order the Registrar to vary the requirements of the Act and do something which they have no power to do. Persons making the appeal must do so in a proper way and follow the procedure laid down.

Refusal of Application for Initial Registration

Where an application for an initial registration is refused there is normally little to dispute. Whether the person has passed the examination, possesses the required full licence or has been under a disqualification are all matters of fact. The most likely area for disagreement therefore is over whether the person is a fit and proper person to be an Approved Driving Instructor. Aggrieved persons may appeal in writing within 28 days of the date on which the Registrar's notice of refusal was given.

Lapse of Registration

Registration will automatically lapse after the last day of the four-year period if by that day:

- no application for renewal has been received by the Registrar;
- the only application to renew registration is incomplete;
- the renewal fee has not been received.

Department of Transport

Register of Approved Driving Instructors

Application for a Trainee Licence

ADI3L

✍ in CAPITALS   ✓ the boxes   ◈ See the Notes sheet

1. Your Details

Title

Mr ☐   Mrs ☐   Miss ☐   Ms ☐

Surname

First name(s)

Home address

Postcode

☎ (incl. STD Code)

What is your personal reference No?

What is your Driver No.? (shown on your licence)

◈ Have you ever been issued with a licence to give instruction?

Yes ☐   No ☐

◈ Have you passed both the written and driving ability parts of the qualifying exams in the last two years?

Yes ☐   No ☐

Please give exact date and centre where you passed the driving ability test.

Date

Centre

Please give the name and address of the training school from which you will give instruction

Postcode

☎ (incl. STD Code)

2. Character Details

◈ Have you been convicted of a non-motoring or motoring offence since the date you applied for registration?

Non-Motoring ☐   Motoring ☐   None ☐

If you have, please give details

Offence(s) (Use separate sheet if necessary)

Name of Court

Date of conviction

Penalty imposed (including any endorsements)

Are court proceedings of any kind pending against you?

Yes ☐   No ☐

If '**Yes**', please give details

Alleged offence(s) (Use separate sheet if necessary)

Name of court (if known)

Date of hearing (if known)

DTp trainee application form

3. Declarations

Your declaration

I apply for a licence and declare that:

The details given in this form are to the best of my knowledge true and correct;

I have read the Department's booklet ADI14;

I understand and accept that failure to receive the required training and / or supervision when it is a condition of the licence issued to me will result in revocation of my licence.

Signed

Dated

Warning

Any applicant who, for the purpose of securing registration, knowingly makes a false statement or gives instruction without being in possession of a licence, is liable to a fine of up to £1000.

Declaration of manager / owner

I declare that, as manager / owner of the establishment named on the licence:

I have read the Department's booklet ADI14;

At this date the required ratio of instructors to trainees is being maintained at the address shown on the licence;

The grant of the licence will not breach this ratio; and

At no time while the licence is in force will the ratio be breached.

Signed (manager / owner)

Name in CAPITALS

ADI No (if applicable)

Dated

Have you:

- Signed the form?
- Enclosed the fee?
- Enclosed two passport type photographs?
- Had the declaration of the manager / owner signed?

Now send this to your local Traffic Area Office

For Our Use only	
Form checked	
Filing position	
Business code	
Ratio	
Issued	

DTp trainee application form (continued)

Refusal of Application for Renewal of Registration

An instructor whose name is in the Register is entitled to have registration
extended for a further four years providing:

- the necessary information is supplied to the Registrar;
- the required fee is paid; and
- the Registrar is satisfied that the applicant still possesses the necessary
- qualifications, has not refused to undergo the prescribed test of
  continued ability, has maintained a suitable standard of instruction;
  and is still a fit and proper person to be a driving instructor.

As many of the requirements are 'matters of fact', where an application for
renewal of registration is refused, the area most likely to be under dispute is
whether the instructor is attaining a suitable standard of instruction and is
still a fit and proper person to be a driving instructor. Aggrieved instructors
have 28 days to make representations to the Registrar as to why the application should be accepted. During this time registration will continue to be in
force. After the 28 days the Registrar will reconsider the application. If it is
still refused the Registrar will write to the applicant to this effect. The decision will take effect 28 days after the date on which the notice is given.
Aggrieved persons may appeal to the Secretary of State in writing within this
28-day period. In the event of an appeal being lodged the Registrar's decision
will not take effect until the appeal is withdrawn, struck out for want of
prosecution, or dismissed.

Removing Instructors from the Register

The Registrar may remove an instructor from the Register at any time if he
is satisfied that the person no longer has the necessary qualifications, has
refused to undergo the test of continued ability, failed to pass the test of
continued ability, is not a fit and proper person, is under disqualification or
obtained the registration by mistake or fraud.

Before removing a name from the Register the Registrar must give notice
of his intentions and reasons in writing to the instructor concerned. The instructor has 28 days from notice being given in which to make representations
to the Registrar with a view to reversing the decision. After 28 days the Registrar will reconsider. If the decision is unchanged, the Registrar will write to
the instructor to this effect. The decision will come into effect 28 days after
the date on which the notice was given. Aggrieved persons may appeal to the
Secretary of State in writing within this 28-day period. In the event of an
appeal being lodged the Registrar's decision will not take effect until the
appeal is withdrawn, struck out for want of prosecution, or dismissed.

Refusal of Application for a Licence to Give Instruction

Only one licence will normally be granted. Applicants for licences must satisfy
the Registrar that they are fit and proper persons and possess the required
qualifications concerning the driving licence. In addition they must have
passed the tests of driving and instruction ability within a two-year period of
passing the written examination. The Registrar has discretion to issue further

licences but does so only in exceptional circumstances. Six months is considered an adequate time to gain the requisite experience. Therefore the Registrar refuses nearly all applications for second licences. However, the Act provides that if a second licence application is made before the expiry of the first licence and that application is refused by the Registrar and an appeal is lodged, the first licence is deemed to continue in force until the appeal is determined. An application made after the expiry of the first licence carries no such entitlement because there is by then no longer anything to extend.

Revoking a Licence to Give Instruction

The Registrar may revoke a licence at any time, if he is satisfied that the licensee no longer possesses the required qualifications, if the conditions on which it was granted are not observed or if it was granted by mistake or procured by fraud.

Before revoking a licence the Registrar must give notice of his intentions in writing to the instructor concerned stating the reasons why. The instructor has 14 days to make representations to the Registrar. At the end of this period the Registrar will reconsider the decision. A decision to revoke the licence will not come into effect for 14 days during which time aggrieved instructors can appeal to the Secretary of State. In this case the decision will not take effect until the appeal is withdrawn, struck out for want of prosecution, or dismissed.

The Appeal

Notice of appeal should be sent in a letter to the Secretary of State at the main office of the Department of Transport, giving the Registrar's decision and grounds for it. The Appeal must also include the appellant's name and address and the address to which papers concerning the appeal should be sent. The appellant must also send a copy of the notice of appeal to the Registrar.

On receiving an appeal, the Secretary of State will arrange for an inquiry into the appeal to take place and give both parties not less than 21 days notice of the time, date and place of the appeal which is, as far as possible, arranged in a large town in the part of the country where the appellant lives. Appeals can be withdrawn by giving notice in writing at any time before the inquiry, and no further action will be taken.

The Appeal Board may consist of one, two or three people appointed by the Secretary of State, who are not Department of Transport officials. Up to three assessors may be appointed to advise the board on matters arising from the inquiry.

The inquiry is normally held in public but either party may request parts to be held in private. Both parties may be represented by counsel or solicitor or by any other person. The Secretary of State has the power to order any person to attend or produce documents. Failure to do so without reasonable excuse may result on summary conviction in a fine not exceeding £20.00.

The Appeal Board reports its findings and may make recommendations to the Secretary of State who will in due course notify both the appellant and the

Registrar of his decision and reasons for it. If the decision is against the appellant he may also order that no future application relating to the ADI Register will be accepted for a specified time not exceeding four years from the date of the order. The appellant may also be ordered to pay the whole or part of any costs incurred by the Secretary of State in connection with the appeal. Alternatively the Secretary of State may decide to pay for the appeal.

**THE DEPARTMENT
OF TRANSPORT**
2 Marsham Street London SW1P 3EB

Register of
Approved Driving
Instructors

Your personal ref no

Date

Dear Candidate

Register of Approved Driving Instructors

I am sorry to have to tell you that you were not successful in the driving ability part of the Register qualifying examination.

The details underlined on the attached statement relate to your test and you should give them your attention if you decide to take the test again.

If you decide not to take the test again, no further action will be taken on your application for the entry of your name in the Register.

To qualify for registration you must pass all three parts of the qualifying examination within the space of two years. Otherwise you will have to pass the written part again and then pass both of the practical tests. All appointments are subject to waiting times and you should make allowance for this when applying for tests.

If you wish to make a further attempt at the test of driving ability and you are still eligible to do so, you should fill in the details overleaf and forward the complete letter, together with the appropriate fee, to the Traffic Area Office for the area where you wish to take the test. The addresses of the Traffic Area Offices and the centres where tests are held, are listed overleaf. It is essential to nominate a second choice of centre. You may then be invited to an earlier test. Cheques etc should be crossed and made payable to the "Accounting Officer, Department of Transport".

Yours faithfully

Supervising Examiner
Register of Approved Driving Instructors.

This portion is for official use

WE   DT   SE

Details of appointment   Supervising Examiner

Date   DT

Time

Place

ADI 9D sent   **ADI 10D
                                               (09/88)**

ADI application form (Part II)

TEST OF DRIVING ABILITY

1 Surname and initials (in BLOCK LETTERS) _____

2 Centre at which I wish to be tested   1st choice _____   2nd choice _____

3 Any dates when I will not be able to take the test _____

4 I apply for admission to the test of driving ability which forms part of the qualifying examination for the Register of Approved Driving Instructors. I enclose the required fee of £ _____ Cheque/PO (No _____

Signed _____

Address _____
(in BLOCK LETTERS)

_____

_____ Postcode _____

Tel No. _____

Date _____

Traffic Area	Centres where tests may be taken	Traffic Area	Centres where tests may be taken
Metropolitan Traffic Area P.O. Box 2224 Charles House 375 Kensington High Street London W14 8TY	Barnet Brentwood Dartford Epping Guildford Isleworth Redhill Surbiton Watford	Eastern (Cambridge) Traffic Area Terrington House 13–15 Hills Road Cambridge CB2 1NP	Bedford Cambridge Ipswich Luton Norwich
North Eastern (Newcastle) Traffic Area Westgate House Westgate Road Newcastle upon Tyne NE1 1TW	Darlington Newcastle upon Tyne	South Wales Traffic Area Caradog House 1–6 St. Andrew's Place Cardiff CF1 3PW	Cardiff Swansea
North Eastern (Leeds) Traffic Area 386 Harehills Lane Leeds LS9 6NF	Hull Leeds Sheffield	Western Traffic Area The Gaunts' House Denmark Street Bristol BS1 5DR	Bristol Plymouth Taunton
North Western Traffic Area Portcullis House Seymour Grove Manchester M16 0NE	Chester Liverpool Preston Rochdale Sale	South Eastern Traffic Area Ivy House 3 Ivy Terrace Eastbourne BN21 4QT	Eastbourne Gillingham Oxford Southampton
West Midland Traffic Area Cumberland House 200 Broad Street Birmingham B15 1TD	Coventry Stafford Wolverhampton Worcester	Scottish Traffic Area 83 Princes Street Edinburgh EH2 2ER	Aberdeen Edinburgh Glasgow Inverness
Eastern (Nottingham) Traffic Area Birkbeck House 14–16 Trinity Square Nottingham NG1 4BA	Derby Leicester Lincoln Northampton		

NOTE: Some centres may be temporarily unavailable. It may be necessary for the Department to invite candidates to a nearby alternative centre.

Dm 272507/1/61*e902 15m 2/39 P

ADI application form (Part II) (continued)

**THE DEPARTMENT
OF TRANSPORT**
2 Marsham Street London SW1P 3EB

Register of
Approved Driving
Instructors

Your personal ref no.

Date

Dear Candidate

Register of Approved Driving Instructors

I am glad to tell you that you reached the approved standard in your recent test of instructional ability, which is the final part of the Register qualifying examination.

Provided that you still satisfy the other conditions of registration your name may be entered in the Register and a Certificate of Registration issued to you. To enable us to proceed with your earlier application for registration will you please answer questions 1 to 4 and sign the statement overleaf.

You should then return this complete letter together with the fee for registration and two passport type photographs. The fee should be in the form of a cheque or postal orders made payable to the "Accounting Officer, Department of Transport" and crossed.

This letter and your enclosures should be sent to the following address:

The Clerk to the Traffic Commissioners

Yours faithfully

Supervising Examiner
Register of Approved Driving Instructors.

ADI 12
(09/88)

ADI application form (Part III)

QUESTIONS

Tick appropriate box

1 Since the date you applied for registration have you been disqualified for driving?   Yes ☐   No ☐

2 Since the date you applied for registration have you been convicted of a non–motoring offence?   Yes ☐   No ☐

3 Are Court proceedings of any kind pending against you?   Yes ☐   No ☐

Note: If you have answered 'yes' to any of the above questions please give details .

....

....

....

4 From what address will you operate as an Approved Driving Instructor?

....

....

.... Postcode ....

STATEMENT

I confirm that the particulars I have entered on this document are to the best of my knowledge and belief correct.

I enclose herewith the two passport type photographs for use in my Certificate of Registration and the registration fee of £ _____ for the entry of my name in the Register of Approved Driving Instructors.

Signature ....   Date ....

It is important that you let the Registrar's office know if you change your address whilst you are on the Register.

Bas 272808/2/8196903 15m 2/89 TP

ADI application form (Part III) (continued)

Details of the Department of Transport ADI (Part III) syllabus are shown in Appendix IV.

Chapter 15

The ADI Examinations

The Qualifying Examination

Subject to Section 84 of the Road Traffic Act 1972 (Driving Licences), persons wishing to take the Register examination before they have held a full licence for the four-year qualifying period described in Chapter 14 may do so. This permits successful examination candidates to have their name placed in the Register as soon as they qualify under the licensing requirements.

The qualifying examination consists of:

Part 1   Written Examination.
Part 2   Test of Driving Ability (Tests of Eyesight and Driving
         Technique).
Part 3   Test of Instructional Ability.

Applicants must apply separately for and pass each part of the examination in sequence. Applicants must pass Part 1 before applying for Part 2 and they must pass this before applying for Part 3.

To qualify for registration, applicants must pass all three elements within a two-year period. Where candidates fail to do this they must start again from the beginning and pass them all again.

The Examination Syllabus

Although there is no legal requirement to do so, applicants are advised to seek professional guidance before sitting the Written Examination and attend properly structured courses before taking the Tests of Driving and Instructional Ability. Candidates are unlikely to succeed without adequate preparation and the cost of repeated failure and retaking each part of the examination can exceed the cost of properly structured training. The examination requires a high standard of knowledge of the following subjects:

(a)   the principles of road safety in general and their application in
      specified circumstances;
(b)   correct and courteous driving techniques including:
      – control of the vehicle,
      – road procedure,
      – hazard recognition and proper action,
      – dealing properly with other road users and pedestrians,
      – the use of safety equipment;
(c)   the tuition required to instruct a pupil in driving a car, the

correction of errors, the manner of the instructor, instructor/student relationships and vehicle adaptations for disabled drivers;

(d) the Highway Code and other matters included in the booklet in which it is contained;

(e) the DL68 'Your Driving Test';

(f) the interpretation of the DL24 (The Statement of Failure to Pass the Driving Test);

(g) adequate knowledge of the mechanisms and design of a motor car relating to driving instruction;

(h) the book 'Driving' (the official Department of Transport manual).

Note: Subjects (a) and (b) are covered in *The Advanced Driver's Handbook* and 'Driving'. Subjects (c) and (d) are dealt with in *Learn to Drive, The Driving Instructor's Handbook* and *Instructional Techniques and Practice*. Subjects (f) and (g) are covered in *The Advanced Driver's Handbook,* 'Driving' and *The Driving Instructor's Handbook*.

Applicants can take each of the tests at the centre of their choice. Applications should be made to the Traffic Area office which deals with the area in which the applicant lives. (See Appendix III, page 357.)

To cancel or postpone an appointment for any part of the examination without losing the fee, applicants must give the centre ten clear days' notice. This must not include the day of cancellation, the day of the test, Saturdays, Sundays or public holidays.

Part 1 – Test of Theory

This part is conducted at centres in London, Aberdeen, Birmingham, Bristol, Cambridge, Cardiff, Glasgow, Leeds, Leicester, Manchester, Newcastle-upon-Tyne and Plymouth.

Multiple Choice Objective Questions

This part of the examination consists of 100 multiple choice questions. For each question candidates are given a choice of three answers. Only one of these is correct. The minimum pass mark for the examination is 85 per cent. However, the questions are now 'banded' in the following subject groupings:

1.   Road Procedure
2.(a) Traffic Signs and Signals
  (b) Car Control
  (c) Pedestrians
  (d) Mechanics
3.(a) Driving Test
  (b) Disabilities
  (c) Law
4.(a) Publications
  (b) Instructional Techniques

Candidates have to attain a minimum of 80 per cent in each of the four 'bands'. It is therefore possible that some candidates will obtain a mark above the total pass mark but still fail the examination because they have not gained the minimum percentage in one or more of the groupings. Banding has been introduced to ensure that candidates have a proper knowledge of the subject matter across the whole syllabus. For that reason candidates are not told in which band or bands they have failed.

Example Questions	*Example Answer Sheet*

1. On motorways parking is allowed:
   (a) in service areas;
   (b) on slip roads;
   (c) on hard shoulders.

1.   a [ ]   b [ ]   c [ ]

2. In icy conditions tyre pressures should:
   (a) be reduced;
   (b) be increased;
   (c) remain as normal.

2.   a [ ]   b [ ]   c [ ]

The question sheets are re-usable. Candidates must not write or make any marks on them. The Registrar will take a serious view of candidates who mutilate or mark them. Candidates are required to indicate their choice in *pencil* in the appropriate box on the answer sheet. The answer sheets are marked by computer.

To compensate for the guess factor in this type of question, a very high proportion of correct answers is required to pass. The result is usually issued within two weeks. Successful candidates receive a letter to this effect and an application form enabling them to apply to take the practical test of driving ability. Unsuccessful ones receive a letter to this effect and an application form enabling them to re-apply for the written exam.

The examination calls for a very high standard of knowledge and candidates are advised by the Department of Transport to prepare themselves thoroughly for it.

The time allowed for the examination is 1½ hours but the presence of candidates is required for longer than 1½ hours to allow for documentation, issue of instructions and collection of papers etc.

Rules for the Examination

Suitable applicants will receive an invitation to attend for the written examination at the time and place stated in the letter. Candidates should take this letter with them to the examination centre. Anyone who fails to produce it to the supervisor at the time of the examination may not be allowed to participate.

Candidates will be provided with a question book, a separate answer sheet, a pencil and an eraser.

Department of Transport

Room
2 Marsham Street London SW1P 3EB

Telex 22221

Direct line 01-212
Switchboard 01-212 3434
GTN 212

Your reference

Our reference DTT3

Date

Dear Sir/Madam

REGISTER OF APPROVED DRIVING INSTRUCTORS

I acknowledge with thanks your application for registration and receipt of the fee for the written part of the qualifying examination.

You are invited to attend the written examination which is to be held at the time and place shown below. Please bring this letter with you. You may not be able to participate in the examination if you cannot show this letter to the Supervisor.

You should read the regulations for the conduct of the examination, which are overleaf.

The fee you paid for this appointment cannot normally be refunded unless you give to this office at the above address at least three clear days' notice (day of receipt, day of examination, weekends and public holidays excluded), before the date of appointment, of your inability to attend. The details below should be completed and this letter returned. The Department is generally not prepared to consider a refund of the fee (or offer you a further appointment without the payment of a further fee) where less than three clear days' notice is given.

If you are unable to attend please return this invitation immediately so that we can give your place to someone else and so help to avoid long waiting lists.

Yours faithfully

for Registrar
Approved Driving Instructors

Time ....   Place ....

Date ....

                                                 ....

DO NOT DETACH

Notice of Inability to Attend

I shall not be able to attend the examination as indicated above.

Would you please arrange for me to attend a subsequent examination:

*a.   as soon as possible

*b.   not before .... (date)   Signature ....

Address ....   Date ....

*Delete as appropriate   ADI 6 (revised July 1986)

DTp ADI application form (Part I)

RULES FOR EXAMINATION

1. You will be required, before going to your seat, to leave behind your hat, coat, and any case, books, papers, etc. Reasonable precautions are taken to safeguard the property of candidates, but the Department of Transport can accept no liability for loss or damage, and you are expressly warned to keep any valuables in your custody.

2. You may not leave the examination room until 45 minutes after the beginning of the paper.

3. If you leave the examination room after papers have been distributed, you may not be re-admitted until they have been collected.

4. You must remain in your place until you have handed your work to the Supervisor or the assisting officer. No work should be left on your desk.

5. Silence must be maintained during the examination. The Supervisor will exclude from the examination any candidate causing or responsible for noise or disturbance.

6. You may not remove from the examination room, or mutilate, any paper or other material supplied.

7. If you obtain any irregular assistance from books, papers, etc. or from other candidates, or if you give such assistance to other candidates, or allow them to see your papers, you are liable to be disqualified from the present examination and from any other examination held by the Department in connection with the Register.

8. During the examination you will be known by the number assigned to you by the Supervisor when you arrive.

9. If you are suffering from an infectious or contagious disease you cannot, in the interest of other candidates, attend the examination centre. You should report the circumstances to the Department at once; in writing if there is time, if not by telephone 01 212 3434. If you have been in contact with a person suffering from an infectious or contagious disease, you should not attend the examination centre unless your doctor or local Medical Officer of Health advises you that you may do so without risk to other candidates.

10. If you do not comply with these instructions, or with any other given orally by the Supervisor or printed on question papers, you are liable to be disqualified; the Department will feel bound to disqualify any candidate who gains, or could gain, an advantage over the other candidates, whether he intended to or not.

The Examination

1. The written part of the Register qualifying examination consists of a single paper of 100 questions. Each question gives you a choice of three answers, and only one of these three answers is correct. Candidates are required to indicate the correct answer by marking the appropriate box. The following question is an example from one of the subjects being examined:

QUESTION PAPER   ANSWER SHEET

Q1. On most cars the hand-   1 ⊂⊃ ⊂⊃ ⊂⊃
     brake operates on the: a   b   c

a.   front wheels only

b.   rear wheels only

c.   all four wheels

2. The time allowed for the examination is 1½ hours but the presence of candidates will be required for longer than 1½ hours to allow for documentation, issue of instructions and collection of papers etc. The examination will call for a high standard of knowledge. Candidates are therefore advised to prepare themselves thoroughly for the examination and, in particular to study carefully the booklets and manual mentioned in Appendix 1 of the booklet ADI 14 'The Register of Approved Driving Instructors - What it is and how to apply'.

DTp ADI application form (Part I) (continued)

(a) Candidates are not permitted to take hats, coats, cases, books, papers etc to their seats. While steps are taken to safeguard property the Department of Transport accepts no liability for loss or damage. Candidates are expressly warned to keep valuables in their custody.

(b) Candidates may not leave the examination room until 45 minutes after the beginning of the paper.

(c) Candidates leaving the room after papers have been distributed may not be re-admitted until they have been collected.

(d) Candidates must remain in place until their work has been handed to the supervisor or assisting officer. No work must be left on the desk.

(e) Silence must be maintained during the examination. The supervisor will exclude any candidate causing or responsible for noise or disturbance.

(f) Candidates may not remove from the examination room, or mutilate, any paper or other material supplied.

(g) Candidates who obtain any irregular assistance from books, papers, or from other candidates or who give assistance to others, or allow others to see their papers are liable to be disqualified from the examination and any other examination connected with the Register.

(h) During the examination candidates will be known by the number assigned to them by the supervisor when they arrive.

(i) To safeguard the health of others, candidates suffering from infectious or contagious diseases cannot attend the examination centre. The circumstances should be reported to the Department of Transport at once; in writing if there is time, if not by telephoning 01-276 3000. Candidates who have been in contact with a person suffering from an infectious or contagious disease should not attend unless a doctor advises there is no risk to the other candidates.

(j) Candidates failing to comply with the examination rules, or with any instructions given orally by the supervisor, or printed on the question papers, are liable to be disqualified. The Department also feels bound to disqualify any candidate who gains, or could gain, an advantage over others whether intended or not.

Instructions for Candidates sitting the Examination
Note: The answer sheet is marked by computer.

(k) Please use *pencil.*

(l) Write in your *reference number* in the boxes provided on the answer sheet. If this number has only five digits, fill in the first box with 0.

(m) Write in your *desk number* and fill in the boxes provided.

(n) Write in the *paper number* of the question paper you are answering and fill in the boxes provided.

(o) Fill in the box of the *test centre* where you are taking this examination.

(p) Write in your *name* and *home address* in the spaces provided using block letters.

(q) Each question has three possible answers lettered a to c. Select your answer for each question and indicate it on the answer sheet by filling in the box like this (   ) below the letter of your chosen answer.

(r) If two answers are shaded in any question, that question will carry no mark.

Parts 2 and 3 – Tests of Driving and Instructional Ability

The Parts 2 and 3 tests of driving and ability to instruct are conducted at various centres throughout the country. Lists of these can be found in the ADI14 pamphlet.

When attending for Parts 2 and 3 of the examination candidates must provide a suitable saloon or estate car, not necessarily fitted with dual controls, in which the test can be conducted.

The vehicle provided must:

(i) be in a roadworthy and proper condition and capable of normal performance for a vehicle of its type;

(ii) have an orthodox manual transmission system;

(iii) have right-hand drive steering;

(iv) have a readily adjustable driving seat and a forward facing passenger seat;

(v) be properly insured and cover the examiner for all third party and damage risks and his liability to any passenger;

(vi) not display any advertisements or signs during the Test of Driving Technique which might cause others to believe it is being used for driving instruction;   •

(vii) in addition, candidates attending for the Part 3 test must have two regulation 'L' plates which they can attach to the vehicle;

(viii) it should also be noted that if a candidate provides a vehicle which does not conform to construction and use regulations, the test will be abandoned. For example, where door mirrors have been fitted and then removed, or adjusted so they cannot readily be used.

Failure to fulfil any of these requirements means the examiner will be unable to proceed with the test.

With effect from 1 December 1989 candidates are allowed a maximum of three attempts at the driving ability (Part 2) test and the instructional ability (Part 3) test within the two-year period after passing the written examination. An applicant who has had three failures at either of the practical tests will have to wait until the two-year period expires and then start the re-qualification period again, starting with the written (Part 1) examination.

Transitional arrangements apply to those applicants who had not passed the practical tests by 1 December 1989. Anyone who had made one or more attempts at either practical test by that date is allowed a further two attempts at that test. The two-year limit for qualification still applies.

Department of Transport

Room C9/18
2 Marsham Street London SW1P 3EB

Telex 22801

Direct line   01-212 3166
Switchboard 01-212 3434

P Ref number

Date

Dear Candidate

Register of Approved Driving Instructors

I am glad to tell you that you have been successful in the written part of the qualifying examination for the Register of Approved Driving Instructors, and it is now open to you to take the practical test of driving ability.

In order that an appointment may be made, would you please fill in the details overleaf. It is recommended that you specify more than one test centre where you are willing to attend as it may be possible to offer you an earlier appointment. You should forward this complete letter, together with the test fee, to the Traffic Area Office which deals with the centre you have specified as your first choice. The addresses of Traffic Area Offices and the centres where tests are held are listed overleaf. Cheques or postal orders should be crossed and made payable to the "Accounting Officer, Department of Transport". The correct fee is

You must provide a car for the test. It must be a suitable saloon motor car or estate car in proper condition including seat belts in working order. It must be free from advertisements and signs which might cause other road users to believe that it is being used for the purposes of giving driving instruction or that it is not being driven by a qualified driver. It should have an orthodox (ie non-automatic) transmission system, right-hand steering, a readily adjustable driving seat and a seat for a forward-facing passenger.

We will write to you again to let you know where and when to attend for the test. If you have not received an invitation for your test within four weeks of submitting this application you should contact the Traffic Area Office to where you sent the application.

Yours faithfully

for Registrar
Approved Driving Instructors

This Portion is for Official Use

Details of appointment   Supervising Examiner

Date.. D/T

Time..

Place..

ADI 7 (Revised 1985)

DTp ADI application form (Part II)

TEST OF DRIVING ABILITY

1. Surname and initials (in block letters) Mr/Mrs/Miss/Ms ....

2. Centre(s) at which you wish to be tested   1st choice ....

                                           2nd choice ....

3. Dates when you will NOT be available to take the test ....

4. I apply for admission to the test of driving ability which forms part of the qualifying examination for the Register of Approved Driving Instructors. I enclose the required fee.

Cheque/PO (No..............................).

Signed..

Address..

....

....Postcode..................

Tel No..

Date..

Traffic Area	Centres where tests may be taken	Traffic Area	Centres where tests may be taken
Metropolitan Traffic Area, Government Buildings Bromyard Avenue The Vale Acton, W3 7AY 01-743-5566	Brentwood Epping Dartford Guildford Isleworth Redhill Surbiton Watford Orpington	Eastern Traffic Area Terrington House 13—15 Hills Road Cambridge CB2 1NP 0223-358922	Cambridge Norwich Bedford Luton
North Eastern Traffic Area Westgate House Westgate Road Newcastle upon Tyne NE1 1TW 091-261-0031	Darlington Newcastle-upon-Tyne	South Wales Traffic Area, Caradog House 1—6 St Andrew's Place Cardiff CF1 3PW 0222-24801	Cardiff
North Eastern Traffic Area 386 Harehills Lane Leeds LS9 6NF 0532-495661	Hull Leeds Sheffield	Western Traffic Area The Gaunts' House Denmark Street Bristol, BS1 5DR 0272-297221	Bristol Plymouth Taunton
North Western Traffic Area Portcullis House Seymour Grove Manchester, M16 0NE 061-872-2333	Chester Liverpool Manchester Preston Rochdale Nelson	South Eastern Traffic Area Ivy House 3 Ivy Terrace Eastbourne, BN21 4QT 0323-21471	Brighton (until Winter 1986) Gillingham (from Spring 1987) Oxford Southampton Tunbridge Wells (until Winter 1986) Eastbourne (from Spring 1987)
West Midland Traffic Area Cumberland House 200 Broad Street Birmingham, B15 1TD 021-643-5011	Coventry Wolverhampton Worcester	Scottish Traffic Area 83 Princes Street Edinburgh, EH2 2ER 031-225-5494	Aberdeen Edinburgh Glasgow Inverness
Eastern Traffic Area Birkbeck House 14—16 Trinity Square Nottingham, NG1 4BA 0602-475511	Leicester Northampton Nottingham		

DTp ADI application form (Part II) (continued)

No responsibility is accepted by the Department of Transport for any risks not covered by insurance. This includes loss of 'no claims bonus' and the cost of excesses not covered by the insurance.

Examination Decisions

Where a candidate believes any part of the ADI Register examination has not been conducted in accordance with the regulations, the method of appeal should be to the Magistrate's Court or, in Scotland, to the Sheriff. The decision itself cannot be changed.

Part 2 – Test of Driving Ability

Candidates receive a letter stating the time and place of the appointment and they must have this in their possession when they attend for the test.

Unsuccessful candidates will receive a letter of confirmation and a further application form enabling them to re-apply. Successful candidates will receive a letter of confirmation and an application form enabling them to apply for the test of instructional ability.

The Test of Driving Ability lasts for about an hour and is split into two parts (Test 1 Eyesight; Test 2 Driving Technique).

Form 42/DT is the ADI equivalent to the DL24 (the driving test statement of failure) and contains 21 main objectives with extra provision for examiners to add additional remarks.

Item 1 relates to the eyesight test. Items 2 to 21 are concerned with driving technique. Items 2 to 8 are under the sub-heading of Control. Items 9 to 21 are under the sub-heading of Road Procedure. Item 22 enables the examiner to add additional remarks.

The Test of Driving Technique

A very high standard of driving will be expected and candidates must demonstrate:

- proper anticipation;
- consideration for the safety of others at all times;
- sound judgement of distances, speeds and timing;
- correct road procedures.

It should also be noted that:

the ADI42/DT contains provision for marking additional faults to those contained on DL24;

candidates who incur more than six minor faults or one or more serious fault will fail;

candidates are assessed as experienced drivers with expert handling skills;

candidates are expected to make reasonable use of the vehicle's performance within the law;

candidates are expected to take advantage of suitable and safe opportunities to overtake, proceed and/or make progress;

the emergency stop may well take place at speeds in excess of 40 mph;

Department of Transport

	Your personal reference no.
	Our reference
	Date

Dear Sir/Madam

Register of Approved Driving Instructors

I acknowledge with thanks receipt of the fee for the test of driving ability which forms part of the Register qualifying examination. You are invited to attend at the time and place shown overleaf so that the test may be carried out. Please be punctual.

You must bring this letter with you when you attend for the test.

You must provide a suitable saloon motor car or estate car in proper condition, with seat belts in working order, and capable of the normal performance of a vehicle of its type. It must be free from advertisements and signs which might cause other road users to believe that it is not being driven by a qualified driver. It should have an orthodox (ie non—automatic) transmission system, right—hand steering, a readily adjustable driving seat and a seat for a forward—facing front passenger.

ADI 9D

DTp ADI notification of appointment (Part II)

If the vehicle does not meet these requirements, it will not be possible to proceed with the test.

The Department cannot accept responsibility for risks not covered by insurance including the loss of any No Claims Bonus or the cost or repairing minor damage.

The fee you have paid for this appointment cannot normally be refunded unless you give to this office at the above address at least three clear days' notice (day of receipt, day of examination, weekends and public holidays excluded) before the date of the appointment, of your inability to attend. The details opposite should be completed and this letter returned. The Department is generally not prepared to consider the refund of the fee (or offer you a further appointment without the payment of a further fee) where less than three clear days' notice is given.

Yours faithfully

for Registrar
Approved Driving Instructors

DTp ADI notification of appointment (Part II) (continued)

Test of driving ability

Date .... Place ....

Time ....

Name in Full ....

**On arrival please ask for
the Supervising Examiner, Mr** ....
In case of FOG, ICE OR SNOW on the day please telephone ....

Notice of Inability to Attend

I shall not be able to attend for test at the time shown.

Would you please arrange another appointment:—

*Delete and
complete as
appropriate*

(a) as soon as possible

(b) not before .... (give date)

Signature ....

Address ....

....

....

Date ....

DTp ADI notification of appointment (Part II) (continued)

candidates are expected to reverse into a road both to the left and the right;

routes will be varied to take in both urban and rural areas;

although there is no specific requirement to test the candidate's knowledge of the Highway Code, examiners may ask questions relating to the drive.

Candidates must also satisfy the examiner on:

(a) precautions before starting the engine;

(b) expert handling of the accelerator/clutch/gears/footbrake/handbrake/steering;

(c) moving away straight ahead/at an angle/safely under control;

(d) stopping the vehicle quickly and under control;

(e) driving the vehicle backwards and while so doing enter limited opening to the right;

(f) driving the vehicle backwards and while so doing enter limited opening to the left;

(g) causing the vehicle to face in the opposite direction by the use of forward and reverse gears.

(h) making effective use of the mirrors well before signalling/changing direction/overtaking/slowing down or stopping;

(i) indicating intended actions at appropriate times by giving appropriate signals clearly and in an unmistakable manner.

(j) acting correctly and promptly on all signals given by traffic signs and traffic controllers and taking appropriate action on signals given by other road users.

(k) exercising proper care in the use of speed;

(l) making progress by driving at speeds appropriate to the road and traffic conditions/avoiding undue hesitancy and taking advantage of suitable safe opportunities to proceed/overtake;

(m) following other vehicles at a safe distance;

(n) making use of proper road procedures and acting properly at road junctions including the regulation of speed on approach/observations before emerging/emerging with due regard for approaching traffic/positioning the vehicle correctly before turning right and left/avoidance of cutting right-hand corners;

(o) overtaking/meeting/crossing the path of other vehicles safely;

(p) positioning the vehicle correctly during normal driving and exercising proper lane discipline;

(q) allowing adequate clearance to stationary vehicles;

(r) taking appropriate action at pedestrian crossings;

(s) selecting safe positions for normal stops;

Department of Transport
Register of Approved Driving Instructors

ADI 42/DT

TESTS 1 and 2

P/Ref No ....

Eyesight and Driving Technique

1 . Comply with the requirements of the eyesight test.

Driving Technique

Control

2 Take proper precautions before starting the engine.

3. Make proper use of/accelerator/clutch/gears/footbrake/handbrake/steering.

4 Move away/safely/under control.

5. Stop vehicle in emergency/promptly/under control.

6 Reverse into a limited opening to the left/under control/with proper observation/with reasonable accuracy.

7 Reverse into a limited opening to the right/under control/with proper observation/with reasonable accuracy.

8 Turn round by means of forward and reverse gears/under control/with proper observation/with reasonable accuracy.

Road Procedure

9 Make effective use of mirror(s) well before/signalling/changing direction/overtaking/slowing down or stopping.

10 Give signals/where necessary/correctly/properly timed/by direction indicators/by arm.

11 Take prompt and appropriate action on all/traffic signs/road markings/traffic lights/signals given by traffic controllers/other road users.

12 Exercise proper care in the use of speed.

13 Make progress by/driving at a speed appropriate to the road and traffic conditions/avoiding undue hesitancy and taking advantage of suitable safe opportunities to proceed/overtake.

14 Follow behind another vehicle at a safe distance.

15 Act properly at road junctions:-
 - regulate speed correctly on approach.
 - take effective observation before emerging.
 - emerging with due regard for approaching traffic.
 - position the vehicle correctly/before turning right/before turning left.
 - avoid cutting right hand corners.

16 Overtake/meet/cross the path of/other vehicles safely.

17 Position the vehicle correctly during normal driving/exercise proper lane discipline.

18 Allow adequate clearance to stationary vehicles.

19 Take appropriate action at pedestrian crossings.

20 Select a safe position for normal stops.

21 Show awareness and anticipation of the actions of/pedestrians/cyclists/drivers.

22 Additional remarks

Supervising Examiner ....   Date ....

DTp ADI test of driving ability (Part II)

(t) showing awareness and anticipation of the actions of pedestrians, cyclists and other drivers and taking appropriate action.

After the test it takes a short time for examiners to assess the candidates' overall performance and announce the result. Providing candidates are prepared to wait a few minutes, the result will be made known to them on the day of the test.

Part 3 – Test of Instructional Ability

In this test candidates are expected to demonstrate their ability to instruct learner drivers at different stages of tuition. The examiner will select any of the following topics as the subject of instruction to be given:

(a) Safety precautions on entering the car and explanation of the controls.
(b) Moving off.
(c) Making normal stops.
(d) Reversing and while so doing entering limited openings to the right or to the left.
(e) Turning the vehicle round in the road to face in the opposite direction using forward and reverse gears.
(f) Parking close to the kerb, using forward and reverse gears.
(g) Using the mirror, and explaining how to make an emergency stop.
(h) Approaching and turning corners.
(i) Judging speed and making normal progress.
(j) Road positioning.
(k) Dealing with road junctions.
(l) Dealing with crossroads.
(m) Dealing with pedestrian crossings.
(n) Meeting, crossing the path of and overtaking other vehicles, and allowing adequate clearance for other vehicles and road users.
(o) Giving correct signals.

The test consists of two phases. Each of these is of about 30 minutes long. In each phase the examiner will give the candidate a briefing and short description of the learner to whom instruction must be given. The examiner will then simulate the role of the learner described in the briefing.

Phase 1 involves giving instruction to the examiner who will be acting either as a complete beginner or an intermediate learner with some experience.

Phase 2 involves giving tuition to the examiner who will be acting as a pupil at about driving test standard.

During the test the examiner will be assessing the candidate's instructional ability and the technical correctness of the instruction given to the learner.

Candidates should listen carefully to the briefing and background detail given by the examiner. They are expected to cover the subject area specified by the examiner at a level of instruction that is appropriate for the description of the learner. The specified topics are:

Subjects Specified in Phase 1

    (a) Safety precautions on entering the car and explanation of the controls.

    (b) Moving off – making normal stops.

    (c) Reversing into an opening.

    (e) Turning the vehicle round in the road.

    (e) Emergency stop – use of mirrors.

    (f) Approaching and turning corners.

    (g) Judgement of speed – making progress – general road positioning.

    (h) Dealing with road junctions – crossroads.

    (i) Meeting – crossing – overtaking other vehicles/allowing adequate clearance for other road users.

    (j) Dealing with pedestrian crossings – giving appropriate signals in a clear and unmistakable manner.

Subjects Specified in Phase 2

    (k) Parking close to the kerb, using reverse gear.

    (l) Reversing into an opening.

    (m) Turning the vehicle round in the road.

    (n) Emergency stop – use of mirrors.

    (o) Approaching and turning corners.

    (p) Judgement of speed – making progress – general road positioning.

    (q) Dealing with road junctions – crossroads.

    (r) Meeting – crossing – overtaking other vehicles/allowing adequate clearance for other road users.

    (s) Dealing with pedestrian crossings – giving appropriate signals in a clear and unmistakable manner.

During the test the examiner will also be looking at various other aspects of the candidate's performance. These include personal characteristics such as patience, tact, firmness and enthusiasm as well as the overall confidence and general manner of the candidate.

It takes only a few days for candidates to be notified of the result. Unsuccessful candidates will receive an application form enabling them to re-apply for another test.

Providing they still satisfy all the other conditions of registration, the name of successful candidates can be placed in the Register and a Certificate of Registration issued. To enable the Department of Transport to proceed further, the reverse of this confirmation letter should be completed and returned together with the registration fee and two passport-type photographs not larger than 2½ x 2 inches or smaller than 2 x 1½ inches.

Details of the subjects and topics covered in the ADI Part III examination are shown in Appendix IV.

Chapter 16

ADI Training and Supervision of Licence Holders

Training for the Examination

Applicants to the Department of Transport Approved Driving Instructor Register are advised to seek professional guidance before sitting the Part 1 Test of Theory and attend properly structured courses before taking the Part 2 Test of Driving Ability and Part 3 Test of Instructional Ability. Although there is no legal requirement to do this, it makes good sense as candidates are unlikely to succeed in any part without adequate preparation.

It is widely recognised that good drivers don't always make good instructors. Similarly, good instructors don't always make good staff tutors. When making enquiries and selecting a course, it is worth keeping in mind that staff tutors require specialist skills which are quite different from those used to teach leaner drivers. The wrong choice of tutor can cause disappointment and result in re-examination fees which can far outweight the cost of attending a properly structured course in the first place.

The ADI National Joint Council has trained a number of specialist staff tutors from all parts of the country. They have all passed a special test conducted at the Department of Transport Examiners' Training Establishment and attended an intensive four-week course. Before enrolling on a course trainees should establish, as far as possible, that the person conducting the course is suitably qualified. Details about the NJC tutor training scheme are available from the Secretary of the NJC at: 41 Edinburgh Road, Cambridge CB4 1QR (Tel: 0223 359079).

Courses should adequately cover the requirements of the official syllabus outlined in the previous section, be conducted by professionally recognised staff tutors and be properly structured and organised to meet the different needs of each of the three separate parts of the examination.

When Examination is structured. To be realistic candidates should allow for between four and six months before applying for the Part 1 test and taking the Part 3. In many instances it is known to take considerably longer than this. It normally takes about two months from applying to receiving the result of Part 1 Test of Theory. Only if the result is favourable may candidates apply for the Part 2 test. It usually takes a further four or five weeks to obtain an appointment and then another four to five weeks to obtain one for the Part 3. This time factor can cause a serious lack of continuity where the course covers both the theoretical and practical elements at the same time.

With any course trainees should consider the extra expense such as travel and accommodation.

Types of Course Available

When selecting a course make adequate enquiries so that you can find the one which most suits your own requirements. Some courses consist of the following elements:

(a) Short group briefings in a classroom, followed by three or four students being sent out in a car to practice together unsupervised.
(b) Prospective instructors being sent out unsupervised with learner drivers.
(c) Long periods of passive observation where the prospective instructor sits in the back of a car watching an experienced instructor teach.
(d) Passive observation where the prospective instructor sits in the back of the car watching another candidate being trained.
(e) Training being given by inexperienced tutors who hold no special professional qualification other than ADI registration.
(f) The theoretical elements being combined with the practical, when the practical examinations may be some six months away and no supplementary training is given nearer the examination appointments.
(g) Where the prospective instructor is asked to teach paying learners (monies being paid to the training organisation). Experience at teaching real learners can be useful in the later stages of a course but thorough training should be given before this 'practice' takes place as the prospective instructor may be 'perfecting' the wrong things.

Note: Some establishments offer finance facilities for large sums of money to cover course and examination costs. Candidates should carefully consider this kind of expenditure; at least until the Part 1 Test of Theory has been passed.

Preparation for the Part 1 Test of Theory

Properly organised 'home learning' programmes can prepare candidates for the Part 1 test and provide a solid foundation before trainees attend practical courses. Systematic study also plays an important part in preparing candidates for the Parts 2 and 3 tests and reducing the need for extended practical courses.

A structured 'home-study programme' is available from the authors. This identifies the key learning points and systematically prepares candidates for the Part 1 Test of Theory. Additional support materials are included to help with preparation for the Parts 2 and 3 tests.

Preparing for the Part 2 Test of Driving Ability

All candidates, including members of advanced driving organisations, are advised to obtain some guidance from a recognised tutor before presenting themselves for the Test of Driving Ability. Reasons for this include:

   (i) the standard is much higher than the standard assessed on advanced driving tests;

  (ii) candidates generally require some training for the test conditions;

 (iii) deficient knowledge still contributes to many failures even though the candidates have passed the Part 1 Test of Theory;

 (iv) candidates who just manage to scrape through the test are at a severe disadvantage when attending the instructional element of their training;

  (v) it is important to remove any false assumptions many have about Department of Transport Driving Tests;

 (vi) time spent under corrective tuition provides a first-hand object demonstration of the teaching techniques to be learnt in the Part 3 course and used on the Test of Instructional Ability.

Candidates for this test are expected to have an expert understanding of the vehicle and procedures and should drive as experienced drivers. They should be above lowering their own standards with elementary styles of car control and superficial shows of overcaution.

Common sense is one of the most important qualities required of candidates on the Part 2 Test of Driving Technique. Unfortunately, common sense is not as common as commonly thought, particularly when under pressure. A common cause of failure is due to the candidates' misconception of how they think the Department of Transport want learners to drive. It should be made clear that learners should be taught to drive competently and not to behave in an artificial or superficial way. Candidates for the ADI driving test who drive in this way lack confidence in themselves and should not expect to pass.

Organised study can also play a vital part in preparing candidates for both the Parts 2 and 3 and reduce the need for extended practical courses.

Preparing for the Part 3 Test of Instructional Ability

Each topic selected by the examiner contains a number of key points. In the time allowed, it may not be possible for you to cover them all. However, if the points you cover are adequate for the level of ability of the learner you will not be penalised providing the tuition given is satisfactory.

1. Explanation of the controls (instruction given to a beginner)
Some instructors try to tell complete novices everything they need to know about a car and its controls during the first driving lesson while others attempt to teach them to move off, stop and/or change gear. While instructors should endeavour to get learners moving and changing gear as soon as possible, these are not the main purposes of the first lesson. The purpose of the initial driving lesson with a complete novice is to:

- reassure them and gain their confidence; and
- familiarise students with the operation and effects of using the main controls.

Don't expect too much too soon! Most people are anxious or excited on their first driving lesson while others are impatient to get moving. Quite obviously these are not states of mind conducive to learning unnecessary detail or masses of technical information about the controls which are irrelevant to assisting students in following instructions to carry out simple tasks.

Properly timed verbal assistance from competent instructors is usually sufficient to get even the most inept of students to follow simple instructions to move off, change gear, steer and stop during this first lesson.

Use this first lesson to demonstrate to hesitant and nervous pupils that driving is not as hard as they think and to fulfil the expectations of the more confident and able learner.

On arriving at the chosen location, change seats and establish an organised sequence for getting into the car. Get the new driver to carry out the 'cockpit drill' (eg doors, handbrake, seat, mirrors, belt). Inform them this is the standard procedure whenever they get into a car.

Once the student can carry out the 'cockpit drill', get them to start the engine. Give them plenty of practice in 'suitable precautions' before starting the engine and get them to switch it off.

Unless the learner has had some previous experience on the same make and model of vehicle, some explanation of the controls will be required.

How deep this goes and how long it takes will vary according to the students experience, ability and aptitude.

On this first outing, it is normally sufficient to explain only the main controls and such others that may actually be needed during the initial drive; the other ancillary controls and instruments are usually better left to another time.

The average time spent on this explanation should be approximately five to ten minutes for someone with considerable previous experience, extending to 30 to 35 minutes for those with little or no experience at all. On very rare occasions it may take longer than this before the learner is able to assimilate sufficient information prior to moving the car. Wherever possible the lesson should be timed to enable the client to move the vehicle and stop it on his first outing.

Give students plenty of 'hands on' practice and feel for all of the controls before you let them move off. Even those who have driven before are unlikely to be familiar with your car. They will need to develop a feel for the steering, gears, pedals and handbrake.

Show the student how the main controls are used and what they do. Start with how to hold the steering wheel and get them to operate the indicators without removing the hand from it. Get them to carry out your instructions concerning the handbrake, gearlever, and pedals.

Give plenty of practice at applying and releasing the handbrake. Let them develop a feel for the gears and moving the lever from one gear to another.

Get their feet positioned correctly for using the pedals. Get them used to covering and feeling for the pedals without looking at their feet. let them start the engine and practice 'setting the gas' for moving off.

Let them hear and feel the 'biting range' of the clutch. Remember that explaining is unlikely to be enough. Tell the students what you want them to do and let them do it. Tell them one thing at a time. Don't go on until they can do it to your satisfaction.

Let the students drive as soon as they can understand and follow instructions. These first attempts to follow your instructions on the move will show the student how the controls affect the car. Moving off and changing gear at an early stage will have a beneficial effect on the over-anxious and help to satisfy the expectations of the more able.

Key Learning Points:

- enter and leave the car safely (safety of opening doors);
- carry out cockpit drill, eg doors, handbrake, seat, mirrors, belt;
- assume a correct seating posture and grip of the steering wheel;
- start the engine, taking suitable precautions beforehand;
- identify the function of and locate the main driving controls (accelerator/footbrake/clutch/handbrake/gears/steering indicators);
- carry out simple instructions relating to moving off, changing gear, steering, use of MSM routine and stopping in a safe position.

2. Moving off and making normal stops (instruction given to a beginner)
Insist that learners check the mirrors and blind spots before moving off, but at first you should concentrate more on developing the students' control of the vehicle. As this improves get them to think more about the proximity of other road users. Encourage them to anticipate and allow for the movement of others. Emphasise the importance of the timing of moving off and making progress on busier roads.

Use fairly quiet roads at first and encourage the student to make proper progress at normal speeds but within their own ability. Explain that the frustration of being held up can cause others to take risks and overtake when unsafe.

Key Learning Points:

- importance of front and rear vision before moving off
- mirrors before signalling/changing direction/overtaking/braking
- keeping to the mirror-signal-manoeuvre routine
- co-ordination of accelerator, clutch, handbrake and steering
- moving off at an angle/on a gradient/level
- responding correctly to the presence/actions of others
- stopping in a safe position.

3. Reversing into an opening.

4. Turning the vehicle round in the road.

5. Parking close to the kerb using reverse gear.

At first use roads which are level, traffic-free and of generous width. At first use round corners for reversing. Avoid roads with trees, lamps, other kerbside obstructions, high kerbs or steep cambers for initial practice. Introduce these only as students improve.

Emphasise the importance of low-speed control and encourage the development of this skill. Point out the different steering characteristics when driving in reverse gear. As control improves place more emphasis on awareness of other road users.

Don't insist on perfect accuracy in the early stages. Place more emphasis on reversing in a straight line along the new road than on distance from the kerb. Explain the value of exercises and their uses, eg in turning round. Give examples of safe places to reverse and of dangerous practices such as reversing from a minor road into a major road.

Encourage students to use the mirror-signal-manoeuvre routine before stopping and avoid commencing exercises near parked vehicles and kerbside obstructions unless they are reversing into a parking space. Encourage students to look out for other road users throughout a reversing manoeuvre and to act sensibly on what they see.

Key Learning Points:
   – the selection of a safe place to carry out the manoeuvre;
   – observations before and throughout the exercises;
   – responding correctly to presence/actions of others;
   – co-ordination of controls and steering to achieve reasonable accuracy.

A qualified driving instructor can legally remove his seatbelt while teaching a provisional licence holder to reverse/manoeuvre. During the Test of Instructional Ability however, and because the examiner is a fully qualified driver only acting as a learner, the Law does not permit the candidate to remove the belt. Candidates may, however, advise the examiner acting as the learner to remove his seat belt if so required.

6. Emergency stop – use of mirrors

Emphasise the importance of using the mirrors frequently in case of emergencies. At first let the student practice the pivot from the accelerator to the footbrake in a stationary car. When moving encourage the use of firm but progressive braking before pushing the clutch down. Explain how to avoid skids caused by harsh braking and how to correct them should the wheels lock. Initially practise 'quicker normal stops'. Gradually build up braking pressure until 'emergency' pressure is reached.

Always insist on correct mirror adjustment. Although at first the use of the routine tends to be superficial it should be developed as a habit.

As the student's car control skills develop encourage fuller use of the MSM routine when moving off, slowing down and stopping, changing direction and overtaking. As the student improves more emphasis should be placed on awareness and the correct judgement of the speeds, distances and actions of others. Insist that the action taken is appropriate to the situation behind.

Key Learning Points:
   – the importance of quick, controlled reactions;
   – the application of footbrake and then clutch before stopping;
   – two hands on the wheel when braking;

- avoidance and correction of skidding;
- the importance of rear vision;
- when and why mirrors should be used;
- the mirror-signal-manoeuvre routine;
- the limitations of mirrors.

7. Approaching and turning corners (see also 9 and 10)

At first let the student practice the MSM routine on the approach to corners and, subsequently, quiet junctions. Emphasise the importance of approaching under control at a proper speed. Let students practice braking and selecting appropriate gears at the right time and speed. Encourage the student to slow down enough to look effectively into side roads and round corners and bends before making any commitment to proceed. As the student improves discourage the practice of crawling unnecessarily up to corners and of uncontrolled coasting.

Let the student develop their steering on the approach and arriving at the junction or corner in the correct position. Discourage the cutting of right-hand corners and driving too close to the kerb or swinging out to the right before turning left.

Ensure the students start looking early when approaching junctions and corners. Make sure they understand that this does not involve superficial head movements. Explain the kind of things they are to look for and where they are most likely. As skill increases point out things which restrict their sightlines and let them practice dealing with these for themselves. Encourage the development of students' judgement of the speed and distances of other traffic and their ability to emerge without causing danger or undue concern to others.

Try to develop proper attitudes towards pedestrians who are crossing the road near corners and get the students looking for and being prepared to give way to oncoming traffic before turning right. Explain what to expect, where to look and what to look for.

Key Learning Points:

- the use of mirror/signals/brakes/gears approaching;
- approaching under proper control at a correct speed;
- avoidance of excessive speed or crawling on the approach and coasting;
- the correct line on the approach and position on corner;
- giving way to pedestrians and oncoming traffic;
- observations into side road/waiting before point of turn/avoidance of cutting right-hand corners.

8. Judgement of speed – making progress – general road positioning

Encourage proper attitudes towards the use of speed and ensure students understand and practice the principle of being able to stop well within the distance seen to be clear. Ask questions about stopping distances and then ask them to convert these into reality. For example, do they know how far 75 feet is along the road or is it just a figure in their head?

Where students have difficulty in judging speeds and distance the observation of other traffic while they are parked may help. This is also a useful exercise with mirrors.

Not all students will have the same perception of the word 'slow'. Where they have difficulty in judging their own speed on approach, demonstrate the speeds required.

Discourage hogging the middle of the road, hugging the kerb and driving too close to pedestrians. Explain the effect of positioning too close to the kerb when turning left and of cutting right-hand corners.

Encourage students to look and plan ahead and take up position early, particularly when driving in lanes. Point out the consequences of failure to do this. Encourage students to read road signs and markings. Discourage the changing of lanes unnecessarily or suddenly without using the mirrors and checking blind spots. Encourage students to drive in the middle of their selected lane and discourage the straddling of lane markings.

Key Learning Points:

- dangers of and avoidance of excessive speed for conditions;
- making progress at speeds appropriate to conditions and avoidance of undue hesitancy;
- maintenance of correct driving position, eg not hugging kerb or hogging road centre; driving in centre of lane; selection of lane and early observation of road signs and markings.

9. Dealing with road junctions.

10. Dealing with crossroads (see also 7).

At first let the student practice the MSM routine on the approach to corners and, subsequently, quiet junctions. Emphasise the importance of approaching under control at a proper speed. Let students practice braking and selecting appropriate gears at the right time and speed. Encourage the student to slow down enough to look effectively into side roads and round corners and bends before making any commitment to proceed. As the student improves discourage the practice of crawling unnecessarily up to corners and of uncontrolled coasting.

Let the students develop their steering on the approach and arriving at the junction or corner in the correct position. Discourage the cutting of right-hand corners and driving too close to the kerb or swinging out to the right before turning left.

Ensure the student starts looking early when approaching junctions and corners. Make sure they understand that this does not involve superficial head movements. Explain the kind of things they are to look for and where they are most likely. As the students skill increases point out things which restrict their sightlines and let them practice dealing with these for themselves. Encourage the development of students' judgement of the speed and distances of other traffic and their ability to emerge without causing danger or undue concern to others.

Try to develop proper attitudes towards pedestrians who are crossing the road near corners and looking for and being prepared to give way to oncoming traffic before turning right. Explain what to expect, where to look and what to look for.

Key Learning Points:

- using the mirror-signal-manoeuvre routine;
- correct speed on the approach/proper use of gears/avoidance of coasting;
- taking effective observations before emerging;
- proper judgement of speeds/distances and emerging with due regard for others;
- selection of the correct position before and after turning;
- judgement of speeds and distances of oncoming traffic/giving way when turning right;
- avoidance of cutting right-hand corners;
- giving way to pedestrians crossing at/near junctions.

11. Meeting-crossing-overtaking other vehicles – allowing adequate clearance for other road users

Encourage proper attitudes towards the movement of other road users and the risks involved in emerging, crossing oncoming traffic, passing parked vehicles and meeting oncoming traffic and overtaking.

Try to develop the students' awareness of speed and judgement of distance and clearances when passing parked vehicles, pedestrians and cyclists. Explain that higher speeds need more clearance and that small clearances require very low speeds. Develop students' awareness of risks when they are approaching and passing parked vehicles and cyclists.

Let the students practice the holdback position behind parked cars when giving way to oncoming traffic. Ensure they practice a safe following position prior to overtaking cyclists.

Encourage a normal driving position which allows safe clearances between their vehicle and oncoming traffic. Make sure students understand the principles involved in giving way to oncoming traffic. Try to develop the students' awareness of restrictions in their field of view when passing on the left side of right-turning vehicles. Encourage students to look out for emerging or turning motorcyclists, cyclists and other vehicles.

As the students' driving develops, encourage them to overtake where progress is severely held up by slow moving vehicles. Point out the dangers involved and discourage overtaking for the sake of it. Provide practice in situations where overtaking may be carried out safely. Ensure the student understands the dangers of overtaking and try to develop a safe attitude towards the selection of place and timing of this potentially very dangerous manoeuvre.

Explain why the MSM and PSL routines are reversed. Ensure proper observations before overtaking and encourage the development of the students' anticipation of the actions of other road users. Make a particular reference to the possibility of vehicles emerging from side roads.

Key Learning Points:

- mirror-signal-manoeuvre routine;
- approaching at safe speeds and provision of adequate clearance when meeting traffic coming from the opposite direction;
- giving way to oncoming traffic when turning right;
- overtaking – assessing the risks and benefits; overtaking safely;
- following traffic/cyclists at a safe distance/stopping distances;
- allowing adequate clearance to stationary vehicles/risks involved when passing/additional risks of dangerously parked vehicles;
- anticipating the actions of pedestrians/cyclists/other drivers crossing path/restrictions to sightlines, eg stationary vehicles.

12. Dealing with pedestrian crossings – giving appropriate signals in a clear and unmistakable manner.

Encourage the development of proper attitudes towards pedestrians and crossings. Make sure the student knows what to look for, where to look for it, what to expect and how to respond. Encourage students to check crossings and approach at speeds which permit them to stop if required. Ensure students understand the rules concerned with overtaking on the approach and giving precedence. Discourage the practice of beckoning people across.

Point out that many crossings may be found just out of sight round corners near junctions.

Try to develop the students' awareness of other road users and encourage them to discriminate between which signals are necessary and those which are not.

Give the student plenty of practice in situations requiring the special timing of signals. For example due to the close proximity of vehicles to junctions and of junctions to other junctions.

Key Learning Points:

- mirror-signal-manoeuvre routine/value of arm signals to pedestrians and others;
- approaching pedestrian crossings at a proper speed/avoidance of overtaking on the approach/invitation signals to pedestrians;
- stopping when necessary;
- give signals where necessary/correctly/properly timed;
- discrimination between necessary and unnecessary signals.

Notes for Guidance – Part 3 Test

Real learner drivers are not used on the Part 3 test because of the dangers this may cause. In addition they make it extremely difficult for the examiner to control the test conditions. During the practical training for the Part 3 test most of the time should be spent on simulation exercises. In these the staff instructor will select the topic for instruction and give the background information on the age, sex, experience and personality of the learner. They should say what is required and give a brief outline of the type of faults most likely to occur. The staff tutor will then simulate the role of the learner described. This format is similar to that of the examination and will ensure candidates are prepared for the test conditions.

Test candidates should listen carefully to the briefing and ask questions to clear up any areas of doubt before the exercise begins. After the initial briefing candidates should try to think of the examiner as a 'learner' driver befitting the description given. Once the exercise has commenced, candidates should ask questions of the 'learner' and encourage the 'learner' to ask questions.

Candidates should be sympathetic towards the 'learner' but with a preparedness to be firm if necessary. Visual aids should be used as they would on a normal lesson. Candidates should explain, demonstrate and provide plenty of opportunities for the student to practice as on a normal lesson. Where appropriate, the Highway Code and other publications should be used to support the points under instruction.

During each exercise the examiner will be looking to see if candidates:

   (a) tell the learner what they are going to do and what to expect;
   (b) answer questions satisfactorily;
   (c) treat the learner unnecessarily as a novice;
   (d) expect too high a standard for tuition so far received;
   (e) adapt the level of tuition to the student's ability;
   (f) use the dual controls unnecessarily or excessively;
   (g) fail to tell the learner when/why the dual controls were used;
   (h) give clear and to the point instructions;
   (i) are excessively verbose or irrelevant;
   (j) allow faults to be repeated without taking corrective measures;
   (k) give correct instruction;
   (l) show lack of patience, tact or firmness;
   (m) inspire confidence;
   (n) give the learner sufficient encouragement;
   (o) are over-critical and destructive;
   (p) give sufficient praise when deserved.

During the test the examiner will also be looking at various other aspects of the candidate's performance. These include personal characteristics such as patience, tact, firmness and enthusiasm as well as the overall confidence and general manner of the candidate.

There are various degrees of impatience from sarcastic comments, tone of voice, impatient body movements, to total loss of self-control and open hostility towards the student. While you should be firm you should also be sympathetic to learners and be prepared to repeat yourself as many times as necessary without making them feel inadequate.

It should go without saying that you should not smoke when giving lessons. Physical contact with a learner is undesirable and should be avoided. There are obvious exceptions such as when diverting the steering wheel to prevent danger. Speak clearly. Your route directions should be specific and easy to follow.

Listen very carefully to the examiner's briefing and address the learner according to your interpretation of this. This is a difficult area to define precisely and will depend on the background, personality, age and sex of both the candidate and the learner. The use of first names is becoming more socially acceptable and usually leads to a more relaxed atmosphere. However, great tact is required as it may be considered disrespectful by some social and professional classes and older people particularly if you are quite a young person.

Try to create a relaxed atmosphere in the car, but there will be times when you must be firm. For example, to ensure dangerous situations do not develop, to avoid damage to the vehicle, to keep within the law, to make learners face up to things they may not like doing.

Be alert and look for ways in which to help or improve the performance of your students. Try to build the learners' confidence and encourage them to think for themselves. The examiner will not be very impressed if you are indifferent, bored or disinterested in what is happening.

Listen carefully to the examiner's briefing and ask questions to remove areas of doubt. Think about the briefing, plan the lesson accordingly and then proceed to give it in an orderly manner, in the correct sequence. If you set off without giving the learner a clear briefing, or without obvious purpose, you should expect to be penalised.

Explain things simply and clearly. Emphasise the main points without losing them in excess verbiage or repetition. Be sure that what you are saying is correct.

Teach at a level that is appropriate to the learner's ability. Don't expect the less able learners to deal unaided with situations they cannot cope with. Talk them through difficult situations. Restrict the information you give them to the basics until they have mastered these. Remember however that over-instruction will inhibit the more able and that it suppresses initiative.

Assess the examiner's actions and understanding as though he were a real learner. Ask questions which test knowledge and encourage the learner to think more about what he is doing and the decisions he makes. For example, if the examiner is driving too close to parked vehicles, ask: 'What kind of things do you expect and look out for when approaching a row of parked cars?'

It should go without saying that if the examiner asks a question as the learner, it must be answered satisfactorily.

Do not allow faults to be repeated without correction, but avoid being petty and over-critical. Try to identify the cause of a fault and point out the action required to prevent recurrence. Point out the consequences of recurring faults.

Try not to emphasise a fault in a negative manner. For example, 'Don't drive in the middle of the road.' It is more effective to state the remedy, for example 'Try to drive about three feet from the kerb'.

Try to isolate and treat the cause of an error rather than its effect. For example, if the examiner continually drives too fast through minor crossroads making only superficial observations, it may show the learner does not appreciate the danger of emerging vehicles. This lack of awareness may be causing the excessive speed. Make the learner more aware of the dangers by pointing them out beforehand.

Very little is learnt in total isolation from previous lessons. At the start of each lesson instructors normally revise or refer to matters they have covered previously. You may find doing this on the examination will help to add more realism to the situation and get you started.

Many instructors only look for faults. While it is important to be able to identify these and correct them, it is equally important to look for improvement and reinforce progress. Instructors who only look for faults provide learners with little incentive to try harder.

Give plenty of praise and encouragement for any improvement and progress you notice in the learner's performance.

At the end of each lesson instructors should summarise or re-state the points covered on it. You should try to do this on the examination.

Supervision and Training of Licence Holders

Twenty per cent of the instruction given by a licence holder during the first three months of the licence must be supervised by an ADI. This supervision does not contribute to the requirement for 40 hours of Core Curriculum Training for licence holders.

Supervision records must be signed by both the licence holder and the supervising ADI. They must be legible, unambiguous and clearly set out on Form ADI 21 S. At the end of three months, the completed records must be sent to The Register of Approved Driving Instructors, Department of Transport, 2 Marsham Street, London SW1 3EB.

The supervising instructor signing the records must ensure they are factual as the Department of Transport takes a very serious view of falsified work ratio records. The Registrar will examine whether or not a supervising ADI signing falsified records is a fit and proper person to remain on the Register.

A driving school manager in Leeds was recently fined £3 200, and two of his staff £800 each, relating to illegal instruction.

The records must clearly show:

   (i) the name of the licence holder;
  (ii) the licence number;
 (iii) the name of the establishment from which the holder is working;
 (iv) the name of the supervising ADI;
  (v) for each working day the records must give:
         – the date;
         – the total number of instruction hours;
         – periods of supervision.

Core Curriculum Training and Records for Licence Holders

All trainee licence holders must receive a minimum of 40 hours of individual in-car instruction from an ADI. This training is separate from the requirement to supervise 20 per cent of the trainee's work and includes instruction on all of the matters listed below:

Department of Transport

Register of Approved Driving Instructors

LICENSED TRAINEE SUPERVISION RECORD

Record required by Regulation 11(4) of the Motor Cars (Driving Instruction) Regulations 1977.

ADI 21 S

Notes 1. For the first 3 months of the trainee licence the holder must keep this record of the number of hours he spends giving driving instruction and of the number of hours he is directly supervised by an Approved Driving Instructor. He must be supervised for at least one fifth of the time he gives instruction during this period (see para 15 of the booklet ADI 14 for details).

2. The record must be clearly set out, legible and unambiguous.

3. Promptly at the end of the 3 months the form must be sent to "The Register of Approved Driving Instructors, Room C9/10, 2 Marsham Street, London SW1 3EB."

4. Please complete the details below using BLOCK LETTERS

Serial No on Licence ....

Name of Licence Holder .... Personal Ref. No ....

Home Address ....

....

Name and Address of ....

Training Establishment ....

on Licence ....

Details of ADI(s) who have signed below and overleaf

Name	ADI Certificate No.	Signature

Date	Hours Instruction	Hours Supervised	Signature of Trainee	Signature of ADI	Date	Hours Instruction	Hours Supervised	Signature of Trainee	Signature of ADI
					(continued)				
				Total Hours on This Page					

DTp ADI Register – trainee supervision record

(a) explanation of the controls of the vehicle;
(b) moving off;
(c) making normal stops;
(d) reversing and entering limited openings to the right and left;
(e) turning to face the opposite direction with forward and reverse gears;
(f) parking close to the kerb, using forward and reverse gears;
(g) using the mirror, and explaining how to make an emergency stop;
(h) approaching and turning corners;
(i) judging speed and making normal progress;
(j) road positioning;
(k) dealing with road junctions;
(l) dealing with crossroads;
(m) dealing with pedestrian crossings;
(n) meeting/crossing path of/overtaking other vehicles/allowing adequate clearance for other vehicles and road users;
(o) giving correct signals;
(p) comprehension of traffic signs and traffic control signals;
(q) the method, clarity, adequacy and correctness of instruction;
(r) the observation and correction of the student's errors;
(s) the instructor's manner generally, eg patience, tact, firmness, confidence and level of encouragement given to students.

The Instructor Training Declaration certificate (ADI 21 T) can be obtained from the Registrar. The completed certificate must be signed by the licence holder and ADI responsible for training. The Department of Transport takes a very serious view of falsified training records and the Registrar will examine whether or not an ADI signing falsified records is a fit and proper person to remain on the Register. The records must show:

(i) the licence serial number;
(ii) the name and home address of the licence holder;
(iii) the name, ADI certificate number, and business address of the ADI responsible for training;
(iv) the name and address of the training establishment on the licence;
(v) the date;
(vi) the number of hours of instruction received.

For each core curriculum topic the certificate must show the date the training was received and the number of hours involved. Each section must be signed by the trainee and countersigned by the ADI.

The completed certificate must be sent to the Registrar so that it is received not later than five weeks from the date of issue of the licence. Send the certificate to The Register of Approved Driving Instructors, Department of Transport, 2 Marsham Street, London SW1 3EB.

Notes for Sponsoring Instructors

Because there is a considerable overlap between the core curriculum subject

---

ADI 21 T

Department of Transport

Register of Approved Driving Instructors

INSTRUCTOR TRAINING DECLARATION

Declaration under Regulation 11(6) of the Motor Cars
(Driving Instruction) Regulations 1977

Notes 1.   **Please use BLOCK LETTERS**

2.   This completed declaration must be sent to the Registrar so that he receives it not later than 5 weeks from the date of issue of the licence. The address to which it should be sent is "The Register of Approved Driving Instructors, Room C17/O ,2 Marsham Street, London SW1 3EB."

Serial No. on Licence

Name of Licence Holder

Home Address

Name and Address of
Training Establishment
on Licence

To be completed by the Licence Holder	A. I hereby declare that within the past 13 months I have received a total of not less than 40 hours training in the giving of driving instruction comprising the matters referred to in Regulation 11(6) of the Motor Cars (Driving Instruction) Regulations 1977 and listed overleaf. A record of such training is set out overleaf.

Signed   Date

To be completed by the Approved Driving Instructor responsible for the training.	B. I hereby certify that within the past 13 months the above named licensed trainee driving instructor has been given a total of not less than 40 hours training in the giving of driving instruction comprising the matters referred to in Regulation 11(6) of the Motor Cars (Driving Instruction) Regulations 1977 and listed overleaf. A record of such training is set out overleaf.

Signed   Date

Name   ADI Certificate no.

Business Address

DTp ADI Register – training record

RECORD OF TRAINING

Name and address of establishment from ....

which instructor training was received ....

....

Training matters	Date training given	No of hours	Signature of Trainee	Signature of ADI
Explaining the controls of the vehicle, including the use of dual controls				
Moving off				
Making normal stops				
Reversing, and while doing so entering limited openings to the right or to the left				
Turning to face the opposite direction, using forward and reverse gears				
Parking close to the kerb, using forward and reverse gears				
Using mirrors and explaining how to make an emergency stop				
Approaching and turning corners				
Judging speed, and making normal progress				
Road positioning				
Dealing with road junctions				
Dealing with cross roads				
Dealing with pedestrian crossings				
Meeting, crossing the path of, overtaking and allowing adequate clearance for, other vehicles and other road users				
Giving correct signals				
Comprehension of traffic signs, including road markings and traffic control signals				
Method, clarity, adequacy and correctness of instruction				
Observation and correction of driving errors committed by pupils and general manner				

Total Hours   (Not less than 40 hours)

DTp ADI Register – training record (continued)

topics, those responsible for training may sometimes find it difficult to know precisely where to allocate the time devoted to individual aspects on the instructor training declaration certificate (ADI 21 T). As long as they cover the listed topics, staff instructors need not restrict experiences they create to those falling strictly within the borders defined by the certificate. An artificial restriction to training such as this may limit the overall value of it and not satisfy the long-term needs of the trainee.

The requirements for supervising 20 per cent of the instruction given by trainee licence holders is in addition to and separate from the training specified in the regulations. ADIs responsible for supervision should allow the trainee authority to conduct the lesson and not rebuke or belittle him in front of the learner. The trainee can usually be corrected later in private but the supervising ADI must rectify any incorrect information given to the learner driver immediately. The ADI will need tact and experience to discreetly make good instructional errors without embarrassment to the trainee and loss of confidence in the school.

The Cost of Training and Supervising Licence Holders

Due to the high degree of close supervision and 40 hours of core curriculum training involved, the cost of qualifying under this system can be higher than a full course of professional training. The cost of the licence fee must also be taken into account and consideration should be given to loss of earnings while carrying out in-house training and supervision.

Chapter 17

Driver and Vehicle Licensing

Driver Licensing

The professional driving instructor should have a good working knowledge of the regulations covering the issue and use of driving licences. He may frequently be called upon to offer advice to customers and to assist pupils with applications for various licences.

In this chapter we deal with the requirements of the law relating to driving licences, how to apply, the minimum ages for driving, eyesight and health regulations and information on vocational licences.

Anyone wishing to drive a mechanically propelled vehicle on a public road in Great Britain must hold a provisional or full licence covering the type of vehicle being driven. Alternatively, a foreign licence or international driving permit may be used for a limited period. When an application for a renewal of a licence is made, the applicant may continue to drive if he is not disqualified from driving and has no medical condition which would prevent him from driving.

It should be noted that driving without a current and valid licence may invalidate the insurance cover.

Licence Groups

The groups of motor vehicles for licensing purposes are:

Group	Class of vehicle	Additional groups covered
A	A vehicle without automatic transmission, of any class not included in any other group	B, C, E, F, K and L
B	A vehicle with automatic transmission, of any class not included in any other group	E, F, K and L
C	Motor tricycle weighing not more than 450kg unladen, but excluding any vehicle included in group E, J, K or L	E, K and L
D	Motor bicycle (with or without side-car) but excluding any vehicle included in group E, K or L	C, E and motorcycles in group L
E	Moped	—

273

Group	Class of vehicle	Additional groups covered
F	Agricultural tractor, but excluding any vehicle included in group H	K
G	Road roller	—
H	Track-laying vehicle steered by its tracks	—
J	Invalid carriage	—
K	Mowing machine or pedestrian controlled vehicle	—
L	Vehicle propelled by electrical power, but excluding any vehicle included in group J or K	K
M	Trolley vehicle	—
N	Vehicle exempted from duty under section 7(1) of the Vehicles (Excise) Act 1971	—

Provisional Driving Licence

A provisional driving licence must be obtained in order to take a vehicle on the road for the purpose of learning to drive and for taking the driving test. The holder of a provisional licence may drive a vehicle only when accompanied by, and under the supervision of, a driver who holds a full licence for that type of vehicle. This rule does not apply under certain circumstances and when driving certain vehicles (when taking a driving test and when riding a motorcycle) but see licence or leaflet D100 for full details.

The vehicle must display 'L' plates which are clearly visible from both the front and back of the vehicle. The holder of a provisional licence must not ride a solo motorcycle with an engine capacity of more than 125cc. When riding a solo motorcycle a pillion passenger must not be carried unless the passenger holds a full licence for a motorcycle.

'L' plates should be removed from a vehicle before it is driven by a person holding a full licence.

Your entitlement to a licence depends on your age and the type of vehicle on which you have passed your driving test. Passing a test for a particular group may entitle you to drive vehicles of some other groups, and may also entitle you to use the licence as a provisional for all other groups. Full details will be found on the driving application form DL26 or DL26M, but a summary is given below of some of the main groups.

A driving test taken on a vehicle in column 1 will also entitle you to drive a vehicle of the groups shown in the appropriate section in column 2.

1	2
Motor car without automatic transmission	Motor car *with* automatic transmission Motor tricycle Moped Agricultural tractor Mowing machine Pedestrian-controlled vehicle Electrically-controlled vehicle

1	*2*
Motor car with automatic transmission	Moped Tractor Mowing machine Pedestrian-controlled vehicle Electrically-controlled vehicle
Motor tricycle	Moped Mowing machine Pedestrian-controlled vehicle Electrically-controlled vehicle
Motor bicycle (with or without sidecar)	Motor tricycle Moped Two-wheel electrically propelled vehicle
Moped	None

You will see from the table that there are certain restrictions:

1. If you pass the test on a moped or motorcycle you are not allowed a full motor car licence.
2. A test passed on a moped does not entitle the candidate to a full motorcycle licence.
3. A test passed on an electrically propelled vehicle does not permit the candidate to drive a car or heavy duty motor vehicle.
4. A test passed on a car with automatic transmission does not entitle the candidate to drive vehicles with manual transmission.

Definitions of different types of vehicles will be found in the D100 leaflet 'What You Need To Know About Driver Licensing'.

Minimum Age of Drivers

No one under the age of 16 is allowed to drive a motor vehicle on the roads. The minimum ages for driving different types of vehicles are:

16 years   Moped (not exceeding 50cc)
Invalid carriage
Agricultural tractor (not exceeding 8ft width)
Mowing machine (three wheels or less)
Pedestrian operated vehicle (three wheels or less)
Motor car (when driven by a disabled person receiving a mobility allowance)

17 years   Motor scooter
Motorcycle (with or without sidecar)
Three-wheeled motor car
Small passenger vehicle (max nine seats)
Small goods vehicle (max 3.5 tonnes)
Road roller (under 11.5 tonnes unladen)
Agricultural tractor

18 years   Goods vehicle (up to 7.5 tonnes laden)
                 Public service vehicle (under the terms of the licence, or if
                     under instruction)

21 years   Heavy goods vehicle (over 7.5 tonnes laden)
                  Road roller (over 11.5 tonnes unladen)
                  Large passenger vehicle

Members of the armed forces are exempt from some of the goods vehicle minimum age requirements.

A 16-year-old may not drive an agricultural tractor on public roads without passing the appropriate driving test.

Disabled young people may (under certain circumstances) drive a motor car at 16 years of age.

A chart showing full details of the age requirements is shown opposite.

Driving Licence Application

A full licence may be issued to an applicant who has, during the past 10 years:

1. held a full GB licence; or
2. passed the GB driving test; or
3. held a full licence issued in Northern Ireland, the Channel Islands or the Isle of Man.

You may also apply for a full licence if you have been resident in GB for less than one year and you surrender a valid full licence issued in the EEC or some other countries. Application for a licence should be made at least three weeks before the date of commencement of the licence. Forms for licence are available from Post Offices and Local Vehicle Licensing Offices. The completed form should be sent to the Driver and Vehicle Licensing Centre, Swansea SA99 1AB. Application may be made at any time within two months prior to the date from which the licence is required. If you need to make an enquiry about your licence you are advised to contact the Driver Enquiry Unit, DVLC, Swansea SA6 7JL (tel: Swansea 72151) quoting your Driver Number. It is worth making a note of this number in case your licence is mislaid.

Driving Licence Fees

The fee for a first GB driving licence (full or provisional) is £17. This fee also covers the first full licence after passing the driving test. Licences are normally valid until the applicant's 70th birthday, at which time a new licence may be issued for one, two, or three years at a time. Renewal in these circumstances is free of charge.

A duplicate or exchange licence costs £5 and is valid for the period of the original licence. The issuing of a new licence at the end of a period of disqualification also costs £5.

An exchange licence may be required by a driver who is entitled to an extra group on an existing licence, or where the applicant requires motorcycle entitlement, or whose existing licence contains endorsements which are no

Driving Licence Groups and Minimum ages for driving

Table 1

Use this table to check whether your licence and age entitle you to drive the vehicles you wish to drive.
Please also read Definitions below Table 2.

VEHICLE	MINIMUM AGE FOR DRIVING	LICENCE ENTITLEMENT NEEDED FOR DRIVING
Four - (or more) wheeled vehicles		
Motor car*	17	A
Motor-car* with automatic transmission	17	A or B
Goods vehicle with maximum wieght not more than 7.5 tonnes	18	A
Goods vehicle with maximum weight not more than 7.5 tonnes and with automatic transmission	18	A or B
Goods vehicle with maximum weight more than 7.5 tonnes	21	A
Goods vehicle with maximum weight more than 7.5 tonnes and with automatic transmission	21	A or B
Large passenger vehicle (ie a passenger vehicle with more than 9 seats including the driver's seat)	21	A
Large passenger vehicle with automatic transmission	21	A or B

*For the purposes of driver licensing, the term 'motor-car' includes goods vans up to 3.5 tonnes maximum weight and mini-buses with not more than nine seats including the driver's seat.

Two-wheeled vehicles		
Moped	16	E or D
Motor-bicycle (with or without side-car)	17	D

Three-wheeled vehicles (other than invalid carriages)		
Motor-tricycle or three-wheeled car or van with unladen weight not more than 410 kg Heavier three-wheeled vehicles are classed, according to weight and design as motor-car, goods vehicle, or large passenger vehicle.	17	C or A or B**

Special vehicles		
Agricultural tractor	16	F or A or B**
Agricultural tractor which a is mounted on wheels b has an overall width not exceeding eight feet c is exempt from duty under Section 7(1) of the Vehicle (Excise) Act 1971 or is specially licensed d is not drawing a trailer other than with an overall width not exceeding eight feet and which has either type wheels or is of the four-wheeled 'close coupled' type. 'Close coupled' means that the wheels on the same side of the trailer are 33 inches or less apart and are so fitted that when it is moving they remain parallel to the longitudinal axis of the trailer	17	F or A or B**
Electrically propelled vehicle	According to vehicle type	L or group containing vehicle type
Invalid carriage	16	J
Mowing machine (with 3 wheels or less and Pedestrian controlled unladen weight not more than vehicle 410 kg) Other mowing machines and pedestrian controlled vehicles are classed according to weight as motor car or goods vehicle	16	K or A or B**
Road Roller	21	G
Road Roller which: a is propelled otherwise than by steam b has an unladen weight not exceeding 11,68 tonnes c is not constructed or adapted to carry a load other than water, fuel, accumulators, and other equipment used to drive it, loose tools, loose equipment and any object which is specially constructed for attachment to the vehicle so as to temporarily increase its weight d is fitted with hard (eg metal) rollers	17	G
Track-laying vehicles steered by its tracks	According to vehicle type	H
Trolley vehicle	21	M
Vehicle exempted from duty under Section 7(1) of Vehicle (Excise) Act 1971	According to vehicle type	N, or group containing vehicle type

** If with automatic transmission.

longer relevant. The fee for exchanging a Northern Ireland full licence for a GB licence is also £5.

A duplicate licence is needed to replace a licence which has been lost, mislaid or defaced. Replacement of a licence following a change of address is made free of charge.

Health and Eyesight

When a driver applies for a licence he has to make various declarations regarding health and eyesight. He must declare, for example, any disability and any illness which might affect his driving. The law also requires the driver to notify the licensing centre if there is likely to be any worsening of any condition and if there has been a change in any disability since the issue of the licence. Failure to give such information can incur a fine of up to £100. Examples of the kind of health conditions in question are listed in the leaflet D100, but if there is any doubt about whether or not the condition should be reported the driver is advised to consult his family doctor. It is not necessary to report any medical conditions which are not likely to last more than three months.

Epilepsy: Under certain circumstances a licence may now be issued to someone who has been free of attacks for two years.

Pacemakers: people who are subject to sudden faintings or giddiness have, in the past, not been issued with a licence. The law, however, has been changed, and a licence may now be granted if this disability is corrected by the fitting of a cardiac pacemaker and if other medical conditions are satisfied.

Disabled: if the driver is physically and mentally capable of driving but is otherwise disabled he may be issued with a licence which restricts him to driving a vehicle of special design or construction. This type of licence does not entitle the driver to use it as a provisional licence for other groups of vehicles. If the disabled driver wishes to learn to drive a vehicle of a different type, he must first apply for the appropriate provisional entitlement to be added to the original licence.

Eyesight: in order to conform with the law there is a minimum standard of eyesight which must be reached (with glasses or contact lenses if necessary). The requirement is to read a motor vehicle number plate in good daylight at a distance of 75 feet (if the symbols are 3½ inches high) or 67 feet (if they are 3⅛ inches high). In the case of the driver of a mowing machine or pedestrian controlled vehicle the relevant distances are 45 feet and 40 feet.

If you need glasses or contact lenses in order to attain these standards, then you must wear them every time you drive. It is an offence to drive if your eyesight does not meet the required standard.

An applicant who declares a disability to the DVLC may be asked for permission to obtain a report from the applicant's doctor. A licence may be issued for a limited period so that the condition can be reviewed or the licence may be restricted to certain types of vehicle.

Motorcycle Licences

A full licence for a car acts as a provisional licence for a motorcycle and as a full licence for mopeds. A provisional motorcycle licence is issued for a maximum of two years. If in this time a full licence has not been gained a further provisional licence will not be issued for a further 12 months. A provisional licence entitles the rider to use a solo motorcycle with a maximum engine capacity of 125cc. A learner rider on a solo motorcycle is not permitted to carry a passenger unless the passenger holds a full motorcycle licence.

Sidecar outfits – There is no restriction on the engine capacity of a sidecar outfit ridden by a learner motorcyclist. The two-part test does not apply to his class of machine, but the two-year provisional licence limit does.

Mopeds – A full licence for a moped is valid only for that class of machine. The learner rider who moves on to riding a bigger machine must then display 'L' plates and pass the tests to gain a full motorcycle licence. A full moped licence enables the holder to ride a motorcycle on 'L' plates indefinitely – the two-year limit does not apply.

A full licence for a car counts as a provisional licence for motorcycles and as a full licence for mopeds. There is no restriction on the amount of time allowed as a learner motorcyclist.

HGV and PSV Driving Licences

To drive heavy goods vehicles or public service vehicles an additional driving licence is needed.

The HGV and PSV licence schemes are operated by the Licensing Authorities at Traffic Area Offices and the decision whether to grant a licence to an applicant rests with the Licensing Authority.

Heavy Goods Vehicles

An HGV licence is required for driving a rigid goods vehicle which has a maximum permissible weight of more than 7.5 tonnes and for any articulated vehicle. A rigid goods vehicle and trailer combination (other than an artic) is regarded as an HGV if the vehicle has a maximum permissible gross weight of more than 3.5 tonnes and if the total maximum gross weight of the combination is more than 7.5 tonnes. If the outfit is over these weights an HGV driving licence is required – even if the vehicle is being used privately or without a load.

There are different classes of HGV depending on the number of axles and whether the vehicle is articulated. A provisional HGV licence covers all classes of vehicle and may be obtained only on production of a current, valid ordinary licence (either full or provisional). If you take a test on an HGV when you hold only a provisional ordinary licence you will be given a pass certificate for both car and HGV. If a test is passed on one class of HGV the pass certificate will include the lower grades of vehicle.

Application for HGV licences should be made to a Traffic Area Office using the form DLG1 which is available from the Department of Transport or from most training organisations. A medical examination report is required for first-time applicants and for applicants over the age of 60. Licences are normally issued for a period of three years. The application must be supported by an ordinary licence (either full or provisional). The minimum age for driving an HGV is 21 years except for drivers in the Armed Forces and in connection with the young drivers' scheme operated by the National Joint Training Committee.

There is also a 'restricted' Class 3 or 3A licence which was introduced when changes in weight limits took place. The holder of a restricted licence is limited to driving HGVs with a maximum permitted weight of 10 tonnes.

When a draw-bar outfit is being used a Class 2 or Class 3 licence is required, depending on whether the towing vehicle has two or more axles.

HGV Driving Licence Classes

Class	Definition	Additional classes
1	an articulated vehicle, without automatic transmission	1A, 2, 2A, 3 and 3A
1A	an articulated vehicle with automatic transmission	2A and 3A
2	a heavy goods vehicle, without automatic transmission, other than an articulated vehicle, designed and constructed to have more than four wheels in contact with the road surface	2A, 3 and 3A
2A	a heavy goods vehicle, with automatic transmission, other than an articulated vehicle, designed and constructed to have more than four wheels in contact with the road surface	3A
3	a heavy goods vehicle, without automatic transmission, other than an articulated vehicle, designed and constructed to have not more than four wheels in contact with the road surface	3A
3A	a heavy goods vehicle, with automatic transmission, other than an articulated vehicle, designed and constructed to have not more than four wheels in contact with the road surface	

Provisional HGV Licence

The HGV learner driver must hold a provisional HGV driving licence and a full or provisional ordinary driving licence. A full HGV licence for a lower class may be used as a provisional for vehicles of a different class. The provisional licence holder must be accompanied by a person who holds a full licence for that class of vehicle.

An 'L' plate must be displayed on the front and rear of the vehicle. If the provisional licence holder also holds a provisional ordinary licence an ordinary 'L' plate must also be displayed.

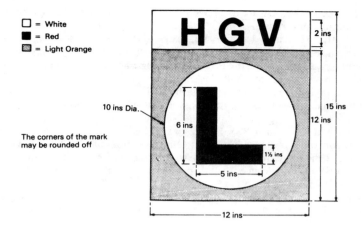

□ = White
■ = Red
▨ = Light Orange

The corners of the mark
may be rounded off

The holder of a provisional HGV licence who holds a full ordinary licence may drive the HGV on motorways. If a provisional ordinary licence is held the driver is not allowed to use motorways.

HGV Licence Fees
A full HGV driving licence is valid for three years and the fee is £10.
A provisional HGV licence costs £5 and is valid for six months.
Exchange and duplicate licences cost £5.

PSV Licences
A PSV driving licence is required for driving a public service vehicle which is carrying passengers for hire or reward.

The PSV licence is not required when the vehicle is not in use for public service, for example:

– when the vehicle is being road tested;
– when the driver is under instruction and during the test;
– when the vehicle is being used privately (or for works transport);
– when the vehicle is used for certain non-profit making services
  covered by the permit.

The minimum age for driving a PSV is normally 21, but certain vehicles may be driven at 18 years under particular circumstances.
The main classes of PSV are:

Category 1:	Double deckers
Category 2:	Single deckers longer than 8.5m
Category 3:	Single deckers longer than 5.5m
Category 4:	Single deckers up to 5.5m

PSV 1A, 2A, 3A, 4A are as above but restricted to automatic (including semi-automatic) transmission.

PSV 4B is similar to 4 and 4A but restricted to specific uses.

When learning to drive a PSV a full or provisional ordinary driving licence is required. After passing the PSV test a full licence is obtained for the class of PSV in which the test took place. This licence is valid for smaller PSVs.

When taking the PSV test, if the ordinary licence is provisional, the same test will enable the driver to obtain pass certificates for both the ordinary and PSV licences.

An application for a PSV licence has to be accompanied by a medical report form, the ordinary licence and the appropriate fee. If you apply for the test at the same time, the licence will be issued after you pass the test.

The PSV driving licence is valid for five years and the cost is £22.50.

An exchange licence costs £5.

When you apply for a PSV driving licence, you have to mention any recent penalty points or endorsements on your ordinary licence and any recent court convictions.

In deciding whether to grant a licence, the Licensing Authority can have regard to any information including court convictions. If a court takes away your ordinary licence, you are required by law to surrender the PSV licence to the Licensing Authority. An application for re-issue will be considered at the end of the period of disqualification.

Driving Abroad

Some countries do not accept a British driving licence. For example, Italy will accept a translation of the GB licence. For driving in the countries which do not accept the GB licence (which include Bulgaria, Poland, East Germany, Hungary and West Berlin) an International Driving Permit is required. This can be obtained from the Royal Automobile Club, the Automobile Association or the National Breakdown Club for a fee of £2.50. A passport-type photograph is required with the application.

Visitors and New Residents

Visitors to the United Kingdom are permitted to use their domestic driving licence or an international driving permit for a period of up to 12 months from the date of entry into the UK.

Anyone taking up permanent residence in this country is allowed to use their national driving licence for 12 months only, during which time they must apply to take the regulation driving test to obtain an ordinary British Driving Licence. If, after this time, the test has not been passed the driver must take out a provisional licence and comply with the conditions.

However, a driving licence issued in any of the member countries of the EEC may be exchanged for a British ordinary driving licence within one year of taking up residence. This concession also applies to holders of a licence issued in Australia, Austria, Barbados, Republic of Cyprus, Finland, Gibraltar, Hong Kong, Japan, Kenya, Malta, New Zealand, Norway, Singapore, Sweden, Switzerland, Zimbabwe and the British Virgin Islands. This also applies to anyone who holds a British Forces Germany licence.

Vehicle Documents

Registration Document

You must not use a motor car on the road until you have registered the vehicle. When a vehicle is first registered, a registration document (form V5 – occasionally called a 'log book') is issued in which the appropriate details are listed. The licensing authority will also issue a 'registration mark' for use on the number plates of the vehicle.

The document should normally be kept in a secure place away from the vehicle. The registration document is not in itself an indication of the ownership of the vehicle. It is issued to the 'registered keeper' of the vehicle. Should a registration document be accidentally lost, destroyed or defaced, application for a duplicate can be made to the DVLC, Swansea, for a fee of £2. Any alterations to the registered particulars of the vehicle should be notified immediately.

Vehicle Excise Licence (Tax Disc)

Application for vehicle excise licences can be made to the DVLC, Swansea, or to the local vehicle licensing office in whose area the vehicle is normally kept. The following conditions apply:

1. Licences are valid for 12 months or six months – the current rate for a motor car is £100 per annum and £55 for six months.
2. Duty must be paid if you 'keep' your vehicle on a highway, even if the car is never driven.
3. You must renew the licence before it expires. A reminder is usually sent by the DVLC when the current licence is due to expire, and this reminder may be used as an application form so long as all the particulars shown on the registration document are still correct.

When applying for a new licence the following documents are required in addition to the registration document and the appropriate fee:

1. Valid certificate of insurance.
2. Department of Transport test certificate. (If the car is more than three years old.)

Where the vehicle is kept on a public road, application for renewal of the excise licence must be made before the expiry of the old one. Where a new licence has been applied for before the expiry date of the old one, there is a legal defence against the offence of failing to display a current licence. A vehicle cannot be used or kept on the road within this period unless application was made before the expiry date of the old excise licence.

Renewals may be made at any main Post Office. When the licence disc has been issued, it should be displayed on the windscreen nearside so that all particulars are clearly visible from that side of the road. The licence may be surrendered during its currency and a refund for any unexpired period claimed.

MOT Test Certificate

A Department of Transport test certificate is required for most vehicles which have been registered or used for three years.

The test is based on the standards laid down in the Construction and Use Regulations and covers the braking system, steering, lighting, reflectors, tyres, indicators, washers, wipers, exhaust, wheels, bodywork, suspension, seatbelts and horn.

Cars are tested at approved garages which display the sign of three white triangles on a blue background.

The certificate lasts one year. The car may be taken for test within a month before expiry. Where a certificate has expired you may drive to and from a test appointment without a certificate providing that the car does not have a serious fault which would contravene the Construction and Use Regulations.

The current cost of a test is £13.22. The certificate must be produced when applying for a vehicle licence, and on the request of a police officer.

Chapter 18
Vehicle and Traffic Regulations

Legal Obligations of a Supervising Driver

Whether using or simply keeping a motor vehicle on a public highway, all drivers, keepers and supervisors of 'L' drivers have, in addition to certain moral obligations concerning the safety of passengers and other road users, many legal obligations which, if abused, will render the offender liable to prosecution with the subsequent inconvenience, fines, endorsements, disqualifications and sometimes prison sentences. Where a driving instructor commits a traffic offence the subsequent punishment resulting from any successful prosecution is likely to have disastrous effects on his livelihood. Even relatively minor offences will attract a disproportionate amount of bad publicity which not only causes disgrace and embarrassment to the instructor concerned, but also stains the character of the driving school industry as a whole. In addition to the obvious responsibilities as the driver of a motor vehicle, the driving instructor has further responsibilities as the supervisor. Where the supervisor of an 'L' driver sees that an unlawful act is about to be committed by the driver and takes no physical or verbal action to prevent it, then he is liable to prosecution for aiding and abetting such an offence. For example, if a pupil were about to ignore a red traffic light and the instructor allowed the car to stop on the wrong side of the line, he would have committed an offence, even though it may have been the instructor who finally brought the car to a stop. There are many other similar examples which illustrate the point including the action taken at pedestrian crossings, one-way streets and give way signs.

Tuition Vehicle
The driving instructor must pay particular attention to ensure that the tuition vehicle is in a roadworthy condition and that it is taxed and adequately insured for driving tuition purposes.

The vehicle must carry 'L' plates of the prescribed size showing clearly to the front and rear of the vehicle.

Driving Licence and Eyesight
He must satisfy himself before allowing a client to drive a motor vehicle that his pupil is in possession of a current, valid and signed driving licence and that his pupil can meet the eyesight requirements. He must check this even though the pupil may have signed a declaration to this effect on the licence

application form. Where glasses are required to meet the minimum standard they must be worn at all times while driving.

Tuition in Client's Vehicle

On occasions where a client may choose to provide his own car for professional driving lessons, the instructor must give special consideration to all the foregoing points, but in particular to the roadworthiness, MOT certificate and insurance cover of the vehicle.

Before agreeing to give tuition in a non dual-controlled vehicle, the instructor should give serious consideration to the standard, or estimated standard, the client has, or is assumed to have reached, where the instructor has not yet had the personal means of making a valid assessment (for example a new client booking the lesson by telephone).

Due consideration should also be given to the type of vehicle to ascertain if the handbrake is in easy reach of the instructor (ie some cars have under-dash handbrakes, or handbrakes set to the right of the driver's seat). Your livelihood and both public safety and that of your client may be at stake.

A final point which should be remembered by the instructor is that any period of disqualification from driving will also entail a further period of disqualification from the ADI Register.

For example, one year of disqualification for a driving offence will be followed by a four-year disqualification from the Register of Approved Driving Instructors. The professional driving instructor would be unable therefore to earn a living at his trade for a total of five years.

Vehicle Regulations

There are many laws which lay down the requirements about the way in which cars are manufactured, what equipment they must have and the condition of vehicles when used on the roads.

Most of these rules are contained in the Motor Vehicles (Construction and Use) Regulations. Some of the rules apply only to cars first registered after a specified date; older vehicles may, therefore, not have to include some of the items of equipment mentioned.

Some of the basic rules apply to vehicles of any age. These include the strict rules relating to brakes and steering gear – each part of the braking system and all steering gear must be maintained in good and efficient working order at all times when the vehicle is being used on the road.

The car must be roadworthy. It is sometimes thought the MOT test certificate is a certificate of roadworthiness, but this is not so. The test system looks at the condition of certain main components, but does not necessarily consider the overall roadworthiness of the car.

The regulations contain rules about the dimensions of cars, and about the maximum overhang. The car must have wings or mudguards. The speedometer must work to within an accuracy of plus or minus 10 per cent. Driving mirrors must be fitted, and other compulsory items are: safety glass, windscreen wipers, horn, silencer, seat belts and direction indicators. Lighting regulations are dealt with as a separate section.

Lighting
The regulations require that lights and reflectors must be kept clean and in good working order. They must be maintained so that the vehicle may be driven during the hours of darkness without contravening the regulations.

This chapter includes only a summary of the main requirements, as the original equipment fitted to a modern vehicle will usually comply with the specifications.

Headlamps must be permanently fitted and must have a minimum rating of 30 watts displaying a white or yellow beam. The lamps must be matched and the beam must be capable of being deflected to the nearside so as not to dazzle oncoming traffic.

Sidelamps must be fitted at the front of the vehicle. The two lamps must have a maximum power of seven watts each (or they may be diffused).

Rear lamps must be visible from a reasonable distance to the rear of the car. There must be at least two lamps, each with a minimum power of five watts. Reflectors are also required.

Rear number plate lamp: the plate must be illuminated so that the letters and figures are easily legible from a distance of 60 feet.

Direction indicators on cars registered after 1965 must be the amber flashing type. On older cars they may be either flashing or semaphore arm and may be white at the front and red at the rear. Flashing indicators must wink at the rate of 60 to 120 flashes a minute. The indicators on each side of the car must be operated by the same switch and there must be a warning light or audible warning inside the car to show that the indicators are working.

Reversing lamps may be fitted using one or two lamps of not more than 24 watts each. The beam produced must not dazzle anyone 25 feet away at an eye level of 3½ feet from the ground and must only be used when the car is reversing. The lights may be operated automatically when reverse gear is selected or may have a separate switch which includes a warning light.

Fog lamps are to be used as two front fog lamps (or one fog lamp and one headlamp) in darkness and fog, falling snow or conditions of poor visibility. The lights must be placed symmetrically and must be placed more than two feet from the ground unless they are to be used only in fog and falling snow.

Rear fog lamps are obligatory on cars first used on or after 1 April 1980. If one lamp is fitted it must be positioned on the offside of the car, and if two are fitted they must be symmetrical. Rear fog lamps may only be used during adverse weather conditions and when the vehicle is in motion, or during an enforced stoppage.

Stop lamps are compulsory on cars built since 1971. The lamps must be matched and placed symmetrically at the rear of the car. They must operate automatically when the foot brakes are applied and show a steady red light visible from the rear.

During the hours of darkness (half an hour after sunset to 1 ½ hours before sunrise) a vehicle must display:

    (a) 2 headlamps (when the vehicle is driven on unlit roads);
    (b) 2 side lamps;
    (c) 2 rear lamps;
    (d) 2 red rear reflectors;
    (e) 1 or 2 rear fog lamps (for vehicles after 1 April 1980).

Headlamps must be used when the vehicle is being driven on unlit roads (ie a road where there are no street lights or on which the street lamps are more than 200 yards apart). Headlamps must be switched off when the vehicle is stationary (except traffic stops).

During daylight hours headlamps must be used when travelling in conditions of poor visibility such as fog, smoke, heavy rain, spray or snow. If matching fog or spotlights are fitted, these may be used in the place of headlights.

Parking lights at night. A car or light goods vehicle may park at night without lights if the following conditions apply:

    1. The vehicle is parked on a road with a speed limit not exceeding 30 mph.
    2. No part of the vehicle is within 10 metres of a junction.
    3. The vehicle is parked with its nearside close to, and parallel with, the kerb, except in a one-way street.

The lighting regulations also permit a vehicle to park without lights in a recognised parking area, and within the confines of an area outlined by lamps or traffic signs. If these conditions are not met lights must be shown (ie side and rear lights).

Dim-dip lights. New vehicles registered from 1 April 1987 must be fitted with a dim-dip device which causes 10 or 15 per cent of the dipped beam intensity to show when the engine is running (or the ignition is switched on) and the sidelights are on.

Hazard Warning Lights may be used only when the vehicle is stationary for the purpose of warning other road users that the vehicle is temporarily causing an obstruction.

Parking
Common law states that a public highway is specifically for the free passage

of the general public and vehicles, and there is no legal right to park on the road except in specially designated parking places or with the express permission of a police officer or traffic warden. There is no legal right even to park outside your own home. A stationary vehicle in the road or on the grass verge is technically an obstruction, even where no other road user is inconvenienced.

It is a more serious offence to park a vehicle in a position where it might constitute a danger to others. (See Highway Code for examples of what might be considered dangerous parking.) Parking within the zig-zag lines at a pedestrian crossing is an offence punishable by an endorsement. It is illegal to park on an urban clearway at the stipulated times and on a rural clearway and motorway at any time.

Parking in Controlled Zones

A controlled parking zone is indicated by waiting restriction signs situated on all entrances, and is marked with yellow lines along the kerb. Restriction times vary from town to town and care should be taken always to read the signs. Parking meter zones are marked with signs saying 'Meter Zone' and 'Zone Ends'. It is an offence to park at a meter without paying or to overstay the time paid for, or to feed the meter on return for an extended period.

Use of Horn and Flashing Headlamps

1. Motor vehicles must be fitted with an instrument capable of giving audible warnings of approach. The tone of the horn must be continuous and uniform, with the exception of emergency service vehicles which may use a two-tone horn, gong or bell. Some goods vehicles are permitted to use an instrument to announce goods for sale, but the vehicle must also carry the standard audible warning device.
2. The horn should be regarded as a warning instrument. It should not be used in order to assert a right of way and should not be used aggressively. There are some legal responsibilities regarding the use of the horn. It must not be used when the vehicle is stationary on the road, except to avoid danger due to another vehicle moving, and may not be used in a built-up area between the hours of 11.30pm and 7.00am.
3. The flashing of headlamps has the same meaning as the horn. It is an indication of your presence to other road users. The lamps should not be used to tell other people what you intend to do, or to tell them what to do.
4. Flashing headlamps can be useful in certain driving conditions – high speed roads and where there is a high level of noise – but should not be regarded as an indication of another driver's intentions. The signal may not be directed to you.

Noise and Smoke

There are very detailed rules regarding the maximum number of decibels that may be emitted from a car, and it is an offence to drive a car which does not conform to those rules, or to cause a nuisance by making unnecessary noise. It is also an offence to use a motor vehicle which produces smoke, vapour or sparks which may damage or affect other road users and property. Smoke which affects the visibility of other road users is regarded as excessive.

Seat belts

The law requires that seat belts are fitted to the front seats of modern motor cars and that they should be maintained in good order. Any additional non-compulsory seat belts which are fitted must also conform to the regulations.

The use of seat belts may be an important factor in the assessment of compensation by a court. Recent cases have shown a reduction in the amount of compensation awarded to non-users of seat belts.

Front seat belts are compulsory on cars and three-wheeled vehicles made after 30 June 1964 and first registered after 31 December 1964 and on light vans made after 31 August 1966 and first registered on or after 31 March 1967.

The use of front seat belts by drivers and passengers is compulsory. The maximum penalty for failing to wear a seat belt is £50. Drivers are not responsible in law for the non-use of belts by adult passengers.

There are several exemptions provided in the regulations. For example you do not have to wear one under the following circumstances:

1. When driving and carrying out a manoeuvre which includes reversing.
2. If you hold a valid medical exemption certificate.
3. When you are making a local delivery or collection round using a specially constructed or adapted vehicle.
4. If a seat belt has become defective on a journey, or previously, and arrangements have been made for the belt to be repaired.
5. If an inertia reel belt has temporarily locked because the vehicle is on, or has been on, a steep incline. The belt must be put on as soon as the mechanism has unlocked.
6. If you are a qualified driver supervising a learner who is carrying out a manoeuvre including reversing.
7. A driving test examiner need not wear a seat belt if he feels that the wearing of a belt would endanger him or someone else.
8. When driving a taxi during normal taxi-ing work, so long as the vehicle displays a plate showing it is licensed as a taxi.
9. While driving a private hire vehicle displaying a plate showing it is licensed as such, or that it is licensed at the Hackney Carriage rate and while used for that purpose.
10. If you are driving or riding a vehicle displaying trade plates and you are looking into or repairing a mechanical fault.

Other exemptions apply to people in special jobs and in certain circumstances, for example the police.

From 1 September 1989 a new Act of Parliament introduced regulations relating to the wearing of seat belts by children in the rear seats of cars. The new law states that children under the age of 14 travelling in the rear of cars should be restrained where an approved restraint is available. The essential point is that the seat belt or restraint should be appropriate for the age and weight of the child. The law does not require that all children in the rear of cars should be restrained, only that if an appropriate device is available it should be used. An appropriate child restraint is deemed available if carried in or on the vehicle where there is space for it to be fitted without the aid of tools. Children can be exempt from the regulations on medical grounds.

Mirrors

All new motor cars must now be fitted with two rear-view driving mirrors — one inside, the other mounted on the exterior offside. Interior mirrors must have protective edges to minimise the risk of injury in the event of an accident. This regulation also applies to the dual mirrors used by driving instructors.

Windscreen Washers and Wipers

The law requires that all windows are kept clean so that the driver has an unobscured view of the road. This includes keeping the windscreen free of stickers, novelties and mascots. There is a legal requirement for automatic windscreen wipers capable of efficiently cleaning the screen. The driver must have an adequate view of the road in front of the vehicle and in front of the nearside and offside of the vehicle.

There must also be windscreen washers which work in conjunction with the wipers.

Vehicle Defects

A new procedure known as the Vehicle Defect Rectification Scheme (VDRS) is now being operated in some areas. Under the scheme some minor vehicle defects such as lights, wipers, speedometer, silencer may not result in a prosecution if the driver agrees to participate and to the following procedure:

1. A VDRS notice is issued.
2. The defect must be rectified within a limited time.
3. The repaired vehicle and the VDRS notice are presented at an MoT garage.
4. The MoT garage issues a certification that the defects have been rectified.
5. The certificate is then sent to a local Central Ticket Office.

Failure to follow the correct procedure will normally result in a prosecution.

Speed Limits

A speed limit of 30 mph normally applies to all vehicles on a road where street lamps are positioned at intervals of less than 200 yards. On occasions a higher speed is allowed on such a road, in which case the higher limit is shown by appropriate signs.

Speed limits apply to roads and vehicles, and where there is a difference the lower limit applies. The maximum speed on motorways and dual carriageways is 70 mph and on single carriageways 60 mph. However, these limits apply to cars, car-derived vans and dual-purpose vehicles adapted to carry not more than eight passengers. A different set of speed limits apply to other types of vehicles.

New speed limits have been introduced for cars and light vehicles, touring caravans and trailers. These outfits may now travel at 50 mph on normal roads and 60 mph on motorways.

Vehicle	Motorway	Dual carriageway	Single carriageway
Cars, including car-derived vans	70	70	60
Cars, towing trailer	60	60	50
Goods vehicles (rigid) – up to 7.5T	70*	60	50
Heavy Goods Vehicles over 7.5T and artics	60	50	40
Buses and Coaches	70*	60	50

*60 mph if articulated or towing a trailer.

Accident Procedure

An 'accident' is generally and legally regarded as one which causes injury to another person or animal, or damage to another vehicle or property.

A driver who is involved in such an accident must stop and give his name, address and vehicle registration number to the other person involved. If there is personal injury he must also produce his insurance certificate to anyone who has reasonable cause to see it. He must also give information regarding the ownership of the vehicle. Where it is not possible to exchange these particulars the accident should be reported to the police as soon as possible and in any case within 24 hours.

These responsibilities apply regardless of who is to blame for the accident so that even if you feel that the accident is relatively trivial and that it was not your fault, you must carry out the procedure described on page 293.

A police officer may also ask for driver and vehicle details if he believes the driver to have been involved in an accident. The chart gives guidance to the instructor who requires detailed information for instructional purposes. With regard to the responsibilities of an instructor it should be noted that the duty to carry out the above procedures apply to a person accompanying the holder of a provisional licence and not only to the driver of the vehicle.

The vehicle must carry 'L' plates of the prescribed size showing clearly to the front and rear of the vehicle (see page 294).

Accident Procedure

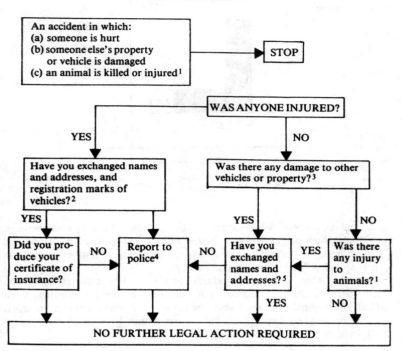

```
An accident in which:
(a) someone is hurt
(b) someone else's property
    or vehicle is damaged        ──────▶   STOP
(c) an animal is killed or injured¹
```

WAS ANYONE INJURED?

YES   NO

Have you exchanged names and addresses, and registration marks of vehicles?²

Was there any damage to other vehicles or property?³

YES   YES   NO

Did you produce your certificate of insurance?   — NO —   **Report to police⁴**   — NO —   **Have you exchanged names and addresses?⁵**   — YES —   **Was there any injury to animals?¹**

YES   NO

NO FURTHER LEGAL ACTION REQUIRED

Note:
The chart shows the *minimum* legal requirements.

Notes:
1 Animals: horse, cattle, ass, mule, sheep, pig, goat, dog.
2 With any person who has reasonable grounds to ask for them.
3 Includes roadside 'furniture' eg lamp posts and other fixtures.
4 Report as soon as possible, and at least within 24 hours, and produce certificate of insurance either when reporting or within five days.
5 With the owner of the vehicle property or animal.

MOT Test

Most small cars, small goods vehicles and passenger vehicles are subject to an annual test starting three years after the date of the original registration.

Testing is carried out at designated garages for an initial fee of £14.26 per vehicle. A duplicate certificate costs £8.56.

The test requirements include brakes, lights, steering, stop lamps, tyres, seat belts (correct fitting, condition and anchorage points), direction indicators, windscreen wipers and washers, exhaust systems, audible warning

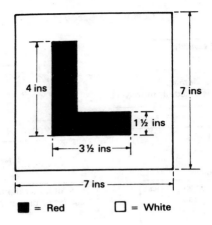

4 ins

7 ins

1 ½ ins

3 ½ ins

7 ins

■ = Red   □ = White

instruments, bodywork and suspension (in relation to braking and steering). A vehicle which passes the test is issued with a test certificate which is valid for one year. The certificate has to be produced along with other documents when applying for a vehicle excise licence.

A vehicle which fails the annual test but which is left at the testing station for rectification of the faults does not incur a further fee for retesting. A fee of half the original is charged when the vehicle is removed and then returned for the necessary repairs to be carried out within 14 days of the original examination.

Chapter 19
Motor Vehicle Insurance

Compulsory motor vehicle insurance was introduced in 1930. It was decided that insurance was necessary to make sure that people who were injured in a road accident were not left uncompensated. Property damage should be included within the *minimum* insurance and this cover is required by the Road Traffic Act 1988.

Types of Insurance

Compulsory Insurance

Users of motor vehicles must be insured with an authorised insurer against third party injury risks. The cover must include compensation in respect of death, injury to another person and also the cost of any emergency medical treatment. All passengers must be covered and no 'own risks' agreements are allowed between passengers and the user of the vehicle. This type of insurance policy (which is very rare) is sometimes known as a 'road traffic only' policy, and leaves the user with a vast amount of risk. As an alternative to insurance, application may be made to the Secretary of State at the Department of Transport for a warrant to enable a deposit of £15 000 in cash or securities to be made at the Supreme Court.

Third party property damage is now a compulsory requirement under the Road Traffic Act 1988 which came into force on 31 December 1988.

Third Party Insurance only

A 'third party' insurance policy usually provides at least the minimum cover described earlier, together with legal liability for claims for damage to the property of a third party.

This type of policy would normally cover liability for injuries to other people (including passengers in your car), liability in respect of accidents caused by them (for example – causing injury to a passer-by, or damaging his property by opening a car door), liability for damage to other people's property (eg damage to another vehicle may be paid in full or in part by your insurance company). For an additional fee the policy may be extended to include the risks of fire and theft. An additional premium may be required if the car is not kept in a locked garage overnight.

A 'third party fire and theft' policy offers slightly more than the bare minimum but still leaves a lot of risk withg the driver/owner/operator.

Comprehensive Insurance

In view of the heavy cost of repairs, most owners these days take out a 'comprehensive' insurance policy. However, there is no such thing as fully comprehensive insurance and care should be taken in reading the small print. The term 'comprehensive' as applied to motor insurance means that a variety and a great deal of protection is provided under one policy document, but it does not mean that cover its provided against every conceivable contingency of whatever nature.

Most motorists (two out of three) use this type of insurance cover which will normally include the risks for third party, fire and theft, together with cover for accidental damage to your own car, medical expenses, and loss or damage to personal effects in the car. These risks are also covered by a third party fire and theft policy.

The policy will specify the uses to which the car may be put. For instance, a policy restricting use to social, domestic and pleasure purposes will not provide cover for any business use (including use by a driving school). There may also be a restriction to cover driving by specified drivers only, or it may exclude driving by certain persons.

Other restrictions will vary from one insurance company to another, but it is normal practice for the company to specify an 'excess' when the car is being driven by a young or inexperienced driver. The excess will generally be from £25 upwards and is the amount you have to pay towards the cost of repairs to your vehicle.

Policies can be invalidated if the vehicle insured is not maintained in a safe and roadworthy condition. Proof that the vehicle is insured in accordance with the Road Traffic Act is given by insurers in the form of a Certificate of Insurance. The certificate is quite distinct from the policy of insurance itself. It is the certificate which has to be produced when renewing the car licence; it must also be produced to a policeman on request.

Driver's Responsibilities

As a driver you must provide details of your insurance to the person who holds you responsible for an accident which results in damage to their property. The law also requires you to give insurance details following an injury accident.

For your own convenience you should be prepared to give your insurance details following an accident, or to a police officer who can ask to see evidence of your insurance at any time.

Therefore it is in your interest, as well as those of accident victims, to keep your insurance details to hand when driving. You are advised, however, not to leave them in the car in case they are stolen.

Even with the new insurance requirements drivers and other road users can find themselves without a source of compensation. This can happen where the accident is nobody's fault, or where you yourself are in some measure to blame. It is for you, as a driver, to consider whether you take out additional insurance cover against such risks as injury to yourself or damage to your own car in these circumstances.

EC Requirements

All British motor insurance policies must include cover against any liabilities which are compulsorily insurable in any other member state of the EC.

These regulations, however, only provide very limited cover and although a 'green card' is no longer legally necessary, it may be prudent to obtain the card from the insurance company to provide evidence of the minimum legal requirements. Possession of the green card can also help to eliminate some of the problems of procedure and language.

Motor Insurance for Driving Schools and Instructors

As a driver (or instructor, or the operator of a vehicle) you are responsible for your own motoring misconduct, but it is possible to pay an insurer to act for you in civil law.

We have discussed in the previous section the various types of insurance available to the ordinary motorist; in this section we review the needs and requirements of insurance cover for the driving instructor.

In order to decide on the right policy and insurance for driving instruction vehicles, it is worth noting that the duty of being insured is a personal one. It is the *person using the car* who must be insured: not the car itself. A car cannot be made to pay damages for injuries and so it would be wrong to assume that a car is insured and that anyone driving it would be covered.

The person who takes out the policy is, of course, covered when he is driving or is in charge of the car, but the policy may not cover anyone else using the car unless the policy specifically includes that person. The policy may exclude or restrict many categories of driver and may exclude or restrict or make an extra charge for various uses of the vehicle.

It is normal practice for many insurance companies to charge an extra premium for young drivers, inexperienced drivers, business use or off-road driving by non-licence holders.

The driving instructor will need to be covered for all or some of these risks. It is important therefore to consider the extent and depth of cover provided by an insurance company.

All motor insurance policies issued by UK motor insurers are subject to the provisions of Part VI of the Road Traffic Act 1988 which stipulates the minimum insurance requirements re: third party bodily injury and property damage (ie 'act' cover). The Motor Vehicles (Third Party Risks) Regulations 1972 detail the requirements; for example, regarding the issue of cover notes and Certificates of Insurance. The additional covers provided under third party fire and theft and comprehensive policies are not controlled by legislation; it is left to the individual insurer to provide a wide range of benefits under the policy. The following rules are some of the requirements imposed by insurers:

1. Care should be taken when completing an application form because false or misleading statements can invalidate the insurance.
2. Any subsequent changes should be notified to the insurers immediately.
3. Some insurance companies may require that driving instruction cars are fitted with dual controls.
4. There may be an 'excess' for drivers or instructors under a minimum age.
5. Each driver must be properly licensed for the type of vehicle being driven. The driver who has never held a licence to drive or who is disqualified by being underage or by a court order is not covered. In this case, both driver and instructor are committing an offence.
6. You will usually be covered under your own policy while driving a car belonging to someone else (but this is not always the case). Even if cover is included, it is limited to third party risks and will not include accidental damage to the car. If one person is borrowing another person's car the driver should ensure that the owner's policy is comprehensive and does not restrict the driving to specified persons.
7. The provision for driving another car does not normally apply to policies issued in the name of a firm (eg a partnership).

Insurance for the Driving Instructor

Specially written insurance policies are available to the driving instructor from the Trade Associations (see page 360). When deciding on a policy not only the cost should be considered but also the extent and depth of cover provided. The following is a list of questions you could ask a potential insurer:

(a) What happens if my car is stolen?
(b) What happens if my vehicle is damaged by fire/in an accident/ maliciously?
(c) Does the insurance extend to property stolen from the car or damaged in the car as a result of an accident?
(d) Am I and any other occupants covered against medical charges incurred as a result of an accident?

(e) Does the policy include compensation for injury or death of passengers?

(f) Does the insurance cover medical expenses and compensation to other people after an accident?

(g) Does the policy include legal costs incurred through an accident?

(h) What cover do I have as a result of consequential damage? For example, the car burns down my garage.

(i) Does it include windscreen cover and the cost of vehicle recovery after an accident and subsequently to the repairers?

Every individual will have their own personal insurance requirements, so these questions are not the only ones you may want answered. You should consider all possible uses for the vehicle such as continental holidays and towing caravans or trailers.

Tuition in Customer's Own Vehicle

For the reasons previously given, it is essential that the instructor takes particular care over insurance matters when considering giving instruction in a customer's own vehicle.

A number of insurers are prepared to interpret the cover under their standard private car policies as extending to include use when a permitted driver under the policy is receiving driving tuition from a professional driving instructor. This would be subject to the driving limitations under the policy being on an 'any driver' basis or, alternatively, where the driving instructor is included as a named driver. Additional premium may or may not be required.

Certain insurers provide business use under their Class 1 private car policies which allow the policy holder and the policy holder's spouse to use the car for their own business purposes. If they employ the services of a driving instructor, however, they would construe that, for the duration of the tuition, the private business use lies with the instructor and not the insured/insured's spouse. In these circumstances a revised cover note of Certificate of Insurance is issued for the tuition period. Once again, additional premium may or may not be required.

Some insurers are prepared to extend the driving instructor's policy to provide tuition in pupils' own cars. This would include the instructor's liability for injury or damage arising from accidents during the driving tuition in a pupil's own car, at an appropriate additional premium. If damage to the pupil's own car were to be covered, then such cover would be limited to liability flowing directly from the negligence of the driving instructor and not from the negligence of the pupil alone. The benefit of this extension to a driving instructor's policy is that immediate response can be made to any requests for tuition in a pupil's own vehicle.

Example Indemnity Form

'We, the undersigned, indemnify (Name . . . .)

and ensure that the existing policy, No: . . . .

expiring . . . . in the name of . . . .

. . . .

Registration number of vehicle . . . . is extended as below:
To indemnify whilst professional driving tuition is being given in the above-
mentioned vehicle against third party personal injury (third party property
and including passenger liability the instructor himself).

Name of Insurer . . . .

Address of Insurer . . . .

. . . .

Signed for and on behalf of the above . . . .

Position held: . . . .

Date . . . .

NB: This form MUST be signed by a person authorised to act on behalf of
the insurance company.

Further information on the subject of motor insurance is available from the
British Insurance Association, Aldermary House, Queen Street, London
EC4N 1TT. However, where any detailed or specialist advice is required, it
is advisable to use the services of a reputable local insurance broker, and/or
to insure with a well-known company.

Chapter 20
Driving and Traffic Offences

Most people are unsure about the law for motorists although at any time when driving or using a car they may find themselves faced with some aspect of it. The purpose of this section is to enable the driving instructor to find out how the law affects him and his pupils.

The motorist is affected by the *civil* as well as by the *criminal* law, and an offence in a criminal court may well be followed by another case in a civil court. For example, a driver who injures a pedestrian and is found guilty of dangerous driving may then find himself being sued for damages in a civil court.

Most of the criminal law is found in the Road Traffic Act which has now been amended on many occasions in recent years, and which is now being reviewed. A new act – the Transport Act 1981 – effectively summarises all the revisions and previous acts which have existed.

Apart from the criminal law, the Road Traffic Act gives the Secretary of State for Transport the power to make other regulations regarding various motoring matters. The most important of these regulations are the Motor Vehicles (Construction and Use) Regulations.

Much of the civil law which affects motorists is not contained in special rules relating to the roads. It is part of the general law of the land. For example, the law of negligence applies to anyone, whether he is driving or not. The motorist is most likely to encounter the civil law after he has been involved in a road accident in which there has been an injury to a person or damage to property. In these cases, the law allows the person injured to claim against the other driver, or the insurance company.

However, the motorist may be guilty of an offence under criminal law even if no accident has taken place. He may have committed an offence even if he had not intended to do so; for example, driving without lights at night is an offence even though the driver may have checked the operation of the lights before starting his journey. There is also a certain amount of confusion regarding the Highway Code. Although the Code is drawn up by the Department of Transport under the specific rules of the Road Traffic Act, a breach of it is not necessarily a punishable offence. However, it is often the case that the Highway Code is used as a reference in a court when assessing the actions of a driver, and a breach of a particular part of the Highway Code may in some cases amount to a breach of a specific part of the Road Traffic Act. Nevertheless, the offence will be found to be against a section of the Road Traffic Act.

Questions of liability may arise when a driver is using a vehicle while carrying out his normal work or when the vehicle is being used for driving instruction. These questions of liability often arise under the Construction and Use Regulations when the driver, supervising driver and the employer may all be equally guilty of an offence.

Driving Offences

It has been estimated that there are well over 2 000 offences for the inconsiderate road user to perpetrate. While some of these may be of a fairly minor or perhaps obscure nature in modern conditions, many are not and are liable to entail the prosecution of offenders.

The following offences will, on conviction, automatically mean disqualification from driving:

- (a) Manslaughter, caused by the driver of a motor vehicle.
- (b) Causing death by reckless driving.
- (c) Reckless driving where it is the second offence within three years.
- (d) Racing on the highway.
- (e) Driving while under the influence of drink or drugs, or with more than the permitted blood-alcohol level.
- (f) Failure to provide a blood or urine specimen.

The 1981 Transport Act introduced a new system of 'penalty points' to replace the old system of 'totting up' for dealing with traffic offences.

Under this system, each traffic offence is given a points rating according to the severity of the offence. When a driver has reached a total of 12 points within three years, a period of disqualification will follow.

	Points
Reckless driving	10
Careless driving	3-9
Exceeding the speed limit	3
Driving, or permitting a person to drive when under age	2
Being in charge of a vehicle when under the influence of drink or drugs	10
Unlawful carriage of passengers on motorcycles	1
Failing to comply with traffic directions given by a police officer, traffic warden, traffic lights, stop sign or double white lines	3
Leaving a vehicle in a dangerous position	3
Contravening traffic regulations on motorways	3
Contravening pedestrian crossing regulations	3
Failure to observe/comply with a signal given by a school crossing patrol	3
Contravention of an order relating to a street playground	2
Contravention of Construction and Use Regulations:	
1. so as to cause or be likely to cause danger	3
2. any breach of requirements as to brakes, steering or tyres	3
Failure to stop and give particulars after an accident	8-10
Driving while unqualified and employing and allowing to drive a person who does not hold a licence to drive the type of vehicle in question	2
Failure to comply with the conditions of a provisional licence	2
Use of a vehicle which is uninsured against third-party risks	6-8

	Points
Taking a motor vehicle without authority	8
Stealing a motor vehicle	8
Driving with defective eyesight	2
Driving while disqualified by a court	6

Courts disqualifying a driver for any of the specified offences may order him to undergo another driving test prior to the re-issue of his licence.

Penalty points for some offences are graded according to the seriousness of the offence. A driver who is convicted for more than one offence will have his licence endorsed with the highest number of points awarded for one of the offences. An accumulation of 12 points within three years means that the driver will automatically be disqualified from driving, although the courts are given powers not to disqualify in exceptional circumstances. The three-year period is always measured backwards from the date of the latest offence.

The period of disqualification as a result of an accumulation of penalty points is:

- Six months, if there has been no disqualification in the past three years.
- One year, if there has been one disqualification in the past three years.
- Two years, if there has been more than one disqualification in the past three years.

Disqualification may be imposed for a single offence if the court feels that the offence is serious enough.

A penalty points endorsement can be removed after four years from the date of the offence.

An endorsement of disqualification may be removed four years after the date of conviction (eleven years for drinking and driving offences).

After a disqualification for a period of more than two years you can apply for the disqualification to be lifted after a period of:

(a) Two years if the disqualification period is less than four years.
(b) Half the period of disqualification if between four and ten years.
(c) Five years if the disqualification was for more than ten years.

Disqualification and the ADI

An important point to be remembered by professional driving instructors is that any period of disqualification from driving will involve a further period of disqualification from the ADI Register. For example, one year disqualification for a driving offence is followed by a four-year disqualification from the official Register. The instructor would, therefore, be unable to practice his trade for a total period of five years.

Fixed Penalties

Traffic wardens and police officers are empowered to enforce the law in connection with various offences by use of the fixed penalty system. The relevant offences include waiting, parking, loading and obstruction as well as offences relating to vehicle tax, lights and reflectors. Driving offences such as making 'U' turns and driving the wrong way in a one-way street are also included.

The ticket is given to the driver or is fixed to the vehicle. Payment must be made within 28 days or alternatively the offender may request a court hearing. If the driver who committed the offence cannot be identified or found, the registered owner of the vehicle is ultimately responsible for payment of the fine. However, in the case of hired vehicles, special rules apply and the person who hires the vehicle will become liable for any fines or excess charges.

An extended fixed penalty scheme came into operation in 1986 covering various moving traffic offences including speeding, failure to comply with traffic directions and vehicle defect offences. The following categories are now included in the scheme and for these offences the issuing of the ticket is normally the responsibility of the police:

Contravening a traffic regulation order
Breach of experimental traffic order
Breach of experimental traffic scheme regulation in Greater London
Using a vehicle in contravention of a temporary prohibition or restriction of traffic on a road, ie where a road is being repaired, etc
Contravening motorway traffic regulations
Driving a vehicle in contravention of order prohibiting or restricting driving vehicles on certain classes of roads
Breach of pedestrian crossing regulations
Contravention of a street playground order
Breach of a parking place order on a road
Breach of a provision of a parking place designation order and other offences committed in relation to it, except failing to pay an excess charge
Contravening a parking place designation order
Breach of a provision of a parking place designation order
Contravention of minimum speed limits
Speeding
Driving or keeping a vehicle without displaying registration mark or hackney carriage sign
Driving or keeping a vehicle with registration mark or hackney carriage sign obscured
Failure to comply with traffic directions or signs
Leaving vehicle in a dangerous position
Failing to wear a seat belt
Breach of restrictions on carrying children in the front of vehicles
Driving a vehicle elsewhere than on the road
Parking a vehicle on the path or verge
Breach of Construction and Use Regulations
Contravention of lighting restrictions on vehicles
Driving without a licence
Breach of provisional licence provisions
Failure to stop when required by constable in uniform
Obstruction of highway with vehicle

Penalty tickets for endorsable offences are handed to the driver as the driving licence will have to be surrendered for possible endorsement with the appropriate penalty points. If the licence shows an accumulation of points which, together with the current offence, would bring the total to 12 points or more, then the fixed penalty ticket would not be issued. In those circumstances a prosecution for the offence would follow.

If the licence is not immediately available, it must be produced within seven days at a nominated police station. A receipt for the licence is then issued and this is an accepted document if for any reason the licence has to be produced at a later date.

The fixed penalty fines of £12 for non-endorsable and £24 for endorsable offences are payable within 28 days (or as specified in the notice). If payment is not received in time the charge is increased by 50 per cent to £18 and £36 respectively. A driver may request a court hearing if he considers that the issue of the ticket was wrong or unfair.

Driving Licence Endorsements

Endorsement offences appear on a driving licence in a coded version which includes details of the court, the offence and of the fine and endorsement.

Code	
	Accident Offences
AC10	Failing to stop and/or give particulars after an accident.
AC20	Failing to report an accident within 24 hours.
	Undefined accident offence
AC30	Undefined accident offence.
	Driver banned from driving (disqualified)
BA10	Driving while disqualified.
BA20	Driving while disqualified by virtue of age.
	Careless Driving
CD10	Driving without due care and attention.
CD20	Driving without reasonable consideration for other road users.
CD30	Driving without due care and attention or without reasonable consideration for other road users.
	Construction and Use Offences
CU10	Using a vehicle with defective brakes.
CU20	Causing or likely to cause danger by reason of use of unsuitable vehicle or using a vehicle with parts or accessories (excluding brakes, steering or tyres) in a dangerous condition.
CU30	Using a vehicle with defective tyres.
CU40	Using a vehicle with defective steering.
CU50	Causing or likely to cause danger by reason of load or passengers.
CU60	Undefined failure to comply with Construction and Use Regulations.
	Dangerous Driving
DD10	Driving in a dangerous manner.
DD20	Driving at a dangerous speed.
DD30	Reckless driving.
DD40	Driving in a dangerous or reckless manner, etc.
DD50	Causing death by dangerous driving.
DD60	Culpable homicide while driving a vehicle.
DD70	Causing death by reckless driving.
	Drink or Drugs
DR10	Driving or attempting to drive with blood alcohol level above limit.
DR20	Driving or attempting to drive while unfit through drink or drugs.

Code	Accident Offences
DR30	Driving or attempting to drive then refusing to supply a specimen of blood or urine for laboratory testing.
DR40	In charge of a vehicle while blood alcohol level above limit.
DR50	In charge of a vehicle while unfit through drink or drugs.
DR60	In charge of a vehicle then refusing to supply a specimen of blood or urine for laboratory testing.

Insurance Offences

IN10	Using a vehicle uninsured against third party risks.

Licence Offences

LC10	Driving without a licence.
LC20	Driving when under age.

Miscellaneous Offences

MS10	Leaving a vehicle in a dangerous position.
MS20	Unlawful pillion riding.
MS30	Playstreet offences.
MS40	Driving with uncorrected or defective eyesight or refusing to submit to eyesight test.
MS50	Motor racing on the highway.
MS60	Offences not covered by other codes.
MS70	Driving with uncorrected defective eyesight.
MS80	Refusing to submit to an eyesight test.

Motorway Offences

MW10	Contravention of Special Roads Regulations (excluding speed limits).

Pedestrian Crossings

PC10	Undefined contravention of Pedestrian Crossing Regulations.
PC20	Contravention of Pedestrian Crossing Regulations with moving vehicle.
PC30	Contravention of Pedestrian Crossing Regulations with stationary vehicle.

Provisional Licence Offences

PL10	Driving without L' plates.
PL20	Driving while not accompanied by a qualified person.
PL30	Carrying a person not qualified.
PL40	Drawing an unauthorised trailer.
PL50	Undefined failure to comply with conditions of a Provisional Licence.

Speed Limits

SP10	Exceeding goods vehicle speed limit.
SP20	Exceeding speed limit for type of vehicle (excluding goods or passenger vehicles).
SP30	Exceeding statutory speed limit on a public road.
SP40	Exceeding passenger vehicle speed limit.
SP50	Exceeding speed limit on a motorway.
SP60	Undefined speed limit offence.

Traffic Directions and Signs

TS10	Failing to comply with traffic light signals.
TS20	Failing to comply with double white lines.
TS30	Failing to comply with a 'Stop' sign.
TS40	Failing to comply with directions of a traffic constable.
TS50	Failing to comply with a traffic sign (excluding 'Stop' signs, traffic lights or double white lines).
TS60	Failing to comply with a school crossing patrol sign.
TS70	Undefined failure to comply with a traffic direction or sign.

Code	*Accident Offences*
	Theft or the Unauthorised Taking of Vehicle
UT10	Taking and driving away a vehicle without consent or an attempt thereat.
UT20	Stealing or attempting to steal a vehicle.
UT30	Going equipped for stealing or taking a vehicle.
UT40	Taking or attempting to take a vehicle without consent; driving or attempting to drive a vehicle knowing it to have been taken without consent; allowing onself to be carried in or on a vehicle knowing it to have been taken without consent.
	Special Code
XX99	Signifies a disqualification under the 'totting-up' procedure.

Aiding and abetting offences are as listed above, but with the 0 changed to 2 (eg UT20 becomes UT22).

Causing or permitting are listed, but with the 0 changed to 4 (eg PL20 becomes PL24).

Inciting offences are as listed, but with the 0 changed to 6 (eg DD10 becomes DD16).

Chapter 21

Driving School Administration

Most driving instructors work for themselves, in isolation from the rest of the profession, operating one-car driving schools and using their own limited systems of administration. Others run larger multi-car schools incorporating other ancillary services. The *Driving Instructor's Handbook* is written for both new and experienced instructors whatever their kind of business operation. It is also useful to others who are only indirectly involved with the driver training industry.

The section on administration and management may make the self-employed instructor more aware of some of the difficulties and problems involved in the expansion of any business.

Some of the basic principles of operation should be considered before deciding upon which type of business to operate, whether it be as a self-employed sole proprietor, in partnership with another, or as part of a franchise scheme. For example, the following checklist may be helpful:

1. Consider the disadvantages of working for yourself.
2. Make sure that you fully understand the risks involved.
3. Make an accurate appraisal of the competition in your area.
4. Ensure that you have adequate financial resources while the business establishes itself.
5. Commit yourself completely to the business.
6. Understand the law as it affects your business and keep within it.
7. Use professional advice sensibly.

Whatever the type and size of business these principles will help you to avoid some of the pitfalls and to enjoy some of the benefits of running a business.

Most instructors work as self-employed proprietors of one-car schools, although there is a move towards partnerships and various forms of franchising.

This section looks at the options open to those starting up and running their own business.

Legal Structure

There are three principal types of business. Most driving instructors operate within the first category.

1. The sole trader

There is very little to prevent anyone running a business within this category. It is not even necessary to register the business name. Care should be taken in choosing a name, however, and those which are likely to imply association with the Crown, the government, a local authority, or any which are likely to mislead, should be avoided.

Avoid choosing a name under which someone else in the area is operating. A quick look through the Yellow Pages, industrial and commercial directories, will help you in this respect.

It is advisable to choose a name which describes the business you are in such as 'Smith School of Motoring', 'Smith Driving School' or 'Smith — Driving Tuition' etc.

If you choose a name other than your own personal title, you must display the owner's name prominently on the business premises and on all business stationery. The notice on the premises should read: 'Particulars of ownership of (trading name) as required by Section 29 of the Companies Act 1981. Full names of proprietors: (insert names). Addresses within Great Britain at which documents can be served on the business (insert addresses).' You must also provide this information on request to any customer or supplier.

If you want to protect a trade name or trade mark and prevent others from using it, you must have it registered at the Trade Marks Registry, Patent Office, 25 Southampton Buildings, London WC2A 1AY.

Operating under this category is suitable for businesses where there is little financial risk. It enables you to employ staff and take all the profits. It also means you must pay all the taxes and bear any losses. Creditors can claim against your personal possessions, which include your home, if you run into difficulties.

2. Partnership

A partnership is an agreement between two or more persons to run a business together. Each partner is individually responsible in law for business debts incurred by the business as a whole and the agreement is based on mutual trust. Otherwise, it is in many respects similar to the sole trader category. Taxes are paid on the partnership profits as a whole rather than by the individuals.

It is advisable to have a solicitor draw up a partnership agreement.

3. Private limited company

A company has similar rights to an individual and is a separate entity in its own right. It costs around £100 to £200 to incorporate a new company or buy a ready-made company name 'off the shelf'.

A company requires a minimum of two shareholders, one of whom must be a director. It also requires the appointment of a secretary. The shareholders own the company and appoint the directors.

All the debts incurred by the company remain the company's debts and if it goes bankrupt the shareholders are not personally liable beyond the face value of their shares. In practice, though, the directors have probably had to put up personal guarantees to obtain company loans and obviously are responsible for these.

A limited company is obliged to prepare annual accounts for the inspector of taxes, which must be audited by an independent auditor; the profit and loss account and balance sheet must be included in an annual return to the Registrar of Companies, as well as information about share ownership and changes in the company during the year.

The objectives and operating rules of a limited company are set out in its memorandum and articles of association; do make sure that these objectives are expressed in broader terms than you may require at present, so you are covered if you wish to expand the business or diversify into other activities later on.

Franchising

Franchising facilitates the marketing of a particular product or service at a quicker rate of expansion and on a larger scale than would otherwise be possible. It primarily cuts out the expensive middle management of large companies and, in effect, passes this responsibility on to the franchisee.

It is a method of starting up a business at less risk, whereby the franchisee buys the right to sell a tried and tested product or service of the franchising company and to carry on the business using the name and other services provided by or associated with the franchisor. The franchisor provides a business package which is operated within a specified area or location under the corporate name of the parent company.

Franchisees should be provided with training and expert backing which would not normally be available to the person setting up his own business, on precisely how the operation is to be run and on the standards to be maintained. In the case of a driving school, a franchisor should provide a complete 'blueprint' for every aspect of operating the business. This should include:

Complete training in instructional skills
Complete training in the business operation

backed up by:

Fully documented training programmes
Teaching notes
Student notes and other literature
Training aids for the learner
A business administration system
Management and business advice
Regular visits by experts from the franchising company
A system of supervising and monitoring standards
A system of communication between franchisees
Regional or national promotions by the franchisor
Regional and national advertising by the franchisor of the service.

A franchise normally contains two cost elements: a pre-launch service involving an initial payment for training, equipment, documentation and services to set up the business; a continuous service, after the initial launch, which normally involves commission charges on the services provided and/ or payments for the products supplied by the franchisor and used in the day-to-day operation of the business.

The system of monitoring the standards of the individual franchisees may at first seem an unnecessary imposition. However, any franchise offered without such monitoring should be avoided. Monitoring is absolutely essential to protect the interest of each individual franchisee and also the reputation of the parent company.

Where adequate controls do not exist, a bad franchisee will have an adverse effect on the overall name and reputation of the services provided, which can result in a chain reaction on the trading of other franchisees. Once obtained, bad reputations are difficult to get rid of!

Avoid those franchisors with heavy 'enrolment' fees and those seeming to charge no fees at all. Where the ongoing commissions or fees seem too low to support the claims of the parent company, particularly in relation to its monitoring of the franchisees' operations, the company should be avoided. It is always wise to meet an existing franchisee before committing oneself. Avoid the company who will not make such an introduction for you.

Before making decisions either to franchise out a particular service which *you* have developed, or to become a franchisee it would be wise to obtain professional advice. *Taking up a Franchise*, published by Kogan Page, is recommended, and two booklets which may help can be obtained from Franchise World, 37 Nottingham Road, London SW17. They are 'How to Evaluate a Franchise' and 'How to Franchise Your Business'.

In practice, and with the exception of the British School of Motoring, franchisors do not have a good reputation within the driving school industry and have so far failed to provide franchisees with the expertise and services required and for which they have often paid. It has been estimated that the minimum cost of setting up a soundly-based franchising company within this field, with all the necessary services and training, would be in the region of £500 000.

Registration of Businesses

It is not necessary to register the name of a business of a sole trader or partnership. However, anyone trading under a name other than their own must disclose on all stationery the details of the owners of the business. Limited companies must register their names with the Registrar of Companies who keeps an index of company details.

Disclosure of Business Ownership

If a business name other than a personal name is used the names of the owners and the official address of the business must be displayed prominently at any of the premises to which customers have access. It is a criminal offence not to comply with these regulations.

Employing Staff

Before employing new staff, a driving school proprietor should consider the costs, responsibilities and risks involved in expanding. As a driving school proprietor you must recognise that staff, no matter how conscientious, are unlikely to work as hard promoting your business as you do yourself. To increase demand it may be necessary to lower prices or offer costly incentives in order to fill the additional car. A hasty decision to expand may result in a previously healthy and profitable school starting to lose money unless the increased demand can be sustained. The situation is likely to be aggravated further if staff leave and set up in opposition. In some cases the driving school proprietor with more work than he can cope with may find it more profitable to increase his prices rather than struggle to fill the extra car.

Selecting New Staff

Once you have made a decision to employ a new instructor, the next step is to select the right person.

1. *Conditions of eligibility for the ADI Register.*
   If these cannot be met there is no point proceeding any further with an application.
2. *Past employment record.*
   Too many jobs over a short period of time may be a bad sign. Caution is required where an applicant is prepared to take a big drop in salary. Take up and check references.
3. *Depth of driving experience.*
   Where an applicant with a poor driving standard is accepted for training, the cost of such training will be considerably increased. A test need only be carried out on short-listed applicants. Eyesight requirements should also be checked at this stage.
4. *Personal qualities.*
   A pleasing appearance and personality are desirable. General attitude, enthusiasm and ability to communicate ideas should also be taken into consideration.

Employing Qualified Instructors

This may not be as simple as it sounds. Standards, abilities and ethics differ widely among qualified instructors.

Driving and instructional ability should be vetted thoroughly as driving techniques and methods of instruction vary a great deal. Obviously a standard system of driving and instruction should be adopted by all employees within the same school. Where a qualified instructor is neither willing to consider new methods nor prepared to change a little, then he or she is probably the wrong person to employ.

Conditions and Contract of Employment

An employed person must be given a contract within three months of starting work. It must contain details of hours of work, job title, salary or wages, holiday entitlement and termination of employment. It should also include details of pension schemes and any disciplinary procedures. It should specify which days qualify for sick pay, the amounts involved for short and long periods off work and any rules applying to the notification of the illness.

Standard employment contracts are available from most commercial stationers but you will need to define the job specification yourself. It should outline the general duties of an instructor, such as procedures for booking and cancelling tests and lessons, professional standards of conduct and relations with clients and how to deal with complaints. You may choose to include reference to personal hygiene, appearance, vehicle maintenance and cleanliness and use of the school car for private purposes.

Driving school proprietors who provide sensible training programmes for new instructors should protect themselves from those instructors who are simply using them as a cheap way to train and qualify. You may decide to include agreement on 'restraint of trade' in the contract on such items as not giving instruction other than through the school, not starting up in opposition in the same area within a specified time or teaching the school's clients after leaving your employment, and payment of full or part costs of training if they leave within a specified time.

When employing a new instructor and deciding on the commencement date, you should consider whether the person has passed Parts 1 and 2 of the ADI exams and the time it may take for the Department of Transport to grant a trainee licence. When working out the cost of training, consideration should be given to:

- cost of the course;
- cost of board and lodgings;
- wages, travel and other expenses while on the course;
- examinations and ADI registration fees.

Several other matters also need to be resolved:

1. *Financial arrangements:*
   (a) payment of training, examination and registration fees;
   (b) recovery of fees if person leaves your employment.

2. *Training and supervision:*
   (a) who is responsible for training and supervision?
   (b) arranging core curriculum training and supervision.

3. *Termination of contract.* What happens if:
   (a) an employee fails the Part 3 exam?
   (b) the trainee licence expires or ADI registration is revoked?
   (c) the employee leaves soon after qualifying?

Self-Employed Instructors

A different agreement is required where instructors are self-employed and working for you on contract. For persons to be legally employed in this way they must accept an element of risk and have the freedom to carry out the terms of the contract in their own way. Legal advice should be sought before entering into such agreements.

Contracts may vary greatly from one situation to another, but in addition to the items previously mentioned concerning the protection of your business, the basic document may include agreement on:

- hours and days of work;
- provision and use of instruction vehicle;
- provision of office facilities, advertising, spare car;
- vehicle costs: tax/insurance/petrol/repairs;
- payment of pupils' fees to school and instructor;
- commencement and termination of the agreement;
- holidays, sickness and insurance.

Health and Safety at Work

An employer must provide a safe working environment for the employee. This includes, in the case of driving instructors, vehicle, office and the training area. The Health and Safety at Work Act 1974 requires all employers with five or more employees to prepare and keep an up-to-date, written safety policy. Its aim is to get employers to think about premises and working conditions. The statement does not need to be long but should be appropriate to the circumstances and brought to the notice of employees. Some employers may feel that, because there is little risk, it is not necessary. However, there are no exemptions and even employers of less than five staff should formulate a policy and work out how to carry it out.

The main elements in the written statement should include:

1. A declaration of intent to provide the safest and healthiest working conditions possible.
2. Who is responsible for implementation.
3. Procedures for dealing with common risks.
4. Identifying any special risks and procedures for dealing with them.
5. Laying out safe systems and methods of work.
6. Accident reporting and investigation procedures.
7. Provision and use of protective clothing and equipment.
8. Emergency procedures.
9. Training for health and safety.
10. Supervision of work in relation to health and safety.

Equipment and Services

Services provided by the national trade organisations include insurance, car hire, training and updating courses. With few exceptions, there appears to be little or no cost saving, or other benefit, in obtaining goods or services from these sources. The equipment and services involved are normally available at lower cost.

Instructor Training Services

The Department of Transport issue a list of instructor training establishments situated throughout the country. The authors appear on this list and provide a comprehensive three-part training programme linked to the examination system. Their home study course has been vetted by the Department's own technical section. It prepares candidates for the Part 1 Test of Theory as well as providing background information for the practical examinations. Many other training establishments now use this to supplement their own course material.

Car Signs and Dual Controls

Headboards and other car signs/panels can normally be supplied by the national instructor associations. Other suppliers include M & M Signs, 81 Arundel Road, High Wycombe, Buckinghamshire; Tel 0494 26592; Amberley Signs, 81 Hamesmoor Road, Mytchett, Camberley, Surrey GU16 6JB; Tel 0252 542503; RCM Marketing Ltd, 80 Tenter Road, Moulton Park Business Centre, Northampton NN3 1PZ; Tel 0604 790890; BIG G Products, 1 Centre Way, Claverings Industrial Estate, Edmonton, London N9; Tel 01-803 7346.

Driving School Aids, East View, Broadgate Lane, Horsforth, Leeds LS18 4DD; Tel 0532 580688, can supply dual controls and car signs.

Dual controls are also available from HE-MAN Equipment Limited, Princess Street, Northam, Southampton SO1 1RP; Tel 0703 26952; Porter Controls Ltd, Forval Close, Wandle Way, Mitcham, Surrey CR4 4NE; Tel 01-640 3200.

For reusable cable dual controls contact AID, Queensdale Works, Queensthorpe Road, Sydenham, London SE26 4PJ; Tel 01-778 7055.

Long-Term Car Hire

Jackson's Driving School Hire, 28 Hermitage Road, Hitchin, Hertfordshire; Tel 0462 34557, can offer long-term contract hire vehicles for between one and three years' duration.

Frank E Conway & Co Ltd, 3a Clifton Square, Lytham FY8 5JT; Tel 0253 737494, offer contract hire services to driving instructors.

Buying or Renting the Vehicle

There are two ways of financing your school vehicle. You can buy it by paying cash or through a hire or lease purchase plan. Alternatively, you can rent it on a lease option or contract hire.

If you have cash to spare and you are sure you will not need it for anything else, a cash purchase from your own savings is probably the cheapest way of financing the vehicle. Alternatively, you may obtain a bank loan which is usually a close second. Then there are the hire and lease purchase options. The difference between them includes the amount of deposit needed and the manner in which tax benefits are calculated. Lease purchase usually involves a smaller initial outlay but with higher monthly payments.

Leasing is a popular method of financing large fleets. It frees capital resources for other things and the VAT on payments is recoverable. Although the initial costs may seem low, contract hire is probably the most expensive way of financing the vehicle. Before entering into a contract hire agreement you should seek professional advice.

Selling the Old Vehicle and Buying a Replacement

Selling the old tuition vehicle privately reduces the depreciation by cutting out the dealer's profits and enables you to negotiate a higher discount on the new car. This often requires the capital to finance the new vehicle while you are disposing of the old one. You can get round this by selling the old one first and then sorting out a quick deal on a replacement before releasing it.

Negotiating the best possible deal should be largely a matter of common sense. Unfortunately, common sense seems a lot less common than is commonly thought! Driving instructors often pay too much for replacement vehicles and get too little for the old ones. Tell the dealer that it is in their interest for you to use their cars and offer £7500 for a £8000 car. Be prepared to shock them a little with your first offer. Be realistic though or you may be shown the door. After negotiating your discount do not let them push the price back up with extras.

Once you have got the deal sorted you can turn your attention to negotiating a discount on the cost of spares and servicing and organising the special service arrangements you will need. You can save yourself a lot of money, time and worry by negotiating your requirements beforehand.

Tuition Vehicles

Next time you are shopping for a replacement vehicle remember that some are better suited to tuition than others and as the perfect driving school car does not exist it is not the intention to compare the faults and virtues here. However, some of the factors influencing your choice are mentioned below.

1. *Initial cost and value for money.* When buying or hiring the car, shop around to get the best deal. Make sure you get an 'on the road' price and that there are no hidden extras. Negotiate at least a 12½ per cent discount or buy elsewhere. Some companies offer special incentives for instructors to buy their particular models; it is worthwhile making enquiries about this but take a hard look at the offer – in some cases you are probably better off with the discount. Find out what the interest charges are and the total price you will pay for the vehicle.

   Check the insurance grouping and the costs of this before acquiring any particular vehicle. Some insurance companies are reluctant to cover certain vehicles for tuition purposes and insurance for foreign cars will usually be higher priced than for similar models produced in the UK.

When comparing the initial cost or outlay of the vehicle you should take account of the subsequent costs. It may be more economical to pay a higher initial figure to obtain lower running costs; for example, the extra cost of a diesel engine option.

There are two important factors to be considered in the cost of vehicle purchase and replacement. These are 'depreciation' and 'replacement value'. Depreciation is the difference between what you paid for the car and what you might receive when it is sold. For example, a new car costing £7500 might only have a value of £2500 after three years of driving school work. This means that the car is depreciating by about £32 per week. However, the replacement value of the car may be £9000 in three years' time. So, in addition to providing for the depreciation on the existing vehicle, you must also budget for the projected increased cost. These additional costs bring the weekly cost to about £42 each week.

Care should be taken when purchasing or acquiring the vehicle from dealers or companies not within, say, 30 minutes' travelling time. For example, where are you going to get the vehicle serviced and repaired when it needs instant attention? Local dealers may not be so sympathetic to your case if you purchased the car elsewhere.

2. *Ease of driving.* A good driving school car will have well positioned controls, a wide range of seat adjustments, central floor gear change with light positive gear positions and a well-protected reverse gear (to avoid accidental selection). A centrally-mounted handbrake is also desirable from the point of view of ease of reach by the instructor in any emergency. The steering should be light and precise, the accelerator, footbrake and clutch smooth and progressive. Servo-assisted brakes are desirable and the engine should be smooth in both first and second gears at tickover speed on a level road. It should also be comfortable in fourth at about 25 to 30 mph.

Choose a car with good all-round visibility, a large interior mirror and two externally-mounted door mirrors. In general terms, the higher the seating position is, the better the driver can see.

3. *Running costs, servicing, repairs and reliability.* Think about the likely depreciation costs. Consider the running costs and the reputation the manufacturer has for reliability. Fuel consumption should be one of the instructor's first considerations. A cheap but unreliable car may turn out to be very expensive through lost lessons and repairs. Good mileage per gallon is of obvious importance and so is the cost of spares. When considering the latter, remember that it is less expensive to pay £150 to replace a clutch which gives you 50000 miles of usage, than to pay half as much, four times as often.

Diesel-engined cars give improved economy. However, they are more expensive to buy and tend to be more sluggish.

Find out the cost and frequency of servicing recommended by the manufacturer. Before committing yourself to any purchase, try to establish what trade discounts the company is prepared to give on spares and servicing. Do this before you buy the car, while you are in a stronger bargaining position. Check the availability of spare parts, particularly for new models and when buying imported vehicles. Do not just take the salesman's word for it! If you do your own servicing, check its effect on the manufacturer's warranty.

If possible, it is better to buy from a local dealer providing you are able to come to mutually agreeable terms. The vehicle will need instant attention if anything goes wrong. Tuition vehicles off the road mean lost income so, before buying the vehicle, establish the kind of service you will require.

4. *Size, design and comfort.* For tuition purposes, the small and medium-sized models are most popular. While there are advantages in choosing a small car they often fail to stand up to the rigours of the job. Very small ones may be too noisy and cause additional stress and fatigue. It is also far from certain that small capacity engines give better fuel economy when used for tuition.

Instructors often buy cars to satisfy their personal needs as well as those of clients. The larger, more powerful cars tend to be more comfortable but rather unwieldy for tuition. However, comfort is an important aspect to consider. Remember, you may be sitting in your car for up to ten hours a day. Ensure the seats provide adequate support and the driving seat has a wide range of adjustments to suit a variety of shapes and sizes of driver. People with small feet may find high pedal positions tiring and troublesome.

Suggestions for 'Conditions of Service' Document

1. Make sure you have a valid driving licence for motor cars before attending for your first on-road practical lesson.
2. Check that you can read a number plate with symbols 3⅛ inches in height at a minimum distance of 67 feet. If you are in doubt consult an optician before your first lesson.
3. Do not drive under the influence of alcohol or drugs. Heavy drinking the night before a lesson may mean you are still over the legal limit for driving the next morning. If you are taking any drugs, ask your doctor if they will affect your driving.
4. Wear comfortable lightweight clothes and low-heeled walking shoes.
5. The school will provide a car which is fully insured for driving tuition and tests. If, for any reason, a lesson has to be cancelled by

the school, you will be informed as soon as possible and a convenient, alternative appointment will be arranged for you.

The school will provide you with a Department of Transport Approved Driving Instructor. Ask to see the official certificate with the instructor's photograph on it. Your instructor will ensure you are advised with complete frankness concerning training needs.

The instructor will advise you when to apply for a driving test. This advice will be based on your continued progress and co-operation over lessons and subject to reappraisal nearing the date of the appointment. If you have applied for a test yourself, show your instructor the appointment card as soon as possible so that the date, time and test centre can be entered in the school's diary. No responsibility can be taken for tests which are double-booked.

Documentation

Although the work of an instructor is essentially practical, there is a certain amount of administrative paperwork which is necessary to the efficient running of any organisation whether it is a two-car or 200-car school.

You will need to keep records of the strengths and weaknesses of pupils and how they are progressing through the course. Records should show routes used and what topics have been covered. These records are the only way in which an instructor can reliably recall the important details of each client's progress.

You will need an efficient booking system to ensure you get to the right client at the correct time. Bad time-keeping and unkept appointments are guaranteed to lose customers. Clients will need appointment cards to remind them of the date, time and place of their lessons. If the client forgets the appointment, it will mean financial loss to the instructor, unless this eventuality has been catered for in your 'conditions of service' brochure. It is hoped that some of these documents will be encountered very rarely (for example the accident report) but obviously there are others which form part of the routine day's work.

Daily Work Sheet

This usually consists of the programme of work for a particular instructor for each working day. It includes the starting time and place of pick up for each lesson; the time of any test appointment and provision for pupils to 'sign in' for their lessons. Provision is also made for starting and finishing mileages and for amounts of fuel purchased during the day. In this way a complete record of the day's work may be kept for future reference. It is clearly helpful for the instructor and his employer to be able to check back for confirmation of lessons taken and details of vehicle mileages and costs. The document is normally carried by the instructor during the day's work, together with the pupil progress sheets required for that day's work. The daily work sheet and relevant progress sheets are always carried by the instructor – probably on a small clipboard. It is important that instructors are fully conversant with the completion and subsequent filing of the documents and their relevance to the administration of the business.

Instructor: .... Car No: ...... Date ....
Milometer: **Finish** .... **Fuel** ....
Start .... **Oil** ....
Miles run ....
Repairs ....

Time	Pupil	Place	Signatures

Daily work sheet – rough example

Pupil Progress Sheet

A progress sheet normally carries the basic information relevant to the pupil – name, address, licence details, previous driving experience and driving test information – as well as a brief outline of the driving topics covered at each stage of learning. The details of this particular document may vary from one school to another, but the overall principle involved ensures that one instructor is able to continue with the training in the absence of the original instructor owing to sickness or holiday leave.

The method of recording accurately the progress of pupils is of vital importance in order to achieve uniformity and also so that the individual instructor can satisfactorily monitor progress, particularly when the training is spasmodic or when a verbal progress report is called for.

Pupil Record Card

In a multi-car driving school, the pupil reception record card would normally be located permanently in the office, although in a small school it may be more efficient for the instructor to carry all record cards securely in the car.

The record card serves a dual purpose – one side of the card contains the same information as the progress sheet, but the reverse side consists of a system for recording lessons taken and payments made.

Company policy will vary regarding the completion of this particular document, but whatever the system the instructor should be familiar with the method used. From an administrative point of view, this is probably the most important record as it will show a complete, accurate and permanent means of checking on a variety of statistics including addresses and backgrounds of pupils, number of lessons taken, test results and total number of new pupils booked.

Driver Assessment

From time to time it will be necessary for the instructor to carry out a detailed assessment of a driver's ability. The assessment may be requested in order to offer a progress report or for an independent check on a driver's ability. In either case, the progress sheet may prove to be an inadequate document. In these cases a 'Driver Assessment Sheet' or 'Mock Test Marking Sheet' might be used. These sheets normally contain some abbreviations or coding in order to include as much information as possible on a relatively small document.

It is vital that the instructor is fully conversant with the method used, and with the system and standard for marking of errors.

From the marking sheet it will sometimes be necessary to issue a standard report to the client, or employer, and this may consist of an individual letter or a standardised report.

Standard Procedures

Even in the best run businesses and with regularly maintained vehicles, breakdowns and defects will occasionally arise. It is essential, therefore, that a procedure exists for reporting and dealing with these problems.

In Appendix III we deal with routine maintenance and the need to carry spare bulbs, screwdrivers and other items for carrying out immediate minor repairs in order to keep the vehicle functional and legal, but here we deal with the documents and procedures involved in more severe cases of defect and breakdown.

Vehicle Defects

If a fault on a training vehicle is more complicated than a simple bulb replacement but not sufficiently serious to warrant an interruption of the day's work, it is necessary for the instructor to be familiar with the procedure for the fault correction. Depending on the type and size of the driving school, the system will vary from:

1. The instructor staying on after work to correct the fault.
2. The instructor reporting the fault on a defect list in the office.
3. Leaving a defect note on the vehicle for the maintenance department.

Whichever system is employed, the instructor should be capable of deciding whether the fault can be corrected by him immediately or, alternatively, be able to identify the defect for others to act upon.

Breakdowns

If the fault is more than a minor problem and causes the vehicle to be unroadworthy or unable to be used for instruction, the instructor will clearly need to abandon the lesson in the interests of safety and the law.

Instructors should be familiar with the company procedure in the event of breakdown, and subject to any particular variations, the basic procedure is as follows:

1. Move the vehicle, if possible, to a safe position.
2. Identify the cause of breakdown.
3. Notify the reception office immediately, giving details of instructor's name, pupil's name, time of any test appointments later that day, present location of vehicle, cause of breakdown, details of next appointment.

The way in which a breakdown is dealt with can affect the economy of the school, and the image which is presented to the customers and to any members of the public who happen to be involved or present at the time.

During any delay in recovering the vehicle and the interruption to the lesson, the pupil should be reassured that he will not lose financially because of the breakdown, particularly if there is any question of a driving test fee being involved. This type of incident will not normally require the completion of a formal document except that it is prudent to make a note of the details on the daily work sheet.

Accident Procedure

Sooner or later the driving instructor may be involved in a road accident – usually through no fault of his learner driver. Basic training in this subject and a standard procedure for reporting accidents will ensure that the instructor and his pupil do not inadvertently break the law. It should also be remembered that the learner driver will require assistance and guidance in a difficult situation. Not only should the instructor be able to carry out the correct procedures, he should during the training of his pupils ensure that they have a complete understanding of the legal requirements. Most drivers feel that accidents only happen to other people. Those who have been involved in accidents probably felt the same way before it happened to them. It is, therefore, the instructor's duty not only to obey the law but also be able to provide comprehensive guidance for his pupils.

With regard to driving school procedure, it is recommended that a driving instructor should normally carry with him a standard form for the purpose of noting down details of the accident at the time. Company procedure may vary from one driving school to another and the relevant form may be issued by the school or by the insurance company, but in either case it is imperative that details of the accident are recorded at the time.

An 'Agreed Statement of Facts' is also available from insurance companies. This has the advantage that it is carbonated and therefore the identical details may be supplied to each insurance company. Standard accident procedure within a driving school should include the following points:

1. Stop the vehicle and switch off engine.
2. Arrange for someone to warn approaching traffic.
3. Take fire precautions and/or fight fire.
4. Obtain emergency services by telephoning 999.
5. Check on well-being of pupil.
6. Exchange particulars with other driver and obtain witnesses' names and addresses.
7. Check on condition of school car. If in doubt, obtain assistance.
8. Report to office as soon as possible.

Further advice and information for the driver is available in the DTp manual 'Driving'.

Accident report

Date of accident .... Time ....
Exact location ....
....
School vehicle .... Reg. no............. Fleet no.............
Instructor's name ....
Driver's name ....
Driver's address ....
....
Description of injuries ....
....
Vehicle damage ....
Other vehicle: make and registration ....
Other third party damage ....
Driver ....

Example of an accident report form

Appointment Card

Some form of appointment card is normally issued by the driving school to each individual pupil. The card usually includes reference to the time and date of lessons booked, and may include a receipt for payments made.

When any money is paid to the instructor by a pupil during a lesson, it is essential that the instructor should initial the appropriate section on the card as well as making a note of the payment on his daily work sheet. When it is

When any money is paid to the instructor by a pupil during a lesson, it is essential that the instructor should initial the appropriate section on the card as well as making a note of the payment on his daily work sheet. When it is not possible for this type of receipt to be given, the alternative may be for the instructor to issue a receipt from a small duplicated book. Whichever system is used, care must be taken that the fees are paid in to the office promptly in order to avoid any misunderstandings or doubt over payment.

The other important point in relation to the appointment card is that either the instructor or receptionist should ensure on each lesson that the time and date of the next lesson is checked against the work diary in order to avoid unnecessary errors and in case of any unforeseen alterations to the schedule.

Summary

Verbal communication between instructor and pupil, and between instructor and reception office will play an important part in the smooth running and efficiency of the school. Internal documentation and standard procedures are important, but these will need to be supplemented by good teamwork in order to 'link' the instructional and administrative sections of the school. A reasonably straightforward system of documentation and procedures will help you be more efficient by enabling you to concentrate your attentions on the task of instructing. It is important, therefore, that you receive some form of training in the use of these procedures and that you are familiar with the internal documentation at the earliest possible opportunity.

Bookkeeping in a Small Business

Adequate bookkeeping in any business, large or small, is essential. Businesses frequently fail because of inadequate record keeping and financial control.

For the person starting a new business such as a driving school it is easy to feel that personal contact with customers or potential customers is the only important part of the business. Keeping a complete set of books is time consuming but must be considered an essential requirement in order to control the running of the business.

Although there is no specific legal requirement it makes good sense for the sole trader to keep a written record of receipts and payments for the purpose of producing a yearly account of assets and liabilities and for an assessment of the tax liability.

A company's obligations are much more specific. The law requires a limited company to keep a complete record of receipts, expenses, sales, purchases, assets and liabilities. Details of the transactions of the company will normally have to be made available to shareholders and directors and some aspects of the company's business will have to be published.

Adequate and accurate records are necessary for the small trader for two main reasons:

1. A quarterly account may be required by Customs & Excise for VAT purposes. A business which has (or is likely to have) an annual turnover of £23600 or more will need to register for VAT.

   The instructor working completely on his own will not normally be obliged to register but a business involving two or more cars will almost certainly have to. One of the advantages of having to prepare a quarterly VAT account is that it does provide a measure of the progress of the business.

2. An annual account will be required for income tax purposes. Most businesses will have to produce an annual balance sheet and for this

an accountant's services will be necessary. It is essential therefore that full details of trading are recorded throughout the year.

When starting a new business on a part- or full-time basis the usual method of keeping records would include:

(a) a notebook for recording small items of expenditure for which receipts may not always be available – fares, postage etc; and
(b) a file or clip for receipts, invoices, statements and delivery notes.

As the business grows a cash book will probably be needed. This book sets out details of income and expenditure, including a breakdown of the VAT content and an analysis of the type of expenditure. A cash book may consist of a normal A4-sized book which is ruled off to provide different columns for various types of expenditure and should be kept up to date, preferably on a daily basis. By this means you will be able to see at a glance how much the business owes and is owed.

For a small business the system described above would be quite adequate for an accountant to prepare the end of year, or end of quarter, accounts for VAT and income tax purposes.

Credit cards can also provide a useful means of keeping a record of payments made as well as being a satisfactory way of paying for larger items. Card companies provide a detailed breakdown of purchases on a monthly basis and these records will give your accountant the information which he requires. The other advantage of paying by this means is that a certain amount of interest free credit is obtained.

As the business grows it may be necessary to consider a more complete system of bookkeeping. At this stage it would be useful to ask your accountant's advice regarding the type of system which would be most appropriate to the needs of your business. There are many books and systems available including the *Self-Employed Account Book* and the *Complete Trader's Account Book*.

One system which is particularly suitable for the small driving school is provided by Safeguard Business Systems, which produces a complete range of 'one-write' sensitised paper, including cheque writing, purchase and sales ledgers, PAYE wages, petty cash vouchers, end of year analysis and quarterly VAT returns.

Time and money saving methods in bookkeeping are just as important in your business as the services you render. Old-fashioned methods waste time – and time is money. The 'one-write' system cuts clerical time and enables you to keep your records up to date at all times. Individual parts of the range may be purchased so that a complete system may be built up as the business grows.

Whichever system of bookkeeping is utilised, whether you use a notebook and a clip for bills and receipts, or a set of analysis books; or the complete system, you will need to know whether your firm is making money or losing it. You will also need to know which parts of the business are weak; whether the outstanding debts are excessive; and what relationship there is between profits and capital employed.

There are of course other points which may be obtained from an up-to-date set of books. The books will provide invaluable information for a prospective purchaser of the business and will act as an indicator of the strength of the business if seeking a loan for expansion.

Establishing an efficient method of record keeping from the start will avoid any unnecessary complications as the business expands.

Points to Remember

Make a point of noting all items of expense as they occur.

File all invoices immediately they are received.

Obtain advice from your accountant regarding suitable records for your particular business.

Set aside a certain amount of time on a regular basis for up-dating your records.

Consider using an appropriate bookkeeping system and/or get some professional help.

Inadequate bookkeeping causes about 80 per cent of business failures. The character of the enterprising instructor who sets up on his own may be very different from that of the trained administrator. However, bookkeeping is going to be an integral and important part of running a successful and profitable driving school.

Inland Revenue and National Insurance Considerations

Use of private residence

If *part* of the expenditure of running the home is wholly and exclusively incurred in the running of a business, a portion of the expenses will be allowed by the Inland Revenue. These expenses may include rent, rates, lighting, heating and telephone. The advantages of allowing some expenses as business costs may, however, be offset by the disadvantages that (a) the rates may be increased by introducing a business element and (b) capital gains tax may be involved if and when the property is sold.

If the home is used as a base without any particular part of it being used for business purposes the apportionment of expenses may be lower, but the capital gains exemption will not be forfeited. This may well prove to be the most effective arrangement for the small-scale home-based business. Any person running a business may employ his or her spouse. The wages are an allowable business expense – so long as the spouse is not paid more than another person would have received for doing the same job, and provided that he/she is actually paid.

A spouse is treated in exactly the same way as any other employee – the normal rules relating to National Insurance and PAYE apply. It is obviously an advantage in a small business for the wife to be employed in a capacity which will enable her to earn a wage which approaches the maximum limit of the earned income allowance. Beyond that limit PAYE deductions are involved. National Insurance contributions are required until the wife is 60 years of age, and the husband 65.

The arrangements for employing both husband and wife in the business will vary from one firm to another, and the advice of an accountant will normally be sought in individual cases.

Books and records must be kept from the start of any business. The Inspector of Inland Revenue will require detailed information annually, and may require answers to any questions. In the absence of answers he will substitute his own estimates which may not be in favour of the business.

If the business is VAT-registered, the Customs and Excise Office will require information every quarter year.

Proper records of your business will be required by bank managers, solicitors and potential purchasers in the event of your seeking finance or wishing to sell your business.

The value of the 'goodwill' of the business depends to a large extent on the bookkeeping records showing that the business is worth purchasing.

Vehicle Controls and Operation

Vehicle Operation

There are three major operating systems in a motor car:

1. *The main controls:* these enable the driver to start and stop the engine and to control the speed, position and direction of the vehicle.
2. *Driving aids:* these assist the driver to see, to be seen by, and to communicate with other road users.
3. *Instrumentation:* this provides the driver with information about the vehicle, how it is functioning and the speed at which it is travelling.

The Main Controls

The steering provides a means of controlling and changing the direction of the vehicle. To operate the steering, keep both hands on the wheel as much as possible and in particular at high speeds, when braking and also cornering. Position the hands at about the 'ten to two' or 'a quarter to three' position. Try to use the 'pull-push' method of steering outlined in the Department of Transport's manual, 'Driving', but directional control and accuracy of the steering is the most important objective. The mirror should be used well before changing direction or position in the road. Avoid sudden, jerky movements on the wheel and hold it firmly, but do not grip too tightly. Remember that when cornering, the rear wheels cut into a turn.

Direction indicators play a major role in a complex system of communications between road users. They are operated by the fingertips, but without losing total hand contact with the steering wheel. They are frequently required for *moving off, stopping, moving to the left or right* and *turning to the left or right*. Generally they should be used in good time, but some traffic situations require special consideration in the timing of them. They must be correct for the situation and cancelled after use. (Automatic self-cancelling mechanisms are not infallible and it is the driver's overall responsibility to rectify prematurely cancelled signals and to ensure that others are switched off after a manoeuvre is completed.)

The handbrake secures the car when it is parked or stationary for more than a short pause. The handbrake should be used only when the car is stationary, except in an emergency (footbrake failure). The ratchet release should be operated before releasing or applying the handbrake, which is used when parking and also to provide a greater degree of safety and control for some temporary stops. Check that the handbrake is on after entering the vehicle, before starting the engine and particularly before leaving the vehicle.

The gear lever provides a permanent means of disconnecting the engine from the driving wheels (neutral). It also provides a selection of different ratios to allow the optimum and most economical engine speeds to be maintained at all road speeds and load requirements. The gears also provide a means of driving the vehicle backwards. There is usually a centrally-mounted four-speed gearbox, although many models now have five gears. Avoid looking at the gear lever when changing. Use a 'cupped' hand on the gear lever and do not use excessive force when moving the gears.

1st gear: . the most powerful, but slowest. Used for moving off, low speed clutch control and manoeuvre exercises.

2nd gear: also powerful, but faster than the 1st gear. Useful for rapid acceleration and slow speeds through some hazards.

3rd gear: a faster gear, used for acceleration from over 15 mph. Used for driving through some hazards.

4th gear: the most economical gear, with insufficient power for speeds of much lower than 25 mph. Used to provide progressive acceleration from about 25-30 mph and for cruising at constant speeds.

5th gear: used as an aid for cruising at higher speeds and on motorways at a constant speed.

The clutch temporarily disconnects the engine from the gearbox/driving wheels to facilitate changing gear and stopping. It provides the means to engage the power source (engine) smoothly and progressively to the load (the road wheels).

It is operated by the left foot and is used for moving off, low speed control, changing gear and stopping. Clutch control involves finding and holding the clutch plates at the first point of contact, the bottom of which is called the 'holding point' and the top the 'driving point'. The full range is called the 'biting range'. Slipping the clutch is an important part of low speed control. Excessive clutch slip over prolonged periods, however, causes undue wear and should be avoided. Also, try not to rest your weight on the pedal when driving ('riding the clutch'). Moving off, changing gear and stopping should always be preceded by mirror checks.

The accelerator (often called the gas) plays a major role in the regulation of vehicle speed. It works by the pedal operating a petrol/air valve which, in turn, regulates the power and speed of the engine. It is operated by the right foot. Any pedal movement and changes in pressure should be progressive. The response to pedal movement is more pronounced in the low gears. Changes in speed should be preceded by use of the mirror.

The footbrake also plays a major role in the regulation of the vehicle's speed. The footbrake pedal is operated by the right foot. It operates a hydraulic system which presses high friction material against a rotating wheel disc or drum (similar in principle to a bicycle brake). Any changes in pressure should be progressive. The response to pressure changes on the pedal is immediate. Pressure can be varied between the barely perceptible up to the point at which the wheels lock. Braking pressure on bends and corners should be minimised or avoided. Use of the brake should be preceded by mirror checks. When the brake is applied, warning lights on the rear of the vehicle are automatically activated.

The Starter Controls

Ignition switch key: a safety and anti-theft device. This activates the engine electrical circuits essential to its operation. It includes an engine cut-out system when it is switched off. It also activates a number of warning and other electrical circuits. When the key is removed this usually activates a steering lock.

The starter activates the engine via the starter motor. It is usually incorporated into the ignition switch as the final position to which the key is turned. The starter motor should not normally be activated for periods in excess of five to eight seconds. The key should be released as soon as the engine fires. (Some vehicles are fitted with a protection device which will only allow one operation of the starter motor without switching the ignition off.) Before activating the starter circuits, the normal safety checks should be made, ie handbrake on and gear lever in neutral.

The choke is used for starting cold engines and during a preliminary 'warm-up' period. To operate, pull out fully, operate the starter and switch the engine on. Push the choke back halfway after the first few seconds. Drive off immediately when safe. Return choke fully after the initial 'warm-up' period. There are three main factors which influence the initial warm up period: the temperature of the engine, the external air temperature and the maintenance of the engine. On a cold winter morning the maximum warm-up period should normally be no more than four or five minutes. On a summer day this may be only a few seconds. (For automatic chokes refer to the manufacturer's handbook.)

Driving and Safety Aids

Mirrors: interior and exterior mirrors should be clean and adjusted so as to maximise visibility to the rear and minimise unnatural or unnecessary head movements. Even with the most desirable combination of a large interior and two door-mounted exterior mirrors, there will still be areas to the rear and sides of the car not covered by the mirrors' 'fields of vision'. Before making certain types of manoeuvre these 'blind spots' need to be checked, for example, before moving away from the kerb.

The mirrors should be used at frequent intervals on a continuous and systematic basis to take full advantage of the views afforded by side mirrors.

They should be used particularly before any manoeuvre involving a change in speed or direction and specifically well before *moving off, signalling, stopping* and *overtaking*.

Excessively long or staring looks at the mirror should be avoided as these are likely to cause problems with both the steering and/or forward planning.

Sensible use of the mirrors involves demonstrating an awareness and sympathy for the speed, distance, actions and movement of other road users.

Windscreen/windows/wipers/washers/demisters/defrosters/rearscreen heater: these play a major role in helping to maintain good all-round visibility for the driver.

The controls vary from car to car (consult the manufacturer's handbook). Avoid using windscreen wipers on dry glass and wiping the insides of windows with bare hands (rings can scratch!). Avoid leaving rear screen heaters on continually when not required. Keep wipers in good condition and the washer bottle topped up with water/solvent. Keep windows clean at all times, and plenty of fresh air inside the car will help to prevent windows misting up. Familiarise yourself with these controls while the vehicle is stationary.

Lights help the driver to see and be seen by other road users. Controls vary considerably from car to car (consult the manufacturer's handbook). Sidelights must be used when parked outside a 30 mph limit or within 10 metres of a road junction at night. Dipped headlights should be used where visibility is reduced by fog, snow or other extreme conditions.

Horn and flashing headlights warn and inform other road users of your presence. Controls vary from car to car (consult the manufacturer's handbook). Use of the horn is not permitted between 11.30 pm and 7.00 am in a built-up area or when stationary (except where in danger from another moving vehicle). It should be used sensibly to warn others and not as a rebuke. Try to avoid long 'blasts' of the horn in close proximity of pedestrians but use longer blasts for drivers in motor vehicles. On fast roads, eg motorways, headlamps may be more beneficial than the horn.

Instrumentation

This group of controls, dials and displays provides the driver with the necessary information on how the vehicle is performing and functioning.

Information displays are becoming increasingly more comprehensive. Most of the information is of great assistance to the driver but some available equipment has yet to be proved useful and may even be found to be counterproductive by causing unnecessary distractions to the driver.

This section is concerned only with essential information and that which can be justified as necessary to the safe and sympathetic use of a motor car.

Speedometer: this is *legally* required to be in working order and should be accurate to an error of no more than 10 per cent. It is an offence to make the mileage recorder read fewer miles than the car has actually travelled. Speedometers are usually marked in graduated scales showing both miles and kilometres per hour. They sometimes incorporate a trip recorder switch which can be set and used to record journey mileages or petrol consumption. Avoid long staring looks at the speedometer when checking your speed, but where necessary take frequent glances to establish legal status concerning speed limits.

NB: A speed limit means the *maximum* speed permitted for that road, not necessarily the safest!

Fuel gauge: check the fuel level at the start of a journey, remembering some gauges may not be fully reliable. Avoid running on less than a quarter tank of fuel if possible. Ensure that, when topping up the tank, only the correct 'star' grading of fuel is used. Some vehicles are fitted with dual tanks or reserve systems which include 'changeover' switches.

Vehicles fitted with fuel injection systems normally operate more efficiently and return improved performance.

Unleaded fuel causes less pollution, is generally cheaper than leaded but consumption is normally slightly higher.

Petrol engined vehicles can be converted to run on liquid petroleum gas, which requires the fitting of special tanks. When converted, these can run on either petrol or gas.

Where a diesel engine is fitted, do not put petrol into the tank, or allow the fuel to run dry or it may not re-start without professional assistance.

Where a spare can of fuel is kept for emergencies, it must be suitably marked and have no leaks.

Petrol engined vehicles can be converted to run on liquid petroleum gas, which requires the fitting of special tanks. When converted, these can run on either petrol or gas.

Where a diesel engine is fitted, do not put petrol into the tank, or allow the fuel to run dry or it may not re-start without professional assistance.

Where a spare can of fuel is kept for emergencies, it must be suitably marked and have no leaks.

Engine temperature gauge: an internal combustion engine produces mechanical power from controlled explosions (rapid expansion of burning gases) inside the engine cylinders. At precisely the correct time, vaporised petrol gases are ignited by the spark plugs. The force of these expanding gases pushes pistons up and down inside the cylinders. There are usually four of these cylinders, each working in rapid succession and adding continuously to the mechanical power produced by the others.

At a speed of only 30 mph these controlled explosions can be occurring 60 times every second. This generates a tremendous amount of heat which, if allowed to build up inside the engine, would melt the pistons and heat other moving parts until they become one solid mass of scrap metal. These high temperatures require an efficient cooling system if the engine is to operate satisfactorily. Most engines are cooled by water. This is pumped through special channels cut into the engine block to carry the heat away to the radiator where it is then cooled before re-circulation.

The driver requires confirmation that this system is functioning normally. This is provided by the temperature gauge which indicates the normal operating range of temperature. This may sometimes incorporate a separate warning light to provide more visual impact for the driver if the system overheats.

Where an excessive temperature is indicated, the driver should stop and either obtain assistance or rectify the problem before continuing with the journey. The most common causes of overheating are:

(a) *Broken fan belt:* this normally operates the radiator fan and water pump.

(b) *Lack of coolant:* water can boil and leak away. Unless the level is checked regularly it may become critical to the cooling system. Also check hoses for leaks and wear.

(c) *Blocked radiator:* water freezes and will block the radiator with ice during the winter months unless an anti-freeze solution is present in the cooling system. Ice also expands and can crack the engine cylinder block during severe conditions. During the normal course of running, lime scale from hard water sometimes builds up inside the radiator and blocks the water channels.

Oil pressure gauge: without lubrication, an engine can tear itself apart within minutes of driving off. Lubricating oil is forced, under high pressure, along a series of pipes and oilways to all the moving parts. Under extreme pressure, the oil is squeezed between the moving metal-to-metal parts preventing this damaging contact.

Information about oil pressure is provided by an oil pressure failure light and/or an oil pressure gauge. In the event of a drop in oil pressure, pull up and check it is safe as soon as possible. Switch off the engine. Obtain assistance or rectify the problem before continuing with the journey.

Before starting an engine, check that the oil pressure warning system is operational. This can be done by switching on only the ignition circuits and ensuring the oil pressure warning light activates. The light should switch off within two or three seconds of starting the engine. Oil pressure gauges give a more precise indication of oil pressure when the engine is running and sometimes help to pinpoint a problem before it reaches a critical level. They do, however, tend to be more of a distraction from a driving point of view.

Low oil pressure can be caused by *lack of oil, burst oil pipes, inoperative pump*, or *a very worn engine.*

Check oil levels regularly and look for tell-tale leaks under the car first thing in the morning. Remember too, most cars will use some oil and require topping up between normal servicing.

Brake system malfunction: vehicles are now being fitted with various different kinds of brake warning systems. These can inform the driver of low fluid levels in the system, of uneven pressure in dual-lined braking systems and of worn brake pads. Check these with the vehicle handbook and remember, if the warning systems activate, *stop immediately and obtain assistance.*

Handbrake and choke warning lights: these indicate that the controls are on and in an operating condition. They are intended as a gentle reminder.

Ignition warning light: the ignition warning light is activated when the engine electrical circuits are switched on. Before starting the engine, the system should be checked. This can be done by ensuring the ignition warning light is illuminated when the circuits are switched on and before the starter motor is activated. As soon as the engine starts the alternator should generate its own electrical supply and the light should switch off.

The alternator is operated by the fan belt. If this fails, the alternator will cease to provide the electrical requirements for the engine and vehicle which will then be running on battery power alone. In this condition the ignition warning light should activate.

A broken fan belt will also cause the engine to overheat (see Engine Cooling System on page 342). Other causes of the ignition light switching on are *loose wires, burnt out brushes or diodes on the alternator*, and/or *malfunctions in the voltage regulator*.

This does not normally cause any lasting or serious damage to the vehicle but the journey time will be limited by battery power alone. However, there are safety factors which must be taken into account particularly at night and in cold or wet conditions.

Door and seat belt warning/reminders: visual/audible warning systems are sometimes fitted to remind the driver that doors are not properly closed and/ or the seat belt is not fastened.

Main beam/sidelights/high intensity rear lights: warning systems are fitted to remind drivers when these aids are operating.

Rear screen heater: a warning system usually reminds the driver that the screen heater is on. Rear screen heaters consume a fairly large amount of electrical power and can cause a heavy drain on the battery during prolonged periods at tickover speeds.

Direction indicators and hazard flashers: these are usually fitted with both visual and audible reminders when the aids are in the operating mode.

Automatic Transmission

Safety

From a safety point of view, a vehicle fitted with automatic transmission *should be* a *safer* car to drive than a manual change, for the following reasons:

(a) Both hands are free for the steering of the vehicle 99.9 per cent of the time.

(b) Driving an automatic is less tiresome, particularly in heavy and slow-moving traffic.

(c) Because of the human error factor in driving, to which we are all susceptible, the automatic car reduces the chances of making an error with a gear or the clutch.

Driving an automatic

One of the problems experienced by people wanting to learn on automatics is that there are not widespread facilities available for tuition, with the result that they are not used to their full potential. Driven correctly, automatic cars provide drivers with as much control over the gears as manual change vehicles. There are certain aspects of driving automatics however which the instructor must remember when giving instruction:

1. *The handbrake* is generally required to be used more often and applied more firmly. This is to check the tendency of some automatic vehicles to creep when running at tickover speed.
2. *The footbrake* should be firmly applied before starting some variomatic transmissions fitted to Daf or Volvo cars where the manufacturer recommends they are started in gear. This is particularly true when they are 'on choke'. The footbrake should be firmly applied on other makes of automatic transmissions when they are 'on choke' and before drive or reverse gears are selected.
3. *The accelerator* must not be depressed when engaging drive or reverse gears.
4. *Right foot only* – it is advisable to use the right foot only for both the footbrake and accelerator. There may be some occasions where it is advantageous to use the left foot for the brake however – in some low speed manoeuvring exercises, particularly if the transmission is not very progressive at low speeds.

Disabled drivers

Where a right leg disability is present, the driver may use the left foot for both accelerator and brake (the vehicle will need to be suitably converted.)

An automatic gearbox is a tremendous help to disabled clients and older people – or in fact anyone finding it difficult to drive a manual gear change car.

The driving test

A person passing the test in an automatic car will only be issued with a driving licence for that type of vehicle group.

Types of Automatic Transmission

Full automatic with gear hold position: these have selector positions for forward and reverse with a gear hold for low speed driving and/or driving downhill.

Variomatic transmission: this type of transmission system is fitted with a hold device which offers a greater degree of engine braking on downhill gradients.

Multi-hold systems: these can retain any particular gear and are fitted to many makes of vehicle from the BL Mini to Rolls Royce.

Semi-automatic: this generally means the vehicle is fitted with a normal gearbox and clutch but without the clutch pedal. The clutch is engaged or disengaged by the movement of the hand on the gear lever.

Pre-selector systems: on these the gear is pre-selected before it is required. The gear is later engaged by means of a foot pedal in place of the clutch.

Kick down: this is a mechanism fitted to many automatics whereby it is possible to change down quickly to a lower gear ratio, usually for overtaking.

A sharp depression of the accelerator pedal past the full throttle opening will override the normal gear control system.

Using the accelerator: fidgeting on and erratic or excessive use of the accelerator burns fuel wastefully in any car but in an automatic it will be changing up and down gears according to changes in this pressure. This causes unnecessary wear and tear on the mechanisms involved and should be avoided.

Automatics
This type of transmission system normally uses slightly more fuel. However, some models appear to return better mileage per gallon on the automatic version than the manual.

Mechanical Principles

The Engine

The average car is powered by a four-cylinder engine. Each cylinder is set in the engine block. Pistons are forced up and down in sequence inside these cylinders in an operation called the *Otto cycle*. The four strokes of this cycle are called:

1. The *induction* stroke.
2. The *compression* stroke.
3. The *ignition* stroke.
4. The *exhaust* stroke.

The flow of fuel and air mixture into the cylinders and the flow of the burnt exhaust gases is controlled by a system of valves incorporated into the cylinder head.

Induction: as the piston travels down the cylinder it draws a mixture of petrol and air from the carburettor through the inlet valve. As the piston reaches the bottom of the cylinder the valve closes and the induction stroke is complete.

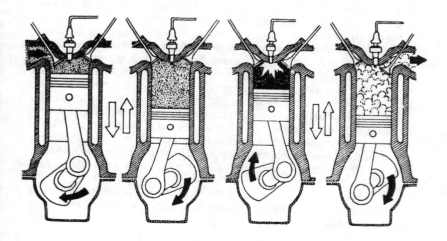

A four stroke engine

Compression: the piston is then forced back up the cylinder compressing the fuel gases into the combustion chamber situated at the top.

Ignition (sometimes called the power stroke): the gases are ignited by the spark plug. The rapid expansion of the burning gases forces the piston back down the cylinder to produce the engine power.

Exhaust: the piston is driven back up the cylinder forcing the burnt gases out of the now open exhaust valve. This completes the *otto cycle.*

Power conversion

The pistons are connected by 'con rods' to the crankshaft, which converts the power produced on the ignition stroke into a rotary motion. This is smoothed by the engine flywheel to produce a continuous flow of power to the gearbox and driving wheels. One complete otto cycle rotates the crankshaft twice.

Valve and ignition timing

The valve and ignition timing gears are arranged to ensure perfect coordination with the motion of the pistons. The camshaft controls the opening and closing of the valves. It rotates at precisely half the speed of the engine and in perfect coordination with the distributor, which controls the exact timing of the spark to initiate the ignition stroke.

The Fuel System

The engine is run on a mixture of petrol and air drawn from the carburettor. The carburettor basically consists of a tube through which the air is drawn, and a float chamber which distributes the fuel pumped from the petrol tank. Air is drawn into the tube of the carburettor through an air filter and is controlled by a flap known as a 'butterfly valve' which is operated by the accelerator pedal. As the accelerator is pressed down, more air is drawn in; this in turn sucks more petrol from the float chamber through small jets which spray petrol into the tube. The combined petrol and air mixture is drawn through a series of pipes known as the inlet manifold into each cylinder. When starting a cold engine a much richer mixture is required and this means a higher proportion of petrol to air than for normal running. This is achieved by restricting the amount of air entering the carburettor by means of a flap in the air intake known as a choke. Some cars have an automatic choke which is controlled by the engine temperature. But in most cars it is operated manually by a knob on the fascia.

In automatic cars an automatic choke can cause the vehicle to creep. It is advisable to get into the habit of pressing one's foot on to the footbrake when starting the engine.

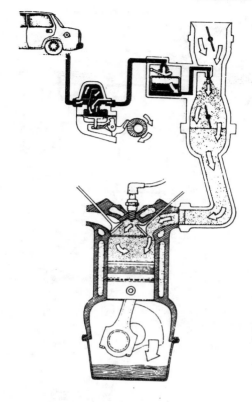

The fuel system

Faults

- *Dirty air filter:* allows air into carburettor and then through into the cylinder causing wear.

- *Sediment in petrol tank:* causes fuel pipe blockage, dirt in petrol pump and carburettor float chamber which will block the jets resulting in starvation of fuel at cylinders.

- *Incorrect petrol and air mixture:* Too rich or too weak. Wrong grade of petrol causing bad engine performance. Driver not returning choke when the engine is warmed up.

The Ignition System

To ignite the petrol/air mixture in the combustion chamber at precisely the correct time, the ignition system converts the low tension voltage from the

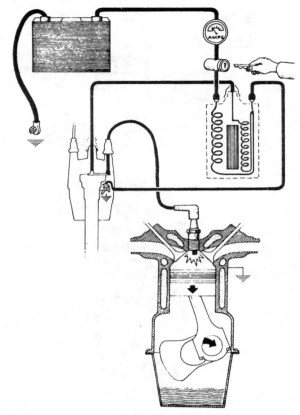

The ignition system

battery into a high tension voltage by means of the coil. The high tension voltage is transmitted through the HT lead from the coil to the distributor cap. As the engine rotates, the rotor arm inside the distributor completes a sequence of contacts to the spark plugs to coincide with the ignition stroke. The timing of the spark is advanced or retarded automatically to ensure it occurs at the correct moment for the load and engine speed. Many modern cars are fitted with electronic ignition systems which involve less maintenance, longer spark plug life and help make starting the car easier.

Faults

- Badly worn, dirty or poorly adjusted contact breaker points or spark plugs.
- Worn rotor arm.
- Poor fitting, dirty, cracked or perished HT leads, faulty or damaged electronic ignition systems.

Engine Lubrication

In normal use the engine is turning from between 700-900 rpm at tickover to about 5 000 rpm at high speed. The need for an efficient lubricating system therefore is absolutely essential.

Oil is stored in the sump at the bottom of the engine and is pumped through a filter up into the engine to lubricate all moving parts. The level of oil in the sump can be checked by the dipstick. It is vital the oil level does not drop too near, or under the low mark. Should this happen the moving parts of the engine will be starved of the lubrication and protection they need. All moving parts must have a layer of oil between them. There must be no metal to metal contact.

Too much oil can also cause problems. Should the dipstick level be above the high mark, excessive pressure might build up in the engine and force oil out. Serious damage could ensue, particularly to the clutch.

The oil is pumped continuously through an oil filter which collects any particles of dirt there may be in the engine. It is essential that the oil and the filter are changed at the manufacturer's recommended intervals. Failure to carry out this fairly basic service will cause unnecessary engine wear and tear. There is no sense at all in putting new clean oil in an engine that has a dirty clogged oil filter.

All cars are fitted with an oil pressure gauge or a low oil pressure warning light. Should these instruments show a low pressure the engine must be switched off immediately.

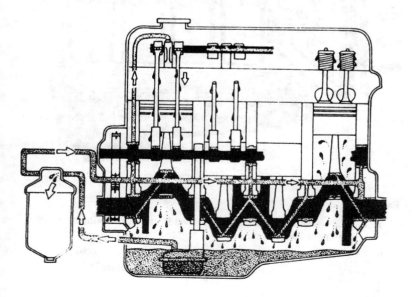

Engine lubrication

Faults

- Lack of oil.
- Blocked oil filter and oilways.

The Cooling System

The high temperature at which the car engine runs demands an efficient cooling system. Driving school cars in particular do a lot of slow town or back street work where there is very little movement of air around the radiator to cool the system.

A typical water-cooled engine comprises a radiator, a water pump driven by a fan belt from the crankshaft, a series of passages running through the engine and a thermostat. Water is pumped from the radiator, up through the engine water passages past the thermostat and back into the top of the radiator where it is cooled by the fan and the natural air flow as the car is being driven.

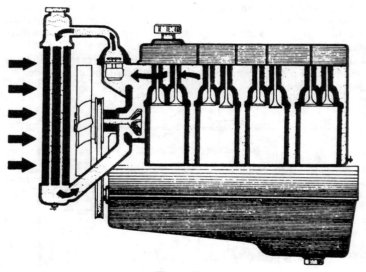

The cooling system

Faults

- Engine overheating: check water level in radiator taking care when removing radiator cap not to get scalded by released steam.
- Fan belt too slack: not operating the water pump effectively.
- Thermostat sticking: not allowing water to circulate.
- Burst hose.
- Ignition timing incorrect.

Some modern cars have an electrically operated fan which comes into operation at a certain temperature.

Anti-freeze should be mixed with the water to give a very low freezing point in winter. Nowadays anti-freeze can be left in the system all year but it is advisable to have the density checked at the start of winter and topped up if necessary.

Transmission

The transmission of a car consists of a clutch, a gear box and a differential. Their combined purpose is to transmit the drive from the engine through to the road wheels.

Clutch

The clutch enables the engine to be disconnected from the transmission in order to engage or disengage the gears. It provides the means for a smooth engagement of the drive between the engine and the road wheels and it also enables the car to be controlled at a crawling pace.

The clutch consists of three main parts. A thrust bearing, a spring loaded pressure plate and centre plate. At the back of the engine there is a flat heavy wheel called a fly wheel. This is attached to the crankshaft and revolves at the same speed as the engine.

The clutch centre plate is made of a friction material similar to a brake lining. It is connected to the transmission and held firmly against the fly wheel by the pressure plate. When the engine is turning the clutch is also turning.

When the clutch pedal is depressed the pressure plate is pulled away from the fly wheel, thus freeing the centre friction plate and disengaging the drive. When the pedal is released the centre friction plate is forced by the pressure plate against the fly wheel and the drive between the engine and transmission is complete.

Partially engaging (slipping) the clutch allows the car to be controlled at a crawling pace.

The thrust bearing is situated behind the pressure plate and provides the means to allow the pedal linkage to operate the clutch.

Faults

- Clutch judder: this can be caused by a faulty clutch diaphragm, loose or worn engine or gear box mountings.
- Thrust bearing worn: can be detected by a rasping squealing noise when depressing the clutch.
- Riding the clutch: resting foot on clutch in normal driving causing partial disengagement of the clutch and unnecessary wear on thrust bearing.

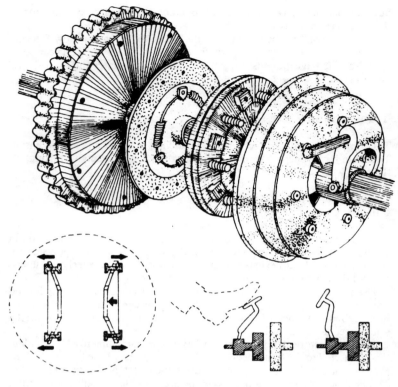

The clutch

● Clutch adjustment: there should be approximately half an inch of free play at the top of the clutch pedal; when this is not the case, the cable must be adjusted.

● Clutch centre plate: the friction lining on each side of the centre plate can wear and cause the clutch to slip. Oil on the lining can also cause it to slip.

Gearbox

The purpose of the gearbox is to enable the car to be driven at varying speeds with the minimum strain on the engine. The lower speeds and harder work will call for the lower gears, while for normal cruising a higher gear should be selected.

The modern gearbox has four or five forward gears and a reverse gear. It also has a neutral position which disengages the engine from the road wheels. All forward gears have a synchromesh coupling which allows changing from

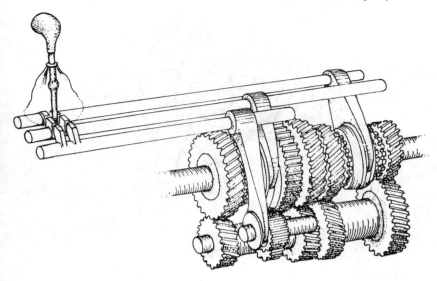

The gearbox

any one gear to another quietly and smoothly. Very simply, they synchronise the speeds of the gears to be engaged before actually coupling them together. Lubrication in the gearbox is as essential as in the engine. Most boxes have a filler/level plug on the side which should be checked at regular intervals. Failure to maintain the correct level of oil could lead to overheating and unnecessary wear and tear.

Faults

- Synchromesh faulty: results in difficult noisy gear change or selection.
- Worn selectors: results in gear lever jumping out into neutral under acceleration.
- Worn bearings and gears: causes excessive noise from gear box.
- Oil leaks.

Differential

The differential enables the inside wheel to turn slower than the outer wheel when on a curve. This effect is made possible by the action of the crownwheel and pinion.

Faults

- Very rare on modern vehicles but requires lubrication and checks for oil leaks.

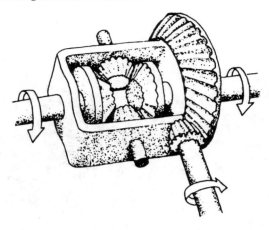

The differential

Brakes

Most modern cars use a combination of disc brakes on the front wheels and drum brakes on the rear. Disc brakes are more efficient than drum brakes because of the flow of cooling air over the discs. When the footbrake is applied, a hydraulic system multiplies the pedal pressure and squeezes the disc between two metal-backed friction pads, thus slowing it down. Drum brakes work on the same friction principle, but with the shoes pressing outwards against the rotating drum. Drum brakes, being enclosed, generate a high degree of heat which is less easily dissipated into the atmosphere. Where excessive heat is generated, this may result in *brake fade*.

The hydraulic system consists of a master cylinder and a fluid reservoir, connecting pipes, hoses and slave cylinders. Footbrake pressure is transmitted from the master cylinder to apply pressure on the brake shoes and disc pads.

Faults

- Brakes out of adjustment: this can cause a pull to one side as the brakes are applied.

- Worn pads or shoes: should the brake pedal travel almost to the floor before reaction is felt, the pads are probably worn and will need to be replaced. With the drum type, adjustment can restore effective braking but these may need to be replaced.

- Air in the hydraulic system: this can be detected by a spongy feel on the pedal. There may be a leak at any of the connections, or a fault in the master cylinder. Bleeding the brakes, which replaces the fluid in the cistern, can be the cure; however, the cause of the fault must be established.

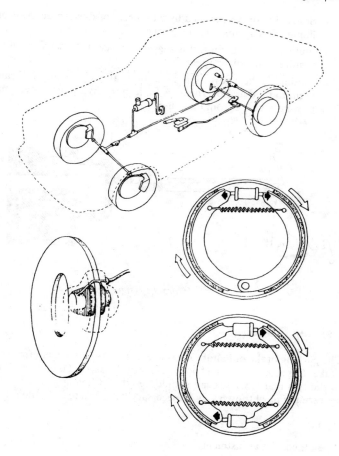

The brake system

- Low fluid level in master cylinder: check all connections and slave cylinders for leaks. Regular topping up establishes that there is a leak somewhere.

- Water in fluid: over a period of time moisture can get into the brake fluid from either the air space in the master cylinder or from the heat generated from braking. This can cause brake failure. Fluid should be changed at regular intervals. See manufacturer's handbook.

- Seized slave cylinder pistons: this will cause the brake at that particular wheel to cease to function and the car will pull to one side when the brakes are applied.

- Squeaking brakes: caused by a build-up of dust on the pads or linings. Pads could also be glazed.
- Fluid on brake linings: this suggests a leak at the slave cylinder and requires immediate attention.
- Binding brakes: adjusting the drum brakes too tightly will cause them to bind and overheat. A fault in the hydraulic system may prevent a brake from releasing.

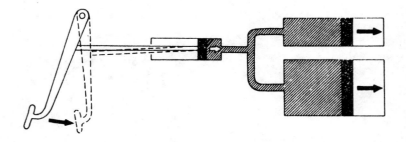

Hydraulic system

Parking Brake

The parking brake or handbrake is a separate braking system from the foot-brake. It is mounted usually on the floor of the car and is connected by cable to the two rear wheels. Care should be taken when applying the brake to squeeze the pawl thus saving unnecessary wear and tear on the ratchet.

Faults

- Incorrect adjustment.
- Worn ratchet.
- Worn, stretched or seized cable.
- Lack of lubrication in linkage.

Suspension

With the varying road conditions bumps, bends, corners and speeds, a car will be subjected to three different types of movement – bounce, roll and pitch, which are rendered stable and therefore comfortable by suspension.

Bounce will occur when a car hits a bump or dip in the road.

Roll is caused when cornering (particularly at speed) when the centrifugal force will pull the car away from the centre of the curve, ie, the car will pull left when you are trying to steer right. In extreme cases a car could roll over.

Pitch is the reaction of the rear wheels following the front wheels over a bump. As the front of the car rises the rear will dip; as the rear wheels strike the bump the front of the car drops causing a forward and backward movement, similar to a ship pitching in and out of waves.

The function of the suspension is to counteract these effects.

Springs connect the axles to the body of the car. There are various types, eg, the leaf spring, the coil or helical spring and the torsion bar. Springs absorb the force produced by a bump or dip in the road and release this force as the spring returns to its natural position. Most cars today have an independent front wheel suspension (coil, spring or torsion bar).

Suspension

The effects of bounce and pitch can be virtually eliminated by the hydrolastic type of suspension. In this system the front and rear of each side of the car has a sealed metal container with an interconnecting pipe. As the front wheel strikes a bump, fluid is forced towards the rear container, thus keeping the body of the car level. As the rear wheel strikes a bump the process is reversed. Loss of fluid pressure in a hydrolastic suspension system will cause it to collapse.

Shock absorbers

To prevent excessive bouncing, cars are fitted with shock absorbers, or dampers. The type most commonly used is the telescopic damper. This consists basically of an internal piston fitted into an oil filled cylinder. The piston moves with the spring and the resistance from the oil restricts quick action preventing a continual bouncing movement.

Faults

- Springs, broken leaf: if the main leaf is broken the whole axle unit is partially disconnected from the body. The car should not be driven.
- Loose clamping (U) bolts: these clamp the springs to the axle. When loose the leaves can spread causing the centre locating bolt to break. The spring is no longer connected to the axle and the car should not be driven.
- Worn or loose mountings: these are the mountings which attach the springs and shock absorbers to the car; excessive wear can cause a noisy uncomfortable ride.
- Hydrolastic suspension: loss of fluid pressure, causing collapse of the suspension on either side.

Tyres

Basically there are two types of tyre in use on the modern car – cross ply and radial ply. It is important that a driving instructor understands the difference and value of each.

The cross ply has a bracing section which goes round the tread and the walls of the tyre. This retains the shape of the tyre irrespective of camber changes and bumps in the road, so the amount of tread actually in contact with the road can vary with the road conditions.

The radial ply tyre, however, has a softly braced flexible wall with a heavily braced stiff tread which ensures an equal amount of tread remains in contact with the road however it is cambered, giving this tyre a much better grip. The radial tyre will also last much longer than the cross ply because the area of tread in contact with the road remains the same; this also ensures that the tyre wear remains even.

Most cars today are fitted with tubeless tyres. The difference between these and the older type is that instead of a separate inner tube they have a lining of soft rubber which makes them airtight; the main advantage over the separate tube is that there is far less danger of a blow-out when punctured.

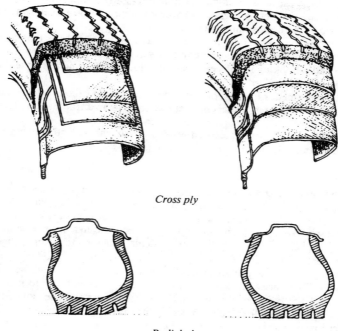

Cross ply

Radial ply

Faults

- Over-inflation: causes excessive wear along the centre of the tread.
- Under-inflation: causes excessive wear around the outer edges of the tread.
- Weak or cut side walls: causes the tyre's outer rubber to separate from its main structure – could cause blow-out. When driving, a separated bulging side-wall gives a bumping feeling similar to driving along a line of studs.
- Balancing: an unbalanced tyre will give a steering wheel shudder and will cause rapid and uneven tyre wear. It will also put excessive strain on all the steering linkage.

It is both illegal and dangerous to mix cross ply and radial ply tyres on the same axle as they have completely different road holding features. It is permissible to have cross ply at the front and radial at the back but it's certainly not to be recommended.

Preventive Maintenance and Service Requirements

To do his job properly, an instructor should not be worrying about the condition of his car. Both he and his pupil must have confidence in the knowledge that the car he is teaching/learning on, is in a sound condition, both mechanically and bodily. Regular servicing and preventive maintenance are therefore of the utmost importance to an instructor.

It is false economy to fall short in the area of car maintenance. Unplanned time off the road causes loss of income as well as the cost of the repair. Cancelling and rebooking lessons causes problems which should not arise if the car is regularly serviced.

The Department of Transport examiners can refuse to conduct a test in a car which their pre-test visual check shows to be in an unroadworthy condition.

Listed below are examples of the regular car checks and services that should be carried out.

Daily

Windows and mirrors should be kept clean and the driver's vision should not be impaired by dangling mascots, badges or self-adhesive 'L' plates. When cleaning use a solvent to remove any windscreen smears, but avoid damaging the rear window heating element with any abrasive cleaner. Operation of the lights should be checked each day with particular attention to the brake lights. Carry spare bulbs in the car in case of sudden failure. In order to save time in the event of bulb failure an instructor should consult the manufacturer's manual to familiarise himself with the instructions on bulb replacement.

There should also be a daily visual check of the car tyres for any cut or bulges, stones in the tread, etc. Checking the operation of the horn, indicator, screen washers and wipers should be part of an instructor's daily routine.

Weekly

Engine oil level

Make sure that the car is standing on level ground. Remove the dipstick, which is usually situated halfway down one side of the engine, and clean it on a piece of cloth or kitchen paper. Replace it in the dipstick hole then remove it again and look for the oil mark. The oil level should be between the high (maximum) and the low (minimum) marks. Should the oil be near or below the low mark one or two pints of fresh oil will be needed to top up to the high mark. Care must be taken not to overfill as this could lead to excessive oil pressure in the engine and cause leaks or damage.

Oil leaks

Oil leaks can be detected quite easily by having a quick look round the engine, gearbox, rear axle and the insides of the wheels. Common places for leaks are drain plugs, oil filters, valve cover gasket or any oil or brake pipe. If the car has a regular overnight parking spot look for drops of oil on the ground. Any leak inside the wheels could mean a faulty brake cylinder which must receive immediate expert attention.

Cooling system

While the engine is cold remove the pressure relief cap from the radiator. Check the water level and top up as necessary. Some cars have a separate expansion tank which must be topped up to the water level mark. If the water level falls regularly, check for leaks or suspect engine overheating, which may require expert attention.

Never remove the radiator cap when the engine is hot. High pressure is built up inside the radiator when the engine is running. The steam released when the cap is removed can cause serious scalding.

Brake and clutch fluid levels

Consult the manufacturer's manual for advice on the fluid levels. When topping up brake or clutch reservoirs always use new fluid. Re-use of old brake fluid may damage the brake or clutch systems. Remember that if frequent topping up is required the fluid must be escaping somewhere. What may be a slight leak one day could be a major loss the next. Never make do with brakes; any suspected fault should receive expert attention without delay.

Windscreen and rear screen washers and fluid levels

It is a legal requirement for screen washers to be in working order and topped up with water. Add a screen washer solvent to the container as water alone is insufficient to clear the combinations of road grit, exhaust fumes, etc that congeal on the windscreen. In winter add about an egg cupful of methylated spirit to prevent the system freezing up. Do not add anti-freeze as this will damage the car paintwork.

Windscreen wipers

Clean the wiper blade rubbers. Dirt and grit stuck on the rubbers could scratch the glass. Renew blades if there is any sign of perishing or brittleness.

Tyre pressures

Check the tyre pressures including the spare at least once a week. Don't forget to replace the valve dust cap. Remove any stones caught in the tread and inspect the side walls for any cuts or bulges. Driving school cars are susceptible to damaged tyre walls as a result of kerbing. Any sign of uneven tread wear should be reported and rectified as soon as possible.

Lights

Check the operation of all lights including indicator flashers and brake lights.

Battery

Check the electrolite level. Top up if necessary using only distilled water to about half an inch above the electrode plates.

Fan belt
Check the tension, look for cuts and fraying. A loose fan belt can affect the operation of the water pump, which will lead to overheating of the generator, which will cause a flat battery. A fan belt is a fairly simple item to replace if broken. We would advise an instructor always to carry a spare and the necessary tools to replace it.

Periodically (as per Manufacturer's Recommendations)

From any practical point of view a driving instructor must be able to carry out daily and weekly checks by himself. Naturally some instructors may have sufficient mechanical knowledge and experience to tackle the larger services which must be made. It is worth considering further study in this field, for example night school classes.

Car manufacturers produce handbooks with service recommendations and do-it-yourself advice. There are many good, clear textbooks starting from the very elementary Ladybird book *The Motor Car*, and the *AA Car Duffer's Guide*. The oil companies, like Mobil, Castrol, Shell BP produce very good, sound manuals explaining car facts and car care. Vehicle maintenance record sheets are also available and very valuable. The majority of instructors will, however, go to a garage or a professional mechanic. Nevertheless it is recommended that an instructor should have some knowledge of the work that must be covered by periodic servicing.

Engine
Renew carburettor air filter
Top up carburettor piston damper
Renew engine oil and oil filter
Check fan belt condition and tension
Check/adjust valve clearances
Check water hoses for leaks
Check fuel system for leaks and fuel pipes for corrosion

Clutch
Check/adjust pedal free play
Check master cylinder and pipes for leaks

Exhaust
Check that there are no leaks and that the system is properly secured

Ignition
Clean/renew spark plugs. Check gap before fitting
Adjust/renew distributor points
Clean distributor cap
Check ignition wiring

Brakes
Check master cylinder and all brake pipes for leaks
Check pipes and unions for chafing and corrosion

Check/adjust handbrake operation
Lubricate handbrake linkage
Check disc pads for wear
Check brake linings
Clean and inspect brake drums

Steering and suspension
Check hydraulic suspension for fluid leaks
Check steering box for oil leaks and wear
Check all linkage for wear, and grease as recommended
Check front wheel alignment
Balance front wheels if necessary
Check and grease front wheel bearings
Check shock absorbers for wear and oil leaks
Check suspension joints for wear

Transmission
Check gearbox oil level
Check differential oil level
Check condition of front wheel drive constant velocity joints and drive shaft gaiters

Electrical
Check all instruments
Remove and clean battery
Check battery electrolite
Clean and grease battery connections
Check headlamp alignment

Seat belts
Check for cuts and fraying
Check release mechanism
Clean with warm, soapy water (oil mechanical parts)

Body
Check operation of all door and boot locks and hinges
Lubricate all door locks and hinges
Grease bonnet lock
Check operation of all windows
Lubricate accelerator, brake and clutch pedal pivots
Lubricate dual controls and check operation

Seasonally

At the first sign of winter get the strength of the anti-freeze checked with a hydrometer at a garage. Top up as necessary. If the radiator requires topping up during the winter use an anti-freeze mixture. In modern cars it is advisable to leave the anti-freeze in all year round as it contains an anti-corrosive additive to prevent rusting in the system. A good quality anti-freeze will keep its strength for about two years after which the cooling system should be drained, flushed and refilled, using the manufacturer's recommended amount of anti-freeze.

In the spring time the car should be thoroughly hosed underneath to remove all the corrosive salt and sand that has accumulated from the gritted roads.

Appendix III

Useful Addresses

Department of Transport

Driver and Vehicle Licensing Centre
Swansea SA99 1AN
(Tel 0792 72134)

Transport and Road Research Laboratory
Crowthorne
Berkshire
(Tel 0344 773131)

Approved Driving Instructor Register
2 Marcham Street
London SW1P 3EB
(Tel 01-276 3000)

Traffic Area Offices

Traffic Area & Office

Eastern
DTp
Birkbeck House
14–16 Trinity Square
Nottingham NG1 4BA

ADI Clerk
(Tel 0602 475511 ext 246)

DTp
Terrington House
13–15 Hills Road
Cambridge CB2 1NP

ADI Clerk
(Tel 0223 358922 ext 308)

Metropolitan
DTp
Government Buildings
PO Box 643
Charles House
375 Kensington High St
London W14 8QU

ADI Clerk
Room C9/11
2 Marsham Street
(Tel 01-276 6677)

North Eastern
DTp
Westgate House
Westgate Road
Newcastle-upon-Tyne
NE1 1TW

ADI Clerk
(Tel 091-261 0031 ext 209)

DTp
Hillcrest House
386 Harehills Lane
Leeds LS9 6NF

ADI Clerk
(Tel 0532 495661 ext 204)

North Western
DTp
Portcullis House
Seymour Grove
Manchester M16 0NE

ADI Clerk
(Tel 061-872 5077 ext 524)

357

Scottish
DTp
83 Princes Street
Edinburgh EH2 2ER

ADI Clerk
(Tel 031-225 5494 ext 327)

South Wales
DTp
Caradog House
1–6 St Andrew's Place
Cardiff CF1 3PW

ADI Clerk
(Tel 0222 225188 ext 220)

South Eastern
DTp
Ivy House
3 Ivy Terrace
Eastbourne BN21 4QT

ADI Clerk
(Tel 0323 21471 ext 278)

Western
DTp
The Gaunts House
Denmark Street
Bristol BS1 5DR

ADI Clerk
(Tel 0272 297221 ext 387)

West Midlands
DTp
Cumberland House
200 Broad Street
Birmingham B15 1TD

ADI Clerk
(Tel 021-631 3300 ext 534)

Training Aids and Services

Autodriva
53 Heanor Road
Ilkeston
Derbyshire DE7 8DY
(Tel 0602 324499)

Autodriva
57 North Street
Chichester
West Sussex PO19 1NB
(Tel 0243 783540)

Amberley Signs
81 Hamesmoor Road
Mytchett
Camberley
Surrey GU16 6JB
(Tel 0252 542503)

AID Dual Controls
Queensthorpe Works Road
Sydenham
London SE26
(Tel 01-778 7055)

Big G Products
1 Centre Way
Clavering Industrial Estate
Edmonton
London N9
(Tel 01-803 7346)

Driving School Aids
East View
Broadgate Lane
Horsforth
Leeds LS18 4DD
(Tel 0532 580688)

Driving Schools Supplies
227 Aston Lane
Perry Barr
Birmingham B20 3HY
(Tel 021-356 7467)

Film Libraries (*see pages 79–80*)

Forest City Signs Ltd
Park Road
Timperley
Altrincham
Cheshire WA14 5QX
(Tel 061-969 0441)

He-Man Duals
Princess Street
Northam
Southampton SO1 1RP
(Tel 0703 26952)

HMSO Bookshop
49 High Holborn
London WC1V 6HB
(Tel 01-211 5656)

Identi-sign
28 Beech Grove
Higham
Rochester
Kent ME3 7AZ

M & M Signs
81 Arundel Road
High Wycombe
Buckinghamshire
(Tel 0494 26592)

Porter Duals
5 Forval Close
Wandle Way
Mitcham
Surrey CR4 4NE
(Tel 01-640 3200)

RCM Marketing Ltd
80 Tenter Road
Moulton Park Business Centre
Northampton NN3 1PZ
(Tel 0604 790890)

Car Hire

Jackson's Driving School Car Hire
28 Hermitage Road
Hitchin
Hertfordshire
(Tel 0462 34557)

Frank E Conway & Co Ltd
3a Clifton Square
Lytham FY8 5JT
(Tel 0253 737494)

Driving Instructor Insurance

Driving Instructor Insurance Services
39 Castle Street
Guildford
Surrey
(Tel 0483 65124)

M J Fish & Co
1 Slater Lane
Leyland
Preston PR5 3AL
(Tel 0772 455111)

Swinton Insurance Services
495 Northolt Road
South Harrow
Middlesex HA2 8JN
(Tel 01-422 4484)

National ADI Associations and Councils

Driving Instructors Scottish Council
5 North Lodge Avenue
Motherwell ML1 2RP

Driving Instructors' Association
Safety House
Biddington Farm Road
Croydon CR0 4XZ
(Tel 01-665 5151)

Motor Schools Association Ltd
182A Heaton Moor Road
Stockport
Cheshire SK4 4DU
(Tel 061-443 1611)

National Joint Council
41 Edinburgh Road
Cambridge CB4 1QR
(Tel 0223 359079)

National Association Approved Driving
Instructors
90 Ash Lane
Hale Barns
Altrincham WA15 8PB
(Tel 061-980 5907)

Royal Automobile Club
Register of Instructors
PO Box 100
South Croydon CR2 6XW
(Tel 01-686 2525)

Associations – Local
(England and Wales)

Blackpool ADI Association
12 Sandyforth Avenue
Thornton
Cleveleys
Blackpool FY5 4BS
(Tel 0253 822811)

Cornish ADI Association
13 Westborne Heights
Redruth
Cornwall TR15 21Q
(Tel 0209 216440)

Derby ADI Association
8 Leopold Street
Derby DE1 2HE
(Tel 0332 683656)

Exeter and District ADI Association
20 Coates Road
Exeter EX2 5PW
(Tel 0392 39926)

Harrow ADI Association
1 Albert Road
Harrow HA2 6PS
(Tel 01-427 4835)

Hemel Hempstead ADI Association
9 Chelsing Rise
Hemel Hempstead HP2 4PU
(Tel 0442 51116)

Isle of Wight ADI Association
11 Town Lane
Newport PO30 1JU
(Tel 0983 523158)

North Hertfordshire ADI Association
36 Exton Avenue
Luton LU2 0LJ
(Tel 0582 30766)

Northampton ADI Association
46 Northfield Road
Northampton NN5 6SW
(Tel 0604 56576)

Northamptonshire ADI Association
3 Holyrood Walk
Corby NN18 9JD
(Tel 0536 744244)

North Manchester ADI Association
179 Hart Road
Fallowfield
Manchester M14 7BA
(Tel 061-225 6934)

North West ADI Association
11 Bakewell Road
Stockport SK7 6JT
(Tel 061-483 3595)

Portsmouth ADI Association
70 Wallisdean Avenue
Fareham PO14 1HS
(Tel 0329 234385)

St Albans ADI Association
121 Marshalwick Lane
St Albans AL1 4UX
(Tel 0727 58068)

Salisbury ADI Association
161 Old Winton Road
Andover SP10 2DR
(Tel 0264 3007)

Sheffield ADI Association
44 Liberty Place
Stannington
Sheffield S6 5QD
(Tel 0742 337234)

Southampton ADI Association
15 Lower Northam Road
Southampton SO3 4FN
(Tel 04892 2104)

South Warwick ADI Association
7 Beech Grove
Warwick CV34 5PS
(Tel 0926 498618)

Teesside ADI Association
320 Marton Road
Middlesborough TS4 2NU
(Tel 0642 243008)

Wigan and District ADI Association
2 Stratton Drive
Platt Bridge
Wigan WN2 5HS
(Tel 0942 862969)

Wirral ADI Association
140A Home Farm Road
Woodchurch
Wirral K49 7LW
(Tel 051-606 9230)

Yorks and Humberside Regional Council
2 North Close
Leeds LS8 2NE
(Tel 0532 656560)

Scotland

Aberdeen and District Driving Schools
Association
Newtonhill School of Motoring
8 Villagelands Road
Newtonhill
Nr Aberdeen AB1 7TU

Approved Driving Instructors of Scotland
49 Prestonhall Avenue
Markinch
Fife

Dundee ADI Association
1 Dysart Place
Barnhill
Dundee DD5 3SN

Edinburgh and District Driving Instructors'
Association
4 Hermitage Terrace
Edinburgh EH10 4RP

Motor Schools Association
(Scottish Region)
96 Angus Road
Scone
Perth PH2 6RB

Disabled Driver Services

Disabled Living Foundation
346 Kensington High Street
London W14 8NS
(Tel 01-602 2491)

Information Service for Disabled
People
Northern Ireland Council of Social
Services
2 Annadale Avenue
Belfast BT7 3JH
(Tel 0232 640011)

Scottish Council of Disability
18/19 Claremont Crescent
Edinburgh EH7 4QB
(Tel 031-556 3882)

Welsh Council for the Disabled
Llyfifor Crescent Road
Caerfili
Mid Glamorgan GF8 1XL
(Tel 0222-869 224)

Clubs:

Disabled Drivers Motor Club
9 Park Parade
Gunnersbury Lane
London W3 9BD
(Tel 01-993 6454)

Disabled Motorists Club
Mobility Information Service
Copthorne Community Hall
Shelton Road
Copthorne
Shrewsbury
Shropshire SY3 8TD
(Tel 0743 68383)

Disabled Drivers' Assessment Centres

Banstead Mobility Centre
Park Road
Banstead
Surrey SM7 3EE
(Tel 0737 351674)

BSM Training Centre
81 Hartfield Road
London SW19
(Tel 01-540 8262 ext 201)

Derby Disabled Drivers' Assessment
Centre
Kingsway Hospital
Kingsway
Derby DE3 3LZ
(Tel 0332 371929)

Mobility Advice and Vehicle
Information Service (MAVIS)
Department of Transport
TRRL
Crowthorne
Berkshire RG11 6AU
(Tel 0344 770456)

Mobility Information Service
Unit 2A Atcham Estate
Upton Magna
Shrewsbury SY6 6UG
(Tel 0743 77489)

Northern Ireland Council on Disability
(NICD)
2 Annadale Avenue
Belfast BT7 3JR
(Tel 0232 491011)

Rookwood Hospital
Llandaff
Cardiff CF5 2YN
(Tel 0222 566281)

Stoke Mandeville Hospital
Occupational Therapy Department
Mandeville Road
Aylesbury
Bucks HP21 8AL
(Tel 0296 84111)

Tehidy Mobility Centre
Tehidy Hospital
Cambourne
Cornwall TR14 0SA
(Tel 0209 710708)

Vehicles for the Disabled Centre
Astley Ainslie Hospital
133 Grange Loan
Edinburgh EH09 2HL
(Tel 031-447 6271 or 031-667 3398)

Wales Disabled Drivers' Assessment
Centre
18 Plas Newydd
Whitchurch
Cardiff
(Tel 0222 615276)

Road Safety Organisations

Accident Officers Association
Aldermay House
Queen Street
London EC4N 1TP
(Tel 01-248 4477)

British Institute of Traffic Education
and Research (BITER)
Kent House
Kent Street
Birmingham BF5 6OF
(Tel 021-742 4902 and 622 2368)

Child Accident Prevention Committee
c/o Faculty of Clinical Sciences
School of Medicine
University College
University Street
London WC1
(Tel 01-387 9300)

County Road Safety Officers'
Association
Highways Department
County Hall
Worcester
(Tel 0905 353366)

Institute of Advanced Motorists
Empire House
Chiswick High Road
London W4 5TJ
(Tel 01-994 4403 –
24 hour answering service)

The Institute of Road Safety Officers
Mrs J A Thornton
The Secretary
21 Windmill Drive
Northowran
Halifax
(Tel 0422 50111 ext 32)

Royal Society for the Prevention of
Accidents (RoSPA)
Editorial and Advertising Offices
Cannon House
The Priory
Queensway
Birmingham
(Tel 021-233 2461)

STEP Management Services Ltd
Federation House
2309/11 Coventry Road
Birmingham B26 3RB
(Tel 021-742 4296/7/8/9)

Vehicle Recovery Services

Automobile Association
Fanum House
Basingstoke
Hants RG21 2EA
(Tel 0256 20123)

Eagle Car Recovery Service Ltd
Trumpers Way
Hanwell
London W7 2QA
(Tel 01-843 9009)

National Breakdown Recovery Club
Bradford
West Yorkshire BD12 0BR
(Tel 0274 671299)

Royal Automobile Club
RAC House
Lansdowne Road
Croydon CR9 2JA
(Tel 01-686 2525)

Business Names and Addresses

Companies House
Business Ownership
Department of Trade
55 City Road
London EC1Y 1BB
(Tel 01-253 9393)

Companies Registration Office
Companies House
Crown Way
Maindy
Cardiff EF4 3UZ
(Tel 0222 388588)

Consumer Credit Licensing Branch
The Office of Fair Trading
Government Building
Bromyard Avenue
The Vale
Acton
London W3 7BB
(Tel 01-743 0611)

HM Customs and Excise
VAT Central Unit
Alexander House
21 Victoria Avenue
Southend-on-Sea
Essex SS99 1AA
(Tel 0702 48944)

National Federation of Self-Employed
and Small Businesses
32 St Annes Road West
Lytham St Annes
Lancashire FY8 1NY
(Tel 0253 720911)

Registrar of Companies
Department of Commerce
43-47 Chichester Street
Belfast BT1 4RJ
(Tel 0232 34121/4)

The Small Firms Division
Department of Industry
Abell House
John Islip Street
London SW11 4LN
(Tel 01-211 5245)

Trade Mark Agency
Forrester, Kettley and Co
Forrester House
Bounds Green Road
London N11
(Tel 01-889 6622/6606)

Trade Marks Registry
Patents Office
25 Southampton Buildings
London WC2 1AY
(Tel 01-405 8721)

**RoSPA Advanced Drivers
Association**

Avon Group
30 Mayfield Avenue
Fishponds
Bristol BS16 3NL
(Tel 0272 659658)

BARSA Group
149 Norris Road
Sale
Cheshire M33 3JR
(Tel 061-962 7508)

Cardiff Bus Group
36 Wordsworth Avenue
Penarth
South Glamorgan
(Tel 0222 709967)

Cheltenham & Gloucester Group
Belgrave House
Imperial Square
Cheltenham
Gloucestershire GL50 1QB
(Tel 0242 239464)

Chester & District Group
17 Geraint Street
Toxteth
Liverpool L8 9HG
(Tel 051-709 1170)

Cumbria & Region Group
11 Teasdale Road
Lowry Hill, Carlisle
Cumbria CA3 0HF
(Tel 0228 35966)

Durham & District Group
'Eureka'
3 Abbey Road
Pity Me
Durham DH1 5DQ
(Tel 091-384 8484)

East Midlands Group
13 Park Grove
Derby DE3 1HE
(Tel 0332 362521)

Eastwood Group
(South Glasgow)
6 Lamont Avenue
Portonfield Estate
Bishopton
Strathclyde PA7 5LJ
(Tel 0505 862649)

Edinburgh & Lothian Group
RoSPA
Slateford House
Lanark Road
Edinburgh EH14 1TL
(Tel 031-444 1155)

Essex Group
1 Addison Road
Walthamstow
London E17 9LS
(Tel 01-521 4995)

Glasgow Group
27 Tulliallan Place
East Kilbride G74
(Tel 03552 31504)

Home Counties South Group
66 Oakfields, Broadacres
Guildford
Surrey GU3 3AU
(Tel 0483 67361)

Isle of Wight Group
243 Upton Road
Ryde
Isle of Wight
(Tel 0983 614614)

Jersey Group
'Seeburg'
St Anne's Terrace
Tower Road
St Helier
Jersey
(Tel 0534 72763)

Kent Group
10 Beechwood Road
Barming
Maidstone
Kent ME16 9HN

Kilmarnock & District Group
33A Kirk Street
Prestwick
Ayrshire
(Tel 0292 74588)

Leicester Group
2 Beechfield Avenue
Birstall
Leicester LE4 4DA
(Tel 0533 676261)

Lincolnshire Group
Area Road Safety Officer
Highways Department
Manby Middlegate
Grimoldby, Louth
Lincolnshire LN11 8SU
(Tel 050782 771)

London Group
21 Graham Court
Eastcote Lane
Northolt
Middlesex UB5 4HT
(Tel 01-422 8282)

Manchester Group
4 Shropshire Road
Failsworth
Manchester M35 0GT
(Tel 061-682 5555)

Mid Anglia Group
21 Ashwell Road
Bygrave
Nr Baldock
Hertfordshire SG7 5DT
(Tel 0462 895988)

Mid-Bedford Group
1 Cherwell Road
Brickhill
Bedford MK41 7AR
(Tel 0234 47865)

North Bucks/West Beds Group
282 Bideford Green
Linsdale
Leighton Buzzard
Bedfordshire LU7 7TU
(Tel 0525 375223)

North Devon Group
Providence House
Landkey
Nr Barnstaple
North Devon EX32 0ND
(Tel 0271 830613)

North Herts/South Beds Group
28 Franklin Gardens
Hitchin
Hertfordshire SG4 0BS
(Tel 0462 56648)

Norfolk & Norwich Group
18 Henley Road
Norwich NR2 3NJ
(Tel 0603 501715)

Nottingham Group
('The Forester Group')
34 Larch Crescent
Eastwood
Nottingham NG16 3RB
(Tel 0773 713157)

South Devon Group
127 Woolbrook Road
Sidmouth
Devon
(Tel 03955 78180)

South East Essex Group
50 First Avenue
Canvey Island
Essex
(Tel 0268 698590)

Southern Group
42 Aster Road
Basingstoke
Hampshire RG22 5NG
(Tel 0256 462776)

South West Group
Fuchsia Cottage
37 Lower Street
Merriot
Somerset
(Tel 0460 76908)

South Yorkshire Group
10 Revill Close
Maltby
Rotherham
South Yorkshire S66 8BN
(Tel 0709 814053)

Taunton & District Group
'Ashley'
Monkton Heathfield
Taunton Somerset TA2 8NA
(Tel 0823 412782)

Thames Valley Group
8 Pine Ridge Road
Burghfield Common
Reading Berkshire RG7 3ND
(Tel 073529 2718)

Ulster Group
RoSPA
117 Lisburn Road
Belfast BT9 7BS
(Tel 0232 669453)

Wessex Group
62 Victoria Road
Warminster
Wiltshire BA12 8HP
(Tel 0985 217013)

West Midlands Group
20 Yew Tree Road
Boldmere
Sutton Coldfield
West Midlands
(Tel 021-373 2695)

West Yorkshire Group
4 Drivers Row
Pontefract
West Yorkshire WF8 4HF
(Tel 0977 700540)

Appendix IV

ADI Examination Part III

Department of Transport
Register of Approved Driving Instructors

ADI 42/ **1**
(rev 1/84)

Test 3 Instructional Ability

P/ref. no.

Safety precautions on entering the car
Explanation of the controls

Phase 1 Instruction given to a beginner

1

2 Instruction on:

  a precautions on entering the car for the first time/doors/seat/seat belt/mirrors/not given

  b precautions on entering the car for the first time/doors/seat/seat belt/mirrors/given but inadequately covered

  c function of controls/accelerator/footbrake/clutch/handbrake/gears/steering/direction indicators/not given

  d function of controls/accelerator/footbrake/clutch/handbrake/gears/steering/direction indicators/ given but inadequately covered

  e procedure for starting the engine/inadequate/incorrect/not given

  f moving away safely/was inadequate

  g stopping normally/in a safe position/using MSM routine/with proper use of controls/was inadequate.

3 Faults committed by the pupil/not corrected/not explained/allowed to be repeated/corrective measures not taken in time/excessive instruction on the move/excessive instruction while stationary/fault analysis/incorrect/inadequate.

4 Incorrect instruction on:

5

6 Insistence on unnecessary signals/before moving off/before slowing down or stopping.

7 Instruction given was/unmethodical/too technical for a beginner/too much time spent on less important items.

8 Dual controls used/excessively/pupil not told why.

9 Pupil expected to perform at too high a standard for amount of tuition received.

10

11 Instructor's questions to pupil/not relevant to lesson/not used/excessive.

12 Pupil's questions/not answered/answered incorrectly/not answered in sufficient detail.

13 Inadequate control of lesson.

14 Lack of clear and concise verbal expression.

15 Lack of/patience/tact.

16 Lack of encouragement to pupil when deserved.

17 Additional remarks.

Supervising Examiner .... Date ....

Department of Transport
Register of Approved Driving Instructors

ADI 42/ **2**
(rev 1/84)

Test 3 Instructional Ability

P/ref. no.

Moving off – making normal stops

Phase 1 Instruction given to a beginner

1 Briefing before moving away/was inadequate/not given.
2 Instruction on:
   a   the importance of rear vision/was inadequate/not given
   b   the use of the mirrors before/signalling/changing direction/overtaking/braking/was inadequate/not given
   c   the correct sequence, mirror-signal-manoeuvre/was inadequate/not given
   d   moving away/safely/with proper use of controls/was inadequate/not given
   e   stopping normally/in a safe position/with proper use of controls/was inadequate/not given.
3 Faults committed by the pupil/not corrected/not explained/allowed to be repeated/corrective measures not taken in time/excessive instruction on the move/excessive instruction while stationary/fault analysis/incorrect/inadequate.
4 Incorrect instruction on:

5
6 Insistence on unnecessary signals/before moving off/before slowing down or stopping.
7 Instruction given was/unmethodical/too technical for a beginner/too much time spent on less important items.
8 Dual controls used/excessively/pupil not told why.
9 Pupil expected to perform at too high a standard for amount of tuition received.
10
11 Instructor's questions to pupil/not relevant to lesson/not used/excessive.
12 Pupil's questions/not answered/answered incorrectly/not answered in sufficient detail.
13 Inadequate control of lesson.
14 Lack of clear and concise verbal expression.
15 Lack of/patience/tact.
16 Lack of encouragement to pupil when deserved.
17 Additional remarks.

Supervising Examiner ....   Date ....

Department of Transport
Register of Approved Driving Instructors

ADI 42/ **3**
(rev 1/84)

Test 3 Instructional Ability

P/ref. no.

Reversing into an opening

Phase 1 Instruction given to a pupil who is partly trained
Phase 2 Instruction given to a pupil who is at about driving test standard

1 Briefing before manoeuvre/was inadequate/not given.

2 Instruction on:

   a co-ordination of controls/with steering/was inadequate/not given

   b observation/just before reversing/while reversing/forward at point of turn/was inadequate/not given

   c being reasonably accurate in positioning/was inadequate/not given.

3 Faults committed by the pupil/not corrected/not explained/allowed to be repeated/corrective measures not taken in time/excessive instruction on the move/excessive instruction while stationary/fault analysis/incorrect/inadequate.

4 Incorrect instruction on:

5 Pupil instructed/allowed/to stop in an unsafe position.

6 Insistence on unnecessary signals/before moving off/before slowing down or stopping.

7 Instruction given was/unmethodical/too technical for a beginner/too much time spent on less important items.

8 Dual controls used/excessively/pupil not told why.

9 Pupil expected to perform at too high a standard for amount of tuition received.

10 Pupil treated as a novice.

11 Instructor's questions to pupil/not relevant to lesson/not used/excessive.

12 Pupil's questions/not answered/answered incorrectly/not answered in sufficient detail.

13 Inadequate control of lesson.

14 Lack of clear and concise verbal expression.

15 Lack of/patience/tact.

16 Lack of encouragement to pupil when deserved.

17 Additional remarks.

Supervising Examiner ....   **Date** ....

Department of Transport
Register of Approved Driving Instructors

ADI 42/ **4**
(rev 1/84)

Test 3 Instructional Ability

P/ref. no.

Turning the vehicle round in the road

Phase 1 Instruction given to a pupil who is partly trained
Phase 2 Instruction given to a pupil who is at about driving test standard

1 Briefing before manoeuvre/was inadequate/not given.

2 Instruction on:

  a co-ordination of controls/with steering/was inadequate/not given

  b observation/just before/while turning/was inadequate/not given

  c being reasonably accurate in positioning/was inadequate/not given.

3 Faults committed by the pupil/not corrected/not explained/allowed to be repeated/corrective measures not taken in time/excessive instruction on the move/excessive instruction while stationary/fault analysis/incorrect/inadequate.

4 Incorrect instruction on:

5 Pupil instructed/allowed/to stop in an unsafe position.

6 Insistence on unnecessary signals/before moving off/before slowing down or stopping.

7 Instruction given was/unmethodical/too technical for a beginner/too much time spent on less important items.

8 Dual controls used/excessively/pupil not told why.

9 Pupil expected to perform at too high a standard for amount of tuition received.

10 Pupil treated as a novice.

11 Instructor's questions to pupil/not relevant to lesson/not used/excessive.

12 Pupil's questions/not answered/answered incorrectly/not answered in sufficient detail.

13 Inadequate control of lesson.

14 Lack of clear and concise verbal expression.

15 Lack of/patience/tact.

16 Lack of encouragement to pupil when deserved.

17 Additional remarks.

Supervising Examiner .... Date ....

Department of Transport
Register of Approved Driving Instructors

ADI 42/ **5**
(rev 1/84)

Test 3 Instructional Ability

P/ref. no.

Parking close to the kerb Using reverse gear

Phase 2 Instruction given to a pupil who is at about driving test standard

1 Briefing before manoeuvre/was inadequate/not given.

2 Instruction on:
   a co-ordination of controls/with steering/was inadequate/not given
   b observation/just before/while turning/was inadequate/not given
   c being reasonably accurate in positioning/steering/was inadequate/not given.

3 Faults committed by the pupil/not corrected/not explained/allowed to be repeated/corrective measures not taken in time/excessive instruction on the move/excessive instruction while stationary/fault analysis/incorrect/inadequate.

4 Incorrect instruction on:

5 Pupil instructed/allowed/to stop in'an unsafe position.

6 Insistence on unnecessary signals/before moving off/before slowing down or stopping.

7 Instruction given was/unmethodical/too technical for a beginner/too much time spent on less important items.

8 Dual controls used/excessively/pupil not told why.

9 Pupil expected to perform at too high a standard for amount of tuition received.

10 Pupil treated as a novice.

11 Instructor's questions to pupil/not relevant to lesson/not used/excessive.

12 Pupil's questions/not answered/answered incorrectly/not answered in sufficient detail.

13 Inadequate control of lesson.

14 Lack of clear and concise verbal expression.

15 Lack of/patience/tact.

16 Lack of encouragement to pupil when deserved.

17 Additional remarks.

Supervising Examiner .... Date ....

Department of Transport
Register of Approved Driving Instructors

ADI 42/ **6**
(rev 1/84)

Test 3 Instructional Ability

P/ref. no.

Emergency stop – use of mirrors

Phase 1 Instruction given to a pupil who is partly trained
Phase 2 Instruction given to a pupil who is at about driving test standard

1 Briefing before manoeuvre/was inadequate/not given.

2 Instruction on:
- a importance of quick reaction/was inadequate/not given
- b applying footbrake before clutch/was inadequate/not given
- c avoidance/correction/of skids/was inadequate/not given
- d the importance of rear vision/was inadequate/not given
- e the use of the mirrors before/signalling/changing direction/overtaking/braking/was inadequate/not given
- f the correct sequence, mirror-signal-manoeuvre/was inadequate/not given.

3 Faults committed by the pupil/not corrected/not explained/allowed to be repeated/corrective measures not taken in time/excessive instruction on the move/excessive instruction while stationary/fault analysis/incorrect/inadequate.

4 Incorrect instruction on:

5 Pupil instructed/allowed/to stop in an unsafe position.

6 Insistence on unnecessary signals/before moving off/before slowing down or stopping.

7 Instruction given was/unmethodical/too technical for a beginner/too much time spent on less important items.

8 Dual controls used/excessively/pupil not told why.

9 Pupil expected to perform at too high a standard for amount of tuition received.

10 Pupil treated as a novice.

11 Instructor's questions to pupil/not relevant to lesson/not used/excessive.

12 Pupil's questions/not answered/answered incorrectly/not answered in sufficient detail.

13 Inadequate control of lesson.

14 Lack of clear and concise verbal expression.

15 Lack of/patience/tact.

16 Lack of encouragement to pupil when deserved.

17 Additional remarks.

Supervising Examiner .... Date ....

Department of Transport
Register of Approved Driving Instructors

ADI 42/ **7**
(rev 1/86)

Test 3 Instructional Ability

P/ref. no.

Approaching and turning corners

Phase 1 Instruction given to a pupil who is partly trained
Phase 2 Instruction given to a pupil who is at about driving test standard

1   Briefing before moving away/was inadeqate/not given.
2   Instruction on:

   a   use of/mirrors/signals/brakes/gears/was inadequate/not given

   b   not coasting/on approach/while turning/was inadequate/not given

   c   excessive speed/not crawling/on approach/while turning/was inadequate/not given

   d   correct line of approach/position on turning/was inadequate/not given

   e   giving way when turning, to pedestrians who are crossing/was inadequate/not given

   f   not turning in front of traffic closely approaching from the opposite direction when making a right turn was/inadequate/not given

   g   not cutting right hand corners/was inadequate/not given.

3   Faults committed by the pupil/not corrected/not explained/allowed to be repeated/corrective measures not taken in time/excessive instruction on the move/excessive instruction while stationary/fault analysis/incorrect/inadequate.
4   Incorrect instruction on:

5   Pupil instructed/allowed/to stop in an unsafe position.
6   Insistence on unnecessary signals/before moving off/before slowing down or stopping/when passing stationary vehicles.
7   Instruction given was/unmethodical/too technical for a beginner/too much time spent on less important items.
8   Dual controls used/excessively/pupil not told why.
9   Pupil expected to perform at too high a standard for amount of tuition received.
10 Pupil treated as a novice.
11 Instructor's questions to pupil/not relevant to lesson/not used/excessive.
12 Pupil's questions/not answered/answered incorrectly/not answered in sufficient detail.
13 Inadequate control of lesson.
14 Lack of clear and concise verbal expression.
15 Lack of/patience/tact.
16 Lack of encouragement to pupil.
17 Additional remarks.

Supervising Examiner ....   Date ....

Department of Transport
Register of Approved Driving Instructors

ADI 42/ **8**
(rev 1/84)

Test 3 Instructional Ability

P/ref. no.

Judgement of speed – making progress – general road positioning

Phase 1 Instruction given to a pupil who is partly trained
Phase 2 Instruction given to a pupil who is at about driving test standard

1 Briefing before moving away/was inadequate/not given.

2 Instruction on:

  a exercising proper care in the use of speed/was inadequate/not given

  b making progress by/driving at a speed appropriate to road and traffic conditions/avoiding undue hesitancy/was inadequate/not given

  c not hugging the middle of the road in normal driving/was inadequate/not given.

3 Faults committed by the pupil/not corrected/not explained/allowed to be repeated/corrective measures not taken in time/excessive instruction on the move/excessive instruction while stationary/fault analysis/incorrect/inadequate.

4 Incorrect instruction on:

5 Pupil instructed/allowed/to stop in an unsafe position.

6 Insistence on unnecessary signals/before moving off/before slowing down or stopping.

7 Instruction given was/unmethodical/too technical for a beginner/too much time spent on less important items.

8 Dual controls used/excessively/pupil not told why.

9 Pupil expected to perform at too high a standard for amount of tuition received.

10 Pupil treated as a novice.

11 Instructor's questions to pupil/not relevant to lesson/not used/excessive.

12 Pupil's questions/not answered/answered incorrectly/not answered in sufficient detail.

13 Inadequate control of lesson.

14 Lack of clear and concise verbal expression.

15 Lack of/patience/tact.

16 Lack of encouragement to pupil when deserved.

17 Additional remarks.

Supervising Examiner .... Date ....

Department of Transport
Register of Approved Driving Instructors

ADI 42/ **9-10**
(rev 1/86)

Test 3 Instructional Ability

P/ref no.

9 Dealing with road junctions
10 Dealing with crossroads

Phase 1 Instruction given to a pupil who is partly trained
Phase 2 Instruction given to a pupil who is at about driving test standard

1 Briefing before moving away/was inadequate/not given.
2 Instruction on:
  a using the mirror-signal-manoeuvre sequence/was inadequate/not given
  b correct regulation of speed on approach/correct use of gears/was inadequate/not given
  c not coasting/on approach/while turning/was inadequate/not given
  d taking effective observation before emerging/was inadequate/not given
  e emerging with due regard for approaching traffic/was inadequate/not given
  f positioning the vehicle correctly/before/after/turning right/was inadequate/not given
  g positioning the vehicle correctly/before/after/turning left/was inadequate/not given
  h giving way when turning, to pedestrians who are crossing/was inadequate/not given
  i not turning in front of traffic closely approaching from the opposite direction when making a right turn/was inadequate/not given
  j not cutting right hand corners/was inadequate/not given.
3 Faults committed by the pupil/not corrected/not explained/allowed to be repeated/corrective measures not taken in time/excessive instruction on the move/excessive instruction while stationary/fault analysis/incorrect/inadequate.
4 Incorrect instruction on:

5 Pupil instructed/allowed/to stop in an unsafe position.
6 **Insistence on unnecessary signals/before moving off/before slowing down or stopping/when passing stationary vehicles.**
7 Instruction given was/unmethodical/too technical for a beginner/too much time spent on less important items.
8 Dual controls used/excessively/pupil not told why.
9 Pupil expected to perform at too high a standard for amount of tuition received.
10 Pupil treated as a novice.
11 Instructor's questions to pupil/not relevant to lesson/not used/excessive.
12 Pupil's questions/not answered/answered incorrectly/not answered in sufficient detail.
13 Inadequate control of lesson.
14 Lack of clear and concise verbal expression.
15 Lack of patience/tact.
16 Lack of encouragement to pupil.
17 Additional remarks.

Supervising Examiner ....   Date ....

Department of Transport
Register of Approved Driving Instructors

ADI 42/ **11**
(rev 1/84)

Test 3 Instructional Ability

P/ref. no.

Meeting – crossing – overtaking other vehicles – allowing adequate clearance for other road users

Phase 1 Instruction given to a pupil who is partly trained
Phase 2 Instruction given to a pupil who is at about driving test standard

1 Briefing before moving away/was inadequate/not given.

2 Instruction on:
   a using the mirror-signal-manoeuvre sequence/was inadequate/not given
   b giving adequate clearance when meeting traffic from opposite direction/was inadequate/not given
   c not turning in front of traffic closely approaching from the opposite direction when making a right turn/was inadequate/not given
   d overtaking other vehicles safely/was inadequate/not given
   e following behind other vehicles at a safe distance was inadequate/not given
   f allowing adequate clearance to stationary vehicles/was inadequate/not given
   g anticipating the actions of/pedestrians/cyclists/other drivers/was inadequate/not given.

3 Faults committed by the pupil/not corrected/not explained/allowed to be repeated/corrective measures not taken in time/excessive instruction on the move/excessive instruction while stationary/fault analysis/incorrect/inadequate.

4 Incorrect instruction on:

5 Pupil instructed/allowed/to stop in an unsafe position.

6 Insistence on unnecessary signals/before moving off/before slowing down or stopping.

7 Instruction given was/unmethodical/too technical for a beginner/too much time spent on less important items.

8 Dual controls used/excessively/pupil not told why.

9 Pupil expected to perform at too high a standard for amount of tuition received.

10 Pupil treated as a novice.

11 Instructor's questions to pupil/not relevant to lesson/not used/excessive.

12 Pupil's questions/not answered/answered incorrectly/not answered in sufficient detail.

13 Inadequate control of lesson.

14 Lack of clear and concise verbal expression.

15 Lack of/patience/tact.

16 Lack of encouragement to pupil when deserved.

17 Additional remarks.

Supervising Examiner .... **Date** ....

Department of Transport
Register of Approved Driving Instructors

ADI 42/ **12**
(rev 1/84)

Test 3 Instructional Ability

P/ref. no.

Dealing with pedestrian crossings – giving appropriate signals in a clear and unmistakable manner

Phase 1 Instruction given to a pupil who is partly trained
Phase 2 Instruction given to a pupil who is at about driving test standard

1 Briefing before moving away/was inadequate/not given.

2 Instruction on:

    a using the mirror-signal-manoeuvre sequence/was inadequate/not given

    b approaching pedestrian crossings at the proper speed/was inadequate/not given

    c stopping at pedestrian crossings when necessary/was inadequate/not given

    d not overtaking at or when approaching pedestrian crossings was inadequate/not given

    e not beckoning pedestrians to cross/was inadequate/not given

    f giving signals/where necessary/correctly/properly timed/by direction indicators/by arm/was inadequate/not given

    g insistence on unnecessary signals.

3 Faults committed by the pupil/not corrected/not explained/allowed to be repeated/corrective measures not taken in time/excessive instruction on the move/excessive instruction while stationary/fault analysis/incorrect/inadequate.

4 Incorrect instruction on:

5 Pupil instructed/allowed/to stop in an unsafe position.

6

7 Instruction given was/unmethodical/too technical for a beginner/too much time spent on less important items.

8 Dual controls used/excessively/pupil not told why.

9 Pupil expected to perform at too high a standard for amount of tuition received.

10 Pupil treated as a novice.

11 Instructor's questions to pupil/not relevant to lesson/not used/excessive.

12 Pupil's questions/not answered/answered incorrectly/not answered in sufficient detail.

13 Inadequate control of lesson.

14 Lack of clear and concise verbal expression.

15 Lack of/patience/tact.

16 Lack of encouragement to pupil when deserved.

17 Additional remarks.

Supervising Examiner . . . . Date . . . .